The Film Archipelago

WORLD CINEMA SERIES

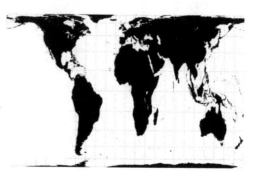

Series Editors:
Lúcia Nagib, Professor of Film at the University of Reading
Julian Ross, Research Fellow at Leiden University

Advisory Board: Laura Mulvey (UK), Robert Stam (USA), Ismail Xavier (Brazil), Dudley Andrew (USA)

The *World Cinema Series* aims to reveal and celebrate the richness and complexity of film art across the globe, exploring a wide variety of cinemas set within their own cultures and as they interconnect in a global context. The books in the series will represent innovative scholarship, in tune with the multicultural character of contemporary audiences. Drawing upon an international authorship, they will challenge outdated conceptions of world cinema, and provide new ways of understanding a field at the centre of film studies in an era of transnational networks.

Published and forthcoming in the World Cinema series:

Allegory in Iranian Cinema: The Aesthetics of Poetry and Resistance
Michelle Langford

Amharic Film Genres and Ethiopian Cinema
Michael W. Thomas

Animation in the Middle East: Practice and Aesthetics from Baghdad to Casablanca
Stefanie Van de Peer

Basque Cinema: A Cultural and Political History
Rob Stone and Maria Pilar Rodriguez

Brazil on Screen: Cinema Novo, New Cinema, Utopia
Lúcia Nagib

Brazilian Cinema and the Aesthetics of Ruins

Guilherme Carréra

Cinema in the Arab World: New Histories, New Approaches
Edited By Philippe Meers, Daniel Biltereyst and Ifdal Elsaket

Contemporary New Zealand Cinema
Edited by Ian Conrich and Stuart Murray

Cosmopolitan Cinema: Cross-cultural Encounters in East Asian Film
Felicia Chan

Documentary Cinema in Chile: Confronting History, Memory, Trauma
Antonio Traverso

East Asian Cinemas: Exploring Transnational Connections on Film
Edited by Leon Hunt and Leung Wing-Fai

East Asian Film Noir: Transnational Encounters and Intercultural Dialogue
Edited by Chi-Yun Shin and Mark Gallagher

Eastern Approaches to Western Film: Asian Reception and Aesthetics in Cinema
Stephen Teo

Impure Cinema: Intermedial and Intercultural Approaches to Film
Edited by Lúcia Nagib and Anne Jerslev

Latin American Women Filmmakers: Production, Politics, Poetics
Edited by Deborah Martin and Deborah Shaw

Lebanese Cinema: Imagining the Civil War and Beyond
Lina Khatib

New Argentine Cinema
Jens Andermann

New Directions in German Cinema
Edited by Paul Cooke and Chris Homewood

New Turkish Cinema: Belonging, Identity and Memory
Asuman Suner

On Cinema
Glauber Rocha, Edited by Ismail Xavier

Pablo Trapero and the Politics of Violence
Douglas Mulliken

Palestinian Filmmaking in Israel: Narratives of Place and
Yael Friedman

Performing Authorship: Self-inscription and Corporeality in the Cinema
Cecilia Sayad

Portugal's Global Cinema: Industry, History and Culture
Edited by Mariana Liz

Queer Masculinities in Latin American Cinema: Male Bodies and Narrative Representations
Gustavo Subero

Realism in Greek Cinema: From the Post-War Period to the Present
Vrasidas Karalis

Realism of the Senses in World Cinema: The Experience of Physical Reality
Tiago de Luca

Stars in World Cinema: Screen Icons and Star Systems Across Cultures
Edited by Andrea Bandhauer and Michelle Royer

The Cinema of Jia Zhangke: Realism and Memory in Chinese Film
Cecília Mello

The Cinema of Sri Lanka: South Asian Film in Texts and Contexts
Ian Conrich

The New Generation in Chinese Animation
Shaopeng Chen

The Spanish Fantastic: Contemporary Filmmaking in Horror, Fantasy and Sci-fi
Shelagh-Rowan Legg

Theorizing World Cinema
Edited by Lúcia Nagib, Chris Perriam and Rajinder Dudrah

Queries, ideas and submissions to:
Series Editor: Professor Lúcia Nagib –
l.nagib@reading.ac.uk

Series Editor: Dr. Julian Ross –
j.a.ross@hum.leidenuniv.nl

Publisher at Bloomsbury, Rebecca Barden –
Rebecca.Barden@bloomsbury.com

The Film Archipelago

Islands in Latin American Cinema

Edited by Antonio Gómez &
Francisco-J. Hernández Adrián

BLOOMSBURY ACADEMIC
LONDON • NEW YORK • OXFORD • NEW DELHI • SYDNEY

BLOOMSBURY ACADEMIC
Bloomsbury Publishing Plc
50 Bedford Square, London, WC1B 3DP, UK
1385 Broadway, New York, NY 10018, USA
29 Earlsfort Terrace, Dublin 2, Ireland

BLOOMSBURY, BLOOMSBURY ACADEMIC and the Diana logo are trademarks of
Bloomsbury Publishing Plc

First published in Great Britain 2022
This paperback edition published 2023
Reprinted in 2022

Copyright © Antonio Gómez and Francisco-J. Hernández Adrián, 2022

Antonio Gómez and Francisco-J. Hernández Adrián have asserted their right under the
Copyright, Designs and Patents Act, 1988, to be identified as Editors of this work.

For legal purposes the Acknowledgements on p. xiv constitute
an extension of this copyright page.

Cover design: Charlotte Daniels
Cover image: *Magic Magic* (CHL/USA 2013) Director: Sebastián Silva 22 January 2013.
Mary Evans/AF Archive/Braven Films

All rights reserved. No part of this publication may be reproduced or transmitted
in any form or by any means, electronic or mechanical, including photocopying,
recording, or any information storage or retrieval system, without prior
permission in writing from the publishers.

Bloomsbury Publishing Plc does not have any control over, or responsibility for,
any third-party websites referred to or in this book. All internet addresses given
in this book were correct at the time of going to press. The author and publisher
regret any inconvenience caused if addresses have changed or sites have
ceased to exist, but can accept no responsibility for any such changes.

A catalogue record for this book is available from the British Library.

Library of Congress Cataloging-in-Publication Data
Names: Gómez, Antonio, 1973- editor. | Adrián, Francisco-J. Hernández, editor.
Title: The film archipelago : islands in Latin American cinema / edited by
Antonio Gómez & Francisco-J. Hernández Adrián.
Description: London ; New York : Bloomsbury Academic, 2022. |
Series: World Cinema series | Includes bibliographical references and index. |
Identifiers: LCCN 2021025427 (print) | LCCN 2021025428 (ebook) | ISBN
9781350157965 (hardback) | ISBN 9781350281752 (paperback) | ISBN
9781350157989 (epub) | ISBN 9781350157972 (pdf)
Subjects: LCSH: Motion pictures–Latin America–History. | Islands in motion pictures.
Classification: LCC PN1993.5.L3 F53 2022 (print) | LCC PN1993.5.L3 (ebook) |
DDC 791.43098–dc23/eng/20211026
LC record available at https://lccn.loc.gov/2021025427
LC ebook record available at https://lccn.loc.gov/2021025428

ISBN:	HB:	978-1-3501-5796-5
	PB:	978-1-3502-8175-2
	ePDF:	978-1-3501-5797-2
	eBook:	978-1-3501-5798-9

Series: World Cinema

Typeset by Integra Software Services Pvt. Ltd.

To find out more about our authors and books visit www.bloomsbury.com
and sign up for our newsletters.

Contents

List of Contributors	ix
Acknowledgements	xiv

Introduction: Islands in Latin American cinema: Film(ing) archipelagos
Antonio Gómez and Francisco-J. Hernández Adrián 1

Part 1 Islands at the end of the world

1   Deserted islands for the nation: Empty land- and seascapes
in three Argentine films of the Malvinas/Falkland Islands
Jason A. Bartles 31

2   Marooned testimony: Chilean islandscape and the politics of
memory in Sebastián Silva's *Magic Magic* (2013)
William R. Benner 55

3   Memory islands: Repeating traumas in Patricio Guzmán's
Nostalgia de la luz (2010) and *El botón de nácar* (2015)
Amanda Holmes 73

4   Insular spaces: A documentary and an affective ethno-mapping
of the Rapa Nui culture
Irene Depetris Chauvin 89

Part 2 Liminal islands

5   Social reformation and the edges of sovereignty: Fernando
Soler's *La hija del penal* (1949) and Emilio Fernández's
Islas Marías (1951)
Ignacio M. Sánchez Prado 115

6   Exposed insularities: Islands, capitalism and waste in Jorge
Furtado's *Ilha das Flores* (1989)
Axel Pérez Trujillo 131

viii   *Contents*

7   Islands in Lucrecia Martel's *Nueva Argirópolis* (2010): Eroding
    and fracturing the national map
    Natalia D'Alessandro   153

8   Gustavo Fontán's films: On faces, spectres, fragments
    of matter
    Laura M. Martins   171

Part 3 Antillean relations on screen

9   The duplicitous empire: Ambiguous representations of Puerto
    Ricans and Japanese-Americans in Herbert I. Leeds's *Mr. Moto
    in Danger Island* (1939)
    Naida García-Crespo   191

10 An archipelago of crossed gazes: Intersections of documentary
    media practices in Cuba and Puerto Rico
    Juan Carlos Rodríguez   209

11 'Irreducible memories' of Caribbeanness: Mariette Monpierre's
    Le Bonheur d'Elza (2011)
    Sheila Petty   229

12 Documenting lifestyle migration: Anayansi Prado's *Paraíso
    for Sale* (2011)
    Carolyn Fornoff   247

13 Raoul Peck's archipelagic cinema: Island contestations of the
    international order in *Assistance mortelle* (2013)
    Jana Evans Braziel   267

Part 4 Reimagining islandscapes

14 Notes on an island film: A journey to Martín García
    Edgardo Dieleke   287

15 Letters from the islands: A visual essay
    Antonio Traverso   307

Index   318

Contributors

Jason A. Bartles is a writer and Associate Professor of Spanish at West Chester University. His scholarly and creative projects are sustained by an interest in restoring the potential for utopian thinking in the present. He has published *ArteletrA: The Sixties in Latin America and the Politics of Going Unnoticed* (2021). His essays on the politics of literature, film and gaming can be found in *Revista Hispánica Moderna*, *Revista de Estudios Hispánicos*, *Revista Iberoamericana*, and *CR: The New Centennial Review*, among others.

William R. Benner is Assistant Professor of Spanish at Texas Woman's University. His research explores the literature and film by children of Southern Cone Dictatorships. He has two articles in progress on digital archiving and testimonial silences in texts by Chilean author Alejandro Zambra. He is concurrently writing his first monograph, *Entangled Specters and Digital Archives*, which will examine how a prolific generation of Argentine writers, bloggers and filmmakers utilizes digital media to challenge traditional notions of producing and sharing testimony.

Jana Evans Braziel, Western Endowed Professor in the Department of Global and Intercultural Studies at Miami University (Ohio), is author of five monographs: *'Riding with Death': Vodou Art and Urban Ecology in the Streets of Port-au-Prince* (2017); *Duvalier's Ghosts: Race, Diaspora, and U.S. Imperialism in Haitian Literatures* (2010); *Caribbean Genesis: Jamaica Kincaid and the Writing of New Worlds* (2009); *Artists, Performers, and Black Masculinity in the Haitian Diaspora* (2008); and *Diaspora: An Introduction* (2008). Braziel has also co-edited five edited collections, two special issues of a peer-reviewed academic journal, and published myriad articles and book chapters.

Natalia D'Alessandro graduated in Modern Literatures at Universidad Nacional de Cuyo (Mendoza, Argentina) and has a PhD in Argentine contemporary literature and film from Tulane University (New Orleans). She has published articles in journals such as *Hispamérica*, *A Contracorriente*, *Iberoamericana*, and *Variaciones Borges*. She is a member of the research group 'Theoretical and Literary Studies on Social Problems' at the Universidad Nacional de Cuyo, and currently works as a researcher at the CONICET and the Universidad de San Andrés (Buenos Aires).

Irene Depetris Chauvin earned her PhD in Romance Studies in 2011 at Cornell University with a dissertation that questions representations of youth vis-à-vis neoliberal discourses in the Southern Cone. She currently works as a Researcher at the University of Buenos Aires and at the CONICET in a project that considers the affective and political uses of music and sound archives in recent films. She has published articles on youth, market culture and affectivity in contemporary narrative and cinema, on memory studies, and on geographical and urban imaginaries. She is the author of *Geografías afectivas. Desplazamientos, prácticas espaciales y formas de estar juntos en el cine de Argentina, Chile y Brasil* (Pittsburgh, LARC, 2019) and has recently co-edited two volumes: *Más allá de la naturaleza. Imaginarios geográficos en la literatura y el arte latinoamericano reciente* (Ed. Alberto Hurtado, Chile, 2019) and *Afectos, historia y cultura visual. Una aproximación indisciplinada* (Prometeo, Buenos Aires, 2019).

Edgardo Dieleke is a filmmaker, professor and editor. He directed with Daniel Casabé the films *La forma exacta de las islas* (released in 2014), shot in Malvinas Islands, and *Cracks de nácar* (released in 2013). These films were nominated as best documentary by the Argentine Academy of Film and the Condor Press Awards, respectively. He earned his PhD in Spanish and Portuguese Languages and Cultures at Princeton University, and teaches Latin American Literature and Film at Universidad de San Andrés in Buenos Aires, where he is also the Academic Coordinator of the PhD Program in Latin American Literatures and the Master's in Cultural Practices. He has also been a Professor of Cultural Studies at NYU-Buenos Aires since 2009. As an editor, he is chief editor of the bilingual film magazine *Las Naves* as well as editor in charge of the essay collection of the publishing house *Tenemos las máquinas*. He has published articles in books and journals in Argentina, the UK, Brazil and Spain.

Contributors

Carolyn Fornoff is Assistant Professor of Latin American Culture at the University of Illinois at Urbana-Champaign. She is co-editor of two volumes in the environmental humanities: *Timescales: Thinking Across Ecological Temporalities* (2020) and *Pushing Past the Human in Latin American Cinema* (2021).

Naida García-Crespo is an independent scholar working out of the Washington, DC area. Her research and publications focus on Caribbean and Latinx film and culture, transnational film and US colonial politics.

Antonio Gómez teaches Latin American literature and film at Tulane University. He is the author of *Escribir el espacio ausente* (2013), and has published articles on Latin American documentary, exile studies, and Argentine and Cuban literatures. He is currently working on a project on Peronism and mass culture.

Francisco-J. Hernández Adrián is Associate Professor of Hispanic and Visual Culture Studies at Durham University. He has published extensively on the contemporary and postcolonial Caribbean, Atlantic island spaces, the avant-garde and Surrealism, and Latin American cinemas and visual cultures. His work has appeared in *Cultural Dynamics*, *The Global South*, *Hispanic Research Journal*, *Journal of Romance Studies*, and *Third Text*, as well as in edited collections and exhibition catalogues. He is an associate editor of *Cultural Dynamics* and the author of *On Tropical Grounds: Insularity and the Avant-Garde in the Caribbean and the Canary Islands* (forthcoming in 2022).

Amanda Holmes is Associate Professor of Hispanic Studies at McGill University in Montreal. Author of more than thirty articles on twentieth-century and contemporary Latin American cultures, she has considered literature and film primarily through the lens of spatial theory and, particularly, urban studies. Her books have studied the Latin American city in literature and culture, as well as national and transnational identities in Latin American cinemas. Publications include *City Fictions: Language, Body and Spanish American Urban Space* (2007), *Politics of Architecture in Contemporary Argentine Cinema* (2017), and *Cultures of the City: Mediating Identities in Urban Latin/o America*, co-edited with Richard Young (2010).

Laura M. Martins is Associate Professor of contemporary Latin American literature, film, visual arts and architecture, and Comparative Literature at Louisiana State University. She has published widely on Luis Buñuel's films and Latin American visual and literary cultures, including her book *En primer plano: literatura y cine en Argentina, 1955–1969* (2001) and an edited volume *New Readings in Latin American and Spanish Literary and Cultural Studies* (2014). Her works have appeared internationally in *Estudios interdisciplinarios de América Latina y el Caribe, Luis Buñuel-New Readings, Revista Iberoamericana, Revista de Crítica Literaria Latinoamericana, Cine y derechos humanos* and *The Cambridge History of Latin American Women's Literature*, among other journals and edited volumes. She is currently writing a monograph on the poetic-cinematic in contemporary Argentine cinema.

Axel Pérez Trujillo is Assistant Professor in Hispanic Studies at Durham University, UK. He is the author of the book *Imagining the Plains in Latin America: An Ecocritical Study* (2021), as well as other articles that explore the intersection between ecology, culture and philosophy in Latin America.

Sheila Petty is Professor of media studies at the University of Regina. She has written extensively on issues of cultural representation, identity and nation in African and African diasporic screen media, and has curated film, television and digital media exhibitions for galleries across Canada. She is author of *Contact Zones: Memory, Origin and Discourses in Black Diasporic Cinema* (2008); editor of *A Call to Action: the Films of Ousmane Sembene* (1996) and co-editor of *Expressions culturelles des francophonies* (2008); *Canadian Cultural Poesis* (2006) and *Directory of World Cinema: Africa* (2015). Her current research focuses on Amazigh and North African cinemas, and issues of citizenship and immigration in French cinemas. She is currently writing a book on Algerian feminist filmmaker Habiba Djahnine (Edinburgh University Press).

Juan Carlos Rodríguez is Associate Professor of Spanish at the Georgia Institute of Technology. He is the co-editor of two books, *New Documentaries in Latin America* (2014) and *Digital Humanities in Latin America* (2020). He also is the co-editor of the book series Reframing Media, Technology, and Culture in Latin/o America, for the University Press of Florida.

Ignacio M. Sánchez Prado is Jarvis Thurston and Mona van Duyn Professor in Humanities at Washington University in St Louis. His research focuses on Mexican cultural institutions with a focus on literature, cinema and gastronomy. He is the author and editor of various books on these topics, including the monograph *Strategic Occidentalism. On Mexican Fiction, the Neoliberal Book Market and the Question of World Literature* and the recently published collection *Mexican Literature as World Literature*. His public writing has appeared in *The Washington Post, Los Angeles Review of Books, Words without Borders* and other publications. He is the editor of two series: SUNY Series in Latin American Cinema at SUNY Press and Critical Mexican Studies at Vanderbilt University Press. He was President of the Association for the Study of the Arts of the Present, and held the Kluge Chair in the Countries and Cultures of the South at the Library of Congress.

Antonio Traverso teaches Screen Studies at Curtin University, Australia. He is the author of *Documentary Cinema in Chile* (forthcoming); editor of *Southern Screens: Cinema, Culture and the Global South* (2017); and co-editor of *Screen Culture in the Global South* (2020), *El Documental Político en Argentina, Chile y Uruguay* (2015), *Political Documentary Cinema in Latin America* (2014) and *Interrogating Trauma: Collective Suffering in Global Arts and Media* (2011).

Acknowledgements

We wish to acknowledge the generous support of the Faculty of Arts and Humanities at Durham University, and in particular Fiona Robertson, Deputy Executive Dean for Research. Special thanks to Andy Byford, Co-Investigator of the AHRC Open World Research Initiative project, for his enthusiastic support of this editorial project in the context of the 'Atlantic Insularities: Languages of Exorbitance in Spanish-Speaking Island Cultures' subproject.

Our heartfelt thanks to our patient and gracious editors at Bloomsbury, Rebecca Barden and Veidehi Hans, and to Lúcia Nagib, World Cinema Series editor, for her encouragement and support. Thanks also to Erna von der Walde for her wonderful dedication and expertise, and to Charles Forsdick, who supported the project with generous suggestions in the earliest stages. Crucially, the volume owes a great deal to the group of anonymous reviewers who commented on the proposal and manuscript with extraordinary generosity, enthusiasm and critical insight. To all of you, thank you!

Introduction

Islands in Latin American cinema: Film(ing) archipelagos

Antonio Gómez and Francisco-J. Hernández Adrián

I claim for everyone the right to opacity, which is not the same as closing oneself off. It is a means of reacting against all the ways of reducing us to the false clarity of universal models.

Édouard Glissant
Treatise on the Whole-World

Latin American island films

Like islands, portions of territory defined by their separation from the mainland but linked to it by multiple connections, island films are part of their corresponding 'national cinemas' (the critical paradigm that has long defined Latin American cinemas) but are also estranged from them. National cinema dynamics determine many of the films analysed in the essays in this volume, but are never enough to comprehend them, confirming the liminal, ambiguous nature of island films. Like islands, fragments of land that, when considered together, make up a distinct notion – the archipelago – island films can be grouped as a separate analytical category in opposition to the 'countries' of Latin American national cinemas, or even to the illusion of the singular 'continent' of a unified Latin American cinema. We conceive of this collective book as a fresh critical engagement with these island films, and as a first critical articulation of the Latin American film archipelago.

In his radical claim for the 'right to opacity' quoted above, Édouard Glissant presupposes those who reduce and those who are reduced, colonizers and the colonized, those standing outside and those who can claim an inside, literally and metaphorically. But these are not static positions. They should be grasped as parts of a conscious commitment to be in the world that Glissant calls 'archipelagic thinking':

> Archipelagic thinking suits the pace of our worlds. It has their ambiguity, their fragility, their drifting. It accepts the practice of the detour, which is not the same as fleeing or giving up. ... it means being in harmony with the world as it is diffracted in archipelagos, precisely, these sorts of diversities in spatial expanses, which nevertheless rally coastlines and marry horizons. We become aware of what was so continental, so thick, weighing us down, in the sumptuous systematic thought that up until now has governed the History of human communities, and which is no longer adequate to our eruptions, our histories and our no less sumptuous wanderings. The thinking of the archipelago, the archipelagos, opens these seas up to us.
>
> (2020: 18)

How might we experience the cultural specificities that Glissant evokes in the riddle of 'our eruptions, our histories and our no less sumptuous wanderings'? He calls for a repudiation of all systematic approaches that cannot account for difference, fragmentation and opacity. Implicitly, he demands an expansive engagement with the imagination of the island as a limitless horizon of relational connections. As spectators and critics, we are encouraged to measure distances and scales in order to situate each island film within a Latin American archipelagic context that affords analogies, tensions and inconsistencies.

Latin American island films appear at the crossing of many categories and practices: utopia and dystopia, independence and confinement, histories and cosmogonies, landscape and motifs, shooting location and locus of enunciation. What we understand by 'island films,' and what these films mean within Latin America, will become apparent in the corpus and critical interventions in this volume. They include analyses of films that narrate the island, and films that show it; films that linger in the materiality of the insular topography, and films that build on the symbolic and imaginary shapes of the island; films that inscribe themselves in the long tradition of representations of insular spaces, and films that excavate new meanings in old spaces and old *topoi*. Drawing from a constellation of topics, images, moods and representations, the chapters outline a cinema where the insular imagination forms the film.

Latin American island films deploy the full range of historical, photographic and cinematic traits that have come to constitute audiovisual islands as intensely attractive cultural constructions and distant mirrors that reflect – and deflect – the social and political imaginaries of late modernity. The discontinuous film archipelago discussed in this volume represents a series of thematic challenges for spectators, film historians, academics and critics. A recurrent theme is the configuration of the islands of Latin American cinema as marginal environments on the fringes of well-defined national cinemas. A less predictable thread will be the critical confrontation with an extraordinary range of common uncertainties that can be summarized as an emerging conceptual and analytical approach. The texts in this volume demonstrate an analytical passion for island visualities within Latin American cinema at a time when there is a global re-emergence of long-lost, forgotten and derelict analytical objects. A renewed critical interest in the aesthetico-political genealogies of the Global South has been evident for some time in national and transnational festival, distribution and exhibition circuits. The driving force behind such analyses has often originated in discussions around archives and precarity; on preservation, access and circulation; and on what is now undeniably a central aspect of Latin American, LatinX and Global South audiovisual cultures: the recovery and reassessment of local, regional and marginal film practices, narratives and protagonists. This volume aims to contribute to those conversations from a series of boldly local, relational and liminal critical perspectives.

Through filmic, photographic, aural and documentary perspectives, Latin American island cinemas mediate our experiences of the physical islands. For local island communities and diasporas, these films constitute an invaluable archival memory of the assemblages, constellations and disparate affinities that are the subjects and protagonists of this volume. Yet, *The Film Archipelago* does not aim to offer a detailed critical exploration of Latin American islands and archipelagos in film, but to establish a concise set of provisional parameters on how islands and archipelagos *perform* in cinema, and on the multiple dialogues and contrasted views that this *performance* entails.[1] The following chapters demonstrate surprising variety and complexity in the modes of negotiation, resistance and articulation that acquire the contours of a cinematic common ground – a common littoral front in vulnerability and representation. Their commonalities rely not only on the well-known tropology of island tropicalizations but, more saliently, on the shared material conditions and cinematic demands of colonial, carceral, extractivist and tourist experience.

Imaginary islandscapes

If, as Natalia D'Alessandro's chapter suggests, 'América' (Spanish for 'the Americas') enters the European imagination as a kind of island – that is, a physical island at first, and eventually the whole continent as an island between the Atlantic Ocean and Asia as object of desire – the notion of isolation will ultimately be key in the historical formation of the American imagination and in the articulation of American selves. After the end of the Spanish and Portuguese empires, a number of nations developed national literatures and, from the early twentieth century, national cinemas, resulting in the complex political scenario of a Latin America with multiple crossings of national cinemas and insular cinemas, that is, national cinemas that are insular, and not, and insular cinemas that are national, and not. But it has become customary to think of Latin American cinemas (individually) as islands in the archipelago of Latin American cinema (as a whole) and of both as part of the larger archipelago of World Cinema.

The tropologies of islands and archipelagos – idyllic paradise, alluring purgatory, tropical limbo and seductive hell – re-inscribe the world-defining Renaissance *topoi* of utopias and dystopias. This collection attempts to revisit, recontextualize and challenge the visualities of island pastiches that became central to Eurocentric imaginaries of islands as generic and eroticized colonial playgrounds, human zoos, tropical gardens and exotic music halls. The careful readings and contextualizations included in the following chapters address the extent to which those archetypal foundations return to haunt the islands of contemporary Latin American cinema, and expose them as mere functional and rhetorical elements in a subtle field of historical and political tensions.

The twentieth century saw an excess of delirious projections in the subgenres of island-based films: horror, monsters, swashbuckler, slapstick adventure, indigenous ethnography, James Bond-style Cold War, neoliberal ventures and endless robinsonades. In light of this, we do not entirely agree with Adam O'Brien when he asks 'whether a small island setting is perhaps ill-suited to film-noir; after all, islands are already places of isolation and vulnerability, and their narrative implications are fairly stable. They do not throw into relief a person's paranoia or self-delusion in the way that film noir so often does. They are too deterministic' (2018: 62). Despite O'Brien's reasoning, many films that were shot fully or in part in various Latin America islands fit these subgenres. They project an imaginary archipelago onto the material and political scenarios of local environments.

The island as pure landscape and sensory bliss is the reverse side of the imagination of island monstrosities, contagious perversion and violence that represses and sublimates deep genealogies of colonial violence and trauma. The visual cultures of exoticism and primitivism that irrigate the early decades of film history resonate still today in fantasies of purity and plenitude, sexual freedom and primitive enlightenment. The duplicitous myth of enlightenment and disillusionment that dates back to Paul Gauguin's fantasy of a personal paradise echoes through the foundational documentary fictions by Robert J. Flaherty, several of which are set on remote islands. Flaherty's films from the 1920s and 1930s, such as *Nanook of the North* (1922), *Moana* (1926), *Tabu: A Story of the South Seas* (1931, directed by F. W. Murnau and produced by Flaherty) and *Man of Aran* (1934), are loaded with an overwhelmingly masculinist sense of cultural and subjective despair that often constitutes ethnographic subjects as cultural commodities. The obverse of this objectifying ideology of cultural and aesthetic primitivism manifests itself in escapes from the feverish Tropics or frozen seas and returns to metropolitan standards after such titillating interruptions.

Discussing Josephine Baker's French island films, *La sirène des tropiques* (1927) and *Zouzou* (1934), Terri Simone Francis writes that 'Baker's films are paradoxically both peripheral to and central to multiple cinema cultures' (2021: 65). Matthew Pratt Guterl further underlines 'Baker's interest in islands and archipelagoes as an intentional disruption – a disruption, that is, of the hegemony of nation time and imperial time ... Baker's islands and archipelagos – those featured in her performances – are arranged without easy hierarchy or too much distinction, which is precisely why any "island" can do the same work' (2017: 341, 352). In tropical island films more generally, such disruptions are commonly steeped in anxieties of persecution and escape that reveal gendered apprehensions, racist fears and barely veiled guilt. As some of the chapters in this collection explain at length, this exoticist genre is far from extinct.

Despite the powerful cultural and economic forces that continue to provincialize Latin American cinemas in a fixed geodesic relation to the north, it would be difficult to disavow Arjun Appadurai when in the 1990s, at the peak of a critical climate dominated by notions of nations and nationalisms, modernity and postmodernism, and globalization and postcoloniality, he affirmed that 'the United States is no longer the puppeteer of a world system of images but is only one node of a complex transnational construction of imaginary landscapes. The world we live in today is characterized by a new role for the imagination in social life' (1996: 31). If such a 'construction of imaginary landscapes' can be reassessed convincingly today, it is worth delving into the primary notion of a plurality of Latin American islandscapes to consider the interwoven dimensions of island films and physical archipelagos not only from the sweeping viewpoint of a vaguely defined transnationalism, but also, and more centrally, from the discontinuous perspectives that are inscribed in the film archipelago.

We have come to assume that the cinematic renditions of the material and profilmic islands are necessarily turned into 'fictional' forms by the act of representation and thus often conclude that all islandscapes in Latin American cinema are constructed, imagined or imaginary. But Appadurai's notion of 'imaginary landscapes' suggests a certain ideology of place and locality that somehow exists autonomously from the realms of representation and the imagination. As Graeme Harper and Jonathan Rayner argue, 'the cinema's power in the depiction of the landscape [...] has driven or led filmmakers of every nationality and political viewpoint, has fed and fed upon definitions of national identity and been read by cinema audiences as one of the most conspicuous and eloquent elements in the idiom of the film culture from which it emanates' (2010: 24). This performative agency of the cinema, its instrumentality in processes of local and national identity, emanates in part from its properties as a prospective apparatus capable of surveying, projecting and altering the three-dimensional spaces that sustain cinematic landscape.

The islands of early cinema bear witness to the beginnings of the cinematographer and to the dominant imperial networks that allowed the new technology to travel, adapt and transform across colonized space through a series of expansionist moves that in an influential essay Ana M. López calls 'peripheral displacements': 'In complex negotiations between national events/ traditions and foreign models and the demands of Westernization, Latin America produced a series of "spectacular experiments" that dialectically inscribed the cinema in national histories while simultaneously recognizing it as the embodiment of always differential dreams of modernity' (2003: 123–4). Many of the films discussed in this collection show an insistent preoccupation with the persistence of dreams, often coded as a meditation on the nature of time in the relatively miniaturized worlds that islands encapsulate, contain and alter.

Island films, ethnographic thinking

Brazilian director Murilo Salles reflects: 'The world has changed, the gaze has not' (Paranaguá 2003: 264). As the Planet changes beyond recognition and enters a dimension of uncertainty on a scale that exceeds all available representational referents and capacities, the gaze too is changing and altering our responses to the current transformation of images, the cinematic and the audiovisual. But where, and in which specific contexts, have these changes begun to emerge, take place and alter our notions of material space? Is it surprising that it is precisely in the islanded spaces of projected purity and idyllic bliss that these films, and we as their audiences and interpreters, must face a burdensome atmosphere of environmental threat, ecological emergency and impending planetary collapse?

Ana M. López comments that 'thinking of Hollywood as ethnographer, as co-producer in power of cultural texts, allows us to reformulate its relationship to ethnicity. Hollywood does not represent ethnics and minorities: it creates them and provides its audience with an experience of them' (1993: 68). The production and co-constitution of cinematic experiences of Latin American islands have been an important aspect of the ethnographic enterprise in Hollywood and beyond. Today, when streaming media services are fast

8 *The Film Archipelago*

establishing themselves as the new 'ethnographers' and 'co-producers' in charge of the play of distant representations for global consumption, it is urgent to consider the film archipelago from different intermedial perspectives.

In the fantastic dreamworlds of influential island films such as *King Kong* (Merian C. Cooper and Ernest B. Schoedsack, 1933) and *Queimada (Burn!)* (Gillo Pontecorvo, 1969), cultural and political climates become sharply contoured projections of national crises that were displaced onto fictional colonial contexts. In *King Kong*, the anxieties of the Great Depression connect a devastated New York City with an unlikely cinematic expedition to a Dutch-colonial archipelago, while *Queimada* negotiates the contemporary political demands of decolonization with critical urgency on a Caribbean island. As Natalie Zemon Davis reflects, 'the film was a fictional parable of linked historical transitions: from slave regime to free labor; from old imperial colony to independent nation dominated by foreign capital. Pontecorvo [...] put together events from Brazil, Saint-Domingue, Jamaica, Cuba, and elsewhere and set them on the imaginary island of Queimada' (2000: 44). In both films, heroic ambition and masculinist excess are tempered by a profound discontent around romantic fantasies of available and effectively colonized island spaces. These are two examples among many where adventure, plenitude and utopian visions contrast with an overwhelming sense of their reverse: political disillusionment and an implicit or avowed recognition of the troubled legacies of colonialism, racialized exploitation and sexist subjugation.

Steven Spielberg's 1993 adaptation of Michael Crichton's novel *Jurassic Park* offers a postmodern alternative to the modern fantasies of *King Kong* and *Queimada*. *Jurassic Park* tells the story of the failed association between the most advanced genomics and the neoliberal model of branding and economic exploitation. When a groundbreaking discovery, funded by a corporation, allows for the resurrection of dinosaurs, a strictly capitalist logic calls only for the generation of benefit. That this imprudent, catastrophic experiment takes place in another Latin American fictional island, Nubia, off the Pacific coast of Costa Rica, is telling. It reveals not only the persistence of neocolonial exploitation and the understanding of Latin America (or the so-called Third World) as the place most appropriate for the exuberant proliferation of the past, but also a perverse upgrading of this logic – the monsters can be easily contained and visited as an attraction for adventurous tourists, while metropolitan locations are kept secure. *King Kong* had taught Hollywood a lesson, and now the T-Rex will remain isolated in Nubia.

Beyond the status of these and other landmark productions as cult island films that comment directly or indirectly on Latin America as an archipelagic territory, this collection asks how the tropes of the old distant view of Latin American islandscapes have fared in recent decades and in the hands of Latin American directors and film industries. While mainstream film traditions (including Hollywood's) pursue endless re-inscriptions of Western fantasies of the Latin American picturesque through franchises, remakes and variations, what are some of the strategies we can discern in the Latin American film archipelago? An unfolding response is taking shape through the recent deployments of affective, sensory, queer, intermedial and planetary detours in Latin American cinema studies. Another detour in most of the films discussed in this collection is an insistence on local temporalities. For example, D'Alessandro's chapter on Lucrecia Martel's short *Nueva Argirópolis* offers an illuminating reflection on the way contemporary cinema dialogues with the discursive tradition of national foundations in South America and confers new meaning to old words by bringing about innovative contexts. This dialogue resonates in Edgardo Dieleke's pensive first-person narrative of a location scouting trip to Martín García Island, and in Naida García-Crespo's critical re-evaluation of classical Hollywood constructions of otherness. Mediated by experimental and self-reflexive investigations into the psychology of places and spaces, this emphasis often centres around figures of absence, loss, disorientation and amnesia, as Sheila Petty's chapter on a young woman's search for family and community histories in Guadeloupe and Amanda Holmes's analyses of Patricio Guzmán's recent melancholy documentaries demonstrate.

Referring to the success of digital technologies such as CGI, Laura Podalsky contends: 'Certainly this type of high-tech travel is somewhat unique to Hollywood films. However, upon surveying contemporary Latin American cinema, one also finds new forms of cinematic routing, not least of which is the plethora of road films that have emerged since the mid-1990s' (2011: 126). Island excursions, like road trips, encourage a critical expansion of Podalsky's insights through the figures of transport and routing in many of the films discussed in the following chapters. As William Benner's chapter on Sebastián

Silva's *Magic Magic*, Irene Depetris Chauvin's work on documenting Easter Island today and Carolyn Fornoff's analyses of land property conflicts caused by booming lifestyle tourism show, the physical islands are often protagonists in cinematic representation, providing much more than mere background. They enable a refocusing and reframing of the scenes of intimate and allegorical conflict, reminding us that cinematic journeys into the spaces of leisure and trauma almost never fail to comment on the uncertain intermedial present of the gaze, with a growing awareness of our fast-changing world.

Staging the island: Cuba and the Malvinas

Two literary (and colonial) motifs have long served as backdrop and paradigm for the Latin American insular imagination: the Shakespearean trope of the island as stage in *The Tempest* (1610) and the fantasy of shipwreck, survival and entrepreneurism in Daniel Defoe's *Robinson Crusoe* (1719). Latin Americanists are familiar with two central interventions in the genealogy of *The Tempest* which, in turn, generated substantial critical discourses: José Enrique Rodó's *Ariel* (1900) and Roberto Fernández Retamar's *Calibán* (1971). Both texts centre on one of two emblematic secondary characters in the service of Prospero, the protagonist exiled on the island where the story takes place, and see in them a cypher of the American experience. While Ariel, an aerial spirit that identifies with his master and serves his cause, is proposed by Rodó as the ideal of the cosmopolitan intellectual at the time of literary *modernismo*, Fernández Retamar (a cultural ideologue of the Cuban Revolution) sees in Caliban, the monstrous native who has been enslaved and who uses the language of the master to insult him, the model of subversive resistance. Francophone Caribbeanists might also summon Aimé Césaire's *Cahier d'un retour au pays natal* (1939) and *Une tempête* (1969), and the writings of Frantz Fanon and Édouard Glissant, in which the 'stage' of archipelagic thinking transcends insular locations, transforming them into moveable scenes that speak through the multiple extraterritorial connections of the Global South. Every island is a potential totality or a 'world in miniature', a vision of radical subjugation, transformation and reproduction where the figures of immersion and boundlessness translate as a continued cornucopia *at the end of the world*.

A fertile offshoot of the long *Tempest* trail has been the *Robinson Crusoe* myth, 'an instance of modern individualism, indeed of colonialist man just as much as of *homo economicus*' (Aravamudan 1999: 74). Defoe's foundational parable has triggered an inexhaustible literary and film 'genre', the robinsonade, which 'only appears with the deliberate rewriting of the generative work taken as source text, and the focalization on what appeared *a posteriori* as constitutive of its genre identity, that is, the motifs of the desert island, social separation and the test of loneliness, even before the invention of the term in 1731' (Racault 2017: 139).[2] Film robinsonades are perhaps less burdened by the allegorical inertia of the *Tempest* tradition and more open to variations and transgressions of its central tropes, as exemplified by the exploration of homosocial bonds in Luis Buñuel's *Aventuras de Robinson Crusoe* (1954). Although none of the films studied in this volume refer directly to *The Tempest* (or to *Robinson Crusoe*), the Ariel-Caliban opposition has left such a profound mark in Latin American cultural production, and in the hermeneutic takes of Latin American cultural studies, that it would be misguided not to acknowledge its haunting presence.

The *Robinson Crusoe* tradition expresses a need to chronicle the excessive demands of island materiality. There is an abundance of detailed accounts of male immersions in an elemental enclave that is anchored in oceanic, tropical and inclement atmospheres. This is a literary and cinematic imaginary of sensory discoveries on the shores of the elemental world – the space of un-civilized and archaic regressions. The temporality of these hallucinatory experiences hinges on nostalgia for continental time. It is expressed through the patient chronicling of identical time, minimal variation and the consciousness of a uniquely insular scale of time and space. The inescapable tropes of the island as productive plantation and leisure garden re-inscribe fantasies of successful settler colonialism and exemplary scientific exploration. Indeed, there is much in the imagination of islands that renders them visible and exciting by suppressing the elements of normality, predictability and boredom that inflect *Robinson Crusoe* as an anxious meditation on cultural alienation and exile where the island is reduced to a stage for paranoid fantasies that reinforce a virtuous self-image of the European entrepreneur. What prevails is a threatening discourse on islanded protagonists, their backs tragically turned to continental civilization. Unsurprisingly, island timespace is perceived as uncivilized, carceral, allegorical and dependable, as Ignacio M. Sánchez

Prado's chapter on the tradition of classical Mexican cinema about the Islas Marías demonstrates.

Any attempt at tracing a comprehensive genealogy of island films in Latin American cinemas would be naive. The island, shipwreck and castaway motifs have a long tradition in Latin American culture that predates European contact and extends from colonial times to the literature and art of the emerging nations in the nineteenth century. Consequently, these motifs figure prominently in early film and throughout the development of national cinemas in the twentieth century. But two particular cases in the Latin American film culture provide a rich contrast for reflecting on the relationship between filmmaking, literary tradition and politics around islands: on the one hand, the appropriation of insular imaginaries as part of the cultural identity of arguably the most archetypal island nation of our times, Cuba, and its prominence (and even hegemony) in the realm of Latin American cinemas in the 1960s and 1970s; on the other hand, the unforeseen role the Malvinas Islands play in the cinematic tradition of Argentina. While these two cases are not representative of the diverse spatial, historical and representational conflicts that characterize the cinemas of the region, they provide a good starting point for describing the trajectory of films on and from islands in Latin America.

The Ariel-Caliban opposition is an integral part of the project of the Cuban Revolution and its cinema. It takes, for example, a peculiar form in Tomás Gutiérrez Alea's *Memorias del subdesarrollo* (1968). During the protagonist's visit to Ernest Hemingway's house (one of several renditions of the 'island within the island' narrative device in the film) we are introduced to the museum guide with this comment: 'His name is René Villarreal and Hemingway found him as a child playing in the streets of San Francisco de Paula ... He molded him to his needs. The faithful servant and the great lord. The Colonizer and Gunga Din.' The reference to Kipling's poem, though lacking the island context, is a late-nineteenth-century version of the master–slave dialectic that has found so many iterations in colonial island thought. It sets the stage for the film's coda on Hemingway: 'He found his refuge here, his tower, his island in the Tropics.'

Memorias del subdesarrollo sets a foundational tone for island thinking in the cinema of the period. Not only does Gutiérrez Alea put forward the alternative between staying on the island and becoming an exile as the key ethical and political conflict of the film, he also reflects on Cuba's insular condition to support the protagonist's first (Shakespearean) impression of the revolution, 'Everything remains the same here. It's like a scenery.' Early in the film, the words of a character about to go into exile, 'we're very small, just a teeny-tiny island', work as a counter-revolutionary argument, or as evidence of Cuba's weakness in the context of confrontation between the superpowers in the Cold War. In the conclusion, when the protagonist seems to have solved his questions about whether to stay or leave, a similar reflection leads to a very different result, 'This island is a trap. We're very small, too poor ... This dignity costs too much.' This comment accompanies images of military deployment in Havana at the height of the 1963 Missile Crisis and is immediately followed by Castro's reclamation of independence and proclamation of isolation: 'Our country will not be inspected by anyone.' Stormy waves hitting the Malecón close the sequence.

Juan Antonio García Borrero assesses the period in these terms: 'The film utopia of the sixties responded to an aesthetics of choral euphoria. We are reminded of this by those films constructed from elaborate long shots that filmed History – a kind of vast and impersonal narrative where, despite everything, the happy ending could be sensed in the future' (2009: 180). Jacques Roumain's novel, *Gouverneurs de la rosée* (1944), inspired *Cumbite* (1964), directed by Gutiérrez Alea with Sara Gómez and Manuel Herrera as assistant directors. *Cumbite*, one of the inaugural productions of the Cuban Institute of Cinematographic Art and Industry (ICAIC)'s vision for a revolutionary film industry, transcends the expectations of Hollywood and European pastiche, resisting the construction of *islandscapes* as mere scenarios or supplements of authorial and discursive requirements rather than an investment in specific locations and environments.

Michael Chanan argues that '*Cumbite* is not only ICAIC's last neorealist picture, it is also visually the most striking: its stark black-and-white photography creates a feeling of tropical countryside better than ever before ... It is the first of a number of Cuban films about Haiti, all of them made with the participation of the Haitian community in Cuba' (Chanan 2004: 157). As Chanan suggests, there is an undeniable ideological investment in the material and social archipelago that comes through in 'several layers of significance, among them the allegorical. [*Cumbite*] is a film of solidarity with the Haitian peasant and a lesson in revolutionary ethics and the practice of collectivism' (2004: 159). Although Sara Gómez's name is only mentioned late in the credits, she was responsible for researching Haitian religion and music, and for casting the female protagonist (García Yero 2017: 95–100). This anecdote allegorizes the gendered and, however tangentially, the racial power dynamics at work in the development of ICAIC's vision and, at multiple temporal and political junctures, in the global scenarios of post-war decolonization. Made on the margins of Cuba's emerging revolutionary project, Gómez's island films are not only important precursors to the work of the women filmmakers discussed in this book. Her work poses fundamental challenges and questions for the articulation of a new Caribbean and Latin American film criticism.

The same year *Cumbite* was released, an extraordinarily ambitious transnational project imagined Cuba from a very different geopolitical and aesthetic angle, and went on to become an international Cold War–era cult film. Made from a script co-written by Enrique Pineda Barnet and Evgeniy Evtushenko, Mikhail Kalatozov's *Soy Cuba* (*I Am Cuba*) (Cuba and Soviet Union, 1964) reproduces an astonishing range of racist, sexist and colonialist tropes. The film sought to stage the strategic alliance between Cuba and the USSR and the coming of age of ICAIC's vision for a Communist Cuba, but it exhibited the risks of cross-cultural collaboration, the limits of aesthetic compromise and the dangers of confusing propaganda with symbolic disorientation. As a Cold War–era construction, *Soy Cuba* illustrates the etymology of isolation.

As *Memorias del subdesarrollo* suggests, it is in the many representations of the possibility and impossibility of leaving the island that Cuban films have reflected the most on the insular condition. The 1994 *balseros* crisis deepened and expanded, in literature and film both from Cuba and the diaspora, the reductionist trope of the island as a culturally secluded territory surrounded by water from which the sea itself is the only way out. This trope finds a juridical and political correlate in the revision of the Cuban Adjustment Act in 1995 that came to be known in the United States as the 'Wet Feet – Dry Feet' policy. Prominent airport scenes in films such as *Memorias del subdesarrollo* or *Lejanía* (Jesús Díaz, 1985) would eventually be replaced in non-Cuban productions such as *Balseros* (Carles Bosch, 2002) and *90 millas* (Francisco Rodríguez Fernández, 2005) by staging the crossing of the Straits of Florida in precarious rafts made from junk and rescued materials.

The rafter motif finally adopted an allegorical tone in *Juan de los muertos* (Alejandro Brugués, 2011), a zombie film shot and set in Havana. A misleading opening sequence shows Juan, the protagonist who would eventually start a business as a zombie killer, floating in a homemade raft, apparently exhausted, thirsty and lost. When his sidekick Lázaro emerges from the waters holding a harpoon, we learn they are actually close to the Cuban shore and Juan was just taking a nap. The raft is not a means to abandon the island (even if the temptation is there, as Lázaro suggests), but an improvised fishing boat. As the action takes place more than a decade after the *balseros* crisis, the raft has become a signifier not only of escape and survival, but also of political dissent. After most of the population of the island have turned into zombies, Juan and a group of survivors design a floating device by attaching empty oil drums to a red convertible of the kind we often see in promotional and melancholy images of Havana. Leaving the island is the only way to flee the zombie apocalypse. The final sequence shows the car jumping over the Malecón and reaching the ocean with the help of a ramp made of dead bodies. Juan helps the rest of the group get going, but decides to stay in Cuba, once again emphasizing the insular condition.

While the Caribbean islands were depopulated and repopulated as part of the colonial and capitalist enterprise, the Malvinas/Falkland Islands, desert islands near a desert continent, were more easily obtainable, as if they had laid there for the taking. The long legal and diplomatic conflict between Argentina and the UK for their 'rightful' occupation is also a conflict between two ways of imagining the world, the nation, global space and national territory, as Jason Bartles shows in the first chapter of this collection, which deals with the 1982 war for the right to occupy, administer and rule the islands. But their presence on screen dates back to about a century ago, with the silent docudrama *The Battles of Coronel and Falkland Islands* (Walter Summers, 1927) about two naval battles between the British and German empires early in the First World War, the Battle of Coronel off the coast of southern Chile (1 November 1914, a German victory) and the Battle of the Falkland Islands (8 December, a British victory). The film, an epic narrative that tells a story of British resilience and resurgence after the first naval defeat in centuries, is also a statement on the endurance of the receding empire and a showcase of Britain's geographic reach. The Falkland Islands, even if stood in by the Isles of Scilly, where the film was

16 *The Film Archipelago*

shot on location, are an utmost illustration of imperial reaffirmation just a few years before the end of the Empire.

In the 1960s, Raymundo Gleyzer, an apprentice reporter for the Buenos Aires news show Telenoche, became the first Argentine filmmaker to shoot on the islands. *Nuestras Islas Malvinas* (1966), originally aired in segments on television, is a portrait of everyday life on the Falklands from a perspective that hints to the then prevalent feeling that the sovereignty of the islands would eventually be granted to Argentina via a diplomatic agreement. That is the tone in which the film ends, 'but another flag still flies over Stanley today. When we arrive at the Darwin for the trip home, there emerges a glimmer of hope: that very soon an agreement might allow the Argentine flag to fly in its stead'. Because the images were meant for public information and this was the first time Argentine media were allowed to film on the islands (which required a special permission from the British Monarch), and because of the political dimension Gleyzer and his films acquired later, the film is usually linked to the emerging radicalized film practices of the 1960s, which would eventually derive in Solanas and Getino's Third Cinema and Gleyzer's Cine de la base. This is, in any case, important evidence not only of life on the islands at the time, but also of the place the Malvinas occupied in Argentine narratives, indicating a historical fracture of the national territory and the possibility of reconstructing it through cultural representation.

José Luis Marqués shot *Fuckland* (2000) clandestinely following the prescriptive guidelines of the Dogme 95 movement. The film follows an Argentine man who travels to the Falklands with the plan of impregnating a native woman to set an example on how to populate the islands with people of Argentine descent. The male chauvinism of the premise provides a key not only to understanding the nationalistic perspective that sees this land as alienated from its perceived natural affiliation to Argentina (a standpoint the war intensified), but also to the constraint of its territory to an insular dynamic. By reproducing or recreating the colonial pattern of tampering with and administering an island population, *Fuckland* replicates the notion that islands are vacant sites, available for the projection of any sort of political fantasy.

Cuba and Malvinas could be thought of as the northernmost and southernmost islands in Latin America, but they also stand at the opposite ends of the sovereignty spectrum as preeminent examples of cultural, political and economic self-determination in the twentieth century. The insular condition of both territories plays a central role in their political and symbolic articulation, but insularity becomes in each case the backdrop for very different scenes. While the island of Cuba is its own centre, an eloquent locus of enunciation, isolated from the world and protected by the surrounding seas, the Malvinas sit on the periphery of both the 'First' and the 'Third World' and seem doomed to be only spoken about. The Prosperos, Ariels, Calibans, Robinsons and Fridays that inhabit both extremes make remarkably different uses of their insularity.

Filming island lives

Arturo Escobar's notion of *redes* resonates with the memories of island environments that travel through diasporic networks and expanded communities. 'The Spanish *redes*, more than the English term *networks* commonly used to translate it, conveys more powerfully the idea that life and movements are ineluctably produced in and through relations in a dynamic fashion ("assemblages" would be a better translation)' (2008: 25–6). Thus, the corpus of island films discussed in this volume may be fittingly described as a *red* that contains narratives of expulsion, tourist exploitation and other facets of 'hospitality' industries in which local and displaced livelihoods are constantly at stake, either centrally (in Carolyn Fornoff's chapter on *Paraiso for Sale* (2011) and in Jana Evans Braziel's analyses of Raoul Peck's films) or in the background, in Laura Martins' discussions of Gustavo Fontán's films. These chapters show how the material conditions in which local populations live and participate in the stories of the film archipelago are inseparable from the dynamics of dependence that characterize most Latin American islands, with their varying conditions of remoteness, isolation, precarity and fragility. In many of these films there is an explicit awareness of the material diasporas that sustain island livelihoods, cultural identity and transformation. In the routine flows of maritime communication and transport, and in the audiovisual lives of island objects, we discern a widespread reflection on commodities, remittances and various kinds of material trafficking. While these are at times symbolic, they are generally interwoven in the life stories of natives, exiles, migrants, inmates and transient protagonists who populate the seasonal rhythms of small tourist islands. Whether explicitly documentary or not, Latin American island films almost invariably reflect on the limited space, challenging social conditions, or unsustainable inequalities that characterize physical and material insularity. Consequently, what links most of the films discussed in the chapters is the analytical intuition that the islands of Latin American cinema perform as 'contact zones' (Pratt, 1992) or laboratory spaces for the staging (and, sometimes, resolution) of conflicts between individuals and groups with different social, ethnic, racial and national affiliations.

Several chapters explore the capillary structures of contemporary neoliberalism, tracing them through long-standing cultural and economic exchanges that centre around tourist extractivism, mobility and monetarization. 'Tourist utopias', perceived as the objects of periodic returns to an idyllic fantasy of natural and ethnic isolation, appear in different fashions and historical periods, registering hemispheric and global phenomena that connect Latin American island films with other Global South contexts. As Timothy Simpson writes:

> The proliferation of such sites is no accident or arbitrary development. Though they share characteristics common to the touristic landscapes formed over the preceding two centuries, they are in other ways definitive products of our contemporary regime. These sites serve inadvertently as laboratories for experimental forms of governance, innovations in architecture and design, and the production of post-Fordist modes of subjectivity. While they certainly reproduce the inequities of global capitalism, they also harbor a palpable utopian affectation.
>
> (2017: 15)

Island and archipelagic environments, in turn, affect visitors' subjectivities on multiple levels. We can speak without hyperbole of the islands of Latin American cinema as altering environments not only because the mythopoeic demands of island imaginaries affect how we experience the elemental world from an island viewpoint, but also because island subjectivities are immersed in the dynamics of unstable exchanges, separations and returns that many of these films interrogate. The difficulty in capturing the island as 'still', whether in the form of a still-life montage, or as a moving cinematic environment, resides in negotiating the two archetypal extremes of the graphic and photographic picturesque, and its dialectical opposite: an adventure-filled and ultimately hallucinatory exploitation of the island as regressive geocultural space.

Capturing the perfect islandscape or producing a memorable island scene remains important for directors and audiences who seek to experience the fantasy island and to participate in the altering experience. But a central challenge we face as spectators is a confrontation with local trauma. We will often enter the tempestuous domains of trauma via the fantasy of an idyllic island microcosm. Encounters with islanders, and transactions between those who might be passing through or have become islanded, are the results of the cinematic exploration of island subjectivities and of the island as a unique altering space. By way of contrast, dialogue and paradox, the objects of filmic and photographic exposure that centre on a specific island become blurred through the traffickings and contestations that traverse the archipelagic flows of Latin American cinema.

Watching Latin American island films

We start from the south to highlight the specific realities of the most remote archipelagos in the hemisphere. A unique set of perspectives from the insular south in the book's first section, 'Islands at the end of the world', interrupts the tropical imaginaries that are central to 'the view from the North'. These chapters suggest connections across geophysical, environmental, ethnocultural and historical limits on the margins of the nation-state in two of Latin America's most prominent national film industries, Argentina and Chile. Jason Bartles' chapter, 'Deserted islands for the nation: Empty land- and seascapes in three Argentine films of the Malvinas/Falkland Islands', scrutinizes the cinema around the conflict between Argentina and the UK at its height during the 1982 war. This intense, short-lived event (it did not last three months, from 2nd April to 14th June) triggered a wave of fictional and documentary representations in novels, *testimonios*, films, plays and television shows. Focusing on three films that evoke the war, Bartles addresses how these films deal with the notion of the 'desert', foundational in the Argentine imaginary, through the depiction of sublime, empty spaces.

With echoes of Michelangelo Antonioni's *L'Avventura* (1960) and insights into different kinds of disappearance and mourning, the essays on Patricio Guzmán's *Nostalgia de la luz* and *El botón de nácar*, and on Sebastián Silva's *Magic Magic*, revisit recent political conflict, unsolved family business and the cinematic construction of islands as mnemonic repositories and burial grounds that can be remembered and exhumed across the archival archipelago. In William Benner's chapter, 'Marooned testimony: Chilean islandscape and the politics of memory in Sebastián Silva's *Magic Magic* (2013)', the island becomes a space in-between geography and history, where a country's traumatic past can be renegotiated. Dialoguing with, and perhaps resisting, an obvious return to the trope of island disappearances, the chapter interprets the cadences and symptomatic constellations of *Magic Magic* as a Latin American film on irrepressible trauma, amnesia and remembrance. In Amanda Holmes's chapter on Patricio Guzmán's first-person documentaries, 'Memory islands: Repeating traumas in Patricio Guzmán's *Nostalgia de la luz* (2010) and *El botón de nácar* (2015)', insular and archipelagic topographies inform how Chile understands itself, and how the documentary film tradition restages history. Holmes proposes that, mimicking the geographical islands, the oppressed communities represented in the films emerge as peripheral memory islands in Chilean society.

Irene Depetris Chauvin's chapter, 'Insular spaces: A documentary and an affective ethno-mapping of the Rapa Nui culture', on Tiziana Panizza's *Tierra sola* (2017), analyses the materiality of the image in the complex interplay of ethnic, geophysical and aesthetic dimensions bearing on the archival reconstruction of Rapa Nui. By following the lives of inmates in an open prison in Easter Island, the film dialogues with the carceral tradition of insular spaces, but offers a new way of representing and understanding the cultural Other.

The chapters in the second section, 'Liminal islands', investigate the conceptual frames of the hemispheric south, opening rather than foreclosing attempts at understanding islands through the exclusive lens of geocultural location and hemispheric remoteness. The texts in this section display a vast panorama of sovereign, environmental and geopolitical visualities that exceed territorial limits and reflect on the geographical diversity that characterizes a pluriregional approach to Latin American cinema. Ignacio M. Sánchez Prado's chapter, 'Social reformation and the edges of sovereignty: Fernando Soler's

La hija del penal (1949) and Emilio Fernández's *Islas Marías* (1951)', charts a historical attitude and a fascinating cultural process in Mexican history around films that interpellate the state from an extreme liminal viewpoint – the penal colony – that is superimposed on the symbolic remoteness of the Islas Marías archipelago. Geographical isolation in these films is tantamount to being on the margins of the national project, almost out of the reach of the pedagogies of post-revolutionary Mexico and classical Mexican cinema. Axel Pérez Trujillo's 'Exposed insularities: Islands, capitalism and waste in Jorge Furtado's *Ilha das Flores* (1989)', brings contemporary environmental theory to bear on the unique documentary construction of a fragile archipelagic context in Furtado's short film. The Guaíba estuary of Southern Brazil is a spectacle that reveals not insular singularity and concreteness, but planetary conditions of precarity, toxicity and injustice. The chapter sheds new light on a now canonical Latin American political documentary to reveal its topicality and pertinence today.

'Islands in Lucrecia Martel's *Nueva Argirópolis* (2010)' by Natalia D'Alessandro analyses Martel's short film (a piece in a collection that celebrates the bicentennial of Argentina) from the perspective of the indigenous groups who have been excluded from the national project. By returning to Sarmiento's utopic national plan in *Argirópolis* (1850), the chapter identifies new conflicts, a new linguistic paradigm and a new insular utopia. Finally, Laura Martins' essay, 'Gustavo Fontán's films: On faces, specters, fragments of matter', considers fluvial insularities in the same region. *El rostro* (2014) and *El limonero real* (2015) put forward, according to Martins, a poetic mode of filmmaking. Her analyses show how the impulse to represent island experiences can be best achieved as a form of sensibility, a way of feeling and an affective structure grounded in the senses.

The chapters in the third section, 'Antillean relations on screen', deploy a provocative critique of the tired imaginaries of the picturesque, exotic and ever-generous Caribbean, in which tourist consumption and audiovisual stimulation foreclose any form of engagement with Caribbean realities. The geographies tackled in this section – Puerto Rico, Cuba, Guadeloupe, the Bocas del Toro archipelago off the coast of Panama, and Haiti – trace no conventional mapping of a stereotypical Caribbean. These essays form a constellation of critical questions that insist on archival, historical, political and environmental junctures. Their investigations into the Caribbean film archipelago expand and complicate the previous sections' mappings of cinematic performances across remote limits, national margins and relational zones. Naida García-Crespo's chapter, 'The duplicitous empire: Ambiguous representations of Puerto Ricans and Japanese-Americans in Herbert I. Leeds's *Mr. Moto in Danger Island* (1939)', raises important questions about the imperialist underpinnings of these hemispheric transactions at the end of the interbellum period. Her approach to Puerto Rico via the classical Hollywood meaning-making machinery exposes racial overtones in the articulation of the island as a space 'in training' to become America, where subjects will also train to become American citizens. The island becomes a symbolic laboratory for the practice of American values in the realms of the law, the economy, gender and race.

Juan Carlos Rodríguez's chapter, 'An archipelago of crossed gazes: Intersections of documentary media practices in Cuba and Puerto Rico', discusses issues of critical and historical method to question prevalent constructions of Cold War–era Cuban and Puerto Rican documentary practices as separate domains that are forcibly divided by strict geopolitical boundaries. This essay encourages us to re-orient our analytical and conceptual practices around (not outside) the compelling evidence of inter-insular archives, political mobilities and fragmented life stories. Sheila Petty's essay, "Irreducible memories' of Caribbeanness: Mariette Monpierre's *Le Bonheur d'Elza* (2011)', argues that Guadeloupe is a site for the examination of not only the history of slavery that shaped the Caribbean, but also the history (and present) of neocolonialism, through the classic narrative vehicle of a personal and family story that, to some extent, allegorizes the Caribbean archipelago. Carolyne Fornoff's chapter, 'Documenting lifestyle migration: Anayansi Prado's *Paraíso for Sale* (2011)', turns to intersections of race, precarity and transnational mobility on the Caribbean fringes of Panama. The essay effectively engages with the material, social and environmental ramifications of Prado's film by highlighting the director's investments in a poetics of island livelihoods and social injustice *against* unequal and destructive migratory practices. Jana Braziel's chapter, 'Raoul Peck's archipelagic cinema: Island contestations of the international order in *Assistance mortelle* (2013)', presents Haiti as an islandscape at the mercy of the powerful forces reigning the world today: neoliberalism, neocolonialism, climate change and forced displacements.

In the closing section, 'Reimagining islandscapes', Edgardo Dieleke's filmmaker's notes on Martín García in the River Plate, and Antonio Traverso's reflections on the visuality of Rapa Nui in the Pacific Ocean, offer a provisional double epilogue on the challenges, paradoxes and inexhaustible attraction of the archipelagos of Latin American cinema. Edgardo Dieleke's chapter, 'Notes on an island film: A journey to Martín García', is an intimate journal that chronicles his experiences during an exploratory trip with fellow filmmaker Daniel Casabé to the island of Martín García. In asking what and where to film on the island, this literary and photographic meditation demonstrates a perceptive awareness of the tensions and potentials of insular filmmaking. Dieleke's reflections on archival, sensory and material immersion anticipate the filmmaking experience as an effort in relational reconstruction. Antonio Traverso's closing chapter, 'Letters from the islands: A visual essay', adopts a poetics of the fragment where the spectre of the carceral island returns as an apt reminder of the many latent dimensions of island films that haunt the film archipelago and, unavoidably, the present volume. The essay's poetic and photographic *excavation* of remote islandscapes and lived memories on Rapa Nui and in Australia applies a fragmentary, 'concentrationary' cinema method and chronicles an emotionally poignant journey across an area of the insular Global South. Colonial violence and systemic injustices perpetrated against Indigenous and Aboriginal populations permeate the entire text in tense dialogue with anxieties about the planetary Covid pandemic.

Nesostalgia: Nostalgia for the islands

The essays in this volume illustrate how dwelling in space through the archipelagic perspective can enable a more sober and intimate understanding of the islands of Latin American cinema. They evoke the old islands of early and ethnographic cinemas, the photographic unconscious that amounts today to a vast archival dispersion and a boundless *nesostalgia*, a painful homecoming desire or *nostalgia* for the elemental island (*nesos*) that we may never visit or inhabit through cinematic experience. As the waters rise and human-driven climate phenomena impact on insular, fluvial and coastal systems, islands are being reconfigured as microcosms of the catastrophic world to come. They are not perfect images of stillness and balance, but rank among the most dangerously exposed zones where ecological and sociocultural catastrophe started a long time ago. In this existential scenario, island visualities can be seen critically in T. J. Demos' words as 'moving images of globalization' (2013: 21). We hope that new appraisals of Latin American cinemas like the ones we propose here can encourage further cultural analyses of geophysical typologies on the fringes of the national film traditions.

The islands and archipelagos of Latin American cinema display an aesthetics of local specificity and hemispheric simultaneity that nuances Appadurai's foresight: 'The complexity of the current global economy has to do with certain fundamental disjunctures between economy, culture, and politics that we have only begun to theorize' (1996: 33). This collection attempts to measure and nuance how the characteristics of Appadurai's contentious 'mediascapes' apply to most Latin American islands and archipelagos. Among the critical and political tools available to the archipelagic spectator, the cinematic practices of precarity and remoteness represent an important challenge posed by a transformed planetarity in which island livelihoods, and the possibility of narrating alternative island perspectives, are crucially at stake.

In the following chapters, a vast historical arch registers the historical traces and archival memories of early colonial displacement and expropriation, asynchronous processes of environmental transformation and ruination, disenfranchisement and diasporas. This has immediate implications for our interrogation of national cinema as the supreme methodological lens to approach both Latin American cinema and its localized varieties. Amitav Ghosh reminds us of this reality when he reflects that 'we live in an era when the body of the nation can no longer be conceived of as consisting only of a territorialized human population: its very sinews are now revealed to be intertwined with forces that cannot be confined by boundaries' (2016: 144). The archipelagic lens permits an asynchronous and wide-ranging understanding of relations across these interlinked processes that displace the centrality of nations in our approaches to cinema. It also lays bare multiple processes of erosion and ruination of conventional modes of cinematic identification along national borders.

Contemporary tropes of nostalgic slowness and elementary connectedness echo the exotic pleasures of early cinema and the long decades of Hollywood hegemony. In today's interlocked environmental, political and economic scenarios, the conceptual and analytical frames of the Latin American film archipelago invite new critical reflections on *nesostalgia* as a relational perspective. More urgently, such frames insist on the material conditions of insularity and displacement that characterize much of Latin American cinema, inviting critical narratives of global and local experiences, in Saskia Sassen's expression, 'at the systemic edge,' where 'the extreme character of conditions at the edge makes visible larger trends that are less extreme and hence more difficult to capture' (2014: 211). The physical islands of Latin American cinema reverberate with the old nesophilic fantasies and new global scenarios in ways that suggest an expanding *nesostalgia*. This film archipelago is traversed by intimate concerns for local livelihoods and displaced communities which must respond to present demands and struggle to project hopeful futures beyond survival and memory. This book addresses this challenge through critical considerations of a *film archipelago* that relates and connects across repeating islands, reaching out to other varieties of Latin American cinematic experience, and never quite exhausting or limiting our curiosity, but encouraging us instead to return differently to the islands of Latin American cinema.

Notes

1   A range of situated discussions on islands in rhetorical and visual representation can be found in Roberts and Stephens (2017); Simpson (2017); Metzger, Hernández Adrián and Crichlow's special issue of *Third Text* on *Islands, Images, Imaginaries* (2014); Edmond and Smith (2003); and in numerous articles in *Small Axe* and *Islands Studies Journal*.
2   All unattributed translations are by the authors.

References

90 millas (2005), [Film] Dir. Francisco Rodríguez Fernández, Spain; Cubaname.
Appadurai, A. (1996), *Modernity at Large: Cultural Dimensions of Globalization*, Minneapolis: University of Minnesota Press.

Aravamudan, S. (1999), *Tropicopolitans: Colonialism and Agency, 1688–1804*, Durham: Duke University Press.

Aventuras de Robinson Crusoe (1954), [Film] Dir. Luis Buñuel, Mexico: Tepeyac.

L'Avventura (1960), [Film] Dir. Michelangelo Antonioni, Italy; Cino del Duca.

Balseros (2002), [Film] Dir. Carles Bosch and Josep Maria Domènech, Spain; Bausan Films.

The Battles of Coronel and Falkland Islands (1927), [Film] Dir. Walter Summers, UK; BIF.

Chanan, M. (2004), *Cuban Cinema*, Minneapolis: University of Minnesota Press.

Crichton, Michael (1990), *Jurassic Park*, New York: Alfred A. Knopf.

Cumbite (1964), [Film] Dir. Tomás Gutiérrez Alea, Cuba: ICAIC.

Davis, N. Z. (2000), *Slaves on Screen: Film and Historical Vision*, Toronto: Vintage Canada.

Demos, T. J. (2013), *The Migrant Image: The Art and Politics of Documentary during Global Crisis*, Durham: Duke University Press.

Edmond, R. and V. Smith (eds) (2003), *Islands in History and Representation*, London: Routledge.

Escobar, A. (2008), *Territories of Difference: Place, Movements, Life, Redes*, Durham: Duke University Press.

Fernández Retamar, R. (1971), *Calibán: apuntes sobre la cultura de nuestra América*, México: Diógenes.

Francis, T. S. (2021), *Josephine Baker's Cinematic Prism*, Bloomington: Indiana University Press.

Fuckland (2000), [Film] Dir. José Luis Marqués, Argentina; Atomic Films.

García Borrero, J. A. (2009), *Otras maneras de pensar el cine cubano*, Santiago de Cuba: Editorial Oriente.

García Yero, O. (2017), *Sara Gómez: un cine diferente*, La Habana: Ediciones ICAIC.

Ghosh, A. (2016), *The Great Derangement: Climate Change and the Unthinkable*, Chicago: University of Chicago Press.

Glissant, E. (2020), *Treatise on the Whole-World*, trans. C. Britton, Liverpool: Liverpool University Press.

Guterl, M. P. (2017), 'The Tropics of Josephine: Space, Time, and Hybrid Movements', in B. R. Roberts and M. A. Stephens (eds), *Archipelagic American Studies*, 341–55, Durham: Duke University Press.

Harper, G. and J. Rayner (2010), 'Introduction – Cinema and Landscape', in G. Harper and J. Rayner (eds), *Cinema and Landscape*, 13–28, Bristol: Intellect.

Juan de los muertos (2011), [Film] Dir. Alejandro Brugués, Spain and Cuba; La Zanfoña.

Jurassic Park (1993), [Film] Dir. Steven Spielberg, USA; Universal Pictures.

King Kong (1933), [Film] Dir. Merian C. Cooper and Ernest B. Schoedsack, USA; RKO.

Lejanía (1985), [Film] Dir. Jesús Díaz, Cuba; ICAIC.

López, A. M. (1993), 'Are All Latins from Manhattan? Hollywood, Ethnography and Cultural Colonialism', in J. King, A. M. López and M. Alvarado (eds), *Mediating Two Worlds: Cinematic Encounters in the Americas*, 67–80, London: British Film Institute.

López, A. M. (2003), 'Train of Shadows': Early Cinema and Modernity in Latin America', in E. Shohat and R. Stam (eds), *Multiculturalism, Postcoloniality, and Transnational Media*, 99–128, New Brunswick: Rutgers University Press.

Man of Aran (1934), [Film] Dir. Robert Flaherty, USA: Gainsborough Pictures.

Moana (1926), [Film] Dir. Robert Flaherty, USA: Paramount.

Memorias del subdesarrollo (1968), [Film] Dir. Tomás Gutiérrez Alea, Cuba: ICAIC.

Metzger, S., F.-J. Hernández Adrián and M. Crichlow (2014), 'Introduction: Islands, Images, Imaginaries', *Third Text* 28.4–5: 333–43.

Nanook of the North (1922), [Film] Dir. Robert Flaherty, USA: Les Frères Revillon, Pathè Exchange.

Nuestras Islas Malvinas (1966), [Film] Dir. Raymundo Gleyzer, Argentina; Telenoche.

O'Brien, A. (2018), *Film and the Natural Environment: Elements and Atmospheres*, New York: Wallflower.

Paranaguá, P. A. (2003), *Tradición y modernidad en el cine de América Latina*, Madrid: Fondo de Cultura Económica.

Podalsky, L. (2011), *The Politics of Affect and Emotion in Contemporary Latin American Cinema: Argentina, Brazil, Cuba, and Mexico*, New York: Palgrave Macmillan.

Pratt, M. L. (1992), *Imperial Eyes: Travel Writing and Transculturation*, London: Routledge.

Queimada (Burn!) (1969), [Film] Dir. Gillo Pontecorvo, Italy; PEA.

Roberts, B. R. and M. A. Stephens (2017), 'Introduction: Archipelagic American Studies: Decontinentalizing the Study of American Culture', in B. R. Roberts and M. A. Stephens (eds), *Archipelagic American Studies*, 1–54, Durham: Duke University Press.

Rodó, José Enrique (2006), *Ariel*, 3rd ed., ed. Belén Castro, Madrid: Cátedra.

Roumain, Jacques (1977), *Gouverneurs de la rosée*, Fort-de-France: Désormeaux.

Sassen, S. (2014), *Expulsions: Brutality and Complexity in the Global Economy*, Cambridge: Harvard University Press.

Simpson, T. (2017), 'Mapping Tourist Utopias', in T. Simpson (ed.), *Tourist Utopias: Offshore Islands, Enclave Spaces, and Mobile Imaginaries*, 13–41, Amsterdam: Amsterdam University Press.

La sirène des tropiques (1927), [Film] Dir. Henri Étiévant and Mario Nalpas, France; La Centrale Cinématographique.

Soy Cuba (1964), [Film] Dir. Mikhail Kalatozov, Cuba; ICAIC.

Tabu: A Story of the South Seas (1931), [Film] Dir. F. W. Murnau, USA: Paramount.

Zouzou (1934), [Film] Dir. Marc Allégret, France; Les Films H. Roussillon.

Part One

Islands at the end of the world

1

Deserted islands for the nation: Empty land- and seascapes in three Argentine films of the Malvinas/Falkland Islands

Jason A. Bartles

Where are the inhabitants? The place seems deserted as well as ruined.

Robert FitzRoy

*Narrative of the Surveying Voyages
of His Majesty's Ships Adventure and Beagle* (1831–6)

Argentine films about the 1982 Malvinas/Falklands War compose more than an archive of a defeated nation; they are the stories of those who were persecuted by a dictatorship in its death throes and a criticism of the widespread nationalist fervour that cheered such exploitation. From this growing archive, I have chosen to study three films: *La deuda interna* (Internal Debt), directed by Miguel Pereira (1987); *La campana* (The Diving Bell), directed by Fredy Torres (2010); and *La forma exacta de las islas* (The Exact Shape of the Islands), directed by Daniel Casabé and Edgardo Dieleke (2013).[1] My analysis of these three films focuses on the frequent appearance of empty land- and seascapes that cannot be reduced to establishing shots or transitions. Films about the Malvinas/Falklands are not always shot on the islands nor do they necessarily take place there. In both *La deuda interna* and *La campana*, the islands are displaced from the screen, referenced only as an extraterritorial and unrepresentable space beyond the national cinematic gaze. Both seek to criticize the dictatorship and those who supported the war; however, in this essay I demonstrate that the recurring appeal to sublime, empty spaces both interrupts and undermines their criticism by reviving essentialist tropes from the national archives, especially that of Argentina as a desert or deserted landscape. In contrast, *La forma exacta de las islas* films land- and seascapes on the Malvinas/Falkland Islands with an innovative technique that does not interrupt, but rather suspends, these spaces and the people inhabiting them. I analyse how this film creates a *mise-en-abîme* (mirroring effect) that allows the viewer to linger and reflect on a dissonant series of narratives of loss and mourning in excess of the war and of any one nation or strident nationalism.

Since the end of the dictatorship in 1983, Argentine cinema has grappled with the painful legacy of those years while also renovating the entire film industry. In the 1980s, Argentine cinema foregrounded the discourse of human rights and sought to shape public discourse related to the dictatorship, its causes and its legacy. According to Jessica Stites Mor, 'among those who rose to the challenge were several directors who wanted to bring a nationalist, realist, and autocritical cinema to the foreground of Argentina's popular film culture' (2012: 96–7). Thus, *La deuda interna* joins *Camila* (1984), *La historia oficial* (1985) and *La noche de los lápices* (1986), among others, to further expose the violent history of the dictatorship through film. Ana Amado describes the goals of such films in the immediate aftermath of the dictatorship: 'Filmed fictions were similar in that they put their interpretative, or simply informative, spin on those social discourses in circulation about genocidal methods and their victims' (2009: 34). Nevertheless, David Oubiña rightly signals the shortcomings of many of these early films: 'The majority of films from the 1980s attempted to approach these great themes, but they did not manage to move beyond an outdated costumbrismo embellished with sensationalist denunciations' (2002: 204). This is to say that many of these films construct sweeping narratives and national allegories that, at times, rely on flat archetypes to carry out their goals of informing the nation about the violence and trauma of the recent past. This will be the case of *La deuda interna* as it employs professional and non-professional actors to represent the real-life events related to an indigenous community in Jujuy that inspired the narrative about an idealistic teacher and his young student who would later be killed in the war.

In the 1990s, the Nuevo Cine Argentino (NCA) radically transformed the entire film industry in ways that can be witnessed to this day. Though this label brings together films and directors who at first glance may not appear to have much in common, Gonzalo Aguilar has mapped out the NCA's innovations, including new technologies for filming and editing, new means of distribution and a new generation of producers who know how to seek global financial support for their films and strategically place them in international film festivals. In aesthetic terms, the films of the NCA are united primarily by their rejection of that realism or *costumbrismo* of the 1980s:

> While the screenplays that respond to the era of the return of democracy have one or two characters who embody the perspective with which the viewer should identify, (the morally correct position, the gaze that most adequately interprets what is going on), a great deal of the films from the New Argentine Cinema eliminate this conciliatory possibility for the viewer.
>
> (2006: 25–6)

When they represent the dictatorship or its aftermath, the films from the NCA eschew overtly didactic messages about what needs to be done or who we are as a nation; instead, these films 'offer us a world: a language, an environment, a few characters ... a *sketch*' (23–4).

Though it was released in 2010, *La campana* more closely models itself after the allegorical films from the 1980s. Set in a small fishing community in Mar del Plata, the film overtly condemns the dictatorship and the war through the vantage point of two, rather flat protagonists: a man who poorly represents the disappeared – he returns home in the end – and a younger man, one of the 'boys' sent to war, who is left shell-shocked and mute upon his return. In contrast to both *La deuda interna* and *La campana*, *La forma exacta de las islas* avoids the appeals to *costumbrismo* and allegory, and it breaks out of the deeply imbedded colonialist tropes that portray the nation as a desert, tropes that overlap with the nationalist cries to reclaim the islands. Rather, the film is a multilayered documentary that develops complex characters centred around Julieta Vitullo, a young Argentine woman who travels to the islands to do research; she interviews locals and happens to become close with two ex-combatants who have returned to the islands for the first time since the war.

Before analysing the empty land- and seascapes of these films in detail, first it will be necessary to review the history of the competing, colonialist claims for these islands that lead to the declaration of war in 1982. Then, I turn to a discussion of how the trope of the Malvinas/Falklands as deserted islands is deeply embedded within the Romantic sublime, an aesthetic that has been deployed to intentionally produce coveted, often indigenous, territories as empty spaces primed for the violent expansion of the state and the market. This history as well as these images and metaphors inform the nationalist fervour surrounding the Malvinas/Falkland Islands in the Argentine imaginary.

Claiming deserted islands

In *Islands of the Mind*, John R. Gillis explains that medieval Europeans ventured into the Atlantic 'in search of a desert in the sea, coveting empty rather than inhabited land' (2004: 23). Deserted islands are ideal sites for utopian thinking, scientific exploration and colonization, but most of the spaces invaded by those Europeans were not actually empty; rather, in order to justify the violent destruction and colonization of other peoples, cultures and territories, those spaces were intentionally perceived, produced and represented as empty regions. Unlike in the Caribbean, the Malvinas/ Falkland Islands appear to have been uninhabited until the arrival of Europeans in the sixteenth century. According to Federico Lorenz, their first sighting most likely took place in 1520 by Jerónimo de Guerra and Esteban Gomes who were sent on an exploration of the South Atlantic by Fernando de Magallanes as he and the rest of his fleet were establishing the settlement of Puerto San Julián (2014: 26–7). The Islas de Sansón, as they were named, appeared on Spanish maps throughout the century, and other British, Dutch and French explorers and conquerors began to chart and lay claim to these deserted islands.

The trope of the deserted island reappears in nineteenth-century natural descriptions of the Malvinas/Falklands, suggesting they comprise a barren, desolate and still uninhabited archipelago. Captain Robert FitzRoy of the HMS *Beagle* – the ship on which Charles Darwin travelled – relates his surprise upon landing at Port Louis in 1831 and finding a 'few half-ruined stone cottages' instead of a 'happy settlement' (1839: 271). By the time of FitzRoy's arrival, the islands were not actually deserted. In 1820, Col. David Jewett claimed possession of the islands for the Provincias Unidas del Río de la Plata, which would become the Argentine Republic, and in 1829, Luis Vernet was named governor and established a colony on the islands. In 1831, the Argentine settlement was attacked by the United States Navy warship USS *Lexington*, and in 1833, the British invaded, expelled Vernet and the Argentine settlers, and colonized the islands in the name of the British Empire.[2] Yet, the image of the archipelago that persists to this day is one of undesirable, wind-swept landscapes – populated more by sheep and penguins than by humans – in the freezing waters of the South Atlantic.

Despite, and because of, the persistence of these images of the Malvinas/Falklands as a deserted archipelago, these islands located less than 500 kilometres off the coast of Patagonia have occupied an important place in the Argentine national imaginary since 1833. In the wake of the British invasion, the theme of their recovery has reappeared as a source of strident nationalism throughout Argentina's history. On 2 April 1982, the military junta ruling Argentina – during which 30,000 Argentine citizens were abducted, tortured, sexually abused and disappeared while neoliberal reforms were imposed on the country – invaded the islands and declared this national territory recovered.

The causes of this war are usually attributed to two factors: first, the economic decline and waning popularity of the military junta in 1982 and, second, the junta's misguided belief that the UK would not respond in force to the Argentine invasion. However, Luis L. Schenoni, Sean Braniff and Jorge Battaglino's analysis of recently declassified documents from the Rattenbach Commission demonstrates a more complex reality underlying the decision to invade. They argue that domestic politics played little role in the decision, since the plans to invade the islands date back to December 1981, months before the greater period of unrest that culminated in the 30 March 1982 protests; they also demonstrate that the military was well aware of the likelihood of a British response and an Argentine defeat (2020: 43–7).[3] Instead, they convincingly posit that 'Argentina's relative decline to peer competitors and territorial losses prompted its government – an insulated decision-making junta imbued by a loss frame [and sunk costs related to outsize military expenditures] – to engage in a long series of offensive, risk-acceptant actions leading to the Malvinas/Falklands War' (61). The military junta ultimately wagered everything on a war they knew they were likely to lose. Even though domestic politics were not the cause of the war, Rosana Guber explains that 'Malvinas was promoted by the regime as the symbol of national unity and continuity, and civil and political society accepted this' (2012: 39). The promise of restoring national unity by recovering a lost territory momentarily displaced the growing, internal dissent towards the regime and even garnered a certain level of popular enthusiasm for the dictatorship until the end of the war.

Argentina suffered a quick and crushing defeat, and General Menéndez surrendered to the British on 14 June 1982. Three Falklanders, 255 British military personnel and 649 Argentines were killed during the conflict. Eight out of ten Argentine soldiers were drafted specifically for this invasion (Lorenz 2014: 141–8). Since the end of the war, around 400 Argentine ex-combatants, as they prefer to be called, have committed suicide (164). The popular support shown to the military junta must be condemned. At the same time, it is important to recognize that those drafted into military service for this war, and all of the casualties of it, are in many ways the final victims of the dictatorship that exploited nationalist sentiments tied to the images of the Malvinas/Falklands as empty, stolen islands.

Sublime land- and seascapes

In 'A Phenomenology of Islands', Peter Hay argues that island studies must engage with real islands, not just with the imagined islands and metaphors that circulate in literature, film and popular culture, because many of these metaphors 'are continental, as well as colonial, constructions' (2006: 30). However, he continues: 'There is one important manner in which metaphorical senses of islandness *are* the appropriate substance of island studies. This is when metaphoric transcriptions of islands rebound upon *real* islands and influence life there' (30). Hay is correct to assert that many of the images and metaphors about islandness are colonialist, reflecting little to nothing of actual islands and islanders. Nevertheless, in the case of the Malvinas/Falklands, the images and metaphors circulating about the islands have had tremendous impact on the global politics surrounding those islands. Responding to Hay's essay, Stewart Williams writes: 'An island is constituted through its proclamations and performances as a political entity that is mythological and scientific, real and imaginary' (2012: 229). This is to say that the ways islands have been imagined, even when fully dissociated from material islands, continue to inform the politics surrounding those islands.

In this sense, it would be impossible to understand the almost-two-hundred-year dispute between Argentina and the UK over these real islands without also engaging the deeply imbedded images and metaphors that have been constructed to represent them. These distant islands are rarely visited by Argentine and British citizens; yet, images of them keep circulating in their respective national imaginaries. Nevertheless, when it comes to representations of the 1982 war, there is a notable lack of archival footage of the actual war. In her analysis of Argentine films about the war, Luciana Caresani notes the repeated use of documentary footage from Galtieri's speech at the Casa Rosada on 2 April 1982 in which the dictator declares triumphantly that the Armed Forces have recovered the islands. This repetitive use of limited footage is due to a lack of other archival materials. Thus, Caresani's analysis points to 'the invisibility at the center of the event (in other words, the images filmed on the battlefield that were censored or destroyed by the Army and by the mainstream media)' (2014: 23). Actual footage from the war does not appear in many of the films that attempt to represent it, primarily because this footage was censored or destroyed by the military junta and the media. Furthermore, it was not always possible to film on the islands after 1982, since Argentines were not permitted to travel there until August 1999, and then only with highly limited options.

Whether or not they take place on the real islands, the three films I analyse in this essay all engage in different ways with the legacy of the Romantic sublime. The sublime has been deployed to represent both national territories and the oceans connecting them as vast, empty tracts of natural space that inspire awe and terror. In the works of both Edmund Burke and Immanuel Kant, the sublime is differentiated from the beautiful, a modern distinction that did not exist in the ancient aesthetic theories of Pseudo-Longinus or Plato. According to Burke, the beautiful is a pleasure sensed in small, delicate and smooth objects: 'For take any beautiful object, and give it a broken and rugged surface, and however well-formed it may be in other respects, it pleases no longer' (1757: 98). The sublime, in contrast, describes enormous, incomprehensible objects that produce astonishment and terror: 'In this case, the mind is so entirely filled with its object, that it cannot entertain any other, nor by consequence reason on that object which employs it' (41–2).[4] In these modern definitions, though hastily summarized here, the beautiful is theorized as a positive aesthetic value, while the sublime is primarily negative.

However, as Byung-Chul Han argues in *Saving Beauty*, the negativity of the sublime is not a negativity of the other; it does not make room for the other, for something radically different, to come into contact with the self. Rather, it is a negativity of the same, because it allows the subject to reason about infinity and feel superior to nature: 'Neither when faced with beauty, nor when faced with the sublime, does the subject end up *beside itself*. It permanently remains grounded *in itself*' (2018: 21). Modern conceptions of both the beautiful and the sublime, regardless of whether they produce pleasure or terror, allow the Western subject to reduce the other to the same and to claim possession of both small objects and vast territories, all the while silencing anything or anyone that does not easily fit within these externally produced images and metaphors.

For this reason, the aesthetics of the sublime found itself at home with colonialist expansions of the Argentine state and market in the nineteenth century. In *Un desierto para la nación*, Fermín A. Rodríguez explains the presence of the sublime in the Argentine archives, especially in relation to the representations of the Pampas and other indigenous territories: 'There is no place on maps for the spatial knowledge of the inhabitants of the plains, nor is there the possibility of hearing their voices when the unrepresentable force of the sublime blankets them with stunning silence' (2010: 77). The overwhelming force of the sublime has the effect of silencing all inhabitants of a space or of completely erasing their bodies and experiences from it.

To mend the silencing effect of the sublime, though not addressing the Argentine case, Han proposes a new mode of conceiving these aesthetic categories: 'Instead of opposing the sublime to the beautiful, one should return to beauty a sublimity that cannot be subjected to inwardness, a *de-subjectivizing* sublimity, and thus undo the separation of beauty and the sublime' (2018: 22). This de-subjectivizing sublimity, this other form of beauty that would not collapse into smooth, homogeneous images, makes space and time for the negativity of the other to manifest itself. It 'invites us to linger' (67). It 'occurs where things turn towards each other and enter into relations with each other' (75). The persistence of the Romantic sublime serves as an ideological tool in the conquest of already-inhabited territories – be it the Pampas in the nineteenth century or the Malvinas/Falklands in the twentieth – and in the erasure of the acts of violence committed at sea, including the slave trade and maritime wars.[5] As I demonstrate below, this silencing, colonialist aesthetics of the sublime is uncritically inscribed within both *La deuda interna* and *La campana*; in contrast, *La forma exacta de las islas* deploys empty land- and seascapes in ways that challenge and repurpose this tradition.

Empty landscapes in *La deuda interna*

La deuda interna opens on an empty, white landscape that extends flat towards a distant, pale mountain range set against a light sky. The cracks in the ground evoke the image of desiccated desert terrain, while the nondiegetic sound of a quena asserts the Andean setting for this film. This first, empty landscape reveals the Salinas Grandes that extend across the provinces of Jujuy and Salta in the Argentine northwest. These sweeping images of the salt plains are more than simple establishing shots. As Martin Lefebvre theorizes, the use of landscapes in film is not limited to establishing the setting; landscapes can provoke an 'interruption of the narrative by contemplation' (2006: 29). They can prompt the viewer to stop thinking about the narrative and instead reflect on symbolic and affective interpretations of the space itself. In my analysis, filming these empty salt plains interrupts the narrative of the exploitation of this indigenous village by redeploying the nineteenth-century trope of deserted landscapes, ultimately undermining the content of its narrative.

Jens Andermann argues that the first image of Argentine literature is that of infinite space – the desert in the first stanza of Esteban Echeverría's *La cautiva* (1837). Throughout the nineteenth century, the fertile Pampas and unincorporated indigenous territory continually reappear in complex and contradictory representations of that space as a sprawling desert. In the writings of Echeverría and Sarmiento, Andermann continues, what is missing is the Argentine archive itself: 'the category "desert" refers first and foremost to a textual absence' (2000: 37). This emptying of the national landscape functions for these self-declared founders not as a realist representation of actually existing spaces but rather as 'the original and legitimating procedure of an ideological and aesthetic project' (37). Such Romantic desert landscapes in literature ultimately produce the image of an essential, but elementary grounds that require the intervention of the Generation of '37 in order to build a civilized nation.[6]

Empty landscapes appear as well in paintings of the Pampas, but landscape paintings practically are non-existent until after 1880 in Argentina. Even Johann Moritz Rugendas, who painted numerous landscapes during his travels throughout Latin America, focused on human dramas in Argentina. According to Laura Malosetti Costa, this absence of Argentine landscape painting 'speaks to an imbalance, to the impossibility of seeing a landscape there or, rather, of the lack of a need to construct one' (2005: 294). The first visual artist to depict landscapes was Manuel José Olascoaga. His drawings and watercolours from the Conquest of the Desert continue in that self-serving Romantic tradition of portraying the Pampas as a deserted territory. In *Choyque-Mahuida* (1880), the Argentine plains undulate like the waves of a vast ocean expanse, and in *La pampa antes de 1879* (The Pampas before 1879) (1909), Olascoaga retrospectively reasserts the emptiness of the Argentine plains with a fictional image that erases the genocidal act, one in which he participated directly, that resulted in the extermination of indigenous cultures and civilizations for the expansion of the Argentine state and market.

In many ways, *La deuda interna* challenges this representation of Argentine space as an empty desert. After the opening landscapes, the camera gradually introduces a rural, indigenous village, its inhabitants and a man who has arrived to reopen a local school. During his time in Chorcán, the idealistic teacher introduces the children to national heroes, using education to incorporate them into the nation – a model that recalls Sarmiento's nationalizing goals from the nineteenth century and, more directly, a certain model of the revolutionary, yet misguided, intellectual of the sixties. When the young Verónico's grandmother dies, the teacher takes him under his care. At the start of the 1976 dictatorship, the teacher is forcibly removed from this village and sent elsewhere, but he maintains infrequent contact with people from Chorcán through letters. By the film's ending, the teacher returns to the village to reconnect with Verónico, only to discover that he had died while serving on the *General Belgrano*, a warship sunk by the British navy during the Malvinas/Falklands War. These scenes of the war are unrepresented in the film.

The film's narrative foregrounds a national paradox in which two separate, but competing, ideologies of the 1960s and 1970s both leave their tragic mark on Jujuy. The film calls into question what Gastón Lillo refers to as 'the emancipatory illusion of the teacher's project that makes use of civic education to integrate otherness into the nation' (2008: 136). The teacher's influence extends beyond the schoolhouse. For example, he lends Verónico a comic book about British pirates and sea captains. Verónico becomes fascinated with the colourful drawings of ships and the ocean. Detail shots of the pages linger on the screen as if seen from Verónico's hypnotized gaze. Then, he asks the teacher, 'What is the sea like?' 'Big. Very, very big', the teacher replies, evoking the sublime and the infinite, as he struggles to catch his breath from the altitude. 'So, there's no sea around here?' Verónico asks despondently. To which the teacher replies, 'No, there's no sea in Jujuy. The sea is in other areas in the south' (00:36:37–00:37:07). Subsequently, the boy's imagination takes flight, and he dreams of going out to the salt plains where the sound of waves, seabreeze and seagulls wash over the scene (00:37:32). Later, after the teacher's departure, Verónico and a local girl return to the salt plains, rinse off shells they find and hold them to their ears as those same nondiegetic ocean sounds play (01:19:00). In this sense, the teacher has sparked an oceanic fantasy that will lead Verónico to abandon this village and join the navy. The final scenes show the teacher's gradual realization that he played an indirect role in Verónico's death and, by extension, in the exploitation of the people he naively believed to be helping. The teacher incidentally lured Verónico into the state with sublime images, but this appeal to the sublime did not create a space to engage with his otherness but rather facilitated the process by which it was consumed and destroyed.

Furthermore, the film never quite frees itself from a nostalgic, *costumbrista* gaze that recreates certain totalizing, essentialist iconography from the Argentine archives. Laura Demaría analyses the uses of the sublime in Joaquín V. González's *Mis montañas* (1893), and she argues that in certain Romantic landscapes nature is constructed as 'the archive that maintains intact the everlasting values of the nation' (2014: 288). Whereas Demaría is able to read against the grain of these Romantic images in González, I argue that the cinematic gaze of *La deuda interna* continually interrupts the critical narrative to return to the Romantic sublime wherein the Jujeño landscape appears to be untouched by the violence of national history and uncontaminated by outsiders. This is confirmed in the final sequence of the film, which shows the teacher in Chorcán walking through the empty village; then, an extreme wide shot showcases an empty hillside with patches of ice (01:31:15), a detail

42   *The Film Archipelago*

shot frames small icicles (01:31:20), and another, melting ice (01:31:22). The camera returns to the teacher's face, introduces the image of a young woman – Verónico's childhood friend, now pregnant, possibly with his Verónico's child – walking through the landscape, and finally returns to the teacher's face who offers the slightest smile. The final image of the film is a close-up that pans down a babbling brook for twenty seconds as a nondiegetic quena plays (01:31:45). These wide and close shots of nature ironically undermine the otherwise critical narrative; as the ice thaws and the sun shines, these landscapes appear as an unharmed, everlasting repository of a more innocent time with purifying powers that might heal the wounds of the recent, traumatic past and give way to a new beginning.

In the end, the flowing waters appear to wash away the violence of the dictatorship and, at the same time, to heal the unintentional harm caused by the archetypical teacher who returns briefly to these provincial lands to confirm that everything is going to be okay. In a hasty and oversimplified manner, the teacher and by extension the nation as a whole appear capable of reconciliation if only they choose to see the sublime instead of the violence that has been erased. By framing and interrupting the narrative with these empty landscapes, the film relies uncritically on the colonialist legacy of the Romantic sublime that has been exploited throughout Argentina's history to justify not only the Malvinas/Falklands War, but also the invasion of territories like Jujuy and the subsequent erasure and exploitation of indigenous communities.

Empty seascapes in *La campana*

The open ocean forms the backdrop and drives the plot of *La campana*. The narrative begins in 1982, just before the war, at the port in Mar del Plata. Juan and Lucho plan to take their small boat past the breakers to see if they will have better luck fishing out on the high seas. A young barmaid, Laura, wants to join them, but they refuse her request. Before they set sail, they are warned by an older man of a mythical region known as La campana in which time stands still, trapping the sailors who pass through it. Juan and Lucho do get trapped for one night in La campana, but they return the next day. Later, Lucho is drafted into the war, and Laura, who has fallen in love with Juan, begs him not to take a second journey into the open seas. Despite her protests, Juan sets sail and spends what he thinks is only an afternoon on the boat, but he returns to port to discover that it is the year 2010. In the final scenes, he grapples with the loss of time and barely recognizes a shell-shocked Lucho who had returned from the war decades prior. Then he attempts to reconcile with a much older Laura who thought he had either abandoned her or disappeared at sea.

Similar to the village in *La deuda interna*, the port town in *La campana* becomes a simple allegory of the nation during the dictatorship with characters who superficially represent drafted soldiers, women searching for the disappeared and militant youths fleeing persecution.[7] Both films also focus on the story of a man who returns, rather unharmed, to the affected town to reflect on the aftermath of the dictatorship. The main difference between these films relates to the types of characters. Aguilar notes that films from the 1980s featured characters who represent and exercise institutionalized power: 'The total absence of this type of character in the new cinema is curious, even in those films that would be positioned to represent them' (2006: n. 22, p. 31). Whereas *La deuda interna* showcases a teacher, the police and the military, *La campana* portrays everyday people caught in these traumatic events. Nevertheless, *La campana* continues in the tradition of representing empty national spaces, but instead of deserted landscapes, empty seascapes interrupt and undermine this film's attempts to critique the dictatorship and the war.

Representations of the ocean are rare in the Argentine cinematic and literary archives. The Río de la Plata appears frequently, but the Atlantic is difficult to locate. Curiously, the Pampa's vast plains become oceanic, invoking the Romantic sublime, as in Sarmiento's *Facundo*: 'It is the image of the sea on land' (1845: 57). In a broader trans-Atlantic context, Philip E. Steinberg describes the long-standing tradition of representing the ocean as an empty, albeit terrifying, surface; the oceans become 'a space of connection that merely unifies the societies on its borders' (2013: 157). Referring to the Caribbean, Ernesto Bassi argues that this supposedly empty ocean surface actually 'was a lived but unarticulated geographical space' (2016: 78). Though sailors expertly navigate the 'mobile markers' traversing oceanic regions – the ships and their flags – they lack 'the fixed markers ordinarily used to make landed territories legible' (79). The mobility and impermanence of the objects and peoples inhabiting these oceanic spaces render them illegible to the territorial logic of the nation-state that interprets seascapes as an empty space that must be crossed as quickly as possible.

Furthermore, Margaret Cohen analyses 'the Romantic evacuation of the sea', or the process that starts in the eighteenth century by which the oceans become empty and therefore sublime (2010: 119). She offers the example of Caspar David Friedrich's *The Monk by the Sea* (1809). Not only does Friedrich portray the seascape as empty, but to achieve this effect he painted over the outlines of two small ships that he had originally placed in the frame (Cohen 2010: 122). The result is the representation of a vast, unknown and awe-inspiring ocean surface that appears to be devoid of human agency and experiences. Of course, neither the Pampas nor the Atlantic were ever as empty as they appear in these sublime land- and seascapes. To invoke the sublime, it bears repeating, serves as the aesthetic procedure for justifying the violence with which these spaces would be invaded and conquered by the flows of empire, state and capital.

The evacuation of the seas is the aesthetic procedure that guides the representation of the ocean in *La campana*. Juan goes to sea twice, and the sequences that represent his journeys are practically identical. The boat is filmed passing through an opening between two breakwaters, Escollera Norte and Escollera Sur, that create an artificial port to shelter the fishing industry (00:12:02; 00:52:16). The Base Naval and the Base de Submarinos de la Armada Argentina are also located at the Mar del Plata port. As the decrepit fishing boat crosses this literal threshold, it symbolically leaves behind the protections of the port and the state. Then, the boat is filmed sailing towards the horizon in a pair of otherwise empty seascapes, with the boat barely visible in the second one (00:12:17; 00:52:28). These empty seascapes evoke the Romantic sublime in an attempt to create suspense. The fantastical elements of the film are also created through another empty seascape in which an eerie light glows intensely at the horizon (00:54:17) in conjunction with a bird's-eye view in which a similar beam of light sweeps across the boat (00:54:22).

In my interpretation, by evacuating the seas, *La campana* undermines its own narrative. It relies on an aesthetic that displaces the experiences of Lucho in the war and of those left behind. Lucho appears only briefly in a quasi-catatonic state at the end (01:03:40). Laura yells at Juan upon his return, but the final image of the film is of her smiling, as if all is forgiven and healed, or at least open to the possibility of reconciliation (01:12:37). Meanwhile, the appeal to the empty seascapes evokes that nationalist trope of open, empty space that is primed for the expansion of the state and the market, in this case, into the waters surrounding the Malvinas/Falkland Islands. This choice to foreground the fantastical elements and sublime seascapes – instead of the experiences of the victims of the dictatorship, for example – displaces and erases a great deal of the narrative about the recent past. The question that remains is what other possibilities exist for incorporating empty land- and seascapes into the films about the Malvinas/Falkland Islands without reverting back to the colonialist legacy of the Romantic sublime.

Islands and memories in suspense

A series of deserted island landscapes appear throughout the opening scenes of *La forma exacta de las islas*. At first glance, the camera held by Julieta Vitullo in 2006 as she documents her trip to the Malvinas/Falklands confirms the long-standing notion that these islands are quite empty and desolate.[8] The shaky camera films a dirt road through a grassy field (00:01:00) and a wind-swept beach (00:03:45). Yet, Vitullo's low-quality handycam is only one of many layers to this complex documentary. The directors, Casabé and Dieleke, return with Vitullo in 2010. Their high-definition camera locates even more empty landscapes with a static gaze that lingers over three images of a low-lying mountain range at the water's edge (00:06:43–00:07:43) and two images of a snowy beach (00:07:44–00:08:38). These opening images situate this film within the tradition of representing the Malvinas/Falklands as deserted islands for the nation. However, in my analysis, *La forma exacta de las islas* disrupts both the allegorical mode of storytelling and the counterproductive deployment of empty land- and seascapes found in *La deuda interna* and *La campana*. Though *La forma exacta de las islas* benefits from filming the actual islands, it is not better for that reason alone, nor because it is a documentary, but rather because of how it deploys an aesthetic sensibility that films these landscapes in relation to the stories and histories of the islands, the islanders and those sent to the islands during the war.

La forma exacta de las islas is indebted to two major aesthetic innovations of the NCA. Aguilar describes these ruptures: 'Two main rejections, drawn in invisible ink, can be found in the screenplays and stories of the new films: a rejection of the political demand (what is to be done?) and of the identity-based demand (who are we?), or in other words, of pedagogy and of self-incrimination' (2006: 23). The NCA does not construct national allegories, nor does it insist on a particular moral lesson for its audience. Continuing in this direction, *La forma exacta de las islas* does not elevate its protagonists as representatives of national types who might showcase either the heroic deeds or the unintended errors of those who fought in and lived through the dictatorship and the war. Rather, it is a more intimate documentary structured through *mise-en-abîme*. Vitullo travels to the islands with a handycam to conduct interviews with Falklanders and to record a journal related to her dissertation research on Argentine literature and films about the war.[9] When she arrives, she meets two ex-combatants, and she joins them as they return to their former battle stations and visit the unmarked graves of Darwin Cemetery. Vitullo's footage is spliced with Casabé and Dieleke's footage from a second trip; they make use of high-quality cameras and lenses to film Vitullo, quote from her dissertation and ultimately reveal that she has returned to mourn the loss of her child who had been conceived during the first trip but died shortly after birth.

In contrast to the other two films, the empty landscapes do not always appear after a cut that clearly interrupts the narrative, nor are they inscribed primarily within the aesthetics of the sublime. *La forma exacta de las islas* becomes a kaleidoscope of narrative temporalities wherein landscapes linger in suspension throughout key scenes. Analysing the functions of suspension in film and literature, Rocío Gordon argues that it typically creates obstacles to slow the development of the plot (2017: 31). However, among many other uses, she locates another definition of suspension from the field of music in which one note of a harmonious chord lingers and creates dissonance with the following chords; from this she argues that in narratives of suspension, 'there are elements that are extended or superimposed, generating a certain "unease" in the (im)possible concatenation of elements' (32). When mobilized for my purposes, I analyse two examples of landscapes in *La forma exacta de las islas* that become suspended in this second sense, creating a dissonant concatenation of temporalities and spaces that upends the allegorical and nationalist modes of the previous films.

The first example comes from the low-quality footage filmed by Vitullo. One of the ex-combatants has returned to a mountainside to build a memorial where he watched another soldier die during the war. Regarding the content of this scene, Irene Depetris Chauvin argues that 'memory seeps into the fabric of the place and lingers there, resisting time' (2017: 9).[10] What is of importance for my analysis is how Vitullo's handycam films the man sitting at the mountain's peak, backlit by the sky. As the camera pans leftward, the man disappears from the frame, and a barren landscape comes fully into view from this vantage point, tempting the narrative with the sublime and its capacity for erasure (01:10:30–01:11:05). But the camera then reverses its course, panning rightward. It withdraws from this landscape, suspending but never interrupting it. On the camera's return, it bypasses the man and finally frames his handmade memorial, cobbled together from local rocks and bits of wood tied together to form a cross (01:11:05–01:11:34). The three focal points – the ex-combatant, the empty landscape and the memorial – are not arranged as distinct elements that can be isolated in separate shots. Rather, the camera works to incorporate each of them, allowing them to linger and overlap with one another; they turn towards one another and into relations with one another without silencing, erasing or consuming the negativity of the others.

When considered as a site of memory, this memorial establishes a curious affinity with the use of empty land- and seascapes in film. Pierre Nora argues that 'the most fundamental purpose of the *lieu de mémoire* (sites of memory) is to stop time, to block the work of forgetting' (1989: 19). Both filmic landscapes and sites of memory interrupt time; the former can stop and even undermine narrative time, while the latter interrupts the present with a reminder of a violent past for the future inhabitants of that same space. In the scene under consideration, Vitullo's amateur camera appears caught in a struggle between these two awe-inspiring poles – the sublime landscape and the precarious memorial – that seek to interrupt time, but their relative gravitational pulls leave the camera suspended, panning back and forth between them and twice capturing the ex-combatant sitting in this place. The empty landscape evokes the power of the sublime to impress upon the viewer the overwhelming scale of the intimate narratives of loss that can only materialize in the tiny, insufficient memorial. Without the memorial, the sublime landscape would erase the violent narratives of the war with abstract universals, whereas without the landscape,

48 *The Film Archipelago*

the memorial might collapse into a story too particular to reverberate beyond those immediately affected by one soldier's death.[11] Together, they allow the particular story of one casualty of war to be remembered and recounted while also unleashing the potential for the film to represent a broader, international narrative of the many forms of loss that have taken place on the islands during the war – Argentine, British and Falklander – and also during events unrelated to that war – a car accident, an epidemic, a stillbirth.

Reflecting on the mutability and various uses to which sites of memory can be put, Nora argues that 'all *lieux de mémoire* are objects *mises-en-abîme*' (1989: 20). This documentary, structured through *mise-en-abîme*, becomes a multivalenced site of memory.[12] The closing sequence, filmed by Casabé and Dieleke, reproduces in high definition the movements of Vitullo's camera, which earlier captured footage of the ex-combatant filming the landscape in which he would construct his memorial with a slow pan (01:06:11). In Casabé and Dieleke's sequence, their camera now sways back and forth across a beach (01:18:57–01:19:11). Then, Vitullo, dressed in white, can be seen in a wide shot walking along an otherwise empty beach, as gentle waves lap the sand (01:19:12–01:19:33). The camera cuts to the rolling waves and then cuts back to a slightly zoomed in shot that showcases Vitullo sitting in the wind-swept sands looking towards the ocean, purportedly reflecting on the loss of her own child and the other stories of mourning narrated throughout the film. The camera then pans leftward, creating an empty seascape at the shores (01:19:51–01:20:05). After a series of images that showcase bridges, houses, farms and penguins in land- and seascapes, the camera cuts to black. The final scene is of Vitullo with a friend at the Monumento a los Caídos en Malvinas – an official and highly contested site of memory in Plaza San Martín in Buenos Aires – during a celebration of the war meant to honour those who died there. This footage is from the first day Casabé and Dieleke began filming, and the documentary ends when the still pregnant Vitullo, walking away from the event, feels her baby moving for the first time.

This final sequence serves two purposes. On the one hand, it recreates the form of the earlier scene, this time blending Vitullo's mourning with the sublime seascape. As this camera pans towards that empty space, her mourning enters the temporal kaleidoscope of the film that narrated so many other forms of loss related to the islands. These stories are refracted and allowed to linger on the screen, because the film refuses both the smooth beauty and the silencing sublime that would otherwise exclude any experience or dialogue with the other. On the other, the film returns to Buenos Aires from the islands, but it ends as Vitullo walks away from the memorial. The contrast between the suspended seascape with Vitullo and the official memorial underscores the empty rhetoric of those who celebrate the Argentines who died in the war by elevating them as silent, national heroes instead of recognizing that they, too, were exploited and killed by a desperate dictatorship with broad public support.

La forma exacta de las islas achieves a new form that can incorporate empty land- and seascapes into film without requiring them to serve as mere backdrop or ironically invoking colonialist tropes from the Argentine archives. Here the islands are no longer represented as deserted or empty; the nationalist appeal to a lost territory loses its enchantment, and new modes of memorializing those who died in the war as victims or suffered other forms of loss on the islands are granted time and space to be mourned. In all, Vitullo's, and later Casabé and Dieleke's, land- and seascapes allow for the dissonant gathering of various temporalities and narratives to reflect and amplify one another. With them, *La forma exacta de las islas* gestures towards a future in which the Malvinas/Falklands finally become unmoored from their representations as deserted islands for the nation.

Notes

1 Other important Argentine films about the Malvinas/Falklands War include *Los chicos de la guerra* (1984), directed by Bebe Kamin; *El visitante* (1999), directed by Javier Olivera; and *Iluminados por el fuego* (2005), directed by Tristán Bauer, which is based on the book of the same title. These three films all centre the experiences of ex-combatants in the war. With different results, two other films place the war and its effects somewhat in the background. *La mirada invisible* (2010), directed by Diego Lerman, adapts Martín Kohan's novel, *Ciencias morales. Un cuento chino* (2011), directed by Sebastián Borensztein, almost appears to have nothing to do with the war until a few flashbacks interrupt the film. More recently, the play and film adaptation of Lola Arias's *Teatro de guerra* (2018) brings together ex-combatants from both Argentina and the UK to

reproduce their experiences. Of course, Argentine literature played an important role alongside cinema in representing the Malvinas/Falklands War. Rodolfo Enrique Fogwill's *Los Pichiciegos* (1982), written during the war, inaugurates the Argentine archive of representations of the war with an anti-heroic story of pure survival that undercuts the nationalist rhetoric surrounding the war. In doing so, Martín Kohan argues that Fogwill's farce pries open a space between 'triumphant zeal' and 'the cries of defeat' which is necessary because 'although they appear to be opposite reactions, both comprise the same idea about the national fable: one that erects heroes who are glorious if they win or sacrificial lambs if they lose, but always heroes in the end' (1998: 6). In *Islas imaginadas*, Julieta Vitullo undertakes a study of the vast archives of Argentine fiction and film through 2011 in which she documents how this corpus continually seeks to dismantle the nationalist tropes around epic narratives and heroes, including novels like Carlos Gamerro's *Las islas* (1998) and Martín Kohan's *Ciencias morales* (2007), among many others. See also Paola Ehrmantraut, *Masculinidades en guerra* (2013). This literary archive continues to grow in new directions. Patricia Ratto's *Trasfondo* (2012) relates the story of a submarine crew waiting in fear deep under the surface of the South Atlantic with little to no details about how the war is progressing or even why they are fighting. In a completely different manner, Carlos Godoy's *La construcción. Metales radioactivos en las islas del Atlántico Sur* (2014) is an enigmatic narrative that seeks to re-invent the islands' foundational myths with an apocalyptic secret society. Furthermore, two recent British novels similarly eschew nationalist rhetoric and the construction of heroes, thus dispelling such tropes from the other side of the Atlantic: David Mitchell's *Black Swan Green* (2006) and Ian McEwan's *Machines Like Me* (2019).

2 See Canclini (2007) for a detailed history of almost every person inhabiting the islands around 1833 who left a paper trail. Canclini asserts that the British chose to colonize these islands for at least three main reasons: (1) to serve as a strategic point of departure and contact for expanding the empire into the Pacific, (2) to create a hub for the sea lion and whale industries and (3) to prevent the United States and France from establishing an important port in the South Atlantic (2007: 26).

3 For an early analysis of the 30 March 1982 protests by the Confederación General del Trabajo (CGT), a major Argentine labour union, see Calveiro (1988). Guber (2012) also studies how the CGT dispute was blunted with the outpouring of nationalist sentiments with the declaration of war.

4 Kant begins to define the beautiful in similar terms: 'as object of a liking devoid of all interest' ([1790] 1987: 53). However, the sublime for Kant is a question of magnitude that exceeds reason: 'When it is judged as [the] absolute measure beyond which no larger is subjectively possible (i.e., possible for the judging subject), then it carries with it the idea of the sublime' (251). He explains that the oceans, for example, are not in and of themselves sublime, but rather it is the mind's attempt to perceive them that causes one to experience the sublime.

5 See Gilroy (1993) for his groundbreaking work that studies the transnational history of the Atlantic to contest these sublime erasures and how the ocean was 'continually crisscrossed by the movements of black people – not only as commodities but engaged in various struggles towards emancipation, autonomy, and citizenship' (1993: 16).

6 See Halperín Donghi ([1982] 2005) for a nuanced study of the competing ideologies within and beyond the Generación del 37.

7 *La campana* received quite a negative critical reception. Horacio Bernades, for example, criticizes the melding of the fantastic elements with the historical realism, stating that the fantastic premise matters little except for 'the allegorical service that it lends' (n.p.).

8 Though beyond the scope of this essay, the islands appear in other Argentine films in which scenes from the war are represented. These include *Los chicos de la guerra* (1984), *Iluminados por el fuego* (2005), *Un cuento chino* (2011) and the mini-series *Combatientes* (2013).

9 See Vitullo (2012), the book based on this research, for a thorough deconstruction of the appeal to heroic figures and the epic in the Argentine literature and film of the Malvinas/Falklands War.

10 See also Depetris Chauvin (2014). Her analysis focuses on the comparison between the fixed landscape images and the scenes that follow the journeys of the different protagonists, creating 'an affective appropriation of geographic space' (60).

11 Mandolessi argues that the rhetoric of the sublime is conceived as existing somewhere else, beyond language and beyond the common space of politics; thus, she affirms the idea that the sublime silences. In contrast, in the case of post-dictatorial Argentine literature, she encounters the language of dialogue, of an encounter with the other, that similarly rejects the aesthetics of the sublime: 'It is not the exclusive ability or inability of a subject to name an event, but rather the exploration of meaning in a community with others, with all the difficulties, misunderstandings, silences, and limitations that the experience of a dialogue

implies. If the sublime is the impossible dialogue with something of the divine order, here, instead, we find the possibility – albeit imperfect – of a profane, human dialogue, even when considering the "impossible" dialogue with the dead' (2018: 514).

12 Corbin and Davidovich argue for the possibility of extending the notion of sites of memory 'in order to encompass those artistic and cultural productions that arise in dialogue with those spaces' (2019: 5).

References

Aguilar, G. M. (2006), *Otros mundos. Ensayo sobre el nuevo cine argentino*, Buenos Aires: Santiago Arcos Editor.

Amado, A. M. (2009), *La imagen justa. Cine argentino y política (1980–2007)*, Buenos Aires: Ediciones Colihue.

Andermann, J. (2000), *Mapas de poder. Una arqueología literaria del espacio argentino*, Rosario: Beatriz Viterbo Editora.

Bassi, E. (2016), *An Aqueous Territory: Sailor Geographies and New Granada's Transimperial Greater Caribbean World*, Durham: Duke University Press.

Bernades, H. (2011), 'Relato fantástico y alegoría de la dictadura', *Página/12*, 17 December.

Burke, E. (1757), *A Philosophical Enquiry into the Origin of Our Ideas of the Sublime and Beautiful*, London: R. and J. Dodsley. Available online: https://archive.org/.

Calveiro, P. (1988), 'Sindicatos y política (Argentina 1980–1986)', in M. Trujillo Bolio (ed.), *Organización y luchas del movimiento obrero latinoamericano (1978–1987)*, 13–53, Buenos Aires: Siglo Veintiuno Editores.

La campana (2010), [Film] Dir. Fredy Torres. Argentina: INCAA.

Canclini, A. (2007), *Malvinas 1833. Antes y después de la agresión inglesa. Un estudio documental*, Buenos Aires: Claridad.

Caresani, L. (2014), 'Representación y memoria en las imágenes de archivo del cine argentino sobre la guerra de Malvinas', *Imagofagia* 10: 1–24.

Cohen, M. (2010), *The Novel and the Sea*, Princeton, NJ: Princeton University Press.

Corbin, M. and K. Davidovich (2019), 'Vestigios del pasado. Los sitios de memoria en el Cono Sur', in M. Corbin and K. Davidovich (eds), *Vestigios del pasado. Los sitios de memoria y sus representaciones políticas y artísticas, Hispanic Issues On Line* 22: 1–36.

Demaría, L. (2014), *Buenos Aires y las provincias. Relatos para desarmar*, Rosario: Beatriz Viterbo.

Depetris Chauvin, I. (2014), 'Paisajes interiores: espacio y afectividad en un documental sobre Malvinas', *Arizona Journal of Hispanic Cultural Studies* 18: 53–63.

Depetris Chauvin, I. (2017), 'Archipelago of Memories: Affective Travelogue and Mourning in *La Forma Exacta de Las Islas*', *Latin American Theatre Review* 50.2: 5–18.

La deuda interna (1987), [Film] Dir. Miguel Pereira. U.K.: British Film Institute.

Ehrmantraut, P. (2013), *Masculinidades en guerra. Malvinas en la literatura y el cine*, Córdoba, Argentina: Editorial Comunicarte.

FitzRoy, R. (1839), *Narrative of the Surveying Voyages of His Majesty's Ships Adventure and Beagle*, London: Henry Colburn. Accessed online: http://darwin-online.org.uk/content/frameset?itemID=F10.2&viewtype=text&pageseq=1.

La forma exacta de las islas (2012), [Film] Dirs. Daniel Casabé and Edgardo Dieleke. Argentina: INCAA Doc.

Gillis, J. R. (2004), *Islands of the Mind: How the Human Imagination Created the Atlantic World*, New York: Palgrave Macmillan.

Gilroy, P. (1993), *The Black Atlantic: Modernity and Double Consciousness*, Cambridge, MA: Harvard University Press.

Gordon, R. (2017), *Narrativas de la suspensión. Una mirada contemporánea desde la literatura y el cine argentinos*, Buenos Aires: Libraria.

Guber, R. (2012), *¿Por qué Malvinas? De la causa nacional a la guerra absurda*, México: Fondo de Cultura Económica.

Halperín Donghi, T. ([1982] 2005), *Una nación para el desierto argentino*, Buenos Aires: Prometeo Libros.

Han, B. C. (2018), *Saving Beauty*, trans. D. Steuer, Cambridge: Polity.

Hay, P. (2006), 'A Phenomenology of Islands', *Island Studies Journal* 1.1: 19–42.

Kant, I. ([1790] 1987), *Critique of Judgment*, trans. W. S. Pluhar, Indianapolis: Hackett.

Kohan, M. (1998), 'El fin de una época', *Punto de vista* 64: 6–11.

Lefebvre, M. (2006), 'Between Setting and Landscape in the Cinema', in M. Lefebvre (ed.) *Landscape and Film*, 19–59, New York: Routledge.

Lillo, G. (2008), 'Nuevas posturas críticas en el cine argentino: *La deuda interna* (1987), *Un lugar en el mundo* (1992) e *Historias mínimas* (2002)', *Canadian Journal of Latin American and Caribbean Studies* 33.66: 129–56.

Lorenz, F. G. (2014), *Todo lo que necesitás saber sobre Malvinas*, Buenos Aires: Paidós.

Malosetti Costa, L. (2005), '¿Un paisaje abstracto? Transformaciones en la percepción y representación visual del desierto argentino', in G. Batticuore, K. Gallo and J. Myers (eds), *Resonancias románticas. Ensayos sobre historia de la cultura argentina (1820-1890)*, 291–303, Buenos Aires: Eudeba.

Mandolessi, S. (2018), 'Memorias sagradas, memorias profanas: Agamben y el discurso de lo sublime en la literatura posdictatorial argentina', *Revista Iberoamericana* 84.263: 497–516.

Nora, P. (1989), 'Between Memory and History: *Les Lieux de Mémoire*', trans. M. Roudebush, *Representations* 26: 7–24.

Olascoaga, M. J. (1880), *Choyque-Mahuida, codo de Chiclana*, Buenos Aires: Ostwalt and Martínez, in J. Andermann and P. A. Schell (eds), *Relics and Selves: Iconographies of the National in Argentina, Brazil, and Chile (1880–1890)*, London: University of London. Accessed online: http://www.bbk.ac.uk/ibamuseum.

Olascoaga, M. J. (1909), *La pampa antes de 1879*, Buenos Aires: Museo Histórico Nacional, in G. Batticuore, K. Gallo and J. Myers (eds) (2005), *Resonancias románticas. Ensayos sobre historia de la cultura argentina (1820–1890)*, 297, Buenos Aires: Eudeba.

Oubiña, D. (2002), 'Un mapa arrasado. Nuevo cine argentino de los 90', *Sociedad* 20–21: 193–205.

Rodríguez, F. A. (2010), *Un desierto para la nación. La escritura del vacío*, Buenos Aires: Eterna Cadencia.

Sarmiento, D. F. ([1845] 1990), *Facundo. Civilización y barbarie*, ed. Roberto Yahni, Madrid: Cátedra.

Schenoni, L. L., S. Braniff and J. Battaglino (2020), '¡' Was the Malvinas / Falklands a Diversionary War? A Prospect-Theory Reinterpretation of Argentina's Decline', *Security Studies* 29.1: 34–63.

Steinberg, P. E. (2013), 'Of Other Seas: Metaphors and Materialities in Maritime Regions', *Atlantic Studies* 10.2: 156–69.

Stites Mor, J. (2012), *Transition Cinema: Political Filmmaking and the Argentine Left since 1968*, Pittsburgh: University of Pittsburgh Press.

Vitullo, J. (2012), *Islas imaginadas. La guerra de Malvinas en la literatura y el cine argentinos*, Buenos Aires: Corregidor.

Williams, S. (2012), 'Virtually Impossible: Deleuze and Derrida on the Political Problem of Islands (and Island Studies)', *Island Studies Journal* 7.2: 21.

2

Marooned testimony:
Chilean islandscape and the politics of memory in Sebastián Silva's *Magic Magic* (2013)

William R. Benner

Reckoning with state terror in contemporary Chilean film

Since the late 1990s, the generations that grew up during the Pinochet dictatorship in Chile have turned to film as a means to reckon with the traumatic past and the transitional government's campaign for truth and national reconciliation. Surprisingly, there remains a dearth of critical reception about this heterogeneous group of Chilean film directors that have begun to achieve both national and international acclaim. This chapter focuses on Sebastián Silva's treatment of landscape in his thriller *Magic Magic* (2013) in order to examine how the island is a site that evokes a performance of disappearance.

Focusing on the materiality of the island space, Silva constructs a performative filmic landscape through a collage of images that relate to disappearance. This is an ethical and aesthetic choice that can be read as a resistance to a memory politics supported by the transitional government's desire to hastily reconcile the collective and individual trauma caused by the Pinochet dictatorship. Rather than seek truth and justice, Chile's transitional coalition government *Concertación* promoted neoliberal socioeconomic policies that claimed to improve economic opportunities for civil society. This chapter engages with notions of filmed space put forward by Martin Lefebvre, Gilles Deleuze and Georges Didi-Huberman to develop a theoretical lens that sees landscape as a performative space. I read Silva's use of island landscape in Chile's Patagonia as a constellation of sites, or archipelago of sites, that encourage the spectator to participate and to discover unexpected meanings that extend outside diegesis to include the current sociopolitical sphere. Finally, I conclude that by bringing landscape to the fore, *Magic Magic* invites a critical analysis that listens to the powerful silences that have marooned the disappeared and censored intergenerational and horizontal modes of memory transmission.

Augusto Pinochet's military regime held the reins of power for seventeen years, from 1973 to 1990. Accordingly, many children had clear memories of living under the dictatorship and many, like their parents, protested and suffered repression. The 1990s therefore led to youth apathy towards reckoning with the terror carried out by the military dictatorship as the *Concertación* political coalition ushered in a neoliberal democracy that purposed a limited project of truth and reconciliation, a move that was strongly criticized by the victims and relatives of the estimated 3,178 *desaparecidos* (Ros 2012: 116; Stern 2010: xxii). However, with the detention of Pinochet in London in 1998, the establishing of truth commissions, and the international influence of human rights groups like the Argentine Hijos por la Identidad y la Justicia contra el Olvido y el Silencio (H.I.J.O.S.), the early 2000s saw a revitalization of public protest in Chile.[1] Inspired by H.I.J.O.S.'s use of *escraches* (a word used to describe outing someone deserving of punishment) in post-dictatorship Argentina, the organization Acción, Verdad y Justicia, Hijos-Chile organized festive protests or *funas* (a word used to describe something putrid) to successfully denounce, in front of the homes of former torturers, the past atrocities of the recent dictatorship and linked them to the perpetrators' present-day impunity which was guaranteed by the silence of politicians and technocrats (Ros 2012: 119). Furthermore, as Steve Stern (2010) explains, young human rights activists looked to connect the traumatic past with the discriminatory neoliberal socioeconomic model that Pinochet's dictatorship first implemented and the *concertación* continued to support (2010: 264).[2]

Cinema has played an important role in revitalizing the desire among those that grew up and survived the Pinochet military regime to examine the traumatic past. Films by Juan Francisco López Balló, Carmen Castillo, Ernesto Díaz Espinoza, Patricio Guzmán, Cristián Jiménez, Pablo Larraín, Sebastián Lelio, Marialy Rivas, Raúl Ruiz, Cristián Sánchez, Dominga Sotomayor, Andrés Waissbluth and Andrés Wood have explored the hidden consequences of state terror and have brought the Chilean case for truth and justice to both local and international audiences. These films reject the reconciliation project espoused by the *Concertación* and instead cast a critical gaze at the present apathy among the general public.

Only recently have critics begun to examine the diversity of genres, generational perspectives and cinematographic strategies of a resurgent Chilean cinema that began in 2011. Further, most of the critical attention has centred on documentary film, whereas recent fictional films have been largely left unexplored. Vania Barraza, Mar Diestro-Dópido, Giovanni Ottone, Pablo Marín and Andrés Waissbluth have identified several tendencies in recent films addressing the aftermath of the dictatorship. Recent documentary and fiction films focus on a theme of loneliness that is brought about through the depiction of broken societal bonds and the lack of a collective dream, positing allegories that orient back to a latent and unresolved trauma left by the Pinochet dictatorship.[3] Vania Barraza (2014) explains that recent films have used estrangement to defamiliarize narrative techniques and provoke a crisis in the referentiality of the image and thus reconfigure its relation to memory and traditional storytelling. Silva is among these filmmakers that utilize spatial defamiliarizing techniques in fictional film in order to communicate historical and collective trauma.

Sebastián Silva and transnational filmmaking

Silva was born in 1979, six years after the 1973 Chilean coup d'état, and belongs to the post-1995 generation that attended film school in Chile and quickly established international acclaim through the use of digital technologies (Diestro-Dópido 2017). Afterwards, Silva left Chile to advance his filmmaking and music career in Canada and most recently New York City. His filmography has shifted from Spanish-language films shot in Chile to English-language films like *Nasty Baby* (2015) that takes place in Brooklyn. However, he maintains a strong connection with Chilean independent filmmaking; the majority of his films have been produced by the internationally recognized Chilean production company Fábula, founded by Juan de Dios Larraín and Pablo Larraín in 2004.[4] Silva has won a variety of international awards, most notably the Sundance Film Festival Grand Jury Prize and Directing Award for his breakout comedy-drama film *La Nana* (2009). As Karina Elizabeth Vázquez (2014) notes, *La Nana* reveals and satirizes the public and private socioeconomic tensions of domestic work within the rigid neoliberal Chilean society.

The neoliberal culture that encourages socioeconomic injustices within Chilean society is a theme that Silva returns to in his fourth film *Magic Magic*. The film was nominated for the SACD Prize at the Cannes Film Festival and won the Grand Jury Prize at the American Movie Awards. In an interview with the *Los Angeles Times* during the Sundance Film Festival 2013, he explains that *Magic Magic* is an exploration of a schizophrenic episode triggered by being an outsider and unable to articulate trauma to an indifferent society. Besides *Magic Magic*, there are few examples of the horror and thriller genres in Chilean cinema. The Director Jorge Olguín is accredited to have pioneered the horror genre within a Chilean context in the early 2000s. His slasher film *Ángel Negro* (2000) follows a coroner who fears that a former classmate, who mysteriously died by falling off a cliff during a graduation party ten years earlier, is killing the survivors one by one. Olguín's film can be read as a truculent allegory of a Chilean society that must fend for itself. Although Silva does not directly reference Olguín's filmography, they share similar tendencies. In particular, both films utilize allegory to criticize Chilean society's neoliberal apathy towards reckoning with the (im)material consequences of decades of state-sponsored terror.

Magic Magic is a coproduced (US-Chile) psychological thriller that follows a group of young tourists from the United States and Chile on a road trip to an island in the Lago Ranco commune of the Chilean Patagonia where the affluent Agustín (played by Chilean actor Agustín Silva) and his sister Bárbara (Colombian actress Catalina Sandino Moreno) have a lake house. The protagonist Alicia (played by British actress Juno Temple) is a naïve and shy American tourist who has come to Chile to vacation with her cousin Sara (played by the British actress Emily Browning), who is studying abroad in Santiago and is dating Agustín. The diegesis revolves around the trauma that Alicia experiences upon witnessing the irresponsible and selfish behaviour of all of the group members, in particular Brink, the US citizen living abroad (played by Canadian actor Michael Cera). Alicia's inability to communicate the trauma that their actions provoke leads to a complete mental breakdown. The film ends with Alicia in a catatonic state, where no one is sure if she is still alive. This degradation of mental health is largely performative, as is Alicia's mysterious relation to the island landscape that triggers her indescribable terror. It is a corporal performance that extends outside of Alicia's narrative function, an allegorical move that inscribes in the film Chilean society's unwillingness to reckon with the hidden consequences of state-sponsored terror. Furthermore, this performance is intimately linked to the island landscape where Silva creates an archive of images and sounds that serve as a constellation of sites of trauma that are revisited throughout the film.

Temps mort: Performative landscape in film

Landscape in film has a double sense; it can refer to the pictorial representation of a space and the objects that comprise that space, and it can also refer to the real perception of a space. In agreement with the analytical suggestions that Martin Lefebvre puts forward in his introductory chapter to *Landscape and Film* (2006), filmic landscape allows for the spectator to contemplate and produce a gaze that extends outside of the immediacy of the narrative, which leads the spectator to interpret how the filmed location speaks to a larger historical and cultural context. Lefebvre refers to these moments in which the landscape briefly comes to the fore, becoming the primary and independent subject matter of the film. For him, landscape must also be a space that is other than the place where the action or diegesis occurs; it is 'a space freed from eventhood' (2006: 22). Lefebvre explains that where the spectator's gaze is drawn to (landscape or the characters) helps to distinguish landscape as autonomous to setting. I would add that the characters can also help give landscape autonomy through corporal performances that contradict or establish meaning that is not subordinate to diegesis. It could be argued that the psychological thriller genre, and consequently *Magic Magic*, is particularly concerned with using landscape as setting. Although the cinematography of *Magic Magic* uses island landscape to build an event-based economy, I argue that it develops an alternative minor narrative centred on the imagery of the island landscape to undermine an excess of words, where the characters are unable to or lack a desire to communicate verbally with each other. This privileging of landscape allows the spectator to see it as autonomous of the main narrative. Furthermore, as I will explain later, *Magic Magic* utilizes the protagonist to perform landscape, culminating with Alicia's immobile and unresponsive body sinking into the material island, a cinematic moment that speaks of a space freed from eventhood.

Magic Magic opens with a series of establishing shots accompanied by haunting film music that is functional to the narrative, establishing the setting as well as foreshadowing key plot points and images that are linked to the diegesis. These opening scenes of the island, the expansive shots of water and the animals that live there also imply island landscape as the focus of the work. This insular space has strong historical connotations for both local and international audiences, and its usage in *Magic Magic* is central to understanding the film's use of landscape to envelop the protagonist Alicia and destabilize the main narrative. The popular imaginary of the Patagonia is that of a space that is boundless and eternal, a centrepiece for the imperial fictions that depicted it as an unconquerable Darwinian space, but nonetheless, a space necessary for national building (Nouzeilles 1999: 35–6). For example, in *Imperial Eyes: Travel Writing and Transculturation* (2007), Mary Louise Pratt examines how the Western literary tradition of travel writing (1750–2007) has influenced Western readership, allowing readers to develop the sense of ownership, entitlement and familiarity within the peripheries of neocolonial power. The Patagonia consistently lacks shape, finiteness, pattern and history under the gaze of the European travel writer. It is a space that is imagined as lacking in Western commodity culture, and where the author is entitled to claim to know about others and that belonging in such a place is impossible (Pratt 2007: 224–44). Pratt explains that imagining the Patagonia in such a way helped to establish the boundaries of the very identities of the cosmopolitan writer and Western readership. Thus, the Patagonia is a space of differences, an Other place that has long been imagined and subjugated under (neo)colonial order, and invited counterhegemonic narratives.

As the title suggests, *Magic Magic* is a game of appearances where what is known and said about the characters and the island landscape unravels mysteriously. By doubling the word 'magic' Silva alludes to the destabilization of the privileged position of diegesis and its ability to verbally communicate the course of events. The Patagonia constructed as an archipelagic domain provides the ideal filmed space to provoke a crisis in the referentiality of the image and the spoken word to narrate. *Magic Magic* subverts characterizations of the insular Patagonia as a real-and-imagined space subordinated to the comfortable flows of a global neoliberal tourist economy. Although the Mapuche community has little visibility in *Magic Magic*, their presence as indigenous caretakers for the whims of the young white tourists alludes to the consequences of the historical genocide suffered by the indigenous inhabitants of the region. The Mapuche and other Patagonian Amerindian peoples were fundamental to the process of nation-building and the making of an antagonistic national *criollo* identity (Andermann 2007: 160–5; Feierstein 2007: 100–6; Nouzeilles 1999: 38). The first contact the main characters have with the Mapuche is indirect. They find a sick and dying puppy on the side of the road near a Mapuche family home. Throughout the film, the Mapuche characters, who have few speaking lines, can be seen transporting the tourists to the island, maintaining the grounds of the second home of Augustín's family, and reluctantly caring for Alicia's deteriorating mental condition. Although the contact the group has with the Mapuche community is minimal, it alludes to a larger allegory of loneliness and isolation that is a product of the transactional (neo)colonial order. The cosmopolitan desires of vacation overshadow the socioeconomic realities felt by those that live in the Patagonia. In the end, the Mapuche ceremony that takes place in the film does not prevent the protagonist's breakdown; thus, the group must take responsibility for Alicia's mental state. The Patagonian island landscape turns from tourist destination to a site of trauma.

Through the experience of individual and collective trauma related to Alicia's mental anguish, *Magic Magic* builds a cartography related to landscape, suggesting that it can connect the individual to a political immediacy. The spectator must interpret the meaning of these natural sites that produce trauma for Alicia and the group through an iconography of insular space. For example, Alicia feels compelled to return to sites of trauma in an attempt to overcome them. When the group decides to jump off a cliff into a swimming hole, it is Alicia who feels terrified and who, despite the peer pressure, decides not to jump. Silva uses a montage of low- and high-angle shots; however, he challenges the conventions of film form by changing the way in which these shots express power dynamics. The low-angle shots usually give the filmed subject an air of superiority and importance. However, it is the high-angle shots of the water below that produce the anxious low-angle shots of Alicia. That is, it is the cliff and the water below that become the main subject and Alicia's identity seems to be crumbling before our eyes with each low-angle shot. Additionally, Silva uses slow motion with the high-angle shot in order to pause the action. This produces a *temps mort* where the camera, looking down from the perspective of Alicia, pauses to see the waves crash over the rocks. It is a momentary lull in the story where landscape becomes autonomous from setting, a cinematographic spectacle and a space that is singled out and detached from its narrative function. It can be described as a slippage between the landscape as setting and landscape as an alternative narrative built on top of a space free from eventhood. The spectator is invited to ponder: Why does Alicia want to return to this space? Is this place in reality an *Other* place?

Later in the film, she returns to the site in the middle of the night and witnesses (perhaps imagines) how a lamb is scared off the ledge by a sheep-herding dog. This time, in her state of flight and despite the group's pleas with her to not jump, Alicia chooses to leap from the ledge. The previous *temps mort* allows the spectator to see through the darkness, to map out the height of the jump and to imagine the water crashing on the rocks below. Ironically, Alicia's choice to jump off the cliff into the darkness, without knowing if it is low tide or high tide, is far more dangerous than the first attempt. The director repeats the underwater shot from the previous scene for Sara's jump, but this time we see that it is Alicia who plunges into the cold water when she emerges from it and is fished out by a Mapuche caretaker. The cliff, the lamb scared off the ledge, the rocks along the water's edge, the mass of bubbles caused by Alicia jumping off the cliff and the Mapuche caretaker provide a new constellation of images that relate to the island's topography. The spectator must choose to gaze at the torment of a US tourist as a spectacle or attempt to create new meaning about the island's topography and its mysterious connection with Alicia.

Alicia's return to the cliff invites the spectator to scrutinize its odd value. In *Being a Skull: Site, Contact, Thought, Sculpture* (2016) Georges Didi-Huberman ruminates on where thought, the mind, is indeed located. He examines how artists have worked on conceptions of the skull and how this relates to different states of being. In the chapter titled 'Être Aître' Didi-Huberman develops the notion of the skull-site, an open site of ontological questioning, a physical dwelling for thought that has yet to be organized into signs but whose powerful intelligibility, prior to any knowledge, founds the possibility itself of signifying. The filmed island landscape in *Magic Magic* functions as a cranium: its topography, its fissures, rocks, cliffs and the surrounding expanse of water become a *magic* cranial box, a vital place that invites the question of the interior, of looking beyond the main narrative. As seen in the cliff scenes as well as the encounters she has with the local animal life, Alicia's own skin makes contact with the materiality of the island space. This contact unleashes anxieties and concerns that turn on themselves, devouring identity. There are numerous scenes where Alicia's anxieties of vacationing in a place she does not know, with people she does not understand, push her to the ground. She is constantly falling to the ground and it becomes increasingly difficult for her to get up. This contact has violent consequences because it carries a historic residue of a past colonial order and the current neoliberal global regime that blankets over individuality and forces rational thought and the subject to become a homogeneous body. The body, especially the woman's body, becomes part of the transactional nature of the global tourist economy. For example, Agustín hypnotizes Alicia with a YouTube video and a simple set of commands that demand that she rest. The group forces her to do a series of increasingly sexual and humiliating acts that culminate with Brink commanding her to place her hand in the fire. She does and screams in pain. The group is repulsed by their own manipulations of the hypnotized Alicia, going as far as blaming her for being so insecure. The woman's body as an object of tourist entertainment extends to Sara, who has to quietly leave to get an abortion before she can rejoin the group. She injures herself when she decides to jump from the cliff. While Agustín hypnotizes Alicia, Sara goes to the bathroom, where she and the spectator see evidence that the jump exacerbated her painful recovery. Thus, there is a doubling of the US woman tourist that is both consuming an exotic place for her own enjoyment and being an exotic body for a man's enjoyment. Both the body and the island landscape are victims of this neoliberal order that views identity as transactional.

The distance between the spectator and the filmed landscape is key to understanding how the tourist body becomes part of this alternative constellation of island imagery. In *The Eye of History: When Images Take Positions* (2018), Didi-Huberman explains that distancing effect in film is used to divide the viewing subject and break the unity of representation in order to show visual-temporal differences and make the image a question of knowledge. This operation of distancing poses an element of surprise for the spectator. He explains that these surprising intervals stem from the simultaneity of showing a unity in the montage and the production of disassembly, a move that 'breaks up our habitual perception of the relations between things and situations' (2018: 81). The filmed landscape produces a distancing effect that disarticulates our perception of the island setting, leading us to cast a critical gaze on the strangeness, the curious phenomena and incomprehensible truths that invite the spectator to shape a critical social point of view about the island sites. Alicia's surprising fall into a schizophrenic-induced catatonic state leaves her with no vantage point from which to survey the viscous nature of the Patagonia landscape which leads to a destruction of identity. In this landscape, her body becomes contaminated by and a filter for the being and objects of the island. This archipelago of images is punctuated by a corporal performance that becomes directly connected to the insularity of the Lago Ranco. As mentioned earlier, Alicia is progressively being absorbed by landscape. It is a performance that begins with the scenes that capture Alicia in the foetal position in the shower after arriving in Chile, and continues with Alicia's submissive responses to the local wild and domesticated animals, her inability to use her phone because of the poor reception, her distrust of the others in the lake house that leaves her with insomnia and her failed attempt to escape at night. These gestures eventually culminate in a total loss of consciousness. Alicia becomes landscape and in doing so produces a disorganized identity that sinks into itself. Alicia's degradation of identity (and point of view) is linked to the disintegration of the diegesis into a series of disorganized images, which, in turn, allows landscape a brief moment of autonomy. Thus, Alicia's corporeal performance is vital to the (re)assembly of non-narrative landscape and the non-narrativity of the body.

The body becoming landscape

As mentioned earlier, how a body moves through filmed space can lead the spectator to recognize landscape as autonomous from setting. *Magic Magic* undoes its own diegesis and setting by allowing an alternative narrative to be secreted by the bodily attitudes, or postures, of the characters. Gilles Deleuze, in 'Cinema, body and brain, thought' (1985) from *Cinema 2: The Time-Image*, explains that the attitudes of the body, its postures, are sites of new thought. In experimental film, the body can vibrate between being a site of the everyday or it can give itself to film; it is born and disappears in a ceremony. Deleuze examines how the coordination of these postures of the body is irreducible to the plot or the 'subject', as they carry with them a social component (1985: 189–94). *Magic Magic*'s intertwining of the postures made by the characters points to a profound isolation due to a distrust of public and private space. The spectator learns very little of the characters through diegesis. There is a deliberate refusal to give any backstory to Sara and Agustín's decision to have an abortion, Bárbara's insistence to focus on her studies or Brink's closeted homosexuality. The lack of character development creates a distancing effect, where the spectator can judge the (in)actions of the main characters.

Alicia's body produces new desires that relate to the powerful silences that have left testimony marooned and the hope of the painful but necessary return to the traumatic past in order to come to a higher understanding of it. This sentiment is echoed by the pop song 'Con razón' (2011) by *Pedropiedra*, or Pedro Subercaseaux García de la Huerta, a former bandmate of the director. The song revolves around an excess of choice, where the singer recounts numerous sexual encounters that have led to nothing more than fragmented and empty relationships with the opposite sex. Early in the road trip in *Magic Magic*, the song is chosen by the group and everyone except Alicia repeat the chorus 'Una más una más y me voy me voy' by memory in Spanish. Ironically, Brink alters the lyrics to be more sexually explicit and recounts how the artist, Pedropiedra, urinated on the audience. It is a song whose message of casual satiation of sexual desire has been internalized by the group and anticipates the superficiality of friendship. Brink's churlish jest reappears with his numerous sexual advances that torment Alicia. Further, it is clear that Brink is struggling with his sexual identity and does not feel comfortable when talking about his presumed preference for women, nor is he aware of his infatuation with Agustín. This uncertainty of sexual identity and the superficiality of the romantic relationships culminate in the disturbing scene where Alicia performs oral rape on Brink. Afterwards, Brink is left confused, humiliated and traumatized. When he tries to kiss Alicia, she rejects him with disgust. She denies the act and Brink is unable to convince anyone that it actually happened. Brink is left stunned, feeling isolated, with no possibility to testify or way to understand the traumatic event. The rape scene and the lack of accountability are haunting reminders of the numerous accounts of sexual torture of men and women suffered during the Pinochet dictatorship. Thus, touch, whether it is Alicia's contact with landscape or other bodies, is corrupted and is the result of the disappearance of identity, of choice and of memory. *Magic Magic* responds to a political immediacy by inviting the spectator to question the *Concertación* coalition's national pacification project. This attempt to silence testimony has left the post-dictatorship generations isolated in a shared feeling of impotence and an inability to build meaningful relationships with each other. Instead, they must look to a neoliberal order that creates subjects that respond to each other through transactional relationships.

Alicia's regression into a catatonic state places her within landscape. Her inactivity leads to an end to the main plot, the continuation of a minor narrative and alternative (hi)stories. The final scenes follow the group as they, once again, look to the impoverished Mapuche community for guidance in curing Alicia. The Mapuche ceremony is conducted in a language that none of the tourists understand and the ceremony's aim remains a mystery. The lack of communication and the view of the native inhabitants as caretakers point to historic injustices suffered by the isolated Mapuche people, the silenced Amerindian voice that resides within the Patagonia. Moreover, Agustín's decision to avoid a hospital alludes to the lack of medical attention the locals receive from the national government as well as the group's selfish desire to avoid accountability. The Mapuche ritual delivers Alicia to a spiritual plain leaving her unable to move or speak. The group rushes Alicia back to the car, in a return to a site of trauma. It is during the car ride to the island that Alicia witnesses the group's irresponsible abandonment of the sick puppy. It is also coupled by Alicia's poor music selection that leads to the CD player looping the same song against the group's will. As the group drives off with Alicia in the back of the vehicle, the spectator and Alicia begin to hear the CD's jazz music return as the off-screen whimpers of the twice-abandoned puppy are doubled by Alicia's own wailing. She soon becomes completely catatonic, a state that provokes a collective reckoning for the group, whose members are inept at helping her. The final scene mirrors the beginning, where landscape moves from marginalia towards a new way of seeing. The spectator gazes on the constellation of meanings of Silva's representation of the Patagonian island landscape. *Magic Magic* concludes by fading to a black screen, the off-screen sounds of Sara crying over Alicia's body and the humming of the motorboat. It is a culmination of the isolation of bodies and the absence of a body, whose meaning the spectator must contemplate. Landscape becomes a vital means in communicating this isolation and absence that, in turn, evoke a haunting return of the figure of the disappeared during Pinochet's dictatorship.

Magic Magic's conclusion is a haunting recreation of disappearance, where a foreign outsider has been forced on a trip against her will, harassed and tortured. The result is that her body is neither alive nor dead, but disappeared. However, the absence of Alicia's body and the archive of images and meanings that Silva produces cannot be reduced to metaphor. These time-images and postures shift and reconfigure themselves, refusing to offer a complete equivalency. Instead, *Magic Magic* can be read as an allegory of loss, a collage of meanings that shift and find new connections in a present neoliberal order while working in tandem with the labour of mourning the traumatic past. Idelber Avelar reminds us in *The Untimely Present: Postdictatorial Latin American Fiction and the Task of Mourning* (1999) of a regime of forgetting that is used to reconcile the violent dictatorial past with a market-driven present that commodifies memory, dooming it to obsolescence. It is through the close examination of this obsolescence, the ruins left by the market's substitutive operation, that a partial form of resistance can subsist. The usage of landscape allows for the spectator to gaze at this loss. Thus, the island serves its narrative function as Alicia's absence serves as a shared spectre, one that becomes a defining loss for all of the characters of the film. It is a visual spectacle, freed from eventhood, that I consider to be highly performative. When placed within the political immediacy of the *Concertación*'s failed reconciliation project, itself a regime of forgetfulness, *Magic Magic* accentuates this collective loss that embodies the figure of the disappeared and the current neoliberal policies that reify the present and the transactional nature of global tourism.

In *Magic Magic*, the resulting identity in ruins is a productive force that resists the substitutive nature of neoliberalism. In agreement with Ana Ros (2012), perhaps the most divisive memory of Salvador Allende's legacy was his socialist government. Ros explains that for many Chileans the socialist project 'pointed to the persisting inequalities and distance between the poor and the rich' that continued under the *concertación*'s embrace of the neoliberal economic model imposed by the dictatorship (2012: 119). Brett Levinson (2003) examines how the *Concertación*-sponsored marketing campaign 'Publicidad. El derecho de elegir' was an attempt to legitimize a false choice between neoliberalism (which the campaign claimed gave the right to choose) and the repressive censorship that was falsely connected to the capitalist reforms that Allende purposed (2003: 104). Levinson concludes that the rapid move to neoliberalism initiated a series of outcomes, among them, 'a shift from citizen to consumer: the state attaches the citizen's debt or duty (as citizen) to his *de facto* obligation to consume' (2003: 99). This contentious public debate between memory and choice, and the resulting apathy produced by neoliberalism's substitutive nature of the past is central to understanding *Magic Magic*'s use of the schizophrenic body. Alicia's ailing body produces desire to such an extent that it interrupts and restarts diegesis, refusing to allow the main narrative to conclude (where did the group go with Alicia's body? Will they be held accountable for Alicia's fate?) and uprooting the social fabric of neoliberal apathy that is content with the façade of unity.

Despite the post-dictatorship generations' important contributions, some of the most unsettling aspects of the past have yet to be addressed in plain sight. Film has become a viable tool to articulate the void left by disappearance and the subsequent broken societal bonds that the dictatorship left behind. Contemporary Chilean filmmakers who lived under the horrors of Pinochet's regime have cast a critical eye on the transitional government's cautious and incomplete reckoning of the traumatic past. Silva's *Magic Magic* evokes this deep frustration of alienation felt by those that cannot find a place to speak about and interpret individual and collective memories related to surviving state-sponsored terror. In the film, this inability to testify manifests itself in the corporal performance by Alicia and her mysterious relationship with the island landscape in the Chilean Patagonia. This destructive but vibrant connection between body and landscape produces a constellation of images that perform disappearance, a performance that requires the spectator's participation. *Magic Magic* attempts to sink into itself and invites the spectator to find meaning beyond the rational order of diegesis.

Notes

1 Augusto Pinochet was arrested in London. However, after a long and contentious international legal battle, he eventually was released in March 2000. According to Stern the arrest and release of Pinochet served as a partial unravelling of memory impasse and a call for social justice.

2 As with the rest of Chilean society, there was no consensus among youth groups in Chile on how to approach the legacy of Pinochet and neoliberalism. This was in part due to Pinochet's popularity and influence on the transition from a neoliberal dictatorship to a neoliberal limited democracy. For example, the Fundación Pinochet included young and old Pinochet supporters who protested Pinochet's arrest and continued to view him as a political saviour. The lack of consensus is also due to the trauma of the assassination of the democratically elected Salvador Allende and his socialist government that promised to address the persisting socioeconomic inequalities (Ros 2012: 112–21).

3 It is important to note that these tendencies do not constitute a movement, nor should they be representative of all recent Chilean film. At a round table discussion at the Seminci Film Festival in Spain (2017), Waissbluth cautioned that Chilean cinema, and Latin American cinema in general, can quickly mirror Eurocentric categories such as Brazil = stories about favelas, Mexico = border crossing, Chile = the dictatorship, which are not representative of the cinema produced in a certain country (Diestro-Dópido 2017). Silva resists categorization by experimenting with the psychological thriller. *Magic Magic* is more concerned with an exploration of the psyche than a series of thrills. I read this as an invitation to discover new meaning through the spectator's participation.

4 Pablo Larraín is accredited with revitalizing Chilean film for international audiences. Pablo and his brother Juan de Dios Larraín founded the production company Fábula in order to connect many Chilean films produced locally and nationally to other international markets. Fábula is a rare case within Chilean cinema as the majority of films depend on state subsidies as well as international treaties with other Latin American and European institutions (Diestro-Dópido 2017).

References

Andermann, J. (2007), *The Optic of the State: Visuality and Power in Argentina and Brazil*, Pittsburgh: University of Pittsburgh Press.

70 *The Film Archipelago*

Ángel negro (2000), [Film] Dir. Jorge Olguín, Chile: Troma Entertainment.

Avelar, I. (1999), *The Untimely Present: Postdictatorial Latin American Fiction and the Task of Mourning*, Durham: Duke University Press.

Barraza, V. (2014), 'Historia y simulacros de la memoria en 31de abril de Víctor Cubillos', in M. Villarreal, et al. (eds), *Enfoques al cine chileno en dos siglos*, 151–60, Santiago: LOM Ediciones.

Deleuze, G. (2003), *Cinema 2: The Time-Image*, trans. H. Tomlinson and R. Galeta, Minneapolis: University of Minnesota Press.

Deleuze, G. (2004), *Desert Islands and Other Texts (1953-1974)*, trans. M. Taormina, South Pasadena: Semiotext(e).

Diestro-Dópido, M. (2017), 'Children of the Coup: Chilean Cinema after Pinochet', *Sight and Sound: British Film Institute*, 27 June. Available online: http://www.bfi. org.uk/news-opinion/sight-sound-magazine/comment/festivals/chilean-cinema-after-pinochet.

Didi-Huberman, G. (2015), *Cuando las imágenes toman posición*, trans. I. Bartolo, Madrid: Antonio Machado Libros.

Didi-Huberman, G. (2016), *Being a Skull: Site, Contact, Thought, Sculpture*, trans. Drew S. Burk, Minneapolis: Univocal.

Feierstein, D. (2007), *El genocidio como prática social: Entre el nazismo y la experiencia argentina*, Buenos Aires: Fondo de Cultura Económica.

La nana (2009), [Film] Dir. Sebastián Silva, Chile: Banco Estado Cine.

Lazzara, M. J. (2006), *Chile in Transition: The Poetics and Politics of Memory*, Gainesville: University of Florida Press.

Lazzara, M. J. (2011), 'Dos propuestas de conmemoración pública: Londres 38 y el Museo de la Memoria y los Derechos Humanos (Santiago de Chile)', *A Contracorriente: Una revista de historia social y literatura de América Latina* 8.3: 55–90.

Lefevbre, M. (2006), 'Between Setting and Landscape in the Cinema', in M. Lefevbre (ed.), *Film and Landscape*, 19–60, New York: Routledge.

Levinson, B. (2003), 'Dictatorship and Overexposure: Does Latin America Testify to More than One Market?', *Discourse* 25.1: 98–118.

Magic Magic (2013), [Film] Dir. Sebastián Silva, Chile: Braven Films.

Nasty Baby (2015), [Film] Dir. Sebastián Silva, USA: The Orchard.

Nouzeilles, G. (1999), 'Patagonia as Borderland: Nature, Culture, and the Idea of the State', *Journal of Latin American Cultural Studies* 8.1: 35–48.

Pratt, M. L. (2008), *Imperial Eyes: Travel Writing and Transculturation*, 2nd ed, New York: Routledge.

Ros, A. (2012), *The Post-Dictatorship Generation in Argentina, Chile, and Uruguay: Collective Memory and Cultural Production*, New York: Palgrave Macmillan.

Stern, S. (2010), *Reckoning with Pinochet: The Memory Question in Democratic Chile, 1989–2006*, Durham: Duke University Press.

Vázquez, K. E. (2014), 'Corre muchacha, corre: estructura de clase y trabajo doméstico en *La Nana* (2009), de Sebastián Silva', *Chasqui* 43.2: 161–78.

3

Memory islands: Repeating traumas in Patricio Guzmán's *Nostalgia de la luz* (2010) and *El botón de nácar* (2015)

Amanda Holmes

Patricio Guzmán's documentary films, *Nostalgia de la luz/Nostalgia for the Light* (2010) and *El botón de nácar/The Pearl Button* (2015), frame Chile as an island through both its unique topography, enclosed by ocean and mountain range, and its human relationships, marked by traumatic collective memories of dictatorship and oppression. While the films underscore the insular qualities of Chile, geography and memory merge to reveal microcosms, a series of both natural and metaphorical islands. The films explore the distinct features of the Atacama Desert in the north, and the archipelagos in the south, and how these natural formations reflect memories and histories from Chile's colonialist and dictatorial past. Here, Guzmán emphasizes the reproduction of these memories across eras and spaces in the stories of community suffering repeated across Chilean history.

Patricio Guzmán (1941–) went into exile in 1973 after his detainment in the national stadium in Santiago, where he was tortured and threatened with death along with other prisoners of Augusto Pinochet's *coup d'état. La batalla de Chile/The Battle of Chile* – Guzmán's highly acclaimed three-part documentary from the 1970s[1] – records the struggle of Salvador Allende and his supporters to retain political control, and the atrocities surrounding his government's overthrow by Pinochet's right-wing coalition backed by the CIA. Along with other powerful films such as the Argentine documentary *La hora de los hornos/The Hour of the Furnaces* (Fernando Solanas and Octavio Getino, 1968), and the Cuban fiction piece, *Memorias del subdesarrollo/*

Memories of Underdevelopment (Tomás Gutiérrez Alea, 1968), La batalla de Chile was produced during the revolutionary era in filmmaking known as New Latin American Cinema that harnessed the region's 'underdevelopment' to exemplify the continent aesthetically, but also to spur political change through the camera lens. Directors from this film movement sought to use the camera as a weapon, a militant attitude depicted most famously in the film manifesto 'Hacia un tercer cine' [Towards a Third Cinema] (1969), written by Argentine film directors, Fernando Solanas and Octavio Getino.[2]

Scholars have noted a shift in Patricio Guzmán's work from a focus on collective perspectives in his films from the 1960s and 1970s to one that has become more individualized and personal in his later projects (Couret 2017: 71). While Thomas Miller Klubock suggests that this change in approach reflects a transition from a more politicized cinema engaged with revolutionary ideology to one that underscores the individual's perspective, Guzmán's current documentary films must not be read as a sea change in political thinking on the part of the filmmaker.[3] The search for a meaningful, egalitarian and ethical community and collectivity still dominates the political ideology of these contemporary works. The transformation occurs, rather, in how the collective is defined and unified.

Nostalgia de la luz and El botón de nácar document the presence of a series of smaller collectivities that can be united philosophically by certain attitudes towards (for the most part) traumatic histories and memories. These groups – the ex-prisoners, the women of Calama and the nineteenth-century indigenous miners (Nostalgia de la luz); the Patagonian indigenous populations and the victims of the Pinochet dictatorship (El botón de nácar) – form communities that repeat themselves in their outlook and suffering. In this way, far from accepting a globalized, individualistic ideology, Guzmán harnesses the power of traumatic memories by proposing that an acknowledgement of their repetition would offer the fragmented collectivity a means to consolidate. By unifying, the suffering felt by the isolated individual can be assuaged.

For the purposes of the study, Nelly Richard's analysis of Chilean history through the lens of the 'cultural residue' becomes particularly potent. Both natural and cultural forms of 'residue' surface in Guzmán's films to mark the historic past, alongside our incorporation into the universe. Certain natural elements such as calcium, salt, water and mother-of-pearl figure centrally, but also accompany the memories related to oppression. By integrating the significance of the permanence of natural elements with the recurrence of individual traumas, the films underscore a constancy of existence that counters the insularity of these memories. In this way, the repetition of 'memory islands' corresponds to the decentred nature of the 'residual' as Nelly Richard understands it:

> The 'residual' as a critical hypothesis connotes the way in which the secondary and the nonintegrated are capable of displacing the force of signification toward borders less favored by the scale of social and cultural values, in order to question their discursive hierarchies from lateral positions and hybrid decenterings.
>
> (2004: 3)

The histories represented in Guzmán's films derive from decentralized communities that have been isolated from society's mainstream. By analysing the 'residue' – both cultural and natural – that is present in the films, Guzmán reveals the recurrence of oppression in Chile from the colonization of indigenous territories to the Pinochet dictatorship of the late twentieth century.

Produced in collaboration between Europe and Chile,[4] both documentaries received critical acclaim with awards for best documentary at festivals predominantly in North America and Europe. *Nostalgia de la luz* notably won the Toronto Film Critics Association Allan King Documentary Award in 2011, and the European Film Award for European Documentary in 2010, while *El botón de nácar* pulled in the Mayor's prize for Patricio Guzmán at the Yamagata International Documentary Film Festival, among ten other accolades.[5] Remarkable for their mesmerizing aesthetic attributes, these documentaries seduce the viewer to confront a past of political atrocities. Bradley Epps aptly captures Guzmán's documentary style in both films when he exclaims in reference to *Nostalgia de la luz*: 'Its scientific trappings do not, however, restrain its poetic, even religious, import, for the film draws on images and words that mix earth and sky, ground and air, bone fragments and stardust, both of which contain calcium salts, just like the desert' (2017: 494).

This chapter first illustrates the three ways in which aspects of Chilean geography can be associated with islands. It then explains the 'residue' presented in both films and its connection to Chilean history and the memory of the survivors of state-guided atrocities. Through an analysis of the cultural and natural residue in the documentaries, I argue that the oppressed communities that Guzmán represents emerge as peripheral, like their geographic island counterparts, while the constancy of their presence in history positions them centrally to become a permanent aspect of Chile.

The islands of Chile

The documentaries underscore three possibilities for understanding Chile in relationship to geographic insularity: (1) the archipelagos in the south; (2) the Atacama Desert in the north and (3) the entire land mass of the country. The thousands of islands, islets and archipelagos in the southern Pacific Ocean that borders Chile are classified into five principal geographic 'sectors': Sector 1, the 134 islands and islets are Mocha Island; Sector 2, the 16 islands far from the continent including Easter Island and the Juan Fernández Islands; Sector 3, 169 islands and islets around Chiloé Island; Sector 4, the Chonos Archipelago; and Sector 5, the 4,553 islands and islets that form around the Isla Grande de Tierra del Fuego, Navarino and Guayaneco Archipelago.[6] In *El botón de nácar*, Martín G. Calderón and Gabriela Paterito, members of the Yámana and Kawéskar peoples respectively, elaborate on the intimate connection that was established between the nomadic indigenous Fuegian populations and the ocean. These peoples navigated the islands of the massive archipelago in the south in wooden canoes, and ate shellfish collected by diving in the ocean. Calderón laments the Chilean governmental restrictions that no longer permit him to move across the ocean in his handcrafted canoe. Paterito speaks nostalgically of the lengthy voyage she took as a child with her family crossing from island to island in the vast archipelago.

The descriptions of these traditional Fuegian water-based lifestyles in the archipelagos contrast with the representation of the second geographic region in Chile that can be equated with islands, namely, the Atacama Desert, commonly known as 'the driest place on earth', underscored primarily in the first documentary, *Nostalgia de la luz*. With the Pacific Ocean flanking its Western border, surrounded by the Andean mountain range on the East, the

Desert spans a little more than 1,000 kilometres from north to south. Guzmán highlights the vastness of this dry expanse by including imagery of the Desert from space: the Atacama stands out for its lack of cloud cover in contrast with the rest of the globe that is covered in a hazy humidity. From outside the earth's atmosphere, looking in, the Atacama appears like an island: a landmass surrounded by the humidity of the clouds.

Finally, the historian Gabriel Salazar affirms Chile's insular nature – the idea of the whole country as an island – in *El botón de nácar*. Salazar makes the poetic claim that the country 'followed the wrong path'. He asserts that Chile has '4,200 kilometers of coastline. Probably the country with the largest coastline in the world'. The 'enormous mountain range' isolates the country from the northern part of the continent, from 'Western civilization', while the archipelagos form a 'long continent in the South'. The historian concludes that 'we are an island in a geographic sense, in human geography, etc. We do not have a maritime tradition and we have built towards the interior' (23:40). Rather than working inland, in Salazar's opinion, Chile should have developed further its relationship with the ocean. Ironically, according to Salazar, by working in the mainland, rather than focusing on the economic opportunities provided by the sea, Chile retained an insularity that it might otherwise have overcome.

Figure 3.1 Chilean archipelagos in *El botón de nácar*.

Figure 3.2 Atacama Desert as island in *Nostalgia de la luz*.

Community isolation, cultural and natural residue

Chile's geographic affinities with islands transfer in the documentaries to the insularity of peoples. Memories of different communities form the cultural residue represented in *Nostalgia de la luz*: the pre-Hispanic indigenous populations who crossed the desert; the atrocities committed under colonial government in the salt mines of the nineteenth century; and the imprisonment and disappearance of political prisoners during the Pinochet dictatorship. As David Martin-Jones notes, the Atacama Desert in this film becomes a veritable archive of Chilean histories. These memories are then juxtaposed in the film with the infinite passage of time represented by the light of stars in the universe, a light that is associated with calcium by the astronomers at the observatory who explain the presence of this element in the graphs that represent the stars. Traces of these peoples' histories surface in the elements of the desert; the salt preserves the bodies, and the calcium – like that of the stars – is found in their bones. Guzmán concludes *Nostalgia de la luz* with a note of hope: since human bodies contain the same substance as stars, we can find comfort in our connection to the infinite light of the universe.

Natural elements preserve and mark the past in a similar way to human memories regarding the recent dictatorship in Chile. A case in point is the experience of the architect, Miguel Lawner, interviewed by Guzmán in *Nostalgia de la luz*, who was held in a number of prisons and concentration camps during the dictatorship. Remarkably, he committed to memory the details of the layout of these holding centres, and managed to recreate them in a series of drawings that he produced in exile in Denmark. Uncannily, the buildings of the Chacabuco concentration camp in the Atacama Desert made use of those of the salt mine from the nineteenth century, a site in which indigenous workers were subject to atrocious working conditions. However, as emphasized by the film's archaeologist interviewee, Lautaro Núñez, even this history is one that the Chileans do not know:

> Notice how little we know about the nineteenth century, how many secrets we keep from the nineteenth century. We have never clearly stated why we marginalized our indigenous peoples. It is almost a state secret. [...] There is a foolishness, as if we do not want to approach our closest pre-history. As if we would encounter an almost accusatory pre-history.
>
> (28:31; 29:20)

Here we see the histories of the salt mines and the dictatorship linked by their association with the desert, more specifically with the element of salt. Even more profoundly, the calcium in the bones of those who suffered and died under circumstances of atrocity connect these victims separated by a hundred years.

One final example from *Nostalgia de la luz* demonstrates the merging of memory with the natural space of the desert, namely, the women of Calama who spend their days scanning and sifting through the expanse of sand to find the remains of their loved ones killed by the dictatorship. These women have spent decades engaged in seeking their relatives whose bodies were discarded in the desert. They cannot finalize their memories and continue with their lives until they have found some or all of their relatives' remains. Clearly representative of the desperation of these women is the painful personal story recounted in the documentary by Vicky Saavedra. She tells of receiving a body part that belonged to her brother, namely his foot that had been retrieved from a mass grave located in the desert. She explains that she spent the day holding and crying over this piece of his body, finally coming to terms with the fact that he had been killed. For these women, material evidence of the death of their family members will not only allow for the possibility of mourning and closure, but will also provide a physical element that will mediate between the different times and histories.

Finding an affirmation of memory in natural elements surfaces as an essential need to alleviate the suffering of these different communities of survivors in *Nostalgia de la luz* – the ex-prisoners, the relatives of the disappeared, those exiled by the dictatorship and, more distantly, the indigenous miners of the nineteenth century. By achieving this, the communities find similar histories of oppression and atrocity written in the sand, and connected to the stars, that provide a sense of a collective continuity, a means to advance with hope.

While *Nostalgia de la luz* links oppressed groups through their connection to the dry 'island' of the Atacama Desert, *El botón de nácar* identifies elemental residues that relate to the archipelagos of the south. This second documentary presents two groups of Chilean inhabitants, whose perspectives are formed by their 'lateral position[ing]' (Richard 2004: 3): the indigenous populations of the archipelagos, and the families and victims of the Pinochet dictatorship. Both groups live with the memory of political oppression, while their experiences are linked to the geographical region of the archipelagos in the south of Chile. Shifting from the Atacama Desert to the southern archipelagos as the film's geographic focus, *El botón de nácar* explores the significance of the ocean to the indigenous populations of the south, as well as to Chile's contemporary history of dictatorship. Cleverly, Guzmán identifies the nacre button as a sombre 'residual' link between these two histories: the Yámana, Jemmy Button, earned his surname for being convinced to board a British ship in 1830 in exchange for a button; in the second event, a pearl button is all that remains of one of the disappeared from the Pinochet dictatorship whose body was submerged in the ocean. The first button marks the beginning of the colonialist oppression of the Fuegian populations. The second signals the savage practices of the recent dictatorship.[7]

The memory of persecution pervades *El botón de nácar*'s presentation of the indigenous populations of the archipelagos. The five nomadic peoples autochthonous to the Tierra del Fuego 10,000 years ago – the Kawésqar, the Selknam, the Aonikenk, the Haush and the Yámana – travelled between islands and maintained an intimate relationship with the ocean. As Guzmán describes, 'they all walked on the sea' (14:32).[8] Interviews with two of the few remaining members of these indigenous groups confirm their symbiotic relationship with the sea. Martín G. Calderón, a Yámana, shows the film director the traditional canoe he is crafting. He explains that Chilean law does not allow them to continue to sail on the ocean in these small vessels. Gabriela Paterito, who identifies as Kawésqar (not Chilean), recounts her 1,000-kilometre voyage as a child with her family around the islands that form the Chilean archipelagos. Following the traditions of her people, at the age of seven or eight, she was taught to dive in the frigid ocean and forage for shellfish, the sustenance for the population.

Throughout the nineteenth century, and into the twentieth until their virtual extermination, the Fuegian populations suffered oppression. During this era, the Chilean government supported the settlement of the archipelagos, and encouraged the indoctrination of the indigenous populations with Western lifestyles. As *El botón de nácar* presents this era, the Fuegians were forced to follow European-based forms of living, and died of Western diseases in enormous numbers. The majority of the population was obliterated in fewer than fifty years. This history emerges even more bleakly in José Luis Alonso Marchante's historical account. While many Fuegians died from Western diseases, many more perished through explicit extermination policies to liberate lands for development by Chilean and Argentinian settlers. The autochthonous peoples of this region were massacred to make room for vast sheep ranches. The film recounts explicitly the abominable episode in Chilean history in which ransom was offered to the 'Indian hunters' for body parts of these populations: 'a pound for each male testicle, a pound for each female breast, and half a pound for each child's ear' (37:40–37:50). Following hundreds of years of persecution, at the time of the film's production, only twenty members of these indigenous populations survive.

When asked to recite words from her native Kaweskar language, as a translation for button, Gabriela offers 'yeḵena-ḵʰar'[9] which incorporates the sounds of the word, 'nácar'.[10] Here too, like the salt and calcium of *Nostalgia de la luz*, the natural element affects and defines the memory. Gabriela's recitation of button in Kaweskar rouses in the viewer a series of references to this item, from Jemmy Button in the initial interaction with the European explorers, to the button found on the ocean floor related to the contemporary Chilean dictatorship.

In the films, and especially in *El botón de nácar*, the memories of the Dictatorship survivors become tied to certain elements of the oppression of the indigenous populations. Guzmán interviews the investigative journalist Javier Rebolledo, who details the 'preparation' of murdered corpses for their inhuman disposal in the Pacific Ocean. A rail would be attached to the bodies with wires, and they would then be wrapped in plastic bags. A monument made of the metal rails has been erected in the Santiago Villa Grimaldi Peace Park – on the site of an infamous torture centre – to commemorate these victims (http://villagrimaldi.cl/parque-por-la-paz/monumento-rieles-2/). The documentary explains that in 2004, when it was decreed by a judge that a diver should exhume the bodies from the ocean, in most cases, all that was found of the remains was the rail. The film focuses on one incredible case regarding the recovery of these rails in which a pearl button was found attached to the rusted metal, confirming its connection with a corpse.

Taken together, the two documentaries suggest haunting links between cultural and natural residue in Chilean history. Salt from the desert and calcium from the bones connect the nomadic indigenous populations to the victims of the nineteenth-century salt mines and the Pinochet dictatorship, all in relation to the Atacama. As an element harvested from the sea, the natural habitat of mother-of-pearl is the source of the livelihood and traditional lifestyle of the

Figures 3.3 and 3.4 Rails monument, Villa Giraldi Peace Park, Santiago, http://villagrimaldi.cl/parque-por-la-paz/monumento-rieles-2/

Fuegian indigenous populations, while also the grave of the murdered victims of the Pinochet dictatorship. Nacre, retrieved and formed into a button for human benefit, also links the European-descended population with their abusive treatment of the Yámana indigenous peoples: Jemmy Button's exchange for his freedom as well as the word for mother-of-pearl button that resembles the Spanish term.

Memory islands

One hour into *El botón de nácar*, the film describes the multiple peoples who suffered atrocities in Dawson Island, Chile: first the indigenous peoples who were sent there to be indoctrinated when the site was used as a Catholic mission; then, Allende's deputies who were incarcerated and tortured in the buildings that served as a concentration camp; and finally, more than 700 of Allende's followers who were imprisoned in Dawson. The film captures the three groups, 'islands,' of victims one after the other. While the first two – the indigenous victims and Allende's deputies – are represented by filmed shots of historical group photographs, the survivors of the final group of prisoners are filmed to underscore the analogies of suffering.

To depict this third group of prisoners, Guzmán gathers approximately fifty Dawson survivors of the Pinochet dictatorship in a room presumably near the jail site. These women and men first stand perfectly still as if waiting for a photograph to be taken of them. In contrast with the historic photographs of the other two groups of victims, these survivors are depicted in colour. Then, gradually, the filmmaker leads them in a powerful choreography. He first asks the survivors to gesture with their hands where Dawson is located, to which they, at their own pace, raise their hands and point over to their left. The image then reverts back to the survivors posing in position as if waiting for a group portrait. Next, in response to the questioner who asks them to all say at once how much time they spent in the prison, the group calls out various numbers – 'four years,' 'three months,' etc. – in a kind of natural rhythm, but not quite in unison. Finally, the camera films their expressions in extreme close-ups to encourage the viewer to contemplate their ordeal.

While this careful staging allows the filmmaker to underscore the horror behind this recycled oppression and victimization supported by the Chilean government, it also frames each group – the indigenous and Allende's deputies in photographs; the Pinochet survivors in film – as their own community, without ignoring the discernible unity across the groups. It is as if the Pinochet

Figure 3.5 The indigenous peoples in Dawson Island.

survivors of oppression stood with the earlier victims of Dawson Island, their choreographed image an homage to the earlier suffering.

Both films explore residues of memory that in turn have created communities of contemporary Chilean peoples. The victims of dictatorship choreographed in *El botón de nácar* find their counterpart in the women of Calama depicted in *Nostalgia de la luz*. The former political prisoners and

Figure 3.6 Allende's deputies.

Figure 3.7 Survivors of the Pinochet incarceration at Dawson.

86 *The Film Archipelago*

the families of the disappeared require connections between the past and the present in order to move forward. While their relationship to isolation might differ, both groups forge links either between island groups in the archipelagos or between historical events in the case of the victims of the Dictatorship. The Fuegians' isolation from contemporary Western politics across the centuries allowed them to continue their traditional lifestyle until the late nineteenth century, and a similar sense of community is sparked for their current survivors, although the scarcity of these peoples reflects the difficulty for them to develop their common memory.

Notes

1   *La batalla de Chile* contains three parts – *La insurrección de la burguesía/The Bourgeois Insurrection* (1975), *El golpe de estado/The Coup d'Etat* (1976) and *El poder popular / Popular Power* (1979) – with a final documentary, *Chile, la memoria obstinada/Chile, the Obstinate Memory*, produced twenty years later in 1996. Guzmán smuggled the footage for the trilogy out of Chile shortly after the *coup* and edited the film in Cuba (Chanan 121–2).

2   See Chanan, López for excellent overviews of New Latin American Cinema.

3   Miller Klubock bases his analysis on the *La batalla de Chile* series including the fourth part, *Chile, la memoria obstinada*, produced after the fall of the Pinochet dictatorship. However, *Nostalgia de la luz* and *El botón de nácar* represent a new style of documentary filmmaking for Guzmán, one that includes more symbolic imagery and balances between the poetic and the factual.

4   *Nostalgia de la luz* is a coproduction between France, Germany, Spain and Chile, while *El botón de nácar* received the auspices of Switzerland instead of Germany.

5   See the IMDb sites on these films for more details regarding awards.

6   'Instituto Geográfico Militar de Chile'. See also http://www.shoa.cl/php/inicio and https://en.m.wikipedia.org/wiki/List_of_islands_of_Chile.

7   In her article on *El botón de nácar*, Brenda Hollweg appropriately expands the significance of the film: 'By means of alignment and condensation Guzmán encourages viewers to consider these structures of violence, not only as constitutive of Chile's past and on-going present, but also in a more general sense as constitutive of any modern industrialized, capitalist society' (Hollweg 19).

8   In fact, the Yámana and the Kaweskar were the 'nómadas canoeros' [canoe nomads]; the others indigenous Fuegian populations hunted and travelled on land (Alonso Marchante 18).
9   The linguistic transcription is from the online dictionary of the Qawaskar language at the *Intercontinental Dictionary Archive*:<https://web.archive. org/web/20110914211708/http://lingweb.eva.mpg.de:80/cgibin/ids/ids. pl?com=simple_browse&lg_id=313>.
10 The filmmaker has her repeat the term so that the viewer clearly hears the connection with the Spanish word.

References

Alonso Marchante, J. L. (2014), *Menéndez, Rey de la Patagonia*, Buenos Aires: Losada.

El botón de nácar (2015), [Film] Dir. Patricio Guzmán, Chile and France: Atacama Productions, Valdivia Film, Mediapro and France 3 Cinéma.

Chanan, M. (2017), 'Latin American Documentary: A Political Trajectory', in M. M. Delgado, S. M. Hart and R. Johnson (eds), *A Companion to Latin American Cinema*, 117–32, Malden, MA: John Wiley & Sons.

Couret, N. (2017), 'Scale as Nostalgic Form: Patricio Guzmán's *Nostalgia for the Light* (2011)', *Discourse* 39.1 (Winter): 67–91.

Epps, B. (2017), 'The Unbearable Lightness of Bones: Memory, Emotion, and Pedagogy in Patricio Guzmán's *Chile, la memoria obstinada* and *Nostalgia de la luz*', *Journal of Latin American Cultural Studies* 26.4: 483–502.

Hollweg, B. (2017), 'A Questioning Situation: Patricio Guzmán's Cine-Essayistic Explorations of Fragile Planetary Configurations', *New Cinemas: Journal of Contemporary Film* 15.1: 13–32.

Key, M. R. and B. Comrie (eds), *The Intercontinental Dictionary Archive*. https://web. archive.org/web/20110914211708/http://lingweb.eva.mpg.de:80/cgibin/ids/ids. pl?com=simple_browse&lg_id=313.

López, A. M. (1997), 'An "Other" History: The New Latin American Cinema', in M. T. Martin (ed.), *The New Latin American Cinema. Volume I: Theory, Practices and Transcontinental Articulations*, 135–56, Detroit: Wayne State University Press.

Martin-Jones, D. (2013), 'Archival Landscapes and a Non-Anthropocentric "Universe Memory"', *Third Text* 27.6: 707–22.

Miller Klubock, T. (2003), 'History and Memory in Neoliberal Chile: Patricio Guzmán's *Obstinate Memory* and *The Battle of Chile*', *Radical History Review* 85 (Winter): 272–81.

Nostalgia de la luz (2010), [Film] Dir. Patricio Guzmán, Chile and Germany: Atacama Productions, Blinker Filmproduktion, Westdeutscher Rundfunk (WDR) and Cronomedia.

Richard, N. (2004), *Cultural Residues: Chile in Transition*, Minneapolis: University of Minnesota Press.

Solanas, F. and O. Getino (1969), 'Hacia un tercer cine', *Revista Universitária do Audiovisual*. http://www.rua.ufscar.br/hacia-un-tercer-cine/.

4

Insular spaces:
A documentary and an affective
ethno-mapping of the Rapa Nui culture

Irene Depetris Chauvin

The first film of Tiziana Panizza's trilogy *Bitácora* (Logbook), *Tierra en movimiento* (Unstable Land, 2014), a travelogue by this film director and the poet Germán Carrasco, begins with Concepción as epicentre – a city severely affected by an earthquake in 2010 – and moves to the edges to go in search of what remained standing: a 'seismic human' community, as the author herself describes it. In thirty-four minutes, this video essay is a journey around the perimeter of an epicentre in search of 'a kind of nation spread throughout the world inhabiting the edges of tectonic plates, a nation that still lacks a name', an intensely affect-laden portrait of a community focusing on the material remains left by the earthquake and a formal exercise that confirms that an 'intimate' cinema is not necessarily a cinema anchored in the first person but one that explores the sensorial and analytical potential of different textures (Depetris Chauvin 2017). It explores the experimental and poetic dimensions of the observational documentary, moving around a space to encounter other forms of community and habitability, at the same time that it deploys an alternative aesthetics to portray the human groups involved (Depetris Chauvin 2016). This 'otherness' of the object as well as of the gaze is maintained throughout the series, but the second instalment, *Tierra sola* (Solitary Land, 2017), offers a deepening, an inflection, of that project.

Like *Tierra en movimiento*, the second film of the *Bitácora* series employs a super 8 camera to portray ways to inhabit an 'other' space: a wall-less prison on the world's most remote island. The island is none other than Easter Island, a territory and a culture that have had a conflictive history of colonial domination with the Chilean national state, a history largely ignored by the general public. A strange space, a strange community, language and culture: the observational documentary becomes an experimental ethnography. After many years of research in the archive, of inhabiting and exploring that space as well as that of the island itself, the cartographic impulse, typical of the logbook, traces a historiographic and anthropological itinerary. Panizza, both a documentary filmmaker and visual artist, 'becomes an anthropologist' when she uses the filmic form to immerse herself in an intensive zone that shapes – perceptively – what is being observed: the textuality and texture of images and of a culture. Geographical exploration, ethnography and documentary come together to make a poetic portrait of the travel experience, of the history and the stories, and of the ways an 'other' culture inhabits a space.

Mobile landscapes and affective mappings

Referring to Third Cinema, Michael Chanan highlighted the political potential of documentaries that make new landscapes and social groups visible. For this author, militant documentaries establish a new 'cognitive geography' that rests on the representative qualities or on the links that the drawing of a filmic map allows to establish between groups and spaces (2010: 150). But the spatial logic of films also opens up the possibility of questioning traditional discourses that characterize geography as a discipline devoid of emotions. In the first decades of the twentieth century, Gabriela Mistral reflected on the affectivity that films could bring to the fore by portraying 'living and sensorial landscapes' that instil movement into what she conceived as a 'paralytic map':

> The map speaks only to the geographer [...] Nothing more abstract, inert, and remote could be invented to illustrate what is otherwise concrete and vital. The wonder of the island becomes a 'mustard colouring'; the fjord a blue scratch; the jungle a stain in faded green [...] This arrogant and paralytic map is going to be brought to life in the cinema, which can offer living landscapes.
>
> (Mistral 1930)

In her critique of the geography taught at school, the Chilean poet finds the cartographic potential of cinema in its ability to provide moving and living landscapes. Contrary to the modern imaginary prevailing at the time,

Mistral points not to the representational qualities of the documentary, but to the very materiality of cinema and its ability to convey the spectres of living beings in a physical or sensorial way. The potential of cinema would be its capacity to offer an 'embodied cartography': a spatial projection by means of a type of 'sensitive light', a diffuse light emanating from the landscapes and the bodies that it makes visible. This cartography would matter not so much for what it reflects or represents, but for it being a trace, on account of its own materiality. Mistral will return to this conception of a cartography of presence when referring not only to the power of cinema to bring life to landscapes but also to the systematic need to expand, by covering different geographical areas, the sensory spectrum of the experience of the National territory. Thus, as if she were imagining a cartography made from echoes or sound shadows, the poet aspires to establish not only visual and tangible maps, but also a 'map of resonances that would turn the land into an "audible" space' (Mistral 1931). In this way, the critical potential of cinema, as the art of space, is played out in the configuration of itineraries and landscapes that allow the design of a sensitive map. Cinema would aim to give an aesthetic rather than a conceptual understanding of concrete and vital elements. However, paying attention to surfaces, traces, remains, lights and shadows is, in fact, a way of thinking space where the dimension of the sensible is not separated from cognition because it is possible to develop from the materiality of the filmic medium, complex significations of a space–time configuration: at the same time construction and 'residue', presence and absence, indexical image and haunting.

The American critic Jonathan Flatley also refers to affective maps in a metaphorical sense when he proposes that certain works or aesthetic practices can be thought of in terms of 'affective mapping' not only because they represent concrete spaces, but because they direct us to the historical world and the affective life of others who inhabited the same landscapes. Following a Benjaminian perspective, Flatley proposes a historical reading that plays on anachronism, in which affects are never experienced for the first time, but rather contain within themselves an archive of objects that have been previously encountered. Works of art open a space where we are confronted with these objects and affects and, in this sense, an affective historical reading constitutes a journey that rejects the linearity of historicism and leads us to think about the ways in which the present carries traces from the past (2008: 81–2). Thus, cinema as a 'peculiarly' spatial art is able to articulate sensitive, cognitive, metaphorical and affective maps. In *Tierra sola*, the materiality of the image records the traces of time through trajectories that describe geographical and perceptual dimensions, putting forward spatial configurations that create a link with the past and with others in the present.

Insular states

Because of their literal isolation, or simply due to a certain sense of separation that their inhabitants experience from continental society, islands acquire a fabulous character in the geographical discourse and in the cultural imagination. Before they are used as locations in works of fiction, islands already function as 'floating signifiers' – as part of a literary procedure that uses those relatively isolated spaces, and their natural boundaries, to contain different narratives and to examine social formations.[1] The image of the island is central to Western thought; however, the purpose here is to reflect not only on the ways in which we think about islands, but also on the ways in which we think through them considering that, in addition to being spaces that can be used as metaphors for philosophical thought, they are real places in which lived stories occur. Thus, for Marc Shell (2014) a study of islands should examine aspects of memory and identity of its inhabitants and, in this sense, he suggests that we recover spatial theories to think of a phenomenology of the archipelago. The island's geography expands metaphorically into the condition of insularity of those who inhabit it and invites us to establish a parallel between the territory, subjectivity and the circulation of affects within these relatively isolated communities.

According to Shell, this space must be understood by means of the dialectic movement that the word suggests: an island is simultaneously a 'land surrounded and isolated by water' (from the Latin word *insula*) and 'the mixture of water and land at the limiting or defining "coast"' (2004: 2), from the Norse 'water-land'. In the first sense, the island is a 'limit', while in the second it is a kind of 'interface', between two worlds happening at the same time. Land that potentially becomes water, island and island effect, insularity: the archipelago is a materially and symbolically unstable territory.[2] From this premise, we can consider how *Tierra sola* works the dimension of insularity in relation to issues of identity and memory from a point of view that privileges the porous and critical dimension of affects.

In Panizza's film a certain subjectivity linked to the 'insular state' is intertwined with geography but without avoiding the historical dimension, as the documentary proposes a reflection on the state of emergency in Rapa Nui history.[3] Easter Island, one of the most remote inhabited places in the world, is a popular destination for Chileans and foreigners. For the latter, the tourist discourse sets in motion an imaginary of the island as a freedom paradise. Yet, the isolation of this 'solitary land' hides another story. After the annexation by Chile in 1888, the island was leased for sixty years to the *Compañía Explotadora de la Isla de Pascua* (Easter Island Exploiting Company), a British-owned company that turned it into a sheep farm; at one point it kept up to 60,000 animals. The company built a fence around the farm and relegated the islanders to a very small portion of the territory, leaving them with limited access to water and food, and preventing them from leaving the island. Many Rapa Nui were killed, others were enslaved, and many others embarked on the almost suicidal adventure of going out on precarious boats to the open sea in search of a future. Of the 14,000 inhabitants that the island had at its peak, only 111 native inhabitants remained at the end of the nineteenth century. After decades of neglect, in 1953 the Chilean government decided to terminate the contract with the leasing company. However, the island remained a 'prison' for its natives as the administration was entrusted to the navy, which managed it according to military regulations. Limits on the freedom of movement of the islanders were maintained and they were prevented from speaking their language. It was not until 1966, after an uprising organized by Alfonso Rapu, a young Rapa Nui teacher, that a civil administration was established, and the Easter islanders were granted Chilean citizenship (Ramírez Aliaga 2004: 15–21).

In her archival research to recover the audiovisual memory of the island, Tiziana Panizza found thirty-two films shot by Norwegians, Belgians, French and Canadians between 1933 and 1970. Framed by a Western gaze of the place as exotic, in most documentaries there are images of the characteristic stone sculptures, but the inhabitants, who have been subjected to conditions of colonial oppression for over sixty years, hardly appear. In her documentary

Tierra sola, Panizza tells the story of that first 'imprisonment' of the Rapa Nui, establishing links between fragments of the recovered films, numerous phonographic records of music in Rapa Nui language that are reproduced untranslated, super 8 recordings of the elders who lived during the colonial era and who bear witness to their situation – never facing the camera, shown always from the back or one side – and other sequences of digital recordings of the routine in the only prison that currently exists on the island.

There is no voiceover narration, but the director's voice appears throughout the documentary as intertitles in English, pointing at a montage exercise with the different audiovisual documents to bring about a new production of meaning. As I argued in another essay, in *Tierra sola*, this attention to montage deconstructs the discursive, media and scientific conventions that prevailed in classical ethnography,[4] not only unveiling the colonial logic in the ethnographic archive but also introducing a poetic and political twist by appropriating the 'gaze' of previous cameramen to anachronistically give 'voice' to those who were subjected to its effects. At the same time, *Tierra sola* enhances the vitality of remains, latent images, echoes and their ability to affect the present. The insistence on spectrality leads us to question not only what we see, but also what looks at us, staging the other bodies and temporalities that participate in the film in a new 'distribution of the sensible'. By collecting hints and remnants that promise to decipher other lives from the images, *Tierra sola* forms a notion of archive inhabited by affects and recovers the expressive nature of the document. The crossover of images from different historical periods and the emphasis on the sensorial character of the filmic record produces an encounter that engages not only the gaze, but also aural and textural dimensions to organize a new staging of memory (Depetris Chauvin 2018).

As a modern cartography, the documentary has the ability to map not only the shape of the territory of the islands, but also the temporal experiences inscribed in it – an itinerary through spectral sites acting as a mapping agency that carves new stories in spaces haunted by a traumatic past. Freedom and its paradoxes in an island space are explored through a crossroads of stories, trajectories, images, sounds and textures that appeal to the critical potential of anachronism. If the construction and deconstruction of the archive carried out in *Tierra sola* establish links between past and present and constitute what Flatley understands by 'affective mapping', working with the found footage is also part of an operation that functions, as Catherine Russell argues in relation to experimental ethnography, as a 'visual historiography in which several layers of mediation render "the primitive" allegorical' (1999: 18) and produces a radical discourse on memory: the critique of 'progress' and of 'cultural representation' makes it possible to 'theorize cultural memory without mystifying it as an originary site' (1999: 8). As in Flatley's, in Russell's reflection there is a Benjaminian perspective, a conception of historiography as a series of disparate, not necessarily related, moments that suggest that allegory itself is a means of expressing utopian desires of historical transformation while reinstating a critical 'distance': experimental ethnography would be an allegorical discourse, a discourse that conceives alterity as something fundamentally strange (Russell 1999: 121–2).

The use of series of frames from previous footage in the documentary *Tierra Sola* is an invitation to reassess not only the past but also the present of a community. They organize an image of the space of the current prison and the relationship of the other inhabitants with the island. Instead of exalting a romantic sublime to direct our gaze towards the recovery of an assumed state of primal admiration, the logbook takes us around Easter Island to collect traces of history and of stories that allow us to resignify a landscape usually associated with the tourist postcard.

Cartography and travelogue

With its 5,035 inhabitants, according to the last census, Easter Island has an atypical prison: an enclosure guarded by native and Chilean gendarmes, with a criminal population of fourteen prisoners who enjoy certain 'freedoms', such as producing handicrafts to sell to tourists visiting the prison, or some flexibility regarding visits from their relatives. Bizarrely the old facilities where the inmates live have no walls, just chicken wire, and no watchtowers. This peculiar space of confinement relates to the limits of the notion of freedom in a place where the possibility to escape from the island in the middle of the Pacific Ocean seems absurd. Where would a fugitive go on the most remote island on the planet? What is the difference between being isolated and being imprisoned?

In *Tierra sola* historical facts are linked to the daily life of the inmates of the island's prison; at the same time, the work of constructing and deconstructing the ethnographic archive is combined with an observational record of ways of inhabiting the island today that makes it possible to fill the fabric of 'threads that weave a community'. According to David MacDougall:

> Observational filmmaking was founded on the assumption that things happen in the world which are worth watching, and that their own distinctive spatial and temporal configurations are part of what is worth watching about them. Observational films are frequently analytical, but they also make a point of being open to categories of meaning that might transcend the filmmaker's analysis. This stance of humility before the world can of course be self-deceiving and self-serving, but it also implicitly acknowledges the subject's story is often more important than the filmmaker's.
>
> (MacDougall 1995: 131)

This opening up to the 'categories of meaning' of the protagonists and to the 'distinctive spatial and temporal configurations' of their world is what makes the observational approach productive in a documentary-making practice that intertwines the portrait of a community with the 'reading of the space' – that is, an approach that involves a critical feedback between film practice, representation of the other and geographical experimentation. Thematically or through montage, filmmaking offers a narrative model of space. The camera becomes a cartographic device, a tool that enables different kinds of geo-spatial storytelling. Giuliana Bruno refers to a 'transit look that transforms the *voyeur* (the one who sees) into *voyageur* (the one who travels)' (Bruno 2002: 11–16). In her *Atlas of Emotion,* the Italian critic envisions cinema as a form of spatial culture that can combine 'panoramic' views with those 'from below' and blur the opposition between 'seeing' and 'walking', between a 'map' and a 'tour'. *Tierra sola* recovers this dual way of understanding the construction of a space, from the perspective of vision and storytelling, but plays with scales and itineraries transforming the stabilizing and demarcating functions typical of traditional cartography.[5]

It is worth noting that the first images of the island from the ethnographic archive, taken from films such as *Island Observed* (Hector Lemieux, 1965, Canada) and *La isla más isla del mundo* (Francisco Efron and Monica Krassa, 1970, Chile), are bird's-eye views, a gaze encompassing the space 'from above'.

Height creates perspective, enlarges the field of vision and changes the point of view. In this gesture, there is a nod to the cartographic question, since the image is projected from a single point of view, indeterminate and impossible to reconstruct from the visual experience (because it has no vanishing point), which transforms the image into a plane without framing, with no physical place of observation. Thus, the zenithal gaze as a whole offers a totalizing and encompassing vision that in the case of *L'Île de Paques* (Henry Storck and John Farnhout, 1935, Belgium) and *Voyage to the Tip of the Earth* (Robert McAuley, 1968, Australia) will be directly replaced by that of cartographic representation of the island that subjects it to the same measuring exercise the bodies of the Rapa Nui are subjected to as objects of field research in ethnographic documentaries.

If there is one type of 'spatial practice' that Panizza privileges in her documentary, it is that of horizontal travel, displacement, moving landscapes and a cartography that is distilled from the travelogue. The only still images of the territory destabilize the traditional cartographic impulse as they are inverted zenithal gazes, leaving the sea where we are accustomed to see the sky and a fine line of the horizon at the lower end of the shot. The emphasis on displacement stresses the importance of the spatial dimension as another source of information in a documentary. In her essay on the use of testimony, Kim Munro suggests 'decentralizing' the role of the speaking subject as the 'indexicality' of this discourse is predicated on 'authenticity' while, in fact, it is constructing a reality. She suggests, then, not to rely only on what is 'said' but also on what is 'shown' and to open the documentary towards recording the landscape and the environment and listening to them as pro-filmic elements that convey experiences beyond the linguistic (2017: 17). Drawing on the concept of 'vibrant matter' coined by Jane Bennett, Munro suggests a 'partition of the sensible' that, by giving agency to 'mute matter', disrupts the conventional structures of documentary discourse. In this sense, as we will see in the following two sections, the work of *Tierra sola*, relying on the expressive nature of the document, finds points of contact with a current of 'sensory ethnography' that destabilizes the assumed dominance of vision – Western occularcentrism – and rescues other senses that in different cultures enable other forms of exploration and reflection, and open new paths for knowledge (Pink 2009: 7–22).

A circle of gazes, a web of textures

Beyond exposing and deconstructing the colonial nature of classical ethnographic approaches, *Tierra sola* stages a circulation of the gaze in which the portrayal of the Rapa Nui culture of the present does not hide the subjectivity of the documentary filmmaker. The first fragment captured by Panizza's camera clearly reveals how she is positioning what we are about to see: by using the same layout used to cite the fragments of the other films, *Tierra sola* shows it is becoming part of the same archive it has unearthed. What is Panizza's point of view? The first image taken by her super 8 camera shows a tree through a window, the wind moves the curtains. It turns around and we see an unmade bed. From the intimacy of her own room the director is adopting the subjective and epistolary inflection inaugurated by Chris Marker in *Letter from Siberia* (1958) by rewriting his opening sentence: 'I am writing to you from a faraway land.' The intertitles tell an anonymous recipient about the discovery of thirty-two films, of 'other gazes', and, as we see the frame of a flower, it states: 'my gaze, next to all others'.

It is a minor gaze, anchored in everyday life. The film's materiality itself takes distance from the idea of ethnography as a non-mediated and objective representation of the other: *Tierra sola* is filmed with two cameras, a digital and a super 8. The imprecise texture of the super 8 is reminiscent of the human gaze: it is fleeting, selective and uncertain, that is, inherently subjective. This visual choice can be interpreted as a gesture that brings Panizza's proposal closer to a self-conscious and critical postmodern ethnography. Catherine Russell coined the concept of 'experimental ethnography' for a methodological exploration into the aesthetics of cultural representation, a coming together of social theory and formal experimentation. Russell seeks to break through the barrier that separates avant-garde and ethnographic cinema to be able to search out the traces of 'the social' by linking 'aesthetic innovation and social observation' (Russell 1999: 16). Following the same process of contemporary documentary film, ethnography is also liberated 'from its assumptions about truth and meaning' (1999: 12). Thus, ethnographic cinema today should see itself as a practice in which aesthetic and cultural theory meets as a critical method to avoid stereotypes around the 'discovery' of the Other. A renewed combination of the gaze as a formal construction and experiences processed through a non-logocentric sensibility would enable experimental ethnography to point out the 'limits' of its status as a filmic text, by historicizing an imaginary 'other' as fiction in progress that is at the same time criticized and reified by the ethnographic approach (1999: 96).

In the case of *Tierra sola*, the use of the super 8 format highlights the status of the filmic text and the gaze of the documentary filmmaker, at the same time that it introduces a textural aspect that becomes additional material to be included in the archive. Thus, *Tierra sola* is evidence of an affective turn on the formal level when it explores the sensible in its visual, textural and aural dimensions. The documentary's performative function is enhanced by a gaze that expands from the visual aspect to the tactile and the auditory. What is at stake, then, is the commitment to create a way of 'looking' and 'listening' that can help to reveal the effects and affects of surfaces.

The introduction of the textural dimension encourages a closer relation between the viewer and the scenes shown. The fragmentary and imprecise images shot with the super 8 camera direct the gaze towards people, spaces and objects. Although dominated by vision, the filmic device, as Laura Marks (2000) suggests, can reproduce a tactile experience. She proposes analysing tactile sensory experiences in cinema, establishing a distinction between 'optical vision' and 'haptic vision'. Unlike the traditional gaze of cinema, touch comes into play when the image reproduces palpable impressions. Vision functions as a tactile organ when the attention turns to a sensorial aspect focusing not only on the gaze that 'penetrates', but on one that conjures up – through both the film grain and the use of scenes of physical contact – a way to look that, in a way, 'caresses' the surface.

A considerable number of images in *Tierra sola* have the formal qualities Marks associates with 'haptic visuality': grainy and unclear images, imagery that evokes memory of the senses (water, nature, light), camera positions close to the body, changes of focus, the use of super 8, posters, prints and handwriting, densely textured images. In *Tierra sola*, images have true sensory power because they are part of a 'haptic' dimension, which comes much closer to the tactile dimension than to traditional 'optical' visuality. The blurred images invite us to perceive things closer to the surface and to their materiality; the eye lingers on grain and texture as minor events occurring on the surface of the filmic image.[6] Here, capturing objects very closely places special value on textures activating the sense of touch in every viewer according to their cultural and sensory memory. At the same time, this closeness opens a dimension of communication with the outside, since touching always implies being touched.

These tactile images also produce a temporal strangeness and build a 'memory of the senses' (Marks 2000). The haptic dimension as an affective intensifier of memory is highlighted numerous times in the film when the present is recorded through the exploration of textures, turning them into memories for the future. As she goes through the archival material, the director wonders which could have been the first film that the islanders saw. It turns out to be a documentary that portrays the Rapa Nui exotically welcoming tourists. This image of themselves already mediated by an exoticizing gaze is subverted as Panizza uses a super 8 camera to film the arrival of a circus to the island. The impressionistic and close takes as the circus people set up the tent and the fragmentary gaze that caresses the bodies of the islanders – men, women, and children – as they await the circus performance become a memory sensation when the intertitle highlights syntactically over the filmed shots: 'Now they all remember.'

The expressive nature of the documents

Very early on in *Tierra sola*, Panizza reveals the methods through which an anthropologist chooses to represent another culture, but also explores the ways a culture represents itself. A lost film, patiently sought after, is found. Some fragments from *Isla de Pascua* (1961) – a Chilean film by Nieves Yankovic and Jorge di Lauro that is currently being restored in the Cineteca Nacional – show a worn and blurred image, a record about to disappear, of the *kai kai*. According to Marcela Garrido Díaz, *kai kai* is an ancestral Rapa Nui practice of shaping with threads an ideogram that tells a story, which, when narrated or sung, is conveyed through a recitation called *patautau*. These woven figures tell the story of the creation of volcanoes, of the arrival of ancestors, of daily experiences. They convey history to younger generations (2013: 115). Like many anthropologists, Garrido Díaz defines *kai kai* as 'a game'. In *Tierra sola* this definition is suggested when we see an image from the archive showing a group of teenagers practising *kai kai* and then, in the next shot, we are brought to the present with an image of a child operating a video game. However, Tamara Vidaurrázaga (2012) argues that the readings that classify *kai kai* as a game reproduce a certain Eurocentric perspective since, from that viewpoint, this would not be a signifying practice in Rapa Nui culture, but merely children's entertainment.

Kai kai has survived to this day; it is orally transmitted within families and in study groups and, more recently, it has been included in formal education. Is the practice of *kai kai* a game, a ritual, a poem, a story, a mode of audiovisual communication? Is it 'image writing', like embroidering, knitting and crocheting in other Tiziana Panizza films? Or is it impossible to classify under Western parameters? *Tierra sola* does not offer an answer to these questions because it avoids falling into the habit of ethnography of imposing meaning on each sign. There is a willingness to approach, to make contact with the other, keeping some level of opacity in that encounter.

Faye Ginsburg has described the impact of indigenous ethnography on visual anthropology as a 'parallax effect' that opens up multiple perspectives for visual anthropology.[7] The cinematic practice of representing other cultures through forms that show both space and time as fleeting contributes to free these cultures from representations that depict them as premodern and ahistorical. If, as Russell argues, ethnography is a practice of representation, then a textual production based on the material history of lived experience, as well as the use of the archive and of movement around the island in the present, points at the existence of an evanescent and transient subjectivity that is both similar and different, remembered and imagined. The strangeness of the other in this representation is the recognition of an excess by which the other represents something unknowable and unattainable. Some of this strangeness is also conveyed spatially when the documentary insists on focusing the gaze on 'amphibian spaces'.

At one point in *Tierra Sola*, the digital camera records a domestic scene in the home of the Chilean gendarme in charge of the prison. While helping her daughter with her homework, the woman dwells on the theories of Thales of Miletus, one of the seven sages of antiquity, who considered that 'Water was the origin of all things', thus establishing that nature was explainable as a dynamic manifestation of a single primal element. From that moment on, the

102   *The Film Archipelago*

images recorded by Panizza's camera and the editing of archival images reflect a specific insistence on characterizing the island as both 'limit' and 'interface': walks along the shore, shots of the horizon, close-up shots of water breaking in the sand and bringing 'remains' of terrestrial objects, volcanic landscapes that resemble islands surrounded by water in the very centre of the island. Archipelagos within archipelagos. The ambiguous and flexible spatiality of the island replicates that of the affects and subjectivity of an 'other' culture.

Trinh T. Minh-ha argues that if the documentary form must pose questions and show multiple forms of knowledge, it must resist its 'totalizing quest' in favour of more open texts that challenge singular didactic knowledge despite its finite and closed form. To go beyond the division between an observant 'us' and an 'other' as object of knowledge, a more fluid conception of reality is necessary, where meaning is not 'closed', but rather avoids and circumvents representation. In *Tierra sola*, cultural meaning is hesitant, slippery; the enigma of otherness remains, as well as some fascination with a sometimes-elusive meaning. At the same time, however, the film avoids reproducing a pure past, free of all contamination. In *Time and the Other: How Anthropology Makes Its Object* (1983), Johannes Fabian argues that one of the forms of visual representation of ethnography is to present the 'other' as living in a different time to that of the observer. He argues that the relationship of anthropology with its object has always been organized around oppositions, as here-there and now-before, which he interprets as distancing devices between the subject and the object of ethnographic practice. In this context, 'authentic' representations of other people imply the elimination of any sign of contemporaneity. But Panizza's images do not erase signs of cultural contamination; on the contrary, they point to the overlapping of places and times, all of which are subject to the deployment of several gazes; the film makes this evident in the structure of shots that show television screens, video games, computers, Bob Marley T-shirts, or handwritten posters in English and Spanish for foreign tourists who visit the prison and buy the handicrafts made by the inmates.

The soundtrack reinforces these cultural contaminations. While the footage reproduces phonographic records of songs in Rapa Nui, the present-day inhabitants of the island listen to music not only in that language, but also in Spanish and English. In his ethnomusical study of the island, Ramón Campbell (1988) explains that, as early as the 1960s, many islanders had Victrola phonographs in which they listened to records from Tahiti, Chile and other countries. These 'modern Polynesian' music and dances – including Tahitian hula and Hawaiian sau-sau – were spontaneously performed by natives for whom, according to Campbell, these songs lacked the *tapu* (sacred) aspect of *kai* songs or *patautau* recitations.

In history and cultural studies, aural memory has been largely neglected in favour of writing and the visual arts, especially since, unlike images or writing, aural memory depends on recorded sound, a type of archive inherently precarious. In its recovery of a phonographic archive, and in the design of sound effects, Panizza's film can be understood, to some extent, as an archaeology of listening in which the inclusion of sound broadens our understanding of the archivable. There is, on the one hand, a topographical function of sound inasmuch as the ear is invited to accompany the journeys around the island.[8] However, beyond its locating function, the documentary explores the affective and transformative capacity of listening. Musicologists argue that music is rooted in a fundamentally asynchronous and spectral temporality. Like cinema, which is structured as future projection and repetition of images captured in the past, music is based on a temporal disjointedness: musical signs cannot coincide because their dynamics are always oriented towards the future of their repetition, never towards the consonance of their simultaneity. Produced at a point in time, the movement of sound, like the movement of images, always travels from and relocates at a time other than its own. Music, like cinema, implies a signifying practice in which we come to understand that what we feel is located both within time and outside it.

In *Tierra sola*, music from the archive generates strangeness not only because, in the absence of Spanish translations,[9] the songs work at the resonance and not the signifying level, but also because their source of origin is uncertain, which creates a spatial instability that only reinforces their intrinsic temporal heterogeneity. Different time models are shaped along the resonance of certain sounds. During one of the first scenes of travel around the island, we hear the humming of a musical phrase that will become a ritornello, recurring time and again at different moments in the documentary. The sound design of *Tierra sola* uses not only old recordings but also some ambient sounds – which, to a large extent, contribute to identify the different places on the island – and that bodyless humming produced by a Rapa Nui native.[10] If, as Barthes theorized, the human voice has a 'grain' that suggests the materiality of the body producing it, this humming of uncertain origin highlights even more the absence of the body, which is then revealed in the final credits when in a kind of coda we see and hear, for the first and only time, in the same shot the body and the singing together, as the camera records an islander singing in Rapa Nui during a family barbecue.

A sound without body, with no visible place from which it springs, suggests spectrality. The disembodied sound makes the temporal detachment – the asynchrony inherent to spectrality – audible. In this light, these sounds resignify the director's decision to choose the cemetery as the first place on the island captured by her camera, as if with that gesture the film intends to summon the dead. The power of sound, like that of images, lies in its ability to touch us beyond absence, distance or death; it thus connects bodies to loss through a structure of spectrality. Music also operates within plural spaces and times: it is not only a form of meaning arising from references and signs but also one that is created through the resonance of sounds and images that are an echo of the past and at the same time move towards their future iterations and reverberations.

Figure 4.1 The elders as eternal guardians of the horizon. Frame from *Tierra sola*.

Figure 4.2 The paradoxes of freedom. Former inmate touring the island. Frame from *Tierra sola*.

Sensitive maps: Poetic ethnography and affective mapping

Critically appropriating pre-existing material is a feature of the essay. Manipulating images of others and its own, *Tierra sola* as travelogue, archival documentary and film essay becomes the place of connection and resonance between images, sounds and events – a discursive system crossed by themes, concepts and values shaped through a staging based on discontinuity, image manipulation, reflection on the filmic device and alternative exploration of heterogeneous expressive resources.

In editing, a kind of archive is created that moves away from hegemonic conceptions and incorporates other types of documents: affective, material and bodily records set in hybrid temporalities and played out with tangible and intangible media. Panizza's documentary can be considered a critical and deconstructive practice of traditional ethnographic cinema, as well as a reinvention of ethnography – a shift towards the poetic that is mindful both of the memory of images and of their ability to displace the gaze from the form to the background, or from the image to the space between images. In *Tierra sola*, images matter much less for their prescriptive capacity or their truth status than for their latent folds and interstices.

Through her work with material media in the film, Panizza allows the viewer to explore other translations of archival effects into affects. The documentary deals with ways of enunciation and of visibility that aspire to become elements of an archive of affects that cannot be conceived outside the intersubjective frameworks imposed by the present or removed from the textures and material conditions of this specific filmic record. In *Tierra sola*, listening, watching and touching are sensory practices and, as such, they are involved in the construction of meaning: if the film highlights listening, hearing and touch, it is because they integrate into a sensorial mode of thought.

Recontextualization procedures turn images into 'indexical' footprints of a relationship with the past whose 'archive effect' is defined by the shift of authority from chronologies to the more performative dimensions of experience and affect. This entails assuming a relative temporality, laden in its reception with an 'archive affect', a new intensity that emerges from disparity, difference, distance and contingency (Baron 2014: 130–4). In this way, *Tierra sola* actively intervenes in the archive – in the archives – by disturbing and re-articulating its boundaries, redistributing agency, altering temporalities, redirecting the effects and affects it produces.

Tierra sola can also be considered as an intervention in the construction of a territorial memory, but that memory is grounded on the critical potential of the affective and sensory dimensions and not necessarily on the dominance of a logocentric representation. If aesthetically the film imposes its own form, the 'ethnographic work' generates its own encounters and commitments. In purely spatial terms, geographical displacements in *Tierra sola* have much less to do with a 'locating' function and tend rather to operate as a 'channel for interactions' where the off-field is an affective dimension that relates to the nature of the link that the director establishes with the Easter Islanders throughout the many years dedicated to the research and filming process. The result is an audiovisual ethnography that experiments with sensations at the same time that it recovers the ethical commitment of documentary practice by decentring the voice. The emphasis in Panizza's documentary on exploring the dimensions of a culture in the present, mediated by an openly subjective device, characterizes it as what Catherine Russell called 'experimental ethnography'; but it is also a new kind of ethnographic cinema that works within an interdisciplinary field of community practices and establishes new – intuitive – relationships between documentary, ethnography and cartography.

The super 8 format of the documentary invites us to establish a closer and more intimate link with a remote archipelago. Through tactile visuality and listening it turns the island into an intensively affective, even heterotopic space, transforming the connection of the people in the film and of the viewers with the territory. If the images of the present-day prison and of the past make us think of the paradoxes of freedom on the most remote island in the world, the porous affectivity of other frames where the characters look from the islands invites us to discover seascapes. Thus, participating vicariously in this insularity, the viewer becomes a permanent guardian of the horizon.

Taking up Gabriela Mistral's intuitions regarding an affective geography that sees in cinema a cartographic device, Panizza's documentary can be conceived as the outcome of a journey and the encounters that it has enabled. This travelogue redefines a concept of cartography as a 'way of writing': the transcription of explorations that, far from objectively representing the world, build their own journeys creating, as Deleuze and Guattari would say in the introduction of *A Thousand Plateaus*, 'a map and not a tracing' (1988: 12). Thus, the anthropologist filmmaker presents a visual ethnography that enables sensory experiences in such a way that the references, fantasies and memories of the viewer, together with the information collected from the environment, will be co-producing the map of the territory. That is, ethnography and cartography are here an exercise in affirmation and delimitation of a cultural and geographical space, at the same time creating and questioning it, of a space for assembly, re-inscription and rereading – a travel space.

Translated from the Spanish by Erna von der Walde

Notes

1   In his essay on 'Desert Islands', Deleuze stresses the philosophical importance
     of the island in contemporary culture: the real and virtual spaces of islands lend
     themselves to exploring the changing relationship between the self and the other,
     between nature and culture: '[The deserted island] is the origin, but a second

origin. From it everything begins anew. The island is the necessary minimum for this re-beginning, the material that survives the first origin, the radiating seed or egg that must be sufficient to re-produce everything' (2004: 13). This idea of a second origin, of a rebirth, suggests that the 'deserted island' is a liminal and exceptional space that impels us to imagine, question and recast social ties. For a follow-up of the conception of the island in Western thought, see also Baldacchino (2006) and Gillis (2001).

2   According to Staniscia (2017), the island's epistemological power as a cognitive tool, and its imaginative appeal as a vehicle for speculation, is a paradox. On the one hand, epistemologically, the idea of the island allows us to demarcate and problematize issues of identity and difference in relation to the existence of borders 'between the territory of pure understanding and the stormy waters of an ocean of ignorance' (51). On the other hand, there is an ambivalence between the use of the idea of the island as a metaphor for thought and the island as a phenomenon that is experienced geographically, an 'island effect' that has an impact on the subjectivity of its inhabitants. These ways of conceiving the island as liminal and as a site from where to question the differences between inside and outside or the duplicity of the island and the implicitly active nature to be found in the notion of the 'island effect' resonates productively with the debates on the 'affective turn' in the humanities, since one of their premises is precisely the dissolution of the dichotomies between inside and outside, between body and mind, between the intimate and the public (see Hardt 2007: 34–7).

3   Rapa Nui or Easter Island is 63 square miles and is located in the South Pacific Ocean at the eastern end of the so-called Polynesian Triangle. To the east, the closest point to mainland Chile is 2,191 miles. The community and the language of the island are called Rapa Nui but, after the annexation by Chile, the inhabitants of the island are also called 'pascuenses' (Easter islanders).

4   In her study on the 'ethnographic spectacle', Tobing Rony (1996) uses the term 'ethnographic cinema' to describe 'the broad and variegated field of cinema which situates indigenous peoples in a displaced temporal realm' (8).

5   The narrative, emotional, symbolic and political dimension of maps in films and of films as maps has been carefully explored by Bruno (2002) and Conley (2006). Conley suggests that maps in cinematic fictions perform various functions, such as stabilizing a point of view, proposing a starting point for a journey, linking distant times and spaces or triggering a memory exercise. It is interesting that Conley reflects both on the presence of maps in the fictions and on the ways in which cinema and the map function as two forms of spatial thought: like the

map, cinema, as a topographic projection, 'plots and colonizes the imagination of the public', but, playfully, it can also trigger contradictions that allow us to think critically about the relationship between the cinematic space and the world in which we live (2006: 1–6).

6 According to Marks, in optical visuality the eye perceives objects from enough distance to differentiate them as shapes in space. As opposed to this separation between the body of the viewing subject and the object, haptic visuality would be a closer way of looking, as 'it tends to move over the surface of its object rather than to plunge into illusionistic depth, not to distinguish form so much as to discern texture'. Thus, haptic vision would be more touch-based and would be closer to a bodily type of perception, as if the eyes themselves were 'organs of touch' (2000: 162–3).

7 Ginsburg argues that indigenous media, along with ethnographic cinema, 'are intended to communicate something about that social or collective identity we call "culture," in order to mediate across the gaps of space, time, knowledge and prejudice' (1999: 171). Ethnography as a sensitive accompaniment experience enables an involvement with other ways of inhabiting this world from which other dimensions of cinematography emerge. As Ginsburg suggests, 'by juxtaposing these different but related kinds of cinematic perspectives on culture, one can create a kind of parallax effect; if harnessed analytically, these "slightly different angles of vision" can offer a fuller comprehension of the complexity of the social phenomenon we call culture and those media representations that self-consciously engage with it' (1999: 158). Ginsburg believes that the knowledge that emerges from this process must be shared with the members of the participating cultures. This is precisely one of the aspects that the production of *Tierra sola* involved: the collection, restoration and reproduction of all the visual footage to make it available to the islanders in the Hanga Roa Museum, where they can access part of the documents that make up the visual memory of Easter Island.

8 This is clear when recording night sounds, replicating thus the mapping of nocturnal space through a sensory perception, which, according to ethnomusicologist Miguel García (2015), is characteristic of many native groups.

9 In conversation with Tiziana Panizza she reveals who he is: 'There is this very unique Rapa Nui called Tote Tepano. He is a kind of collector of ancient sounds of the island (…) he walks around with a microphone he lifts up in the air capturing ambient sounds. I met him when I was looking for old phonographic records for the film. As it turned out, we liked each other, and he ended up

playing a guitar and singing. Claudio, our sound technician, had this idea that maybe he could hum a tune and Tote accepted. It was recorded there with hundreds of other audios that we had collected and I "rediscovered" it during montage. I tried it out and it gave me what I was looking for; it enhanced the intimacy of the super 8, and then when we were on the most "euphoric" stage of montage, I repeated it and repeated it as a mantra. I felt like I was giving it another threshold' (email from the director, November 2017). The fact that the songs are not translated nor their meaning explained replicates the conundrum of ethnomusicological research that sets off considering the sound archive as an unfinished and fragmentary knowledge because its material remains cannot be separated from the listening conditions of those who recorded them in colonial contexts (García 2015).

10 The idea of 'mantra' and the notion of 'threshold' point at a spectral use of sound, inasmuch as sound is here a presence that, paradoxically, suggests an absence.

References

Baldacchino, G. (2006), 'Islands, Island Studies, Island Studies Journal', *Island Studies Journal* 1.1: 3–18.

Baron, J. (2014), *The Archive Effect: Found Footage and the Audiovisual Experience of History*, London: Routledge.

Bennett, J. (2010), *Vibrant Matter: A Political Ecology of Things*, Durham: Duke University Press.

Bruno, G. (2002), *Atlas of Emotion: Journeys in Art, Architecture, and Film*, London: Verso.

Campbell, R. (1988), 'Etnomusicología de la Isla de Pascua', *Revista Musical Chilena* 42.170: 5–47.

Chanan, M. (2010), 'Going South: On Documentary as a Form of Cognitive Geography', *Cinema Journal* 50.1: 147–54.

Conley, T. (2006), *Cartographic Cinema*, Minneapolis: University of Minnesota Press.

Deleuze, G. (2004), 'Desert Islands', in D. Lapoujade (ed.), trans. M. Taormina, *Desert Islands and Other Texts, 1953–1974*, 9–14, Los Angeles: Semiotext(e).

Deleuze, G. and F. Guattari (1987), *A Thousand Plateaus: Capitalism and Schizophrenia*, trans. Brian Massumi, Minneapolis: University of Minnesota Press.

Depetris Chauvin, I. (2016), 'Sobre la destrucción. Memoria y afectividad en dos itinerarios por una geografía sísmica', *Mora* 22: 1–16.

Depetris Chauvin, I. (2017), 'Hilvanando sentimientos. Políticas de archivo e intensificación afectiva en *Seams* de Karim Aïnouz y en la trilogía *Cartas visuales* de Tiziana Panizza', *Imagofagia* 16: 439–64.

Depetris Chauvin, I. (2018), 'Mirar, escuchar, tocar. Políticas y poéticas de archivo en *Tierra sola* de Tiziana Panizza', *452F. Revista de Teoría de la Literatura y Literatura Comparada* 18.

Fabian, J. (1983), *Time and the Other. How Anthropology Makes Its Object*, New York: Columbia University Press.

Flatley, J. (2008), *Affective Mapping: Melancholia and the Politics of Modernism*, Cambridge: Harvard University Press.

García, M. (2015), 'Un oído obediente (y algunas desobediencias)', in B. Brabec De Mori, M. Lewy and M. García (eds), *Sudamérica y sus mundos audibles: Cosmologías y prácticas sonoras de los pueblos indígenas Los mundos audibles de Sudamérica*, 197–210, Berlin: Gebr. Mann Verlag.

Garrido Diaz, M. (2013), 'El Kai Kai: la cultura más allá de la lengua', *Contextos* 29: 113–6.

Gillis, J. R. (2001), 'Places Remoted and Islanded', *Michigan Quarterly Review* 40.1: 39–58.

Ginsburg, F. (1999), 'The Parallax Effect: The Impact of Aboriginal Media on Ethnographic Film', in M. Renov and J. Gaines (eds), *Collecting Visible Evidence*, 156–75, Minneapolis: University of Minnesota Press.

Hardt, M. (2007), 'Foreword: What Affects Are Good For', in P. Clough (ed.), *The Affective Turn*, 34–7, Durham: Duke University Press.

Lettre de Sibérie (1958), [Film] Dir. Chris Marker, France: Argos Films, Procinex.

MacDougall, D. (1995), 'Beyond Observational Cinema', in *Principles of Visual Anthropology*, 115–32, New York: Mouton de Gruyter.

Marks, L. (2000), *The Skin of the Film: Intercultural Cinema, Embodiment and the Senses*, Durham: Duke University Press.

Minh-ha, T. T. (1993), 'The Totalizing Quest of Meaning', in M. Renov (ed.), *Theorizing Documentary*, 90–107, New York: Routledge.

Mistral, G. (1930), 'Cinema documental para América', *Revista Atenea* 61: 52–4.

Mistral, G. (1931), 'Pequeño Mapa audible de Chile', *El Mercurio* 21 de octubre.

Munro, K. (2017), 'Rethinking First-Person Testimony through a Vitalist Account of Documentary Participation', *Frames Cinema Journal* 12: 1–15.

Pink, S. (2009), 'Situating Sensory Ethnography: From Academia to Intervention', in *Doing Sensory Ethnography*, 7–22, London: Sage.

Ramírez Aliaga, J. M. (2004), *Rapa Nui: Manual de arqueología e historia*, Valparaíso: Universidad de Valparaíso, Centro de Estudios Rapa Nui.

Rancière, J. (2004), *The Politics of Aesthetics: The Distribution of the Sensible*, trans. Gabriel Rockhill, New York: Continuum.

Russell, C. (1999), *Experimental Ethnography: The Work on Film in the Age of Video*, Durham: Duke University Press.

Shell, M. (2014), *Islandology. Geography, Rhetoric, Politics*, Stanford: Stanford University Press.

Staniscia, S. (2017), 'The "Island Effect": Reality or Metaphor?', *New Geographies*. 8, 50–5.

Tierra en movimiento (2014), [Film] Dir. Tiziana Panizza, Chile: Domestic Film.

Tierra sola (2017), [Film] Dir. Tiziana Panizza, Chile: Domestic Film.

Tobing Rony, F. (1996), *The Third Eye: Race, Cinema and Ethnographic Spectacle*, Durham: Duke University Press.

Vidaurrázaga, T. (2012), 'Ka tere te vaka. Kai Kai rapanui. Una aproximación crítica a su clasificación como juego', *Cultures populaires et cultures savantes dans les Amériques, Amerika* [En línea], 6 | 2012, Publicado el 15 junio 2012, consultado el 2 julio 2019. URL: http://journals.openedition.org/amerika/2988.

Part Two

Liminal islands

5

Social reformation and the edges of sovereignty: Fernando Soler's *La hija del penal* (1949) and Emilio Fernández's *Islas Marías* (1951)

Ignacio M. Sánchez Prado

Mexican culture's long-standing fascination with the penal colony in the Islas Marías archipelago is palpable in the many stories that have emerged from it. Since its foundation in 1905 as a model place for social reformation and effective prevention of prison escapes, the Pacific Ocean jail and its famous 'muros de agua', as writer José Revueltas named them in his famous novel (2014), were the subject of fascinating stories from the leftist intellectual Djed Bojórquez's chronicle of the island (1937), to the memoir of one of its administrators (Meléndez 1960), to a chronicle by a writer of ethnographic inclinations in the 1970s (Montiel 1976). The social and cultural interest arisen by the penal colony is grounded in its role in a myth of citizen discipline and modernization tied to both the positivistic aspirations of the Porfirian regime, and the social reorganization that followed the Mexican Revolution. As Diego Pulido Esteva has studied, penal colonies have their origins in a utopian idea of social reordering, which sought the reformation of social sectors seen as undesirable (anywhere from indigenous peoples yet to be brought to the fold of citizenship to drunkards and clochards in emerging cities) by deporting them to places requiring labour (2017: 18). As Pulido Esteva notes in his analysis of the prison, the Islas Marías represent a space based on the social erasure of subjects not fitting the Porfirian and the Post-Revolutionary models of development, under the guise of resocialization and a discourse tied to secular morality and development (2017: 205). All the many cultural interventions of the penal colony, from the aforementioned books to the films that make reference to it, participate in the project of making sense of a sovereign state that uses the island as a space in-between the inside and the outside of sovereignty.

The Islas Marías are an archipelago of nine islands located in the Pacific Ocean, off the coast of the state of Nayarit, although only one of them, Isla María Madre, is substantially populated. They were first reached by Diego Hurtado de Mendoza in the sixteenth century. The Islas Marías Federal Prison, which rendered the archipelago visible to most Mexicans, was established in 1905 as part of a penitentiary reform by the government of Porfirio Díaz to prevent escapes. After 1920, it became regulated by the post-Revolutionary government, and during the middle of the twentieth century, a prison for political and social outcasts, from members of the Communist Party to people accused of social crimes like vagrancy. The prison was temporarily deactivated in the late 1990s and the islands would be later declared a biosphere reserve. It was reactivated again in 2004 to relieve stress from other penitentiary systems, now becoming favoured for federal crimes like drug trafficking and kidnapping. In 2019 it was once again closed, and at the time of this writing, in 2020, it is planned to become a cultural centre named 'Los muros de agua' in honour of José Revueltas.

In what follows, I will analyse the two most iconic films on the Islas Marías to reflect upon the cinematic imagination of the biopolitical project underlying the penal colony. First, I will engage *La hija del penal* (Fernando Soler, 1949), a melodrama centred on María (María Antonieta Pons), the daughter of an escaped convict raised in the island, and her misadventures when she moves to Mexico City. Then, I will follow with a discussion of *Islas Marías* (Emilio Fernández, 1951), which follows Felipe (Pedro Infante), the son of a bourgeois matriarch in economic trouble who takes responsibility for the murder of a man committed by his sister Alejandra (Esther Luquín). I will conclude with a short reflection on the crisis of this project by referring briefly to a third film: *Cadena perpetua* (Arturo Ripstein, 1978).

La hija del penal and *Islas Marías* were shot in a telling moment both of the penal colony and of the way in which cinema thought the question of social reformation. The main island in the archipelago, María Madre, suffered an earthquake in 1948, which led to the destruction of existing structures and the reconstruction of camps that fit modern standards of life (Pulido Esteva 2017: 202). It is thus not surprising that both films continue to hold a somewhat utopian notion of the Islas Marías, by establishing narratives of social reformation of exceptional subjects, whose virtues demonstrate the possibility of being restored into citizenship. Yet it is also important to remember that the populist tones of Golden Age film had created two very different indictments of the reformation system in two of the most important films of the period. *Nosotros los pobres* (Ismael Rodríguez, 1948) questions the strategies of social marginalization by showing its virtuous hero Pepe el Toro (Pedro Infante) facing unfair incarceration and becoming vulnerable to violence inside the prison. It is interesting though that Pepe el Toro was not sent to the Islas Marías, a true possibility for someone of his social class. Yet, although Rodríguez enacted what Silvia Rocha Dallos (2017) calls 'cinematic profilaxis', that is, the marking of bodies and spaces on the basis of their purported health and disease, it also shows scepticism regarding the ability of institutions of the state to truly cleanse the body politic of undesirable elements. A more radical take is offered in a famous scene in Luis Buñuel's *Los olvidados* (1950), in which child Pedro (Alfonso Mejía) leaves a farm-school (the Correctional Farm School in Tlalpan to be precise) only to be killed by El Jaibo (Roberto Cobo). The farm-school was a way to transition impoverished migrant children from rural areas into the city (and a way to industrialize activities like egg production in urban settings as Mexico moved away from its majority rural setup). Pressured by his producer, Buñuel shot a second finale, in which Pedro was not killed, but ended up returning to the farm school (Polizzotti 2006: 74–6). That the second finale – the affirmation of social reformation – was an imposition of the producer in case censors objected to the tone of the film is telling: Buñuel's critique of the paternalistic model of social reformation was felt to be contrary to the modernizing project of the state.

Part of the uniqueness of the penal colony of the Islas Marías and the reason why I focus on them in this piece lies in the outsourcing of social reformation to an extraterritorial space, isolated from the rapidly developing urban settings and constructed as a society of its own. The construction of a liminal space of social reformation is quite meaningful if one looks into it in the context of the theory of the state as well as in relation to Mexican history. Nineteenth-century Mexican history was defined in part by the inability of the state to exercise full control within its territory: the secession of Texas, the vast territory lost in the Mexican American War, the Yucatecan Casta Wars were all significant examples of this. The construction of the penal colony of the Islas Marías can be read as an assertion of state authority in the kind of border territory that was the source of national crisis and territorial dissolution during the tumultuous times of the nineteenth century. Speaking of state capitals, Michel Foucault notes that 'a good sovereign, be it a collective or individual sovereign, is someone well placed within a territory, and a territory that is well policed in terms of its obedience to the sovereign is a territory that has a good spatial layout' (2007: 14). The penal colony, particularly at the time of a reconstruction aligned with the aspirations of modern life, was in a way a mirror of this concept of the capital, the full demarcation of a wild territory through positivist designs that would literally place delinquent bodies (marked by their disease, their decadence, their crimes and even their race) into a controlled laboratory of sovereignty. Reformation was thus predicated on the full participation within a parallel society that would later allow re-insertion into the societal core. The strict rules and the fully designed social world of the penal colony realigned bodies into citizenship so that, when they were restored to the space of the capital, they would be able to remain within the bounds of the sovereign and outside of the liminal spaces of crime.

Films about the Islas Marías are part of a major cultural trend to represent and think through crime as a central narrative of a Mexican society experiencing booming economic growth and rapid modernization. As Álvaro Fernández Reyes documents, the Islas Marías were invoked as a frightening referent outside of civilization. This is the case, for instance, of *Hipócrita* (Miguel Morayta, 1949), where the protagonist faces her destiny in a climatic final scene set in the train that began the journey to the Islas Marías (2007: 158). Yet, it is equally important to note that these films were by no means exceptional. As Fernández Reyes catalogues, there were as many as 110 crime films released between 1946 and 1955, and nearly 200 of them when the sampling is expanded from early cinema to 1960 (2007: 285–94). Representing the Islas Marías in literature or cinema did not happen in isolation, but was part of a social code based on what historian Pablo Piccato calls 'criminal literacy', that is, 'basic knowledge about the world of crime and penal law [... which] included eclectic information about institutions, famous cases, everyday practices and dangerous places that helped people navigate the complex practical problems of modern urban life' (2017: 6). Furthermore, 'crime was a central theme in the public sphere', an element of modern life very much in the consciousness of mid-century Mexicans (2017: 4). Thus, the narratives of social reformation became particularly significant for two reasons: they became a way by which the state could reassure its citizens that lawlessness would not impede the consolidation of the nation, and they provided evidence that the scientific knowledges (from psychology and sociology to architecture and urbanism) deployed by the state were a rational way to modernize the country while protecting the body politic. Yet the rise of crime and the visibilization of social problems tied to poverty were connected with the particularities of a model of development based on Import Substitution Industrialization (ISI) which led to the wave of economic growth known as the 'Mexican miracle' (Aguilar Camín and Meyer 1993: 159–98; Morton 2013: 63–99). The combination between fast industrialization, the decline of rural economies and mass migration from the countryside to the cities intensified social marginalization and created a heightened awareness in urban bourgeoisies not only of racial and class difference but also of the perception of danger posed by these lower classes. One way of reading cinema of the late 1940s and early 1950s in this regard is as a cultural debate apropos of class difference. The Pepe el Toro trilogy, for instance, sought to demonstrate that this migrating lower class could become part of the body politic, while Buñuel was highly sceptical that social reformation could overcome deep economic differences.

La hija del penal and *Islas Marías* are fascinating in this context because they invert the logic that locates civilization in the city and fear in the penal colony. *La hija del penal*'s protagonist, María, is presented as an innocent figure who grew up sheltered by the penal colony. To counter the illogical premise of the presence of a happy and beautiful blond girl in the prison, the film informs us early on that her goodness is well known and that all prisoners respect her. The film opens with a documentary-like narration that explains to us that the penal colony in the largest of the islands, María Madre, is a unique place in which male and female prisoners live together, which, in turn, is the reason why the story can only take place in that setting. The scene then introduces us to a set of prisoners, presented as criminals of different types who are nonetheless notable for their good behaviour, until María breaks into the scene, carrying food for the inmates. We learn that María is the daughter of a dancer who was indicted for drug dealing and one of the dancer's accomplices, who escaped the islands, but is presumed have perished in the sea. The setting of the prison is, if not pleasant, quite positive and bucolic. Prisoners are performing their labours, women are generally virtuous (we see them either working, praying or providing good advice) and the director is presented as an enlightened member of the government. In this setting, it is thus not surprising that María grew up to become an innocent woman. Even if the inmates mention that the place is hell, the reality is that we are shown an orderly society.

The logic behind this peculiar representation corresponds to the biopolitical process of quarantine as part of the healing of the social body. As Roberto Esposito notes, commenting on Foucault's idea of the governance of life, the medieval logic of quarantine created social spaces that provided the placement of sick bodies 'into individual settings that allowed them to be numbered, registered and assiduously controlled' (2011: 139). Thusly, penal colonies like the Islas Marías, part of a carefully constructed system of social organization and segregation, can be described in Esposito's terms as enacting an 'immune framework which contains this general process of superimposition between therapeutic practice and political order' (2011: 140). The archipelago's isolation from the mainland is crucial to this project because it occupies a particular place in what Esposito calls 'progressively desocialized spaces' which allow for gradual degrees of immunization 'against anything arising from the community' (2011: 140). María's innocence is a palpable example, within the film's world, of the success of this model. Rather than following a social-Darwinist model in which genetics and 'natural conditions' would irrevocably determine natural selection (i.e. María being doomed because of being a child of convicts growing up around inmates), her beauty, goodness and incorruptible moral sense all signal to the success of biopolitical control to reverse the negative effects of purportedly undesirable lineages. In the end, the desocializing potential of the island is a blank slate upon which the biopolitical project of the prison can be enacted in a more proper way, and *La hija del penal* imagines the utopian possibility of a scientifically based reformation that could at long last integrate the ultimate outcast of society, the criminal, to an all-encompassing rule of law and a system of shared social morality.

Social Reformation and the Edges of Sovereignty

The point is furthered as María's melodramatic downfall takes place once she leaves the penal colony. After the first few scenes, María moves into the mainland to find work as a dancer in a cabaret owned by Aranzuela (Andrés Soler), making use of the abilities learned in the island. In the cabaret she meets Ernesto (Rubén Rojo), and they fall in love with each other. Unbeknownst to them a gangster named Chapa (Alejandro Cobo) harbours lecherous desires for María, and, in jealousy, tricks them into driving a car with drugs, which leads to Ernesto's arrest and deportation to the Islas Marías. The plot line indicates that María's entry into the society of the mainland is defined by crime. Aranzuela is a reformed drug dealer, but remains in contact with criminal elements like Chapa. Thus, by entering society in the crime-influenced world of the cabaret, María's work as a dancer no longer has the idyllic flair it had in the island. Urban nightlife exposes her to the sinful realm of lust and desire.

Insofar as her biological parents were drug dealers themselves, María's growth as a 'good woman' was rendered possible by the isolated space of the island. In the mainland, even though her nature never changes (she marries a good man and seeks to be a good family woman), her character is framed by a deterministic understanding of society, falling into the world of drug dealing that her parents had created. María, we learn, is not actually guiltless. She fails to tell Ernesto about her origins and she only discloses them when they are at the penal colony. This leads Ernesto to disavow her until the very end of the film, when news of his liberation (once his innocence was established) and the birth of his child soften his heart. In this twist, we can see that both María and Ernesto had to be reformed by the penal colony. Ernesto – who is in solitary confinement after a foiled scape attempt – must overcome his pride to accept María's heritage, while María must pay penance for not disclosing it. After being both exposed to the moral effects of the penal colony, they are redeemed and once again deemed ready for societal integration, as they move back to the city after Ernesto's release.

This story unfolds within a cinematic framing characterized by its fidelity for a variety of cinematic conventions, thus conveying different meanings to the world of the island and of continental society. The opening sequence is a documentary-style scene, in which an extradiegetic narrator briefly explains viewers the existence of the prison, against the backdrop of an open shot of the ocean. This pedagogical tone is then transferred to explanatory dialogue in which the prison's warden describes to visitors the cases of various prisoners. This sequence echoes other social films located in the coast (the 1936 classic movie *Redes* is an example) contrasting the idyllic life of working on the beach with the counterpoint of social and state institutions. María is introduced in a dance scene, where we focus on her, surrounded by the prisoners and a musical group, singing 'María del penal', the title song. The scene belongs to a long tradition of *rumbera* dancing performances, providing viewers with an ambiguous ambiance of both innocence and joy (embodied in María's dance) and her exposure to sin in the male gaze of the prisoners, including one that has to be stopped from attacking her. Later on in the film, this scene is actualized by a full-fledged performance by María in a cabaret, this time aesthetically framed by the urban world of gangsterism. The film is fully constructed in this division: an idyllic space of social reformation, presented in its tropical character, and the nightclub sphere of sin and social decay, conjoined by María's dance performances. The ambiguity of dancing as a signifier – innocent in the islands, sinful in the continent – is the clearest allegory of the way in which the film understands social sin and prison redemption.

A final critical twist is provided by the destiny of María's father. Originally known as 'El Comodín' (the Spanish word for the joker in the poker set), we are informed at the beginning of the film that he had escaped and is presumed to have died in the ocean. Yet, at the end of the film we learn that he is in fact Aranzuela. After finding out that Chapa entrapped María and Ernesto, Aranzuela orders his killing and then turns himself in. In the Islas Marías, he seeks his daughter's forgiveness, but she does not grant it, unaware that he is her father. Although Ernesto figures it out, Aranzuela asks him to not tell María, stoically accepting his fate as an inmate, presumably for the rest of his life. This reveal further reinforces the film's presentation of the prison. As an escapee, Aranzuela interrupted his process of social reformation and, unsurprisingly, his reintegration was marred by once again being part of the world of crime that he had escaped. Even if he was a criminal no more, he remained vulnerable to the effects of crime, thus ultimately paying for his incomplete rehabilitation with the pain of his daughter. His return to the Islas Marías is the ultimate recognition of the social desirability of reformation by the target of the reform himself.

Social Reformation and the Edges of Sovereignty   123

Moving on to *Islas Marías*, it could be said that, while Emilio Fernández does not render visible the technology of social reformation, his account of its effects in Mexico's social renewal is even deeper. The film is not one of the major works in the trajectory of either Fernández or Pedro Infante. In his biography of the latter, Carlos Monsiváis recognizes some brilliant sequences in the film, but dismisses it because of the excesses of its melodramatic tone and the forcing of the penal colony into genre conventions and structures (2008: 245–6). It is also one of the few Fernández-Figueroa films from the Golden Age period that has elicited critical work. Yet, the film is very rich: the presentation of the islands is astounding under the eye of Gabriel Figueroa and, within Fernández's nationalist sagas, its plot is one of the most radical representation of Mexico's social transformations. Unlike *La hija del penal*, mostly constructed through mediums shots of indoor and outdoor spaces, Figueroa's cinematography removes the film from the focus on social reformation as such in *La hija del penal* and back into the affective codes of character-centred melodrama, accompanying a plot more in line with Pedro Infante's performance.

The film is basically divided in two halves. The first part chronicles the decline of Felipe's regal family. The beginning of the film notes that the family is facing major economic challenges since the death of the patriarch, a revolutionary general. The family is gathering together to honour Ricardo (Jaime Fernández), who has followed his father's footsteps and joined the military academy. However, Felipe is a musician who dropped out of school and opted to live his life in the cabarets and bars of the underworld. To honour his mother, Ricardo seeks Felipe in the bars and brings them in, and in the process, they witness their sister Alejandra murder her lover. When the police arrive, Ricardo takes responsibility and kills himself. Yet, in court, Felipe claims to be the killer to clean the Ricardo's image, getting himself sentenced to prison and deported to the Islas Marías. In the process, Felipe's mother Rosa (Rosaura Revueltas) and Alejandra must face bankruptcy and ruination.

Felipe's family's downfall clearly enacts Fernández's populist rejection of new aristocracies emerging from the revolutionary process and is almost presented as a punishment for the lavish life of the family of a revolutionary general. We see them celebrating with a dance not different from those held by Porfirian elites right before their downfall. While Ricardo is an upstanding family man (and his suicide shelters him from the full consequences of the family's collapse), Felipe is shown as an insouciant man who is wasting away his social privileges in alcohol and women, while Alejandra carelessly dishonours the family – and, ultimately, in true Mexican-cinema fashion ends up as a prostitute in a brothel. The film's long setup hollows out of the superfluous reputation of a family with privileges built over the revolution and squandered in a lifestyle financed by debt and in the inability of the general's offspring to truly live by revolutionary values, instead becoming each one a version of the kind of decadent elite that the revolution was supposed to overthrow.

The second part of the film completely focuses on Felipe's rehabilitation in the Islas Marías, announced as Felipe is boarding the train to leave the urban prison for the port. There, an officer tells the inmates that the penal colony will give them the elements for their full reformation, from a job that will allow them to accrue savings to the discipline needed to become citizens. Unlike *La hija del penal*, where the Islas Marías are introduced with a documentary voice-off speaking over a sunny, paradise-like landscape, Felipe's journey is far more ominous. It starts with a brutal framing of the prisoners escorted to the station, followed by a mass of desperate family members until they board a train in the middle of the night. All of this is musicalized through Antonio García Conde's dark and melodramatic score, until we see the train depart chased by the relatives of the prisoners and with the troops sitting on top. The open shot of the ship arriving to the islands under a cloudy sky is nonetheless counterpointed by a bucolic shot in which a local woman, María (Rocío Sagaón), is sitting next to a flock of ship and runs to meet the arriving vessel. Felipe and the new prisoners are again lectured on the benefits of reformation and hard work. Felipe's first encounter with María is telling. After being disciplined by an officer for smoking in front of him after being warned not to do so, María helps him and asks the officer to not beat him, providing him with the opportunity of behaving correctly and beginning his new life in the prison.

The visual aesthetic deployed by Fernández is quite different in the first and second parts. The first part relies significantly on closed shots of private spaces like the house and the bar and focuses significantly on close-ups of the characters. Conversely, the Islas Marías appear as a *tableau*, thanks to Gabriel Figueroa's famous work with wide shots and landscapes. Besides

Social Reformation and the Edges of Sovereignty   125

the ocean shot upon Felipe's arrival, one can note the deep shots of the salt fields where the inmates work, in which the white of the ground is skilfully contrasted with the dark bodies of most of the inmates. In contrast, *La hija del penal*'s depiction of prisoner labour in its opening sequences tends to focus on individualized shots in which the characters are doing non-descript work, thus erasing the prisoners' racial dynamics and the prison's concrete labour regime. In the second half of *Islas Marías*, the camera carefully captures discipline: we see, for example, still bodies of soldiers lined up in the port and around the mines, and the tanned, muscular bodies of the inmates are caught performing labour from different angles. To the decadent darkness of urban bourgeois life, Fernández and Figueroa oppose the paradoxical luminosity of life and work in the penal colony. This is a clearer pattern than *La hija del penal*, where light and darkness are used in a less stark distinction. When María appears in the frame, rather than seeing the hardships of island labour, we see a bucolic island setting with her frolicking, as picturesque tropical landscapes appear behind her. As the scenes progress, Felipe occupies a more prominent space in the image, suggesting his gradual incorporation to the regime of discipline. Once he is fully embedded in this regime, he notices María in the beach, dancing. The scene is deliberate, and Fernández insisted in having Sagaón dance in the film. This moment triggers her relationship with Felipe and puts into place the final element of his reformation.

The fact that island women are called María in both films shows parallels not only in terms of the religious connotation of the name as innocent and virginal. It is also obvious that the name indicates both women's embodiment as an allegory of the islands themselves. Both characters and their body are counterpointed in relation to urban decay. Another interesting factor is that they are both dancers, albeit part of different dance cultures. María Antonieta Pons's *rumba* roots are indicative of the risqué nightlife that will come to define her experience in the city, and the tropical elements of this Cuban cultural form are appropriated in *La hija del penal* to construct the binary between redemption and sin. Rocío Sagaón, a foundational figure of Mexican choreography, brings the sensibility of modern nationalist dance to her character, embodying not the type of urban modernity that *rumba* represents but a sense of social authenticity and Mexicanness that allow Felipe to abandon his decaying bourgeois identity to become part of revolutionary society. There is a significant racial underpinning to this distinction. María in *La hija del penal* is blond and white, and the casting of Cuban-born Pons affirms the pigmentocratic notions of purity and beauty common in Mexican media. It was in fact not uncommon in Mexican cinema at the time to whitewash the screen with Cuban and Argentine actors who represented a beauty different from the *mestizo* ideals of the post-revolutionary state. In contrast, the casting Rocío Sagaón, a *mestizo-featured* actress, clearly allows Emilio Fernández to render his María as an allegory of telluric cultural authenticity in contrast to Felipe's bourgeois self and his whiteness.

Both women save their men from foiled escape attempts and they both represent an innocence that emerges from the penal colony's biopolitical project. By locating these women in the islands, their innocence allows for a presentation of the island as a redeeming site of otherness for the modernizing nation. In a piece of dialogue, Sagaón's María tells Felipe that Mexico lies beyond the coast. Both characters represent moral and primal social values that are left intact because of their lack of engagement with the decadent modern society. In *La hija del penal*, the film tests the innocence of the island and of its María by creating a direct encounter with the continent's netherworld, setting up challenges to test the moral fortitude of its protagonist. In Fernández's film, the Islas Marías appear as a space of preservation of the inherent goodness of indigenous Mexican culture, safeguarded in coexistence with the ordered society of the island.

Like Ernesto's in *La hija del penal*, an important feature of Felipe's reformation is his refusal to participate in an escape attempt and his acceptance of rehabilitation in the island. This is more telling in Fernández's film because Felipe is innocent all along and he has always accepted imprisonment as the price to keep his brother's memory guiltless. Even from the consciousness of innocence, his refusal to participate in the escape attempt (which is eventually foiled) at the expense of being stabbed by the ringleader is what allows him to see the day of light. As part of his good behaviour, he is eventually freed, married to María and with a child. In the end of the film, Felipe seeks out his mother Rosa only to find that she went blind in an accident in a brick factory where she was employed. Ultimately Felipe saves Rosa from her life as a beggar in a church. In a significant ending, the last scene shows Felipe and María entering a majestic church in Peralvillo, redeeming their new modern life through the mediation of Catholic values, a frequent gesture in some of Fernández's films.

Two noticeable features emerge from the final sequence of *Islas Marías*. The first one is that the city as presented by Fernández is not a hospitable or even desirable place. He even goes further than Fernando Soler, whose urban spaces were mostly nocturnal in *La hija del penal*. After leaving the island, we see a sequence first of the same ominous train station from which he left (and in which an oversized train's steam release startles María) to then see the dystopian brick factory which, in what could be read as a nod to *Los olvidados*, shows the labour exploitation and aesthetic horror of the elements needed for urbanization. Indeed, it is telling that the manager of the factory denies having responsibility in Rosa's blindness, even though she clearly got hurt in a factory accident. It is a known feature of Fernández's cinema that he conceives the rural as the space of authentic Mexicanness, and many of his more virtuous characters (like Tizoc, the indigenous man that Infante would play a couple of years later in a Fernández film) are those not touched by modernization. *Islas Marías*, though, present a twist in his canon. Even though María follows the mould of virtuous female characters from other films, the orderly, militarized world of the penal colony is a place where inmates are given the choice to become upstanding citizens. The island isolates the disciplining project of the Mexican Revolution from its frictions with urbanism and crime, thus becoming the perfect place to become a citizen once again, in the intersection between a pure version of the biopolitical project of reformation and the original space of a nation before 'Mexico' as such, the natural state that precedes it.

Read in full, *Islas Marías* embodies in Felipe an allegory of social reformation and cleansing that is as much individual as it is societal. Fernández conceives modern society as diseased: ruled by decadent elites, embarked in a process of urbanization that leads to crime and worker exploitation. Felipe, a member of the former, gets redeemed by the combination of virtuous labour (all rural, from salt harvest to agriculture and cattle), his becoming a family man, his renunciation of pigmentocratic rules and sexual decadence by marrying a dark-skinned moral woman, and his acceptance of the process of social reformation that fell upon him. Fernández re-imagines the penal colony not as a place where everyone gets reformed (in fact the failed escape attempt involves about a dozen inmates), but rather as a place where the potential evils

128   *The Film Archipelago*

of Mexican modernity may become rethought and solved. It is a return to the primordial elements of society: the cult of indigeneity and the validation of rural labour as the cornerstone of society. In setting it in the archipelago, Fernández finds a symbolic laboratory through which he could imagine the return to this primordial social state, one challenged by the noise and dirtiness of modernization.

The faith in social reformation invested by these films in their respective fictionalizations of the Islas Marías would find its reversal as scepticism about the state and in its role in social reformation became a theme in carceral narratives of the 1970s. In particular relation to the Islas Marías, Arturo Ripstein's *Cadena perpetua* stands as a key counter to the ideology presented in *La hija del penal* e *Islas Marías*. The story centres in the life of a reformed criminal, Javier Lira (Pedro Armendáriz Jr), who must return to crime when a corrupt policeman, Prieto (Narciso Busquets), begins to extort him. As we learn through flashbacks, Lira's past is marked in his criminal career as El Tarzán, a pickpocket and pimp, who was eventually sent for reformation to the Islas Marías. Unlike the luminous presentation of the colony, Ripstein shows the Islas Marías as a generally hopeless and corrupt place, where El Tarzán is able to reach a certain amount of leeway due not to his rehabilitation, but the favour of Pantoja (Ernesto Gómez Cruz), an officer of the police corps. His stay in the islands is far from ideal.

In the final scene of the island flashback, El Tarzán is brutally beaten by Pantoja in retaliation after his wife (Pilar Pellicer) seduces him. The scene in the Islas Marías is founded on a full reversal of the representation in Soler and Fernández's films. Pantoja's wife, unlike the two Marías, is clearly a lecherous and valueless woman whose role is not to contribute to the rehabilitation of men but to their further downfall. This is the type of female character Ripstein often deploys in his cinema to undermine the cinematic effect of melodrama. Further, the film's cinematographer, Jorge Stahl Jr, breaks with Figueroan landscape cinematography, presenting us the salt fields in a dark silver hue with the male bodies physically diminished and opaque, a contrast to the shiny dark-skinned muscular bodies of *Islas Marías*. Ripstein's is a story of the impossibility, even the undesirability of the biopolitcal project of reformation. As Charles Ramírez Berg notes in his commentary of the film, when he was a criminal, Tarzán 'had freedom, self-sufficiency and self-pride to the point of arrogance. The respectable Lira, in contrast, is a whimpering, robotized, company man' (1992: 112). If the promise of reformation is the centre of the sovereign project of the Islas Marías, *Cadena perpetua* shows that the islands are a lie, crime is a form of freedom and citizenship the ultimate triumph of voluntary servitude to the state project.

The three films discussed here remain as testaments of the ways in which Mexican cinema in the mid-twentieth century imagined the biopolitical imagery of correction and reformation using the Islas Marías as a site of articulation. Fernando Soler and Emilio Fernández crafted films invested in the representation of the islands as frontiers of Mexican modernity, places to imagine the redemptive cures to the ills of modernity – sexual licentiousness and criminal behaviours for the former, the decadent persistent of the bourgeois in the latter. The space of the island defined by corrective labour and personified in female characters. Both films encode in their variations of genre and melodrama the belief in the Islas Marías as a necessary disciplining entity for the functioning of Mexican modernity beyond immorality. By the 1970s, Ripstein's film undermines this notion of reformation by flipping the female character into a temptress, embodying the islands, and the penitentiary system in general, as a system of advancement of violence and decay, a deep challenge to both the melodramatic investments of the precursor films and the ideology of carceral redemption advanced by the Porfirian and Post-Revolutionary regimes. As the Islas Marías closed in 2019 to become a cultural centre, these films will likely become part of an archive to rethink Mexico's modern liminalities.

References

Aguilar Camín, H. and L. Meyer (1993), *In the Shadow of the Mexican Revolution. Contemporary Mexican History 1910–1989*, trans. L. A. Fierro, Austin: University of Texas Press.

Berg, C. R. (1992), *A Cinema of Solitude. A Critical Study of Mexican Film, 1967–1983*, Austin: University of Texas Press.

Bojórquez, D. (1937), *María madre del archipélago. Islas Marías en el Océano Pacífico*, Mexico: Talleres Tipográficos de A. Del Bosque.

Cadena perpetua (1978), [Film] Dir. Arturo Ripstein, Mexico: CONACINE.

Esposito, R. (2011), *Immunitas. The Protection and Negation of Life*, trans. Z. Hanafi, Cambridge: Polity.

Fernández Reyes, A. A. (2007), *Crimen y suspenso en el cine mexicano 1946–1955*, Zamora: El Colegio de Michoacán.

Foucault, M. (2007), *Security, Territory, Population. Lectures at the Collège de France 1977–1978*, ed. M. Senellart, trans. G. Burchell, New York: Picador.

Hipócrita (1949), [Film] Dir. Miguel Morayta, Mexico: CLASA.

Islas Marías (1951), [Film] Dir. Emilio Fernández, Mexico: Producciones Rodríguez Hermanos.

La hija del penal (1949), [Film] Dir. Fernando Soler, Mexico: Ultramar Films.

Los olvidados (1950), [Film] Dir. Luis Buñuel, Mexico: Ultramar Films.

Meléndez, A. (1960), *Las Islas Marías. Cárcel sin rejas*, Mexico: Jus.

Monsiváis, C. (2008), *Pedro Infante. Las leyes del querer*, Mexico: Aguilar.

Montiel, G. (1976), *Yo viví en las Islas Marías*, Mexico: Costa-Amic.

Morton, A. D. (2013), *Revolution and State in Modern Mexico. The Political Economy of Uneven Development*, Lanham: Rowman & Littlefield.

Nosotros los pobres (1948), [Film] Dir. Ismael Rodríguez, Mexico: Producciones Rodríguez Hermanos.

Piccato, P. (2017), *A History of Infamy. Crime, Truth and Justice in Mexico*, Oakland: University of California Press.

Polizzotti, M. (2006), *Los olvidados*, London: British Film Institute.

Pulido Esteva, D. (2017), *Las Islas Marías. Historia de una Colonia Penal*, México: Secretaría de Cultura/Instituto Nacional de Antropología e Historia.

Revueltas, J. (2014), *Los muros de agua*, Mexico: Era.

Rocha Dallos, S. J. (2017), 'Intervenciones contaminantes y profilaxis cinemática en la vecindad de Pepe El Toro: la trilogía del mexicano Ismael Rodríguez (1948–1953)', *Latin American Literary Review* 44.88. DOI: http://doi.org/10.26824/lalr.34.

6

Exposed insularities:
Islands, capitalism and waste in Jorge Furtado's
Ilha das Flores (1989)

Axel Pérez Trujillo

The Guaíba estuary is one of the most unique coastal geographies in Brazil. Located at the mouth of the Jacuí River – before it turns into the Guaíba River and descends unto the giant Lagoa dos Patos – the estuary is divided into several small islands at the heart of the urban sprawl of Porto Alegre, the state capital of Rio Grande do Sul and home to 1.4 million inhabitants. These small islands form an archipelago: Ilha do Pavão, Ilha da Casa da Pólvora, Ilha das Garças, Ilha da Pintada and Ilha das Flores.[1] Together with the Lagoa dos Patos, this hydrographic system is considered the 'most notable case of a paleo-estuary in the entire Brazilian littoral' (Ab'Sáber 2007: 106). The estuary was formed after the glacial melting that took place during the Holocene more than 11,000 years ago, a process of deglaciation that flooded continental coasts. As a liminal site between continent and ocean, these estuary islands are an intersection between geological time and human time. These river islands are also unique because they are a point of contact that exposes the trajectories of commodities as they travel the world over to be discarded in this river delta. One of the islands in the estuary – Ilha das Flores – is a municipal landfill for Porto Alegre, a city that experienced a large increase in population and urban sprawl since the 1920s. Quite literally an island of waste, Ilha das Flores clearly presents the contradictions of consumerism in global capitalism. It offers a glimpse of what Jason Moore argues is the 'capitalist world-ecology' in which 'capitalism takes shape through the co-production of nature, the pursuit of power, and the accumulation of capital' (2015: 46).

Jorge Furtado's short film *Ilha das Flores* (1989) both frames capitalism's co-production of nature in the Guaíba estuary and serves as a challenge to the narrative of the Anthropocene as equally distributed among all humans across the globe. First coined by Paul Crutzen and Eugene Stormer in 2000, the term 'Anthropocene' refers to our present geological time as shaped by human interactions with the planet. All humans are hence responsible for this new geological time, regardless of social class, race or gender – a premise that has sparked criticism from postcolonial and feminist scholars, as well as environmental historians. As T. J. Demos suggests in *Against the Anthropocene*, 'the Anthropocene thesis tends to support such developmentalist globalization, joining all humans together in shared responsibility for creating our present environmental disaster' (2017: 17). Furtado's short film anticipates this important discussion that connects social justice and the environment by tracing the circulation of commodities as they are produced, consumed and discarded on the small island near Porto Alegre.

Ilha das Flores appeared during a key moment of the democratization period in Brazil, the year in which the 'reinstitution of direct popular election' took place with the appointment of President Fernando Collor de Melo (Skidmore 1999: 218). It was also a turbulent economic moment in the country, after the failure of the new currency under the Cruzado Plan and the subsequent inflation that surpassed 1,000 per cent from 1986 to 1989 (Baer 2007: 392). The debt crisis that ensued widened the gap between the rich and poor, placing Brazil as one of the nations in South America with the most inequality. By 1990, approximately 30 per cent of the population had an 'income inadequate to buy sufficient food' (Skidmore 1999: 198). One of the most serious environmental disasters had also occurred only a few years before the film appeared, an accident that took place in the city of Goiânia and involved the improper disposal of radioactive material. As the 1988 report by the International Atomic Energy Agency states, 'the accident in Goiânia was one of the most serious radiological accidents to have occurred to date' (*The Radiological Accident in Goiânia*: ii). The radioactive contamination of Goiânia affected the way Brazilians imagined this new future in which the promises of democracy, nuclear energy and capitalism seemed to only exacerbate the social inequality of the country. In a recent interview for *Itaú Cultural*, Furtado emphasizes that his short film continues to be relevant thirty years later precisely because its core message is a critique of the social injustice that still pervades Brazil (Bandeira: n.p.).

The present chapter will explore how *Ilha das Flores* establishes a critique of current global discourses of the Anthropocene by framing the mesh of consumption and waste in the landfill of the Guaíba estuary. I am particularly interested in exploring the intersection between insularity and ecology as it appears in the film. Although produced in 1989, the film offers a timely discussion of how islands are exposed to environmental crisis generated by capitalism in the southern hemisphere. As Elizabeth DeLoughrey argues, 'anthropocene scholarship cannot afford to overlook narratives from the global south, particularly from those island regions that have been and continue to be at the forefront of ecologically devastating climate change' (2019: 2). By narrating the chain of connections that emerge in all directions from the island landfill, Furtado critically engages with the intersection of capitalism and nature. He includes the presence of the Global South embedded in a river estuary, challenging Western imaginaries of insularity and reframing the Anthropocene as occasioned by capitalism. Not surprisingly, *Ilha das Flores* anticipated current environmental discussions on nature as co-produced by capitalism (Haraway 2016: 47; Moore 2015: 301; Malm 2018: 18; Tsing 2017: 4). It foregrounds the commodity circuit of global capitalism as it affects the livelihoods of those dependent on the disposal of waste on Ilha das Flores.

I will frame the analysis via what I term as an 'exposed insularity', a notion that is indebted to Édouard Glissant's understanding of 'poetics of Relation' and Stacy Alaimo's materialist contribution to a 'trans-corporeality'. I argue that *Ilha das Flores* presents insularity as exposed and vulnerable to the mesh of capitalist trajectories that produce, circulate and discard commodities in the Global South. Glissant and other scholars in the field of island studies offer an approach that portrays insularity as open, never hermetic, whilst Alaimo emphasizes the porosity of bodies as an extended space of vulnerability. Although both perspectives differ significantly – the former is invested in enacting an archipelagic understanding of the world, while the latter is focused on a posthuman and feminist understanding of bodies – both engage with what Furtado considers to be the core theme of *Ilha das Flores*: that 'people still survive on food scraps left by animals' (Bandeira 2019). Glissant and Alaimo engage directly with issues of social injustice through the dialectic between the local and global. I will discuss the notion of openness in island studies, alongside Alaimo's contribution to trans-corporeality in the environmental humanities. Both leverage the exposed insularity that I argue is present in Furtado's short film and which anticipates current debates on the Anthropocene by including the oppressed other that is forced to live off the scraps left in the landfill of the island. In my close analysis of *Ilha das Flores*, I will first examine the significance of garbage in the film as a critique of global discourses of the Anthropocene that do not consider the role of capitalism in co-producing nature. I will then explore how the use of archival footage reinforces the mesh of connections between the rich and the poor, the inorganic and the organic, the human and the nonhuman in the Guaíba estuary.

Scholars in archipelagic studies continue to challenge the peripheral place of islands in Western imaginaries (McMahon 2016: 4). During imperial pursuits in the fifteenth and sixteenth centuries, island archipelagos such as the Canary Islands or the Azores became 'a way station on the routes to and from colonies that did grow money-makers' (Crosby 1986: 75). They were part and parcel of the experimental cartographies of imperialism in its expansion westward, yet gradually became marginalized, as navigation routes lost importance and empires sought resources inland. Colonies established in islands were not unlike biological laboratories, precursors to continental plantations. More importantly, such a 'continentally oriented' modernity typically defined islands as 'fixed' and 'self-enclosed', as opposed to the limitless expanses of plains geographies (Roberts and Stephens 2017: 13). This meant that islands were conceived as disconnected from each other across oceans, interspersed and disposable to empires. Insularity signified a hermetic isolation, a 'narrowness' within a large body of water (2017: 19). Moreover, this colonial conception of insularity is attached to the 'slaving logic' that generates an 'atomization of space' which mobilized capitalism in its early stages as it raced across the Atlantic with Black slaves to occupy and extract resources (Mbembe 2017: 4).

DeLoughrey explains that such rhizomatic repetition of the archipelago 'as an ideological and social template' manifests the colonial underpinnings of these cartographies (2007: 9). A critical insularity would have to 'decontinentalize' the overarching colonial narrative of islands as extractive laboratories spread out in fragmented geographies across bodies of water (Roberts and Stephens 2017: 19). This means that archipelagos bring to the surface unexpected networks of relations. Similar to how Glissant describes the Caribbean, 'each island embodies openness' (1989: 139). Islands are never cut off, for they are sites of fluctuation and transit. As stops in navigational trajectories and commercial ports, islands are sites of exchanges. It is in this sense that 'openness' is linked to 'errantry' in Glissant's poetics: 'One who is errant (who is no longer traveler, discoverer, or conqueror) strives to know the totality of the world yet already knows he will never accomplish this' (1997: 20). Glissant distinguished the 'errant' from the 'traveler, discoverer, or conqueror' insofar as the latter trace a linear route through the world. Conquerors travel taking with them the 'root of their people' (1997: 14). They are not open to the difference of the other, but remain hermetic – rooted in their own culture as they expand outwards. This type of expansion obviates the singularities of islands, attempting to repeat the paradigm of the empire scattered throughout the ocean. It informed the 'trope of the isolated island' as a mode of 'thinking allegorically' about the world (DeLoughrey 2019: 6).

Challenging such a notion of insularity, Glissant looks towards a poetics that sees islands as knots in the fabric of totality, an 'open circle' of relations across the globe (1997: 203). Such an open totality would be capable of negotiating the local and the global through the differing relations possible in such a mesh. DeLoughrey suggests something similar when arguing that allegory can navigate 'our awareness of the planet as a totality and our experience of embedded place' (2019: 11). *Ilha das Flores* frames such a dialectic by tracing the convergence of capitalism in the island. It establishes a mesh of relations via a series of images that Furtado suggests is not unlike that of a hypertext (Bandeira 2019). The archival footage and sequence of definitions narrated explore the global connections embedded in the local lives of those humans forced to scavenge for scraps. The island thus is not presented as an isolated site, a sited outside the gaze of consumers in different places that perhaps have no knowledge of where the product came from and where it will end up. *Ilha das Flores* collapses the binary between outside and inside that sustains consumption and waste through the powerful allegory of the Guaíba estuary in Porto Alegre. The estuary islands that appear in Furtado's short film are open in the negative sense, as they are part of the circulation of commodities that ultimately become waste, and also in the positive sense, as they are precariously porous to other places in the world. As Levi R. Bryant suggests, porosity is crucial for 'environmental thinkers' who explore 'how encounters with other substances change the nature of things' (2013: 292).

From an ecological perspective, islands are highly sensitive to changes in the environment and climate. Rising acidity in the ocean waters, for example, first affects island habitats and the human populations that depend on them. This suggests that islands are not just porous, but also vulnerable and exposed. Alaimo offers a materialist approach to understanding the complexities of the ecological notion of the mesh without being caught in the pitfalls of a hierarchical understanding of the place of humans in the environment. Her contribution to what she terms as 'trans-corporeality' offers some valuable insights into the reframing of insularity, especially concerning the propagation of poisonous substances across bodies in nature that is also a central theme in *Ilha das Flores*. As Glissant and DeLoughrey, Alaimo is invested in leveraging local places within global networks (2010: 16). The concept of 'trans-corporeality' is built on the basis of the body as an environmental category – one that allows Alaimo to not only insist on the materiality of relations in nature, but also to address the exchanges between bodies that are also part of those relations. The prefix 'trans' suggests 'movement across sites', as the 'often unpredictable and unwanted' actions between humans, nonhumans, environments, climate and other possible agents (2010: 2). These exchanges between different bodies in nature underline the toxic interconnections that are also present in our globalized world. The radioactive incident in Goiânia is a manifestation of how a small dosage of caesium-137 could poison the bodies of hundreds of people in a matter of days. From the manufacture of the x-ray machine and its illegal disposal in an abandoned building, to the poisoning of informal garbage pickers and the death of a young girl, the chain of toxicity as it travels across bodies traces a worldwide network of relations. 'Although trans-corporeality as the transit between body and environment is exceedingly local, tracing a toxic substance from production to consumption often reveals global networks of social injustice' (2010: 15).

At the beginning of *Exposed*, Alaimo raises the following question: 'What forms of ethics and politics arise from the sense of being embedded in, exposed to, and even composed of the very stuff of a rapidly transforming world?' (2016: 1). Here she couples the notion of 'trans-corporeality' with that of 'exposure'. If the former critically frames the relations between different agents across sites in the planet, the latter further emphasizes that those relations are always risky. To be part of an ecological mesh of relations between the human and nonhuman can mean the risk of global pandemics, systemic economic crisis, radioactive incidents across nations and climate change. As Glissant anticipates, 'beings risk the being of the world, or being-earth' (1997: 187). To become aware of the open totality that makes up the world is to also come to terms with the vulnerability of being exposed to the other. Alaimo's approach rings true with the archipelagic notion that specialists in island studies advocate as a means to break the Western and colonial 'stolid monadism of the island' (McMahon 2016: 10). An exposed insularity critically traces the dark side of interconnections in the Anthropocene, revealing the often-ignored exchanges between bodily natures that come to the surface in island geographies. Furtado's *Ilha das Flores* offers a fascinating visual narrative that connects the ecological importance of these small and largely unknown estuary islands with the toxicity of waste that ironically brings together the human and nonhuman inhabitants of the island. By tracing this darker side of the ecological mesh in the landfill of the estuary, Furtado establishes a critical exploration of the Anthropocene as ultimately a consequence of capitalism. That is, he reveals what Moore has coined as the 'Capitalocene' beneath the global network of consumption and waste (2016: 6).

An island of garbage

In *Tropical Multiculturalism*, Robert Stam dedicates several pages to analysing a trend in Brazilian cinema that began with the Marginal Cinema movement in the 1960s and that focuses on garbage as an overarching theme (1997: 353–8). Also known as the *udigrúdi*, Marginal Cinema evolved from Cinema Novo and formed part of a larger *tropicalismo* counter-culture in Brazil that resisted the authoritarian military regime that had gained power through a coup in 1964 (Xavier 1997: 7; Dunn 2016: 21). Whereas Cinema Novo aligned itself as a national cinema, the films of Marginal Cinema steered away from institutionalization and consumerist society with low-budget projects that engaged with unusual themes (Xavier 1997: 10; José 2007: 157). The transition from the former to the latter traces the evolution of Glauber Rocha's 'aesthetics of hunger' into an 'aesthetics of garbage' (Xavier 1997: 120). Although produced decades after the emergence of Marginal Cinema, Furtado's *Ilha das Flores* resonates with the movement's aesthetics by invoking 'garbage as a source of food for poor people; garbage as a site of ecological disaster; garbage as the diasporized, heterotopic space of the promiscuous mingling of the rich and the poor' (Stam 1997: 354). Garbage exposes the rampant social inequalities that intersect issues of class and race, especially in Brazil where these inequalities were quickly widening in the 1980s. Furtado's film is a precursor to Eduardo Coutinho's *Boca de lixo* (1993) and Marcos Prados' *Estamira* (2004), both of which also explore the presence of landfills and how these affect the marginalized people in them.

The fact that Furtado chose an insular landfill in Brazil to parody and critique consumerist society serves as a valuable reminder that islands continue to be marginalized in Western imaginaries as places separated from the rest of the world. Insofar as they are sealed away from the rest of the world, they are seen as adequate sites for refuse within the circuit of commodity production and disposal. The Pacific Garbage Patch is one such example of an island of waste floating across the ocean that has only recently garnered the attention of the general public. The intersection between islands and waste manifests the need to consider how capitalism co-produces island landscapes throughout the world, repeating the trope of a hermetic insularity that is no longer a biological laboratory for empires, but a landfill in which the toxic residues of the Global North accumulate. It reminds us of Glissant's experience of an unnamed 'burning beach' that gives off 'the ocre smell of the hounded earth' (1997: 209).

Beginning in the 1970s, landfills across Brazil became sites in which the poor were forced to scavenge for their livelihood, when 'driven by the dire straits in which many urban poor found themselves during the severe economic downturn that followed the so-called economic miracle that Brazil's most recent military dictatorship engineered' (McKay 2016: 135). In Porto Alegre, the rapid increase in population and the limitations to its urban sprawl turned the Guaíba estuary into a makeshift landfill. It was only in 2001 that a much larger landfill was created in an old mining site in the municipality of Minas de Leão, about 90 kilometres from Porto Alegre. In the 1980s, the waste disposal site of Ilha das Flores had hardly any legal or physical infrastructure to maintain minimum safety levels. Its open landfill exposed not only the toxicity of garbage, but also the systematic racism that the poor suffer.

Towards the end of *Ilha das Flores*, a quick reference is made to a particular word, that of 'caesium'. The radioactive isotope points to the toxicity of garbage as point of exposure where the material connections can be traced in consumerist society, one that makes evident the social inequalities produced in capitalism that are life-threatening and ecologically disastrous. As Alaimo argues, toxic bodies manifest an interconnected mesh of trans-corporeality: 'The traffic in toxins may render it nearly impossible for humans to imagine that our own well-being is disconnected from that of the rest of the planet or to imagine that it is possible to protect "nature" by merely creating separate, distinct areas in which it is "preserved"' (Alaimo 2010: 18). To trace toxicity as it spreads is yet another way of showing the precarious mesh that bind humans and nonhumans together, connections that are never entirely stable, but are rather built on shared vulnerabilities.

The reference to caesium in the documentary is accompanied by an image of a child covering his face with what looks like white powder, immediately followed by an image of that same child in a body bag with radioactive signs. On 13 September 1987, several people in Goiânia were contaminated with the radioactive isotope of caesium – caesium-137. The accident shook the nation. It not only showed the negligence of the Federal Government and the owners of a clinic in handling the accident, but also that the poorer communities suffered the most from the spread of radioactive toxicity. It is an example of what Nixon terms 'slow violence' insofar as it manifests how 'chemical and radiological violence [...] is driven inward, somatized into cellular dramas of mutation that – particularly in the bodies of the poor – remain largely unobserved, undiagnosed, and untreated' (2011: 6). Islands continue to suffer the toxicity of waste in many of its forms. For example, the nuclear tests that took place over the Marshall Islands in the Pacific transformed the archipelago into 'the most contaminated place in the world' (Cooke 2009: 168).

Ilha das Flores presents toxicity as a trans-corporeal connection that binds the consumption of commodities with the 'diseases' to which the people on the island are exposed to. A seemingly benign product such as a tomato may become part of a mesh of toxicity in the process of being grown, sold and discarded. 'Consumer products manufactured to do what they are supposed to do – taste like cheese yet squirt out of a bottle – may do other, unwanted things as well, such as cause cancer or litter the planet' (Alaimo 2010: 18). Mr Suzuki and Mrs Anete are unknowingly collaborating in the toxicity of the human and nonhuman bodies inhabiting the island. The narrator of the documentary suggests as much when he explains that what Mrs Anete considers as unsuitable to feed her family – because of the possible diseases it might carry – later becomes the food that the poor women and children will eat. Toxic substances are never really disposed of, for they always find a way back in. That is, there is not inside/outside binary, but rather a circuit that manifests social hierarchies. Much the same way that Western imaginaries think of islands as isolated places, so does the inside/outside dichotomy inherent to our common understanding of waste attach to such a conception of insularity. The exposed insularity of Ilha das Flores in Furtado's film reveals the accountability of the Global North in producing a waste whose toxicity directly affects the lives of the poor in the Global South. Islands are not isolated landfills or laboratories, they are connected into the ecological mesh co-produced by capitalism. Furtado's documentary dissolves that binary, revealing how there is no such 'outside'. The same human beings with 'a highly developed telencephalon and opposable thumb' produce the very waste that they consume – the only difference is that the human beings that consume that toxic garbage are those that have 'no money, nor owner'.

Furtado's documentary also raises questions concerning what scholar Lucy Bell suggests is a 'waste theory' that emerges 'if we turn our attention towards the experience of those whose existences are marked principally not by the production or disposal of waste, but rather by experiences, livelihoods and lives in/with/of waste' (2019: 101). Insofar as Ilha das Flores links together the different phases in the production and disposal of waste – from the growing of vegetables to the experiences of garbage pickers – it engages in what living 'in/with/of' garbage signifies for these people. The film portrays waste as something that is in close range, not something that is at a distance, in some isolated and remote location. The landfill island of Porto Alegre is an exposed site where pigs, landowners, garbage pickers, women, children and garbage coexist minutes away from the urban centre. The island lies at the 'dissolve, where fundamental boundaries have begun to come undone' (Alaimo 2016: 2). It dissolves the binaries associated with waste: near/far and inside/outside. As Bell concludes in her essay on waste in the Global South, 'the very notion of "waste" is problematic since it is premised upon a human/non-human, person/place divide that is rooted in Western modernism and Enlightenment rationality' (2019: 117).

Exposed insularities through archival images

The title of Furtado's short film frames the local experience of social injustice in the Guaíba estuary, yet also ironically plays with the viewer's expectations. 'Ilha das Flores' literally means 'Island of Flowers', which is starkly different to the reality of the island which is home to one of the bigger landfills in Porto Alegre. As the narrator suggests at the beginning, the island does not really smell like flowers at all. The film is composed of a plethora of archival footage from different media, from magazine ads to images of supermarkets. The rapid definitions of terms in tandem with shots taken from commercials and other seemingly unrelated material are deployed to construct the often surprising links that emerge from following the journey of a tomato as it arrives at the landfill in Ilha das Flores. The use of fragmented footage is a strategy that exposes the connections between social classes – the rich who access goods in the market and the poor who live off the garbage piled in the landfill of the island – and also between the human and the nonhuman, whether animal, artificial or geologic.

Ilha das Flores won numerous accolades when it debuted in the Gramado Film Festival and went on to gain international attention at the Berlin International Film Festival a year later, in 1990. Even though the short film did not have any 'production costs', the post-modern assemblage of images and the theme of consumerism and waste disposal hit a chord with audiences (Debs 2005: 8). Its ironic tone establishes a narration that seems to jump from one seemingly arbitrary definition to the next, all the while archival footage and paper cut-outs are juxtaposed to tell the story of a common food item. Lasting only thirteen minutes, the short film blurs the boundaries between the indexical capacity of images and the construction of perspective. Bill Nichols argues that 'commonsense assumptions' tend to 'rely heavily on the indexical capacity of the photographic image and sound recording' to capture the world for viewers (2001: 23). The reproduction of photographs elicits a sense of reliability, as if the image itself does not contain any opacities, a fully transparent window into the world. Susan Sontag discusses this 'presumption' attached to photography: 'Whatever the limitations (through amateurism) or pretensions (through artistry) of the individual photographer, a photograph – any photograph – seems to have a more innocent, and therefore more accurate, relation to the visible reality than do other mimetic objects' (2005: 3). *Ilha das Flores* fractures this common-sense understanding of photographic images in documentaries, for the assemblage of archival footage reminds viewers of the film's artificial construction. Such a challenge to the indexical dimension of photographic images is particularly relevant in discussing the nature documentary genre – especially in the Global North – that has boomed alongside the widespread use of the term 'Anthropocene'. Gustavo Procopio Furtado argues that 'although all filmic modes have an archival dimension, this dimension is crucial for the documentary as a cultural form that embraces cinema's "core and formative indexicality" as a constitutive component of its identity' (2019: 8). This is precisely why *Ilha das Flores* does not exactly fit within the genre, since it deconstructs the 'core and formative indexicality' of documentaries by emphasizing the manipulation of the archive to produce an artificial collage. Yet this strategy is what makes the film all the more compelling, since it creates an assemblage of archival footage and other media that strikingly resembles a landfill. Similarly to how garbage pickers would encounter exam papers, organic refuse, magazine cut-outs and other objects, so does *Ilha das Flores* build a visual narrative through a collection of diverse media. I would argue that Furtado's short film, alongside many other Latin American documentaries that have tackled head on the insidious consequences of neoliberal practices on human communities and the environment, offers a valuable entry into other modes of narrating the environmental crisis that asymmetrically affects the Global South.[2] *Ilha das Flores* is by no means a nature documentary; yet, it makes some valuable points regarding how the discourse of the Anthropocene too quickly ignores how the privileged few consume the resources of the many, only to discard obsolete commodities in landfills throughout the Global South.

The film opens with a few provocative lines of text, which are not unlike a syllogism: 'Este não é um filme de ficção. Existe um lugar chamado Ilha das Flores. Deus não existe.' ('This is not a fictional film. A place named Island of Flowers exists. God does not exist'). Just as in a syllogism, the first two phrases act as linked premises that prove the supposed logical consequence of the third and final phrase, 'God does not exist'. The first sentence ironically plays with documentary expectations, directly pointing to its non-fictional nature right from the beginning, although many of the images used in the short film are an assemblage of fragmented archival footage, newspaper cut-outs, and animations made by the director himself. The second sentence is also significant, especially from an environmental perspective. The film's indexical power is drawn from the fact that the geographical reference is real, for there is such a place as Ilha das Flores. What makes the short film a documentary is its commitment to a real place in the world, with a history of its own. There is a logical chain that binds the first and second clauses of *Ilha das Flores's* opening: insofar as the geographical setting of the documentary exists, the documentary must 'refer directly to the historical world' (Nichols 2001: 5). Furtado thus links the role of his film with that of a specific region of the world – an emphasis made all the more present when the narrator insists that the place of origin for the tomato in the film is Belem Novo, Porto Alegre, located at the longitude 30°12′30″ South and latitude 51°11′23″ West. The stress on the concrete and specific setting serves to anchor the indexical power of the narration and images. Furtado's documentary short is built on the connections between seemingly distant entities and what takes place in the Guaíba estuary, much the same way as the first two clauses are bound together and fixed on that geographical location. From footage of a tomato plantation to the mushroom cloud of a nuclear explosion and the image of a whole pig about to be cooked, the film strives to weave surprising connections through ironic twists and reasoning that builds into a crescendo.

The third clause also points to the epistemic stance of Furtado's documentary, which I argue is central to understanding his use of archival footage and the fragmented ecology of images that he deploys. The last sentence of the opening appears to break the logical connection with the previous two sentences, stating something that at first seems absurd, yet becomes all the more powerful towards the end of the documentary. That 'God does not exist' seems a random statement when arguing for the documentary nature of the film, its non-fictional aspect. However, a closer analysis reveals the modus operandi of this materialist film. What at first seems fragmented and out of place gradually becomes interlinked. The film takes fragments of the world, whether they be tomatoes, pigs, capitalism or islands, and exposes their problematic

144   *The Film Archipelago*

connections. The nonexistence of God may seem disconnected at first, but as the documentary begins showing images of the Holocaust, nuclear explosions and humans eating the scraps left over in the garbage heaps of Ilha das Flores, the viewer realizes that those haunting images become far more real than God. This random statement in the beginning of *Ilha das Flores* drives the powerful observations of the film, which begins light-heartedly, only to lead the viewers to a tragically ironic conclusion which shows footage of humans searching through the island landfill for discarded foods and items; all the while the images are accompanied by the sounds of an electric guitar playing the song from the opera *O Guaraní* by Carlos Gomes: 'What places the human beings of the Island of Flowers behind swine as to the priority of choosing food is the fact that they do not have money, nor owner.' The narrator explains that it was humans with a 'highly developed telencephalon and opposable thumbs' that made possible such a situation on the island.

All the fragmentary pieces – images, words and texts – coalesce together into a mesh that gradually exposes precarious connections. After the initial syllogism, the documentary begins tracing these strata as they sediment in and around the Guaíba estuary. It is in that sense that it 'performs exposure':

> Performing exposure as an ethical and political act means to reckon with – rather than disavow – such horrific events and to grapple with the particular entanglements of vulnerability and complicity that radiate from disasters and their terribly disjunctive connection to everyday life in the industrialized world. To occupy exposure as insurgent vulnerability is to perform material rather than abstract alliances, and to inhabit a fraught sense of political agency that emerges from the perceived loss of boundaries.
>
> (Alaimo, 2016: 5)

Furtado offers a powerful narration of the ecological interconnections between all parts, steering away from innocent views of nature by exploring the points of contact that gradually emerge between trash, humans and consumerist society. His is an ecology that does not ignore how the fact that those most affected by the environmental decisions of the privileged are the poor, much the same way that islands are the first biomes to be affected by climate change. That is, Furtado's documentary is a provocative ecology that engages with the toughest questions faced by cosmopolitan environmentalisms or sustainable ecologies insofar as it links industrial society to the harrowing situation of the inhabitants of Ilha das Flores, reduced to living below pigs in the eating order that reflects the stark social inequalities.

Furtado represents the world, not from an imaginary all-seeing perspective – 'God does not exist' – but from the fragmented concreteness of archival footage and news cut-outs. One of the first images to appear in the documentary is the animation of planet Earth, rotating on its axis as the title *Ilha das Flores* encircles the planet. Ironically playing on the 'Blue Marble' photograph taken on 7 December 1972 by the crew of the Apollo 17 mission, a photograph that would constitute an icon for environmental movements in subsequent years, the simulated image of the Earth in Furtado's documentary stresses its artificial construction. The image of the 'Blue Marble' offers a totalizing view of the planet – naïvely ignoring the discourse of power latent in such a homogenizing perspective, a perspective in which everyone is told that they belong to an abstract humanity, when the truth is that discrimination and oppression in all their forms are pervasive. As in other Brazilian documentaries since the 1980s, there is 'a suspicion of all-encompassing classifications' (Navarro 2014: 76).

In the past decades, the production of documentaries dealing with topics of climate change and nature has increased dramatically. The *Planet Earth* series, launched by the BBC in 2006 with the trademark voice-over of David Attenborough, reached audiences worldwide. Episodes of these nature documentaries exploit the popular assumptions of viewers in regard to being given an unmediated access to natural environments, as if the documentary were a transparent window to these remote places and animals, when it is all actually a montage of cameras to attempt to frame the scene as a spontaneous event available to the viewers for the first time. These and many other instances of environmental documentaries reveal a critical naïveté in their representation of the world, for they offer a mix of expository and observational modes to build narratives that are always constructed and artificial. Behind the high-definition images of animals in a seemingly pure state of nature, there is a simulation and construction of the scenes that is hidden from the viewer. Cinema 'is a machine that produces or discloses worlds' (Ivakhiv 2013: 88). More importantly, these mainstream wildlife documentaries 'offer a glimpse into the cultural logic of ecology by revealing the close-knit ties between economics and cultural perceptions of environment' (Rust 2013: 234). Given the globalizing discourse of the Anthropocene present in mainstream nature documentaries – a discourse that misses issues of environmental justice that affect the Global South – their commercial success is quite troubling. Claire Molloy's analysis of Disney's wildlife documentaries is particularly relevant in pointing to how such films are incorporated into capitalist infrastructure: 'the company's wildlife films as commodities which are produced, distributed, and repurposed by a diversified global entertainment conglomerate within a capitalist industrial structure' (2013:170). They reinforce a narrative of the current climate crisis as caused by all humans and imagine solutions solely predicated on the preservation of wildlife, regardless of the consequences to human inhabitants. In other words, commercial nature documentaries often distract viewers from the role of capitalism in environmental issues.

Yet as Rob Nixon argues in *Slow Violence and Environmentalism of the Poor*, the spectacular images of the media that we have been so acquainted with in the past decades also generate amnesia fed by a capitalist economy that is accelerating the extraction and disposal of resources across the world (2011: 7). Emphasis on spectacular images in state-of-the-art wildlife documentaries depends heavily on the indexical dimension of images to attract viewers. They seem to lack a critical reflection on the role of documentary in representing the world – an aspect which is precisely one of the strongest points in favour of considering *Ilha das Flores* as a frontrunner in environmental documentary as it engages with the themes of capitalism and waste. Furtado's film offers an important contribution to ecocinema that is all the more relevant today, given the ongoing discussions concerning the hidden racism of the globalizing discourse of the Anthropocene.[3]

Just as in the opening syllogism, the choice of names and definitions seems random at first. Why should the definition of the term 'Japanese' be relevant to growing a tomato or the Island of Flowers? Moreover, the condescending tone of the narrator, whose seemingly 'objective' definition seems to miss the mark completely, appears overtly racist. Yet there is a reasoning behind each of the lexical definitions that accompany the images in the documentary. Notice the sequence of terms that are defined throughout *Ilha das Flores*: 'Japanese', 'human beings', 'telencephalon', 'opposable thumb', 'tomato', 'money', 'Christ', 'Jews', 'perfumes', 'profit', 'pig', 'day', 'family', 'garbage', 'island', 'water', 'flowers', 'owner', 'estate', 'organic origin', 'history test', 'women and children', 'seconds' and 'caesium'. The narrative sequence simply moves from one to the other, almost like following hypertext links (Bandeira 2019). Some of the terms are accompanied by powerful archival images. For example, the words 'telencephalon' and 'opposable thumb' are said to help humans come up with 'improvements for the planet', while accompanied by the image of a mushroom cloud from what seems to be a nuclear explosion; the word 'Jews' is juxtaposed to images of the Holocaust and extermination camps; and the word 'water' is linked to images of the brackish waters of the Island of Flowers.

In tandem, both the fragmented images and the chain of lexical definitions expose the injustices of a system in which the following occurs, as the voice-over narration acquires a critical tone towards the end of the film:

> The tomato planted by Mr. Suzuki, exchanged for money with the supermarket, exchanged for the money that Mrs. Anete exchanged for perfumes extracted from flowers, refused for the pork sauce, thrown to the trash, and rejected as food for pigs, is now available for the human beings of the Ilha das Flores.

There is a thread that links the images and words, bringing to the forefront a stratum that evidences the complicity and vulnerability of a system in which human beings – those creatures with 'a highly developed telencephalon and opposable thumb' – create a system in which other humans are placed below pigs in the eating order of the Island of Flowers, which really is not an island of flowers at all, but rather a heap of waste where what Mrs Anete judges as inedible for her family ends up strewn in the ground. The island has few flowers and smells of garbage, the narrator explains. This ironic twist is all the more pronounced when the narrator suggests that the reason for the conditions under which 'women and children' of the island live is due to the fact that they neither have 'money', nor an 'owner'. Just as the notion of archipelago undermines the Western imaginary of insularity, so does *Ilha das Flores* construct an archipelagic epistemology from archival and lexical fragments. Challenging a totalizing and homogenizing view of the environment, Furtado offers a documentary that represents the world by exposing the precarious links between its parts.

———

In this chapter I have discussed how Jorge Furtado's *Ilha das Flores* challenges Western imaginaries of islands by exposing the precarious relations between the human and nonhuman that intersect at a specific geography, that of the Guaíba estuary in Southern Brazil. Postmodern and materialist in its approach to the indexical quality of images, the documentary jars viewers' expectations by establishing an apparently fragmented ecology of images and random choice of words defined by the narrator in a hypertextual play that emphasizes its artificial framing. Yet this performance gradually leads the viewer to make connections between what seemed distant and disconnected, creating a mesh of relations that provocatively makes the journey of a tomato from the field to the landfill in the Ilha das Flores, a path that exposes all entities complicit in the social and environmental injustices taking place there. I have also argued for the material connections in the presence of waste and its toxicity in the film. The reference to caesium-137 in the film is an indictment to the vulnerable situation of those obliged to live in and on garbage just outside cities across Brazil and Latin America. Toxicity traces the precarious relations between the human and nonhuman, also dissolving Western binaries regarding inside/ outside relations with garbage.

Most importantly, *Ilha das Flores* brings to the forefront the importance of reconsidering environmental justice as it affects islands across the planet, whether they be found in oceans or river estuaries. More so than continental biomes, islands are sites of environmental dissolve, where the effects of climate change, ecological disaster and human impact become quickly exposed. Islands are the first places to surface ecological issues that will later affect other geographies. As Nixon argues, 'yet over time, that risk will be passed on, as today's imperiled islanders turn into climate refugees whose desperation will exacerbate the crisis in the richer, high-consumption nations whose profligacy triggered it in the first place' (2011: 266).

Notes

1   From here on out, I will use the non-italicized Ilha das Flores to refer to the island found in the Guaíba estuary. The italicized form will refer to Jorge Furtado's short film by the same name.

2   Some of the Latin American documentary filmmakers whose works offer
     a valuable contribution to discussions on the role of capitalism in the
     Anthropocene from the perspective of the Global South are Margot Benacerraf
     with *Araya* (1959), the work of Fernando Solanas, from his foundational *La
     hora de los hornos* (1968), co-directed with Octavio Getino, to the cycle of
     documentaries that start with *Memoria del saqueo* (2004) to the present; Eduardo
     Coutinho with *Boca de lixo* (1993), and Patricio Guzmán's first-person trilogy,
     Nostalgia de la luz (2010), *El botón de nácar* (2015) and *La cordillera de los
     sueños* (2019). More recently, a generation of young documentary filmmakers
     is continuing in this same vein, including Lucas Van Esso with *Gran Chaco*
     (2015); Ernesto Cabellos Damián with *Choropampa, el precio del oro* (2002),
     Tambogrande: mangos, muerte, minería (2007) and *La hija de la laguna* (2015);
     and André D'Elia with *A Lei da Água* (2015) and *Ser Tão Velho Cerrado* (2018).
3   For a discussion of the racial dimension of the Anthropocene, see Yusoff and
     Vergès.

References

Ab'Sáber, A. (2007), *Brasil: Paisagens de Exceção. O litoral e o Pantanal mato-
     grossense, patrimônios básicos*, São Paulo: Ateliê.

Alaimo, S. (2010), *Bodily Natures: Science, Environment, and the Material Self*,
     Indianapolis: Indiana University Press.

Alaimo, S. (2016), *Exposed: Environmental Politics and Pleasures in Posthuman Times*,
     Minneapolis: University of Minnesota Press.

Baer, W. (2007), *The Brazilian Economy: Growth and Development*, Boulder: Lynne
     Rienner Publishers.

Bandeira, M. B. L. (2019), '30 anos depois: a atualidade de *Ilha das Flores*', *Itaú
     Cultural*, 30 April. https://www.itaucultural.org.br/secoes/noticias/30-anos-
     depois-a-atualidade-de-ilha-das-flores (accessed 15 June 2020).

Bell, L. (2019), 'Place, People, and Processes in Waste Theory: A Global South
     Critique', *Cultural Studies* 33.1: 98–121.

Boca de lixo (1993), [Film] Dir. Eduardo Coutinho, Brazil: CECIP.

Bryant, L. R. (2013), 'Black', in J. J. Cohen (ed.), *Prismatic Ecology: Ecotheory beyond
     Green*, 290–310, Minneapolis: University of Minnesota Press.

Cooke, S. (2009), *In Mortal Hands: A Cautionary History of the Nuclear Age*, New
     York: Bloomsbury.

Crosby, A. W. (1986), *Ecological Imperialism: The Biological Expansion of Europe, 900-1900*, Cambridge: Cambridge University Press.

Debs, S. and J. Furtado (2005), 'Jorge Furtado: Interview by Sylvie Debs', *Cinémas d'Amérique Latine* 13: 4–19.

DeLoughrey, E. (2007), *Routes and Roots: Navigating Caribbean and Pacific Island Literatures*, Honolulu: University of Hawai'i Press.

DeLoughrey, E. (2019), *Allegories of the Anthropocene*, Durham, NC: Duke University Press.

Demos, T. J. (2017), *Against the Anthropocene: Visual Culture and Environment Today*, Berlin: Sternberg Press.

Dunn, C. (2016), *Contracultura: Alternative Arts and Social Transformation in Authoritarian Brazil*, Chapel Hill: University of North Carolina Press.

Estamira (2004), [Film] Dir. Marcos Prados, Brazil: Zazen Produçoes.

Furtado, G. P. (2019), *Documentary Filmmaking in Contemporary Brazil: Cinematic Archives of the Present*, Oxford: Oxford University Press.

Glissant, E. (1989), *Caribbean Discourse: Selected Essays*, Charlottesville: University Press of Virginia.

Glissant, E. (1997), *Poetics of Relation*, Ann Arbor: University of Michigan Press.

Haraway, D. (2016), *Staying with the Trouble: Making Kin in the Chthulucene*, Durham: Duke University Press.

Ilha das Flores (1989), [Film] Dir. Jorge Furtado, Brazil: Casa de Cinema de Porto Alegre.

Ivakhiv, A. (2013), 'An Ecophilosophy of the Moving Image: Cinema as Anthrobiogeomorphic Machine', in S. Rust, S. Monani and S. Cubitt (eds), *Ecocinema Theory and Practice*, 87–106, London: Routledge.

José, A. (2007), 'Cinema marginal, a estética do grotesco e a globalização da miséria', *ALCEU* 8.15: 155–63.

Malm, A. (2018), *The Progress of This Storm: Nature and Society in a Warming World*, London: Verso.

Mbembe, A. (2017), *Critique of Black Reason*, Durham: Duke University Press.

McKay, M. (2016), 'Documenting Jardim Gramacho: *Estamira* (2004) and *Waste Land* (2009)', *Luso Brazilian Review* 53.2: 134–52.

McMahon, E. (2016), *Islands, Identity, and the Literary Imagination*, London: Anthem Press.

Molloy, C. (2013), 'Nature Writes the Screenplays: Commercial Wildlife Films and Ecological Entertainment', in S. Rust, S. Monani and S. Cubitt (eds), *Ecocinema Theory and Practice*, 169–88, London: Routledge.

Moore, J. W. (2015), *Capitalism in the Web of Life: Ecology and the Accumulation of Capital*, London: Verso.

Moore, J. W. (2016), 'Introduction: Anthropocene or Capitalocene? Nature, History, and the Crisis of Capitalism', in J. W. Moore (ed.), *Anthropocene or Capitalocene? Nature, History, and the Crisis of Capitalism*, 1–13, Oakland: PM Press.

Navarro, V. (2014) 'Performance in Brazilian Documentaries', in V. Navarro and J. C. Rodríguez (eds), *New Documentaries in Latin America*, 75–90, New York: Palgrave Macmillan.

Nichols, B. (2001), *Introduction to Documentary*, Bloomington: Indiana University Press.

Nixon, R. (2011), *Slow Violence and the Environmentalism of the Poor*, Cambridge: Harvard University Press.

Planet Earth (2006), [Documentary Series] United Kingdom: BBC.

The Radiological Accident in Goiânia (1988), Vienna: International Atomic Energy Agency.

Roberts, B. R. and M. A. Stephens (2017), 'Introduction: Archipelagic Studies. Decontinentalizing the Study of American Culture', in B. R. Roberts and M. A. Stephens (eds), *Archipelagic American Studies*, 1–54, Durham: Duke University Press.

Rust, S. (2013), 'Ecocinema and the Wildlife Film', in L. Westling (ed.), *The Cambridge Companion to Literature and the Environment*, 226–40, Cambridge: University of Cambridge Press.

Skidmore, T. E. (1999), *Brazil: Five Centuries of Change*, Oxford: Oxford University Press.

Sontag, S. (2005), *On Photography*, New York: Rosetta Books.

Stam, R. (1997), *Tropical Multiculturalism: A Comparative History of Race in Brazilian Cinema and Culture*, Durham: Duke University Press.

Tsing, A. L. (2017), *The Mushroom at the End of the World: On the Possibility of Life in Capitalist Ruins*, Princeton: Princeton University Press.

Vergès, F. (2017), 'Racial Capitalocene', in G. T. Johnson and A. Lubin (eds), *Futures of Black Radicalism*, 60–7, London: Verso.

Xavier, I. (1997), *Allegories of Underdevelopment: Aesthetics and Politics in Modern Brazilian Cinema*, Minneapolis: University of Minnesota Press.

Yussof, K. (2018), *A Billion Black Anthropocenes or None*, Minneapolis: University of Minnesota Press.

7

Islands in Lucrecia Martel's *Nueva Argirópolis* (2010): Eroding and fracturing the national map

Natalia D'Alessandro

What is an island?

Jacques Derrida
The Beast and the Sovereign

Continental islands *are accidental, derived islands. They are separated from a continent, born of disarticulation, erosion, fracture, they survive the absorption of what once contained them.*

Gilles Deleuze
Desert Islands and Other Texts

In Argentine literature and film, the Falkland Islands or Islas Malvinas occupy a central place in representations of insularity. Just to mention a few examples in Argentine cinema, the representations of the Islas Malvinas range from the foundational film on the Malvinas war *Los chicos de la guerra* (1984) by Bebe Kamin to one of the latest contemporary films, *Teatro de guerra* (2018), by Lola Arias. However, Lucrecia Martel's short film *Nueva Argirópolis* (2010) explores some minor and scarcely investigated islands in the Argentine context that are visible, for example, in a few texts by Argentine writers Haroldo Conti, Juan José Saer and Juan L. Ortiz.

Nueva Argirópolis is part of the *25 miradas, 200 minutos* project, a series of twenty-five eight-minute-long shorts, which add up to a total of two hundred minutes. The project was developed by the Ministerio de Cultura and Universidad Nacional Tres de Febrero in the context of celebrations of

Argentina's Independence bicentennial in 2010. It is essential to underline that the film was shot in the provinces of Corrientes, Chaco and Salta, with the assistance of actors from the Qom community, speakers of the Guaraní and Toba languages.[1] *Nueva Argirópolis* stages the struggle of indigenous communities to settle on islands in the Paraná Delta – located in the eastern centre of Argentina, between the provinces of Entre Ríos, Buenos Aires and Santa Fe – to found a new collective territory named Nueva Argirópolis. In addition, the film narrates how the local police, following state orders, searches for members of these occupying groups in order to prevent their actions. The film revolves around the possibility of the radicalization and mobilization of local indigenous communities. By referring to this conflict, Martel intervenes in an urgent contemporary debate in Argentina. What is the role of the state in the systematic violence against indigenous communities?

As a starting point, this chapter interrogates the concept of 'island' at work in *Nueva Argirópolis*. From this perspective, I analyse the cinematic tools for delegitimizing *Argirópolis o la capital de los Estados Confederados del Río de la Plata* (1850) by Domingo Faustino Sarmiento. In this text, a long essay of more than 100 pages published in 1850, Sarmiento imagines Argirópolis, located on the Martín García Island, as the capital of the Confederated States of the Río de la Plata, a modern nation encompassing the current sates of Argentina, Uruguay and Paraguay. I argue that, while in *Argirópolis*, similarly to other insular narratives, the island is seen as the unifying extension or prosthesis of a homogeneous national body, *Nueva Argirópolis* operates from the idea of *fracture*. Martel imagines her island as *detachment* and as the point of arrival of an indigenous resistance movement. This movement works like a small fraction that is capable of disarticulating the historic constructions of a national 'single body'. The cinematic configurations of the Paraná Delta in Martel's film, and the relations established there among islands, rivers and the continent, erode the concept of a homogeneous national map and invite us to rethink territorial distributions in the context of the twenty-first century.

The dialogue between Martel's short and Sarmiento's text is very productive for a debate on contemporary conflicts in the Argentine context in relation to the indigenous communities. Deborah Martin affirms:[2]

> Through its inclusion in the *25 miradas* project *Nueva Argirópolis* inhabits the commemorative discourses of the nation-state, yet it does so subversively,

Islands in Lucrecia Martel's Nueva Argirópolis *(2010)*

overturning the values with which the project of national foundation and its commemoration are associated. It does this primarily through a radical resignification of the text from which it draws its name (…) Martel's *Nueva Argirópolis* meditates on and reimagines crucial terms of its Sarmientian precursor, especially the role of rivers and geography which were central to concepts of national foundation and progress in Sarmiento's text and more broadly within nineteenth-century nation-building.

(2016a: 107)

As Martin argues, *Nueva Argirópolis* redefines hegemonic concepts associated with a national foundation and seeks to rewrite the Sarmientian terms linked to the configuration of a national territory. Deborah Martin focuses her argument on the analysis of water and fluidity, especially associated with 'the role of rivers and geography which were central to concepts of national foundation and progress in Sarmiento's text and more broadly within nineteenth-century nation-building discourses' (2016a: 176). In this chapter, as mentioned before, I question and analyse the concept of 'island' in *Nueva Argirópolis* arguing that, while in *Argirópolis* the island is seen as the unifying prosthesis of a homogeneous national body, *Nueva Argirópolis* operates from the paradigms of *erosions* and *fractures*.

In his text, Sarmiento imagines Argirópolis, 'the city of silver', which would function as capital of the Confederate States of the Río de la Plata, thus neutralizing the conflicts between *unitarios* and *federales*, the two factions that faced each other in the Argentine Civil Wars during the first decades of the organization of the national territory. While the *unitarios* sought the centralization of national power in Buenos Aires, the *federales* defended provincial autonomy.[3]

In Sarmiento's utopia, Argirópolis was to be built on the Martín García Island, located in a central point of the Río de la Plata. It is important to mention here that in the construction of his utopia, Sarmiento seems to have as a literary precedent the *Utopia* of Thomas More, among other texts.[4] Sarmiento's island encapsulates all his alienated dreams about fluvial navigability as the main engine of civilization converged, in the same way the Paraná and Uruguay Rivers converge there to form the Río de la Plata. This insular city, conceived by Sarmiento as a replica of Washington, DC, would become the capital of an imaginary nation which did not include the provinces of Buenos Aires and Patagonia, so as to avoid any proximity between the Confederate States and the indigenous peoples: 'To the South, instead of being able to exchange its products with a civilized nation, the Argentine Confederation suffers the devastation of the savages' (Sarmiento 1850: 93).[5] The Martín García Island would operate as an administrative and commercial centre and the states would fuse 'in one single body the spirit of the time and the needs of modern nations. The human race is moving towards forming large groups, by races, by languages, by similar or analogous civilizations' (1850:130).[6] In this way, Sarmiento proposes to avoid what he calls the tendency to separate into small fractions: 'South American republics have all more or less leaned to decompose into small fractions, provoked by an anarchic and unpremeditated aspiration to a ruinous, obscure independence, unprecedented among nations' (1850: 131).

Insularity is key to Sarmiento because it is precisely Martín García's 'insular form' that would generate the homogenizing effect he so desires. The island 'is naturally detached from any sort of influence from each of the provinces' (1850: 128). Finally, Sarmiento visualizes the location of Martín García in the Paraná Delta as the perfect disposition for the establishment of a long-awaited institutionality: 'Many are the useful applications offered by the labyrinth of channels and islands that form the Paraná Delta!' (1850: 137). The most extreme – and hilarious – extent of this utopia arrives when Sarmiento proposes the urgency of the *gaucho* naval transformation: 'What a change in ideas and customs! If, instead of horses, young men needed boats to move around; if, instead of taming colts, the people had to subdue rowdy waves with their oar' (1850: 144).[7]

Visual unrepresentability of the islands and preeminence of the voice

Martel's *Nueva Argirópolis* represents a meticulous scrutiny of insularity. In direct dialogue with Sarmiento's text, the short investigates the notion of 'island' in the Argentine context through cinematographic specificity. By way of this meticulous investigation of the idea of 'island', Martel inserts her film into a lateral debate in Argentina, not only because *Argirópolis* is less debated than other texts by Sarmiento – one of the most canonic writers in nineteenth-century Latin America – but also because the film proposes an enquiry into a space scarcely represented in Argentine cultural production in recent years, the islands of the Paraná Delta. From these peculiar historic and geographic circumstances, and from a cinematic perspective, Martel's film asks again Jacques Derrida's seminal question in *The Beast and the Sovereign* (2002–3), 'What is an island?' (2011: 3). Derrida's enquiry is part of a wider search, which involves not only reading the word 'island', but also observing its function in different scenarios and in the diversity of texts that have engaged the notion of insularity. Derrida's examples include James Joyce's and Virginia Woolf's readings of the concept of the island in *Robinson Crusoe* (1719) by Daniel Defoe.

Nueva Argirópolis takes on the question 'What is an island?' from different perspectives. In a key scene towards the middle of the film a teacher discusses with her grade school students the formation of the islands in the area where they live: 'When it rains the water goes down and it takes all that soil to the Iruya River, and from there it goes to the Bermejo river, the Paraná river, and reaches the Río de la Plata. As the speed slows down there, that soil settles, and islands are gradually being formed.' One of the girls listening to the teacher adds, almost in a whisper: 'Islands. They are ownerless islands. They don't belong to anyone.' This scene functions as a kind of central axis around which the film revolves, especially because the film is dominated by a geographical enquiry into the Paraná Delta that leads us to reflect on political conflicts that are absolutely contemporary.

The film opens with a brief but fundamental scene to put us in context. We fleetingly see a wide shot of the river furrowed by a small motorboat led by two people. The boat is dragging a kind of *camalote*, a water hyacinth that aggregates to form floating 'islands'. From the riverbank, two policemen and a girl – their backs towards the camera – are watching the forward movement of these people, who will be intercepted by the police. Later on, we will find out that they are part of an indigenous movement coming together around the notion of fluvial navigability and whose long-term goals are to occupy the 'ownerless islands' and to found a new collective space there, 'Nueva Argirópolis'. Behind all this, in a blurry background, we can see the opposite bank of the river. On closer inspection, however, it looks like the two formations towards which the boatmen are moving are islands. This key moment puts us *in medias res* in the context of the Delta and of a specific debate about the Sarmientian text, since the establishing shot includes the banks of the continent, the navigable/navigated river and certain insular formations. This image is also the only one in the film in which we can discern in the distance formations that we could read as 'islands'. These islands, later termed 'ownerless islands', function in the short film as a kind of visual ellipsis; they are something we never see; they are raised cinematically from the idea of unrepresentability. Unlike Sarmiento's highly detailed visual description of his Argirópolis island, in *Nueva Argirópolis* the islands are invisible. Their presence gradually takes shape through voices. Through what the characters say or suggest, possible islands are projected on a blurred out-of-field, barely glimpsed in the initial establishing shot.

Martel states in an interview: 'I always understand space as a cause/effect line, so words generate characters and characters generate space. The characters always come from words' (James 36). Through this preeminence of orality, the insular space seems to work in the film: the islands are shaped cinematically through the voices of the characters. The cinematic work with orality, present in *Nueva Argirópolis,* is key in Martel's cinema. All her films, from *La ciénaga* (2001) to *Zama* (2017), present meticulous sound work via a preeminence of the oral. Martel has broadly displayed in her films her enquiry into different uses of orality, voices and silences – in her own words, 'ways to recognize sound absences'. Her work with orality is a recurring mechanism, sometimes associated with the remembrance of oral tales from the Salta region and, at other times, in relation to the oral cadence of voices from her own family or the drift in conversations typical of the local Spanish of northern Argentina.

In connection with this preeminence of orality, Martin affirms:

Fragments of conversation in both Spanish and indigenous languages are combined on the soundtrack of *Nueva Argirópolis* with unintelligible whispers and murmurs, in this way also introducing textual folds, troubling any sense of univocality, and suffusing the soundtrack literally with rumours. Martel's cinema has been described both as 'aurally conceived' and as an oral cinema, or a cinema of words. In it sound is always potentially more revolutionary, more open to interpretation than the more heavily coded and ontologically defined visual field (…) sound is used to continually suggest

Islands in Lucrecia Martel's Nueva Argirópolis *(2010)*   159

further layers to reality beyond the limits of the visual image, and thus to challenge the hegemony of the visual.

(2016b: 460)

As Martin proposes, *Nueva Argirópolis* is no exception in Martel's filmography. There is a prevalence of conversations and whispers in Toba, Guaraní and Spanish that set themselves up above the visual image. But how do the characters' voices in the film shape insular space? After the scene discussed above, the film brings us to a police station. We see a police officer from behind and, in a blurred background, a group of men and a woman who apparently were in the boat and have been arrested. The camera cuts out the body of the policeman. We do not see his face; we only hear his voice and another voice that comes from a radio. These voices in Spanish play the role of a kind of 'state machiner' of control that runs through the entire short film. 'One female and four males, undocumented. They came down floating on a *camalote* with plastic bottles', explains the policeman. The sequence cuts to a close-up of one of the arrested men when we hear the voice from the radio respond: 'What do you mean "on a *camalote*"? Are they human remains?' 'No, no,' specifies the policeman, 'all is QSL, these are *camalote*-like rafts.'

The oral articulation of the *camalote* as a minimum unit in the voice of the characters begins to outline the concept of an 'island'. The *camalote* is imagined as a tiny mobile island, steered by the indigenous community in resistance, since it is used as a means to navigate the rivers, heading towards certain 'ownerless islands'. As Martin proposes from this initial image, Martel appropriates the Sarmientian topic fluvial navigability as a civilizing engine, transforming it into a vehicle for this community's struggle. The assertion of the policeman who reconstructs the story ('They came down floating on a *camalote*') and the other policeman's question ('What do you mean "on a *camalote*"? Are they human remains?') book-end the voices of the men and the woman, who speak an indigenous language. At the same moment in which the policeman states that 'all is QSL' ('all understood' in police jargon), the camera stops on the faces of the detained men and woman. Importantly, it stops at their voices. They speak to each other in a language that, as spectators, we do not understand, and of which we do not receive any kind of translation. We wonder what they might be discussing. Are they talking about the *camalote*, the arrest or the policemen's claims? We receive no answer to these questions.

160 *The Film Archipelago*

From here on, *Nueva Argirópolis* stages a conflict that persists to the end and can be expressed as the politics of 'no translation'. The film is populated by the voices of the community, which are left untranslated. It reflects on the indigenous languages of northern Argentina, especially Wichi, Mocoví, Pilagá, Toba and Guaraní, and the non-translation mechanisms they deploy for us. In this sense, the film can be interpreted through Walter Benjamin's conceptualizations in 'The Task of the Translator' (1923): first, the fact that 'translation thus ultimately serves the purpose of expressing the innermost relationship of languages' (1996: 255), and in direct relation to this, the understanding that translation is ideological.

The film depicts the relationships that indigenous languages keep with Spanish, which operates as a historical language of domination. However, from this opening scene in which we hear the woman and the men speaking in their language untranslated, the film reverses the traditional perspectives of translation. This mechanism shows the film's effort to equalize the power dynamics between indigenous languages and Spanish. Failing to translate indigenous speech places us as spectators in the position of an *other*, from which we must acknowledge our ignorance of the unknown language, thus challenging viewers and the perspectives granted by their hegemonic position within tradition. In this sense, the film undermines the dominance of Sarmiento's 'civilization or barbarism' trope in *Argirópolis*. The entire film revolves around our lack of knowledge as spectators of the characters' indigenous language, and around the knowledge that police officers do not possess in relation to the movement they are investigating, as they also ignore the language. The film portrays how state-sanctioned ignorance of the indigenous language hinders the possibility of the police suppressing the movement of resistance, while it is used by the activists as a means to circulate information about their actions.

Let us return to the initial question: 'What is an island?' In *Nueva Argirópolis*, the indigenous languages themselves seem to operate cinematically from the notion of insularity. The Wichi, Mocoví, Pilagá, Toba and Guaraní languages function similarly to the initial image of the *camalote* as a minimal and mobile island which takes over the Sarmientian topic of fluvial navigability to turn it into a vehicle of territorial struggle and reappropriation. The staging of indigenous voices as the engine of a film dominated by orality, added to the strategic performance of collective speech acts that take place in front of us and that we do not understand, works in the film as a force of resistance. Thus, indigenous languages are cinematically activated as linguistic systems that effectively transform their historical and insular situation (their isolation, marginalization by a state system, translation as a form of control and the abysmal distance from Spanish as the official language) into a collective force. Like the *camalote*, the use of their own language and the state's ignorance can lead the indigenous communities towards the possibility of founding of a new collective space, which upturns the uneven historical distributions in the national 'Argentine' context. Through its insular condition, the indigenous language helps delineate those other possible 'ownerless islands' that are foreshadowed as the future territory of the fighting community. In this way, the failure to visually represent the islands towards which the group advances, that is, the absence of an image, is supplemented by other 'islands' – the voices of indigenous communities as active elements of political struggle.

Through the imaginary foundation of Argirópolis Island, Sarmiento's centralizing discourse underlined the urgency of a definitive union of the various provinces 'in one single body' to join the great civilized nations of the world as a modern state, and to protest against the anarchic spirit of the South American republics and their propensity to break down into small fractions. Thus, Sarmiento's Argirópolis Island would function as the extension or unifying prosthesis of a homogeneous national body. The indigenous languages in *Nueva Argirópolis* lay the foundation for a reversal of Sarmiento's utopia. The circulation of collective voices functions as that 'small fraction', minimal island or *camalote* which could definitively dismantle the historical and hegemonic construction of a totality – the nation and national identity, the establishment of a centralized territory as a homogeneous body, and monolingualism.

Islands as detachment and fracture

There is in *Nueva Argirópolis* a great emphasis on the idea of the 'island' as a 'small fraction'. This kind of insularity dialogues with Deleuze's concept of 'continental or derived islands', islands that 'are separated from a continent, born of disarticulation, erosion, fracture, and they survive the absorption of what once contained them' (2003: 9). Following the police station scene, we witness again a fleeting long shot of the river and its banks. Four police officers have their backs turned to the camera. Two of them are in a boat with the word 'PREFECTURE' on its side, supervising the situation. The others stand on the shore. One holds a kind of bludgeon in his hand. The other, pulling a rope, draws a *camalote* towards the banks. If we contrast this scene to the opening scene, in which we saw a group moving away from the continent in a boat and a *camalote*, we can describe a kind of oscillation between *detachment* and *absorption* in *Nueva Argirópolis*.

On the one hand, the film dramatizes the inspiration I draw from Deleuze's epigraph on 'derived islands'. That is, the communities appropriate Sarmiento's dictum on fluvial navigability, sailing in boats and *camalotes* and heading towards certain 'ownerless islands'.[8] These function as 'small fractions' separated from the continent in search of a new collective territory, since communal lands have been historically usurped from them. In this sense, Martel, without losing sight of her cinematographic specificity, positions her short film in the distinct and acrid debate around the dispossession of lands indigenous communities endure through to this day, and the brutal police repression they have suffered in several Argentine provinces in recent years.

In his text, Sarmiento is very lucid about this function of insularity. Resonating with Deleuze's epigraph, the islands in *Nueva Argirópolis* stem from disarticulation and fracture as tools for resisting the historical violence of homogenizing absorption by the nation-state. Here, the film again challenges Sarmiento's text, turning his proposal for the marginalization of indigenous populations into a force of resistance. In *Argirópolis*, Sarmiento proposes that the capital island, and the territory regulated from there, should be completely detached from the areas subject to the 'devastation of the savages'. In addition, an obsession in his text is that the insular form of Argirópolis would generate a homogenizing effect, since the island, by its own condition, would separate 'naturally from all influence by each of the provinces'. The homogenizing effect generated from the capital island would underline Sarmiento's yearnings for an ideal nation, as Helen Kapstein states on the functions that many insular stories have fulfilled: 'One of those lies is that island is castaway from its nation, when in fact it is held at a proximate distance, underwriting the nation culturally, politically and economically. Spaces that appear marginal are fundamentally constitutive of the center' (2017, XV).

Islands in Lucrecia Martel's Nueva Argirópolis (2010)

If on the one hand *Nueva Argirópolis* works with the image of 'derived islands' that detach *from* the continent and, on the other, in its oscillating movement, the film lingers at the moment when the officers pull the *camalote towards* the continent, exerting a kind of centripetal violence. Thus, Martel stages the absorption of the *camalote* as a force of resistance which the policemen draw to the riverbank. They are looking for the activists who sail the river to reach the 'ownerless islands', and then arrest them and transfer them to the police station. Later, the film shows that they are examined by state medical officers to check if they are transporting drugs in their bodies, signalling an institutional system based on mistrust and violence towards indigenous communities. Once they are attracted to the continent through this centripetal violence, they enter an 'institutional labyrinth' like the one Sarmiento dreams of in the Paraná Delta, which now operates in the continent in police stations, hospitals and public offices: 'Many are the useful applications offered by the labyrinth of channels and islands that form the Paraná Delta!' For this reason, the fleeting appearance of the word 'PREFECTURE' in capital letters on the police boat is not accidental. Through this intervention, Martel shows her film's particular interest in investigating how the Argentine Naval Prefecture monitors the state and security of the rivers and seas. According to its own official website, 'in concert with State institutions, the Argentine Naval Prefecture is a security force dependent on the Ministry of National Security'. Martel investigates this delta, observing the state of the rivers and the relationships they establish with the islands and the continent. She visualizes Sarmiento's obsession with fluvial navigability as a civilizing engine and as a part of a homogenizing policy, of a centripetal violence still present in the modern day. But she also focuses on the institutional labyrinth, on that 'concert of state institutions' active to this day as 'security forces' that continue to watch over the precarious idea of a 'Nation' with capital letters.

The word 'prefecture' comes from the Latin *praefectura*, which means, among other things, 'organizational and political division of the territory'. The conflict around the 'organizational and political divisions of the territory' marked the formation of the Argentine nation in the nineteenth century and is very much alive today. *Nueva Argirópolis* makes this conflict visible. The film seeks to delineate new maps that redesign the unequal political, economic and social distributions configured at the national level in the last 200 years, and

164   *The Film Archipelago*

in particular those related to indigenous communities, to finally dismantle the nineteenth-century utopia, so prevalent today, of Argentina as a homogeneous national body.

Two other key scenes further elaborate the oscillation between detachment and absorption. In the first one, we see a man and a woman in a small room, and we hear someone else's voice: 'Are you stupid or what? You are an Indian, an idler. You are an ignorant Indian. What could have happened?', declares the voice of a man whom we can now see in close-up. He continues: 'All of us who speak in Wichi, Mocoví, Pilagá, Toba, Guaraní, all poor. What are we? All fools? All ignorant?' The other man responds: 'You are the fool. How will you get there if you cannot swim?' The first man continues: 'We don't like having teeth. That our teeth bother us. That's why we remove our teeth. What could have happened?' After this question, the man continues to speak in his own language and we no longer understand the conversation. In the second scene, we see three girls entering an official establishment to translate a message from a leader of the movement circulating on *YouTube*. In the foreground we see the 'interpreter' girls, and we hear the voice of the leader over the voice of one of the girls, who whispers the translation in the ear of the other girl. We get the message when the girl who receives it repeats it aloud in Spanish: 'We should be extinct, after all the effort this nation has made. Let's get on the rafts. Let us enthrone noble equality.'

In these two scenes, the film again shows its poetics of oscillation, swinging between detachment and absorption, between the fracture of the continent and centripetal violence, and between the possibility and impossibility of reaching the islands. The question 'How will you get there if you cannot swim?' is superimposed over the command 'Let's get on the rafts.' Here too Martel takes possession of the Sarmientian text. Both phrases bring us back to Sarmiento's delirious proposal in *Argirópolis*, calling for a *gaucho* 'naval' transformation as part of the civilizational action of fluvial navigability: 'If, instead of horses, young men needed boats to move around; if, instead of taming colts, the people had to subdue rowdy waves with their oar' (1850: 144).

Martel pauses to examine this oscillatory conflict that dominates the entire short film. Around the question 'How will you get there if you cannot swim?' certain historical slogans from Sarmiento's 'civilization or barbarism' trope are rewritten to visualize their operational violence: 'Indian', 'stupid', 'bum',

Islands in Lucrecia Martel's Nueva Argirópolis *(2010)* 165

'ignorant', 'toothless'. But also to corrode this homogenizing violence through differences. It is here that the names of the languages of the communities appear for the first and only time in the short: 'Wichi, mocoví, pilagá, toba, guaraní.' At this moment in the film, the mention of their own languages functions as a force against homogeneity which hails these differences as an active element of struggle today. In this struggle, the recurring question, 'What could have happened?', summons the spectator to question these *leitmotivs* and the emphatic affirmation, 'All of us who speak in Wichi, Mocoví, Pilagá, Toba, Guaraní, all poor'.

In the second scene, as Martin suggests, the activist leader re-interprets in her own language a phrase from the *Argentine National Anthem* (1813), which now gives expression to the community's struggle: 'Let's get on the rafts. Let us enthrone noble equality.' While the original statement invited listeners to the passive acknowledgement of a given order of things, resulting from the construction of the new republic, 'See noble equality enthroned', the new version is a call for action for the social, territorial and political transformation of an order of things that is now untenable, 'Let us enthrone noble equality.'

A new map, a new positioning and a new gaze

Ian Kinane analyses the textual meditations on the Pacific, and the trope of insularity that emerges from there, as part of a hegemonic literary topic, historically generated from a part of Europe and then also from North America. In this sense, he states:

> The trope of the tropical island has continually been recontextualized for Western European and North American audiences through subsequent textual meditations of the Pacific. These meditations, and the sheer volume of texts produced about or set in the Pacific, have scripted Western cultural assumptions about the Pacific region, reinforcing our beliefs in the symbolic import of the island as a place of wish fulfilment, self-betterment.
>
> (2017: 9)

Sarmiento's inaugural move in *Argirópolis* consists of appropriating the European literary topic of the islands – historically conceived in the experience of colonization voyages – to use in his own articulation of the new 'nation'. As critics have pointed out, although Sarmiento does not make it explicit in his text, Thomas More's *Utopia*, among other texts, clearly resonates in his Argirópolis island. If Europe had generated a textual gaze *from* its own continent *towards* the oceans and islands – and towards 'América' (Spanish for 'the Americas') – that huge island to be colonized, as a future territory that would generate greater 'wish fulfilment and self-betterment', Sarmiento reverses that gaze and brings about, for the first time in the Argentine literary tradition, his very own position. And this is the fundamental Sarmientian feat, the act of generating a new map and a new textual gaze, one that mirrors the European gaze and thus reverses the positions from which the oceans, the islands and the continent ('América/the Americas') are thought of and written about. Sarmiento projects his gaze *from* the shores of the Paraná Delta *to* the South Atlantic. From there, he builds a new viewpoint through which he imagines Argirópolis Island as the capital of the Confederate States of the Río de la Plata and as the absolute centre of his civilizing dream.

Martel takes over the challenge of creating a new map and a new gaze, now cinematically, and carries it to an extreme. She imagines New Argirópolis as an 'ownerless island' in perpetual oscillation. Once again, the final two shots condense this movement. In the first one, we hear a murmur of voices and we see, from a panoramic take of the river and its banks, how this space is being occupied by groups that emerge from different directions and make their way towards the river. In the final scene, two Prefecture officers sail the river looking in all directions, as if they were trying to locate the indigenous groups. One of them repeats aloud: 'I hear voices.'

These two scenes synthesize a central conflict in *Nueva Argirópolis*, the poetics of oscillation between *detachment* from the continent in the departure of the groups towards the river, and *absorption* in the image of the officers as a centripetal force of state violence. In this way, Martel invites us to rethink about an unsolved conflict in the Argentine context. 'I hear voices', the final phrase of the short film, is key. On the one hand, it rewrites the Sarmientian nightmare that has traversed Argentina's history up to our time. It functions as that phantasmatic and paranoid construction of the threat of an 'other' – Indian, 'cabecita negra', 'grasa', migrant and more – that has been the basis of the master narrative since the foundation of the nation. On the other hand, 'I hear voices' works cinematically to signal the latent existence of a minimal island or 'small fraction' that, located in some uncertain place in the river, and observed from the banks of the Paraná Delta, could generate a new map, a new positioning and from there, finally, a new gaze.

Notes

1   Indigenous communities of north-eastern Argentina. In the province of Santa Fe, for example, different communities have joined in the QOPIWINI collective, an organization that groups together the Qom, Pilagá, Wichí and Nivaclé communities of the province of Formosa, as a way of seeking their autonomy. See: http://comunidadlaprimavera.blogspot.com; Karl (2011).

2   Martin's book (Martin 2016) is one of the few available analyses of *Nueva Argirópolis*. See also Martin, 'Lucrecia Martel's *Nueva Argirópolis*' (2016), and Aón and Gómez (2012).

3   For a detailed analysis on the history of *unitarios* and *federales*, see Goldman, dir., *Nueva historia* argentina, vols. 3 & 4 (1998).

4   See Amaro Castro (2003) and Villavicencio (2010).

5   Except where so noted, all translations are mine.

6   The Martín García Island has a long history of violence. During the 'campaña del desierto', it operated as a concentration camp where indigenous *caciques* and their families were imprisoned. See Nagi and Papazian (2011).

7   For a more detailed analysis of *Argirópolis* by Sarmiento, see Rezende de Carvalho (2014), Amaro Castro (2003), Villavicencio (2010), Cerutti Guldberg (2007) and Criscenti (1993).

8   In 1969 American indigenous communities moved from San Francisco to Alcatraz island, occupied the old prison in protest for the usurpation of their lands and lived there for two years (Troy 1997).

References

Amaro Castro, L. (2003), 'La América reinventada. Notas sobre la utopía de la "civilización" en *Argirópolis* de Domingo Faustino Sarmiento', *Espéculo*. Available online: http://webs.ucm.es/info/especulo/numero25/argiropo.html.

Aón, L. and L. Gómez (2012), 'Los relatos de la historia en el cine argentino del Bicentenario', *Question* 1.33: 1–9.

Benjamin, W. (1996), 'The Task of the Translator', in *Selected Writings*, I, 253–63, Cambridge: Harvard University Press.

Cerutti Guldberg, H. (2007), *La utopía de nuestra América: de varia utópica, ensayos de utopía III*, Costa Rica: Universidad Nacional de Costa Rica.

La ciénaga (2001), [Film] Dir. Lucrecia Martel. Argentina: Wanda Visión, Cuatro Cabezas.

Comunidad Qom Toba Derqui. Available online: http://www.qom-toba.com.ar/.

Criscenti, J. T. (1993), *Sarmiento and His Argentina*, Boulder: Rienner Publishers.

Deleuze, G. (2003), *Desert Islands and Other Texts*, Los Angeles: Semiotext(e).

Derrida, J. (2011), *The Beast and the Sovereign*, Chicago: The University of Chicago Press.

Goldman, N. (ed.) (1998a), *Nueva historia argentina. III. Revolución, república y confederación (1806-1852)*, Buenos Aires: Sudamericana.

Goldman, N. (ed.) (1998b), *Nueva historia argentina. IV. Liberalismo, estado y orden burgués (1852-1880)*, Buenos Aires: Sudamericana.

James, N. (2018), 'Mistery Is a Constant Fact of Existence', *Sight&Sound* 28.6 (Jun): 35–6.

Johnson, T. (ed.) (1997), *We Hold the Rock. The Indian Occupation of Alcatraz (1969–1971)*, San Francisco: Golden Gate National Parks Conservancy.

Joyce, J. (1964), *Daniel Defoe*, Buffalo: State University of New York Press.

Kapstein, H. (2017), *Postcolonial Nations, Islands, and Tourism. Reading Real and Imagined Spaces*, London: Rowman and Littlefield.

Karl, I. (ed.) (2011), *Una mirada diferente de quiénes somos. Jóvenes Wichi opinan proponen en la comunidad El Potrillo*, Buenos Aires: Ediciones Ciccus.

Kinane, I. (2017), *Theorising Literary Islands. The Islands Trope in Contemporary Robinsonade Narratives*, London: Rowman and Littlefield.

Martel, L. (2013), 'Territorios transitables', in F. Ingrassia (ed.), *Estéticas de la dispersión*, 67–76, Rosario: Beatriz Viterbo.

Martin, D. (2016a), *The Cinema of Lucrecia Martel*, Manchester: Manchester University Press.

Martin, D. (2016b), 'Lucrecia Martel's *Nueva Argirópolis*: Rivers, Rumours and Resistance', *Journal of Latin American Cultural Studies* 25.3: 449–65.

25 miradas, 200 minutos. Los cortos del Bicentenario (2010), [Film] Various directors. Argentina: Secretaría de Cultura, Universidad Tres de Febrero.

Nagi, M. and A. Papazian (2011), 'El campo de concentración de Martín García. Entre el control estatal dentro de la isla y las prácticas de distribución de indígenas', *Corpus* 1.2. Available online: http://ppct.caicyt.gov.ar/index.php/corpus.

Nueva Argirópolis (2010), [Film] Dir. Lucrecia Martel. Argentina: Magma Cine.

Resistencia Qom. La tierra es nuestra vida. Available online: http://qoomih-qom.blogspot.com/.

Rezende de Carvalho, E. (2014), 'La utopía identitaria en *Argirópolis* de Domingo F. Sarmiento', *Tabula Rasa* 21: 247–65.

San Juan Bayón, D. (2018), 'Lucrecia Martel prepara un documental sobre el activista Javier Chocobar', *Otros Cines Europa*, 24 April. Available online: http://www.otroscineseuropa.com/lucrecia-martel-prepara-documental-activista-manuel-chocobar/.

Sarmiento, D. F. ([1850] 1916), *Argirópolis o la capital de los estados confederados del Río de la Plata*, Buenos Aires: La Cultura Argentina.

Villavicencio, S. (2010), '*Argirópolis*: Territorio, República y utopía en la fundación de la nación', *Pilquén* XII.12. Available online: http://www.scielo.org.ar/pdf/spilquen/n12/n12a02.pdf.

Woolf, V. (2001), 'Introduction', in D. Defoe (ed.), *Robinson Crusoe*, New York: Random House.

Zama (2017), [Film] Dir. Lucrecia Martel. Argentina: Cameo.

8

Gustavo Fontán's films:
On faces, spectres, fragments of matter

Laura M. Martins

The only way to envision a new cinema is to have more regard for the spectator's role. It's necessary to envision an unfinished and incomplete cinema so that the spectator can intervene and fill the void, the lacks.

Abbas Kiarostami
(Nancy 2001: 88)

Amanece y ya está con los ojos abiertos.
[Dawn breaks and his eyes are already open]

Juan José Saer
El limonero real, 11
The Regal Lemon Tree, 15

With its 3,000-mile-long alluvial basin in Argentina, the Paraná Delta region that flows north to south across several provinces and empties into another river in the Buenos Aires area, and then into the Atlantic Ocean, is one of the largest in the world, given its trajectories, the volume of its waters, its biodiversity and its fertile terrain. The Paraná River – a name that comes from a Tupi Indian phrase meaning *as big as the sea* – has a unique topography: it is the only river delta on Earth that empties into another river, the estuary of the Río de la Plata.

Its other great distinctive trait resides in the conflicting and paradoxical tension that runs through it, since its islands, rivers, streams and channels belong to an in-between: between the leafy greens and the precarious, the exuberant and the fragile, the overwhelming and the provisional, the immutable and the mobile, the immeasurable and the insignificant. The Paraná Delta, its islands and islets constitute a seismic territory that blurs all boundaries: Where does the water begin? Where is the land erased? Because rising water transfigures it all in a matter of hours in such a space, banks mutate all the time; they become an abyss. This is an unstable area, changing like few others, always threatened by floods. Clear waters with a brownish hue, totally unpredictable, always alter their course and flow. Uncertainty governs this environment filled by contingency. And yet, as I have pointed out, there is also an unavoidable permanence: the flora, the birds, the insects, the fish, the omnipotence of the water – a biodiversity of ecosystems that is home to a colossal number of birds, amphibians, mammals, arboreal species. It is also a vast, wide, immense scenario that demands of the inhabitant, settled or transitory, a gaze focused on the small or the insignificant: a drop of rain that hangs from the leaf of a willow, a ray of light on the water, the texture of a tree trunk, the shape of a branch. Alberto Muñoz, the Argentine poet, musician and scriptwriter, offers a convincing poetic definition of the Delta region: 'The island isolates, repels, eats everything with its maw of soil and roots, but that animal is the one we love' (Esses 2015).[1]

Of the theorizing and diverse representations pertaining to the topic of islands, Graziadei et al. have observed:

Discussions of islands in literary and cultural studies frequently gravitate towards the meaning of islands and discuss islands as either supremely meaningful and knowable spaces [...] tracing their associations with concepts such as *isolation* [...], *paradise* [...], *antithetical counter-spaces* [...] and *spaces of colonial control* [...] or as *spaces that resist meaning* [...]. Thus, Chris Bongie [...] suggests that 'the island is a figure that can and must be read in more than one way.' Rod Edmond and Vanessa Smith [...] view the island as 'the most graspable and the most slippery of subjects,' while Ottmar Ette [...] views it as a site of semantic oscillation. While these discussions have added much to our understanding of the metaphorical and conceptual appeal of islands in the Western imagination, they have obscured the multilayered experiences of islands conveyed by island narratives. *These discussions have perhaps emphasized textual structure at the expense of sensory, corporeal, and material textures of islands in different media.*

(2017: 240; my emphasis)

I would like to focus on some films by Argentine Director Gustavo Fontán, mainly *El rostro* [The Face] (2014) and *El limonero real* [The Regal Lemon Tree] (2017) that deal with the Paraná Delta region to capture precisely the sensory, corporeal and material textures of islands.[2] In Fontán's films, islands mark a displacement and blurring of objects and human figures in such a way that viewers are left with only contemplation. As I will describe in greater detail later, these films translate the rawness of the world's materiality into a *poetic mode*. What are those faces, sounds and images of an ecosystem that Fontán is chasing after? Are they images of a dream? Are they ghosts? What do those new sounds tell us? In what follows, I will address these questions, emphasizing that Fontán's films foreground living entities: rivers, trees, insects, birds, a girl playing with a red umbrella, a fisherman cooking a fresh fish he just caught, a man diving into a river while escaping from anguish and pain. By filming the islands of the Paraná Delta, Fontán, on the one hand, engages with the literary pieces that he is very interested in 'translating' into cinematic form (for instance, Juan L. Ortiz's poetry or Juan José Saer's novel *El limonero real*), and, on the other, his cinema immerses itself into what it means to inhabit these islands: it takes the senses on a journey (an unparalleled experience of the visible, the audible and other sensorial impressions) and captures the observable tension of living in a land that is constantly changing due to the seismic movement provoked by persistent rains, winds, floods. The constant of Fontán's films consists in registering discreet occurrences, the world in its becoming, a peculiar glance at moving matter, a sound that does not duplicate the diegesis but instead compounds it, by existing independently of the image. Fontán locates the poetic (and therefore political) resolutions of his filmography in the slight disconnection between image and sound. This non-synchronicity between sound and image reveals hidden meanings that will be examined later.

In the end, by filming (in) the islands, through the camera's insistent wandering, Fontán weaves a poetics of haptic space; the camera sometimes pauses this wandering to examine a seemingly trivial detail that becomes special in the pausing. Laura Marks and Giuliana Bruno have theorized about the cinematic in ways that explore its tactile or haptic appeal. *Haptic visuality*, as Donato Totaro adequately summarizes it, is defined as containing some of the following formal and textual qualities: grainy, unclear images; sensuous

174   *The Film Archipelago*

imagery that evokes memory of the senses (e.g. water, nature); close-to-the-body camera positions and panning across the surface of objects; changes in focus, under- and overexposure; images produced through decaying film and video imagery. 'The haptic image is in a sense, "less complete," requiring the viewer to contemplate the image as a material presence rather than an easily identifiable representational cog in a narrative wheel' (Totaro 2002). Keeping this haptic frame in mind, now I would like to stroll over to and through the poetic-cinematic in order to approach Fontán's films.

The poetic-cinematic

Fontán's films are poetic. Now, what is 'the poetic-cinematic'? To understand the link between the two, I had initially thought that long takes enabled me to contemplate the astonishing celebration of the unity of the living. Long takes exhibit a canvas, or a sensible membrane, that allow me to discover the poetic, that is, I was able to observe in them the power of suggestion, the power of something that remains incomplete and invites me to intervene. However, when I came across the short film *The Inhabitants* (1970, nine minutes) by Armenian Director Artavazd Peleshian, a film whose brief, speedy shots result in a poetic film, I realized that the poetic does not depend only on the duration of the shots, but rather on the *intensification of the sensorial experience*. Both poetry and the poetic-cinematic are housed in the indeterminate, preserve indescribability, and are not comprehensible through transparent logical equivalencies. But who can demarcate and characterize the cinematic dimension, or specify what poetry is when poetry has flowed through us since time immemorial?[3] The following body of reflections about two of Fontán's films puts forward an approach to the poetic-cinematic. This approach is necessarily provisional and does not aspire to be complete or to encompass every aspect at play.

The poetic-cinematic is not a language/mode that designates or defines by emphasizing things. Rather, it flashes like a spark, it produces resonances, luminescences that make it possible for us to apprehend (see, feel, sense), for a moment, something of the flow of the world. It is a small puncturing into that which is different, forgotten, that which is surprising or had remained unnoticed up until then. In this cinematic mode of filmmaking, something which is known can be observed or contemplated as if it were unknown, in an activity that endeavours to un-tame our gaze or to debunk certainties that have become fossilized. Although Georges Didi-Huberman refers to spaces of insurgency and resistance that emerge to confront the current capitalist catastrophe, the poetic-cinematic can be found in a cinema of fireflies, as opposed to 'reflectors', a term through which Didi-Huberman alludes to the spotlights of 'lookouts and observation towers, those of political shows, football stadiums, and television studios' (2012: 36) in a cinema of affection and respect for all the living entities and for spectators. The poetic-cinematic resides in that which intensifies our sensory experience, that which stimulates the deep inventiveness of the ear (as Robert Bresson wished) in the possibility of opening a small incision that can re-sensitize our way of seeing the world (1979: 76).[4] When a sound engineer records the vibration of the rain falling on wicker to offer us a storm on the delta, when this engineer creates, in a more abstract way, another storm composed of the sounds of the throwaway recordings of winds, we find in these sound-images something of the poetic, as sound takes on a dimension of its own, instead of operating as a mere duplication of the diegesis.[5] The dearth of words makes way for voices and evocative sounds. These operations carried out in Fontán's films multiply the possibilities of the gaze. They produce a full experience of *seeing* and *listening*. As Roger Koza has accurately posited, '[Fontán's camera] is the invention of a [gaze] and it creates a shot for which we don't even have a name yet' (2016a).

In *The Material Ghost*, Gilberto Perez maintains that 'the projector, the magic lantern, animates the track of light with its own light, brings the imprint of life to new life on the screen. The images on the screen carry in them something of the world itself, something material, and yet something transposed, transformed into another world: *the material ghost*' (1998: 28; my emphasis). Perez's account applies to Fontán's films. Considering the paradoxical tension that defines the delta, the features of life on the islands all facilitate a poetic approach: the persistent force of the water and its unpredictability, the perception of not feeling that our feet are on solid ground, the constant movement of effective but miniscule earthquakes of the elements, and the blurriness or spectrality of the environment produced by the haze and the rain all facilitate a poetic approach. Thus, within Argentine cinematographic

176   *The Film Archipelago*

productions, Fontán's films loom as *islands* themselves, where we see both the camera and the rivers flowing into something new, *isolated* in its uniqueness.

His films set out on a quest that hovers between the senses and matter. I am referring to a *modus operandi* that consists of deactivating the plot in order to activate a dialogue between images and spectators. Such a *modus operandi* makes the spectators seek, observe, stop at what s/he feels compelled to respond sensibly, to touch, to palpate, that is to say the *haptic*.[6] The haptic refers to a mutual con*tact* between the spectator and the 'environment'; it refers to the body's capacity to feel its own movement in space (Bruno 2002: 6). According to Marks, the *haptic gaze* prompts the caressing of the surface of image:

> While optical perception privileges the representational power of the image, *haptic perception* privileges the material presence of the image […]. *Haptic visuality* involves the body more than is the case with optical visuality. Touch is a sense located on the surface of the body: thinking of cinema as haptic is only a step toward considering the ways cinema appeals to the body as a whole.
>
> (2000: 163)

Fontán's films *demand* something from us: they do not function via narration but through a voluntary and fundamental *perceptive will* that intensifies our sensorial experience of images and sound. Cinema, as Argentine writer María Negroni affirms with respect to poetry, is 'a hallucinatory way of knowing. A trip taken without any kind of protection to the realm of dreams, that place where it is forbidden to move backwards and where the question "why?" makes no sense' (2016).

El rostro

El rostro and *El limonero real* are punctuated by a very peculiar conjunction of image and sound: words are scarce, but many hypnotic voices can be heard, vibrations of the landscape, uncertainties of the (in)visible. It is not a difficult task to relate the discreet action in *El rostro*: a man is rowing a boat until he reaches one of the islands of the Paraná Delta.

Once he steps on firm ground, he encounters fishermen, a woman, children, dogs, other human beings and nature that speaks with its own voices: buzzing, roars, humming, murmurs, the singing waves of water. In the end, the farewell. This man returns to who knows where, just as we do not know where he came from. The habitat is lined with trees, plants, soil and, above all, water exposed in its melodiousness, in its repetitiveness, in its vaporous condition: we see fragments of matter that construct images. In *La orilla que se abisma*, *El rostro* and *El limonero real*, all of which are part of the so called 'Cycle of the River', or we should say more accurately 'Cycle of the Paraná Delta', Fontán builds a sort of botanical catalogue or barometric eroticism where the waters copulate with the trembling soil, the insects with their wandering from leaf to leaf, the wind with all that it touches and blows along. In all three films, the camera delights in touring the abundant and diverse species of trees, the reverberations of the water, the creaking of the wood on a boat, the mist that smooths contours. All images are sparsely accompanied by words (or rather, by *voices*). And this economic restraint, among other things, yields to the *textural* (the haptic) nature of the cinematographic image (as opposed to the *referential* value of it). The eye of the camera lingers as much on these infinite inhabitants of the islands and the immense river as on the *textures:* the ripples of the water, the strange shapes of the trunks and branches. The camera captures the reverberations of water hyacinths, ferns and willows, and all kinds of floating beings.

El rostro begins like a documentary experience – a man who rows while he observes the aquatic and vegetal landscape – which it then transforms into a

Figure 8.1 Reaching one of the islands in *El rostro*.

poetic experience: Does what we see belong to the order of dreams, memories or is it a world already gone? Its brief account seems to tell a chronology, but time is an abyss because it is a present inhabited precisely by the past, or dreams, or memories. The memory is like a ghost: Does the man who arrives meet with extinct beings? In both *El rostro* and *El limonero real*, the experience of inhabiting the islands involves a memory and an imminence because life is always in tension. But this mode of inhabiting is marked by permanent contact with the natural and by the ancestral knowledge of this world: the river's movements, its courses, its transformations, its strength and unpredictability, or the experience of fishing on that river. The islands do not offer stability: the sensation of being on *terra firma* vanishes in a haze as does the characteristic haze of sunrises on rivers. Fontán synthesizes as follows what he proposes in *El rostro*: 'The face is therefore not the face of this place, it is not the face of this particular man, but *the face of this way of inhabiting islands*' (Girardi and Pinto 2019; my emphasis).

The organizing 'poetic principle', as Fontán calls it, in this particular case, is the *phantasmagoric*. The film's present transcends towards another time. Therefore, the sound and the image do not exist within the same temporality, even though they are in the same space. There is a drift of time and a drift of sound, since cinema works with perception, words here are not clear because, when they are clear, they tend to anchor meaning. Here, we attend to the word as only a sound image, a murmur or whisper, sometimes barely audible. Fontán's aspiration consists of carefully observing daily living and giving us time to observe, to contemplate, and by doing so, allowing it to transform into something else: a woman who walks can be young and then can become older, as if a luminescence, spots of sunlight in the environment, produces minor mutations. Our gaze anchors itself beyond appearances.

In *El rostro*, nature and rumours appear in amplified sound: an oar that splits the water, some steps on dry leaves or detached branches, voices that do not coincide with the movement of the lips but create a poetic intonation, because sound is not present to function as a mere duplicator of diegesis. Sound does not intensify or illustrate: it is rather an *addition*; it becomes *emancipated* from the image. Thus, we are seeing an audiovisual choreography. The instability of the territory of the islands has its formal echo in the disjunction between the visual image and the sound. Like the artisan and poet that he is, Fontán operates here with black and white in different formats (Super 8, 16mm, expired 16mm, and video with digital editing). It is an aesthetic-political decision, since he films this way due to his idea of time that the film portrays, that is to say, time as drift. From Fontán, we cannot expect a narrative or a traditional story with its characters and dialogues, with their psychological construction and defined spaces. That is, we do not expect a story in conventional terms (non-conflicting situation + appearance of conflict + plot twist + outcome/resolution), nor does our experience of the film rely on chronological sequence. The images present something that traverses memory and sleep, without dialogue. But from Fontán we do expect the primacy of the senses, an experience that is lodged in the sensible certainty of being in the world and being part of something that surpasses us. Fontán films splinters of the world: a boat, a man who rows, water, a dog, faces, ranches, bodies, the meticulous cutting of a fish. Those fragments must be transformed into a vision. 'The experience is not necessarily contact with things that are immensely far from us. On the contrary, it is the immersion *in the contiguous*' (Fontán 2018, my emphasis). So, *El rostro* has nothing to do with a particular human figure; rather, it constructs that way of inhabiting. And the fragmentations (filming those splinters of the world) embody one of Fontán's formal operations, echoing what it implies to inhabit the islands: the unsteady, the uncertain, the imminent. The defiance of *El rostro* consists of – as Silva Rey claims – 'placing right in front of our eyes, for one hour, *that lightning that is our life*: "proofs, feelings, sketches, drafts [...]" without order, without beginning or end' (Silva Rey 2014; my emphasis).[7]

El limonero real

In the 'background' of the film *El limonero real* lies the homonymous novel (1974) by Argentine writer Juan José Saer. Yet, the film is not an adaptation: cinema here demonstrates how the trace left by a story can be picked up. It is true that, through his training in literature, Fontán extracts cinematographic reflections from literature. His approach to the Santa Fe writer does not ignore the compounding fragments of Saer's novels, which are configured as cinema and montage. By approaching Saer's *El limonero real*, Fontán has us enter the island landscape, the tensions of this habitat: between life and death, where

Figure 8.2 Mourning in the islands in *El limonero real*.

islands offer us a perpetual sensation of the diffused and foggy (the mist, the rain and the steaminess of water). And the soil is presented like quicksand, always waiting for an imminent flood. Again, we see islands, water, boats, foliage, men who are rowing, women, children, horses, dogs and some ranches. *He*, Wenceslao, the husband, goes to a gathering with family and friends from other islands to celebrate New Year's Eve. *She*, his unnamed wife, remains at her home on one of the many islands because she continues to mourn the death of her son six years earlier.

Wenceslao feels, and says, that it is he who should have died, not his young son. At a certain moment he dives into the water and swims. He sinks but we do not know if he tries to die by drowning or not. At night, dinner, dancing, faces and wind intermingle. After celebrating the arrival of the New Year, Wenceslao returns by boat, rowing in the dark. We see nothing, but hear only the rhythmic cadences between water, oars and breathing. In the dark night our senses perceive: his physical work, the human being, the environment. Fontán would appear to share Robert Bresson's idea that the eye in general is superficial; the ear, however, is profound and inventive. According to the French filmmaker, the whistle of a train imprints on us an entire station. Fontán gives us access to what is not shown but which we *see* because our ears allow us to. Time appears free of teleology, of totality; it appears as a constant becoming. 'Fontán lets us see what is not meant to be shown' (Oubiña 2016b). The grieving and the continuation of life by choice are not spoken; *they are felt*.[8] Because, what is grief, if not a constant stumble, a feeling that you cannot step on firm ground, a permanent evasion of falling or sinking into the dark depths of a deep and opaque river? Islands and grief coincide ontologically. However, the pain due to the absence of a loved one and Wenceslao's own continuation among the living are not spoken either but rather perceived: his sinking into the golden water of the river triggers in us his affliction. We *feel* his dejection. This is an epistemology of feeling as understood by Marks (in the suggestion that the gaze is tactile): 'Haptic visuality implies making oneself vulnerable to the image, reversing the relation of mastery that characterizes optical viewing' (2000: 185). In this sense, we must take into account what Bruno also maintains:

> Places and affects are produced jointly, in the movement of a superficial projection between interior and exterior landscape. Affects not only are makers of space but are themselves configured as space, and they have the actual texture of atmosphere. To sense a mood is to be sensitive to a subtle atmospheric shift that couches persons across air space. In this way, motion creates emotion and, reciprocally, emotion contains a movement that becomes communicated. It is not by chance that we say we are 'moved.' Emotion itself moves, and the language of emotion relies on the terminology of motion. To address this language involves a tangible redressing of visual space, because the affect is not a static picture and cannot be reduced to optical paradigms or imagined in terms of optical devices and metaphors. *The landscape of affective mediation is material: it is made of haptic fabrics, moving atmospheres, and transitive fabrications.*
>
> (2014: 19; my emphasis)

The haptic cinema of Gustavo Fontán refers to the materiality of small gestures, minimal events. It refers to the discreet. To him, knowledge is corporeal, not hermeneutic. Perhaps we need to return to what Susan Sontag maintained in 1966 in *Against Interpretation*, that, instead of a hermeneutics of art, we need an *erotics of art*.[9] In general, we, as readers/spectators, are characterized by the possession of a hermeneutic compulsion through which we desire to understand and, therefore, interpret texts/films with

Figure 8.3 Diving into the river to escape from lacerating pain in *El limonero real*.

the expectation of unravelling their meanings. A compulsion that if, when facing words/images, not satisfied, leaves us mired in the dissatisfaction of a fervently pursued desire. Such an epistemological anxiety, generated by the frustrated desire to elucidate meanings in order to soothe ourselves, exposes not only something about the order of certain anxieties and, therefore, something about the order of immediacy, but also a major problem that refers to the naturalization of a reading experience/audio-viewing experience that is a learned training – that is to say, an experience that alludes to the existence of a hegemonic narrative that has imposed the necessity of a story punctuated by suspense, enigmas and ellipses. Due to this normalization, it is difficult for us, for example, to realize that the human figures and landscape in Fontán's films facilitate the advancement of time, not of action. Confusion and disorientation are sensations that emerge from the proclivity of a text/film to suspend its meanings. We feel as though we are stripped of our ability to interpret when we are disabled from deciphering films that lack plot progression, that expose the dissolution of characters. We prefer to interpret, instead of experiencing the image in our bodies or encountering the materiality of the image itself in order to observe how we perceive. This sensitive experience of the spectator with that materiality of the image makes it possible for us to see Fontán's films.

What, then, do islands mean in Gustavo Fontán's films?

First, I have aimed here to characterize some of the peculiar features of the 'poetic-cinematic': that which suggests an intensified sensory experience, the possibility of contemplating a feverish state of vision and the principle of indeterminacy that would govern this state. It is that which allows us to multiply the possibilities of the gaze and those of hearing – through those wide eyes that are our ears – that which moves and affects us from the ineffable margin of images. As the poetic is undecidable and indescribable, each of Fontán's films actualizes or characterizes the contours of the poetic-cinematic. Each one exhibits, in its singularity, the poetic-cinematic elements within that dimension of images. In this, I subscribe to the pertinent observations of David Oubiña about the cinema of Abbas Kiarostami: 'If it were possible to determine a fundamental feature of the poetic-cinematic, one would have to seek it out in those places where the impossibility of tracing in the image an accord between take and concept, would itself makes this distinction useless' (2016a).

Secondly, Fontán's approach connects him to James Bennings' ways of understanding cinema:

> The mere exercise of our *raw senses seems almost radical*: a veritable '*total minimal situation*,' as the artist and filmmaker Ryan Trecartin would put it. But it is *looking* and *listening* that have been at the core of Benning's filmmaking practice since it began in 1971. Though we typically consider these tasks of the viewer in the cinematic scenario, Benning challenges this convention, *showing us how looking and listening can serve to defy the stasis of passivity* [...]. *Our senses come alive to the subtlety of detail contained within the frame, and the whole it forms.*
>
> ('On the road' 2016; my emphasis)

And, third, if my purpose is correct in presenting some of the distinctions that make cinema poetic, I find in Fontán's filmography, fundamentally located in the Paraná Delta, a conspiracy against dehumanization. In late capitalism, we are witnessing the proof of the real destruction of many things: our environment severely degraded and overexploited, the adoption of extractivist policies, the mass killings and massacres, the persecution of minorities, the increasing precariousness of our lives and so on, and, at the same time, among so much predation, we realize that if there is art, there is life. And with Fontán we find ourselves before a *mobilizing* gaze. His films are imperative because they urge us to look and listen, to be capable of coming in con*tact* with what we see/we hear, not to expect clear outcomes or soothing closures, instead to experience the materiality of the world, a way of corporeal knowing through which we stop at the fragile, the discreet, the tenuous: the cutting of a fish, the disassembling of a boat plank by plank (*El rostro*), the grazing of a horse, the plunge of a suffering man into the water bathed by sunlight (*El limonero real*). Ultimately, the films propitiate a sensible and emotional encounter with the world and, here in particular, with the Paraná Delta ecosystem and its unique bio-geographic characteristics. By inviting us to see and feel life in the deltas, which are some of the most fragile ecological habitats to protect, these films encourage us to feel and think as a decisive instrument for collective survival.

Notes

1   This image also invokes the idea of landscape as a physical archive in the sense that there are social relations stored within it, or as Andermann points out: 'the way in which the landscape, for being a cultural means of perception and representation of space (like – or through – places), is also the mediator between the social relationships and human politics and the non-human environment' (2008: 5). Historically, the Paraná Delta became a refuge for sexual exiles (gay couples) and for left-wing militants during the seventies and eighties. All translations from Spanish to English are mine, unless otherwise indicated.

2   His filmography until now, in short, mid-length and long films, consists of *Luz de otoño* (1992), *Canto del cisne* (1994), *Ritos de paso* (1997), *Marechal, o la batalla de los ángeles* (2001), *Donde cae el sol* (2002), *El paisaje invisible* (2003), *El árbol* (2006), *La orilla que se abisma* (2008), *La madre* (2009), *Elegía de abril* (2010), *La casa* (2012), *Sol en un patio vacío* (2014), *Sucesos intervenidos* (2014), *El rostro* (2014), *Lluvias* (2015), *El día nuevo* (2016), *El estanque* (2016), *El día nuevo* (2016), *El limonero real* (2016) and *La deuda* (2019). With *El rostro* and *El limonero real* Fontán culminates the 'Cycle of the River' that had started with *La orilla que se abisma* [The River Bank that Becomes an Abyss], which is about the

universe of poet Juan L. Ortiz, resident of one of the numerous rivers that make up the Paraná Delta. Pertaining to *La orilla que se abisma* (2008) and *La casa* (2012), see Martins (2014) and Depetris Chauvin (2017, 2018).

3　These questions take up the reflections that I put forward in Martins (2019).

4　In this regard, Koza maintains the following: 'The *indetermination* that characterizes poetry is related to the very distinct way in which the poet labors *with* and *on* language, and where language hints through specific areas of sensibility, through some specific ways of experiencing the world and emotions. It is in that undetermined place that poetic language is located. The language of cinema is treated in similar ways and it is in this sense that we find a cinema of poetry instead of a cinema of prose (a basic distinction made by the great Pasolini), where, once again, there is an indetermination of all the elements that are combined in the mise-en-scène.' Radio call-in with Koza in his program 'La oreja de Bresson' (University of Córdoba, Argentina, April 2016) following an email that I had sent to him regarding the poetic-cinematic.

5　These poetic uses of sound are what Fontán accomplishes in *La orilla que se abisma* (2008).

6　*Haptic*, from the Greek, means 'capable of coming in contact with'. Marks (2000) and Bruno (2002) propose an approach that bypasses the 'optic gaze' and the 'ocular focus', which have been at the centre of cinematographic canonical criticism.

7　Also, as Lingenti assures, 'Fontán has explained before that in his films he tries to expose the raw recording of his encounters with the world. His roughness/ rawness has nothing to do with the mimetic reproduction of reality but rather with the awareness that films have the capacity to reuse those fragments for the benefit of a poetic vision. That is what *El rostro* sets out to do' (Lingenti 2014).

8　Roger Koza (2017) observes this as well.

9　With this, I do not mean to ignore or annul correspondences between erotics and hermeneutics. I have also engaged with Sontag in Martins (2011: 406–7).

References

Andermann, J. (2008), 'Paisaje: imagen, entorno, ensamble', *Orbis Tertius* 13.14: 1–7.

Bresson, R. (1979), *Notas sobre el cinematógrafo*, Mexico: Nueva Era.

Bruno, G. (2002), *Atlas of Emotion: Journeys in Art, Architecture, and Film*, New York: Verso.

186 The Film Archipelago

Bruno, G. (2014), *Surface: Matters of Aesthetics, Materiality, and Media*, Chicago: University of Chicago Press.

Depetris Chauvin, I. (2017), 'Mirar y escuchar. Percepción háptica y narrativa sensorial en *El limonero real* (2016) de Gustavo Fontán', *TOMAUNO* 6 (2017–2018): 140–51.

Depetris Chauvin, I. (2018), 'Percepción háptica y narrativa sensorial en el "ciclo del río" de Gustavo Fontán', *Cuadernos de literatura* XXII.4 (July–December): 36–62.

Didi-Huberman, G. (2012), *Supervivencia de las luciérnagas*, trans. J. Calatrava, Madrid: Abada.

Esses, C. (2015), 'Paisajes. El Delta poético: un refugio natural para la literatura', *La Nación*, 15 October. Available online: https://www.lanacion.com.ar/opinion/el-delta-poetico-un-refugio-natural-para-la-literatura-nid1838810/ (accessed 30 April 2021).

Fontán, G. (2014), 'Sol en un patio vacío', 7 August, Available online: http://gustavo-fontan.blogspot.com/2014/08/sol-en-un-patio-vacio-3.html (accessed 12 September 2018).

Fontán, G. (2018), 'La casa del cineasta. Ver por primera vez', *Con los ojos abiertos. Críticas, crónicas de festivales y apuntes sobre cine*, 20 June. Available online: http://www.conlosojosabiertos.com/la-casa-del-cineasta-mirar-primera-vez/ (accessed 12 September 2018).

Girardi, A. and I. Pinto (2019), 'Gustavo Fontán, cineasta. 'La única responsabilidad es ser honesto y coherente con la propia película', http://www.lafuga.cl/gustavo-fontan-cineasta/734 (accessed 3 November 2019).

Graziadei, D., B. Hartmann, I. Kinane, J. Riquet and B. Samson (2017), 'On Sending Island Spaces and the Spatial Practice of Island-Making: Introducing Island Poetics, Part I', *Island Studies Journal* 12.2 (2017): 239–52.

Koza, R. (2016a), 'A Shot That Plunges. The Cinema of Gustavo Fontán', *Con los ojos abiertos. Críticas, crónicas de festivales y apuntes sobre cine*, 21 July. Available online: http://www.conlosojosabiertos.com/a-shot-tha-plunges-the-cinema-of-gustavo-fontan/ (accessed 11 September 2018).

Koza, R. (2016b), 'De la buena glosa cinematográfica: un diálogo sobre *El limonero real* con Gustavo Fontán', *Con los ojos abiertos. Críticas, crónicas de festivales y apuntes sobre cine*, 1 September. Available online: http://www.conlosojosabiertos.com/de-la-buena-glosa-cinematografica-un-dialogo-sobre-el-limonero-real-con-gustavo-fontan/ (accessed 27 Sept. 2018).

Koza, R. (2017), '*El limonero real*', *Con los ojos abiertos. Críticas, crónicas de festivales y apuntes sobre cine*, 24 January. Available online: http://www.conlosojosabiertos.com/limonero-real-04/ (accessed 11 September 2018).

El limonero real (2016), [Film] Dir. Gustavo Fontán, Argentina: Insomnia Films.

Lingenti, A. (2014), '*El rostro*', *La Nación*, 4 April. Available online: https://www.lanacion.com.ar/1677913-el-rostro (accessed 26 September 2018).

Marks, L. (2000), *The Skin of the Film. Intercultural Cinema, Embodiment, and the Senses*, Durham: Duke University Press.

Martins, L. M. (2011), 'En contra de contar historias. Cuerpos e imágenes hápticas en el cine argentino (Lisandro Alonso y Lucrecia Martel)', *Revista de crítica literaria latinoamericana* XXXVII.73: 401–20.

Martins, L. M. (2014), 'Contra la museificación del mundo: *La orilla que se abisma* (2008) y *La casa* (2012) de Gustavo Fontán', *Studies in Spanish & Latin American Cinemas* 11.2: 167–77.

Martins, L. M. (2019), 'Algunas consideraciones sobre lo poético cinematográfico', *Revista Icónica. Pensamiento fílmico*, 24 September. Available online: http://revistaiconica.com/algunas-consideraciones-sobre-lo-poetico-cinematografico/c (accessed 4 September 2019).

Nancy, J. L. (2001), *L'evidence du film: Abbas Kiarostami*, Brussels: Yves Gevaert.

Negroni, M. (2016), 'Un saber alucinatorio', *Eterna Cadencia*, 25 July. Available online: https://www.eternacadencia.com.ar/blog/ficcion/item/un-saber-alucinatorio.html (accessed 27 September 2018).

'On the Road: James Benning's Landscape Cinema' (2016), *Ran Dian* 3, 18 August. Available online: http://www.randian-online.com/np_feature/james-bennings-landscape-cinema/ (accessed 28 September 2018).

La orilla que se abisma (2008), [Film] Dir. Gustavo Fontán, Argentina: Insomnia Films.

Oubiña, D. (2016a), 'Abbas Kiarostami: la mirada precaria', *Revista Invisibles* 4.17 (July). Available online: http://www.revistainvisibles.com/abbas-kiarostami-por-david-oubina.html (accessed 23 November 2019).

Oubiña, D. (2016b), 'Lo inefable', *Con los ojos abiertos. Críticas, crónicas de festivales yapuntes sobre cine*, 29 August. Available online: http://www.conlosojosabiertos.com/?s=David+Oubi%C3%B1a+Limonero+real (accessed 23 November 2019).

Perez, G. (1998), *The Material Ghost. Films and Their Medium*, Baltimore: Johns Hopkins University Press.

El rostro (2014), [Film] Dir. Gustavo Fontán, Argentina: Insomnia Films.

Saer, J. J. ([1974] 2002), *El limonero real*, Buenos Aires: Seix Barral.

Saer, J. J. ([1974] 2020), *The Regal Lemon Tree*, trans. S. Waisman, Rochester: Open Letter.

Silva Rey, A. (2014), 'Acerca de *El rostro*, película de Gustavo Fontán, estrenada en el BAFICI 2014'. Available online: http://gustavo-fontan.blogspot.com/2014/05/acerca-de-el-rostro-pelicula-de-gustavo.html (accessed 11 September 2018).

Sontag, S. (1966), *Against Interpretation, and Other Essays*, New York: Farrar, Straus & Giroux.

Totaro, D. (2002), 'Deleuzian Film Analysis. The Skin of the Film', *Off Screen* 6.6. Available online: https://offscreen.com/view/skin_of_film (accessed 27 November 2019).

Part Three

Antillean relations on screen

9

The duplicitous empire:
Ambiguous representations of Puerto Ricans and Japanese-Americans in Herbert I. Leeds's *Mr. Moto in Danger Island* (1939)

Naida García-Crespo

Twentieth Century Fox's *Mr. Moto in Danger Island* was part of an eight-piece series of murder-mystery films, spanning from 1937 to 1939, featuring Peter Lorre as the title character, Mr. Moto.[1] Lorre portrayed a Japanese-American detective with great strength hidden under a small physique, who solved crimes using deductive techniques similar to those of Sherlock Holmes – thus, he was a copy of the popular Chinese-American detective Charlie Chan (Thomas 2012: 67). Although Mr Moto and his band of sympathetic, supporting characters were firmly rooted in the United States, many of the films in the series took place in 'treacherous' foreign locations like Thailand, Egypt, China and, in the case of the film discussed in this chapter, Puerto Rico. The plot of *Mr. Moto in Danger Island* revolves around the investigation of the murder of a local police commissioner by a gang of diamond smugglers and the inability of the Puerto Rican government to solve the crime. Through well-known detective conventions (multiple suspects, double crossings, violent encounters, etc.) the film works to promote a traditionalist vision of the necessity for a very involved system of law and order.

In this chapter, I argue that the film's combination of a Japanese-American detective with a criminal, Caribbean island setting signals to growing tensions inside the United States regarding ethnic diversity and the performance of 'proper' masculinity among its population in the midst of the 'Good Neighbor' years. In 1936, fearing how the global changes of the decade affected the United

States' military and economic status, President Franklin D. Roosevelt made his famous 'Good Neighbor' proclamation, in which he vowed to steer his country away from armed intervention in the Americas. This change in policy, from hard to soft power, from military to culture wars, involved the prolonged dissemination of cultural messages that simultaneously distinguished the American character and marked the country as a saviour. Therefore, American popular culture effectively became state policy, consciously reflecting trends that had already been brewing for decades.

With its representation of immigrants, non-white populations and US colonial spaces, *Mr. Moto in Danger Island* worked to concurrently include ethnic others into Hollywood's arsenal of representation and define them as foreign or improperly American. In this way, as I will show, the film reflects the contradictory discourses regarding inclusion and exclusion present in US political discussions during the first half of the twentieth century. More specifically, discourses in popular culture regarding immigrant populations (like the ones presented in this film) paradoxically demanded the new community members' complete assimilation into US traditions at the same time that both legally and socially, state institutions excluded immigrants from economic, political and cultural opportunities.

Historicizing the colony

The absorption of the islands of Puerto Rico, the Philippines and Guam following the Spanish-American War and the 1898 Treaty of Paris brought new peoples into the discussion of what should be considered an American citizen (Erman 2019). Although the main character in this film, Mr. Moto, is Japanese (thus not a colonial subject), the US discussions regarding the new island colonies, like the film's setting of Puerto Rico, resembled in many ways those that related to Asian immigrants. Therefore, the film's placing of an Asian immigrant within a tropical setting is actually a logical derivative from contemporary political debates. As was the case with Chinese and Japanese-Americans, and the Exclusion Acts enacted during the turn of the twentieth century, the national debates regarding colonial immigration from the tropics were played out on the legal realm in what came to be known as the Insular Cases (Lowe 1996).

The Insular Cases were a series of legal battles dealing with the ability of the newly colonial subjects from Puerto Rico, the Philippines and Guam to immigrate to the US mainland and their citizenship status. Using arguments reminiscent of, and sometimes directly related to, the cases that lead to the Chinese Exclusion Act of 1882, the US Congress ultimately decided not to extend full citizenship rights to the peoples of the newly incorporated territories. Particularly in the case of Puerto Rico, as Edgardo Meléndez lucidly argues, 'one of the most lasting consequences of the Insular Cases has been to sustain the notion that Puerto Ricans, although U.S. citizens since 1917, are "alien" to the U.S.' (2013: 113). Ultimately, through the Insular Cases, Congress decided that geographic location (the colonial space) trumped the legal status of the natives (having American citizenship) when it came to defining the colonized subject's constitutional rights (2013: 130). Specifically, in *Balzac vs. People of Puerto Rico* the Court infamously ruled that 'it is locality that is determinative of the application of the Constitution in such matters as judicial procedure, and not the status of the people who live in it'. Thus, the colonial land came to stand in for the dangerous shortfalls of Puerto Ricans and therefore their inability to be trusted as proper nationals. *Mr. Moto in Danger Island*'s vacillation between presenting Puerto Rico as a lawless, perilous location and a savable American burden consequently follows a historical, cultural and legal tradition relating to immigration and colonialism.

Accordingly, the portrayal of Puerto Rico in US popular culture, historically, has been tied to the US military presence on the island as a consequence of the Spanish-American War. Indeed, the first cinematic representations of the island were staged vignettes like *How the Porto Rican Girls Entertain Uncle Sam's Soldiers* or actualities like *Washing the Streets of Porto Rico*, which portrayed aspects of the military occupation that followed the 1898 invasion (García-Crespo 2019: 47–55). The early discussions of the United States' expanding empire in the Caribbean and Pacific, to which these films contributed, often portrayed the island colonies as uncivilized and in need of careful tutelage. Under this discursive line, as Camilla Fojas argues, 'the people of Cuba, Puerto Rico, the Philippines, and Hawai'i ... were depicted as childlike and immature and thus incapable of self-rule. They were infantilized subjects awaiting the directives and salubrious influence of the colonial master from

194 *The Film Archipelago*

the United States' (2014:199). As part of this imperial rhetoric, throughout the first decades of the twentieth century, the major film producers in the United States consistently portrayed or used Puerto Rico as a generic tropical island location where white characters were seduced (by either the land or the natives) and subsequently redeemed by a fellow white saviour. Melodramatic films such as *Heart and Soul* (1917) and *Aloma of the South Seas* (1926) exemplify the paradoxical colonial anxiety of both desiring and fearing the tropics. For decades, in popular culture, Puerto Rico continued to serve as a problematic site of criminality hidden under beautifully lush tropical flora and seductive natives. By the end of the 1930s, when the outbreak of war became a real threat and Puerto Rico's strategic military position regained significance, American representations of its island empire exhibited heightened concerns about the United States' control of these locations and their populations, as exemplified in Herbert I. Leeds' *Mr. Moto in Danger Island* (1939), the subject of this chapter.

The foreign, domestic subject

The paradoxical fear/desire dynamic relating to the US expanding global influence was manifest not only in its treatment of geographic spaces but also in its objectionable fascinations with 'exotic' subjects. Even though the 1930s saw a surge in the popularity of Asian-American characters (whether as heroes or villains), as the durability of the Charlie Chan and Mr Moto film series evidence, this cultural inclusion did not mean the legal or systemic inclusion of Asian (or other non-white) immigrants into the United States, as the Chinese Exclusion Act of 1882 and the Immigration Act of 1924 (which excluded Japanese) exemplify. Consequently, the alluring exoticism of Japan made Mr Moto an interesting character but it also set him aside as undeniably a foreigner rather than an American. Thus, Mr Moto could be an effective detective who saves the day in his films but he could not be a part of the United States' political establishment. As Mimi Thi Nguyen and They Linh Nguyen Tu point out, 'there are firm if not always clear distinctions between cultural and political representation ... ideas permissible in the realm of culture are not always acceptable in the realm of politics' (2007: 11–12). Consequently,

Mr Moto's superior investigative qualities, as I will show throughout this essay, although desirable for the successful development of a detective story, do not necessarily reflect a vision of the Japanese, or other similarly racialized immigrants, as important contributors to the American polity.

Correspondingly, *Mr. Moto in Danger Island*'s use of Puerto Rican characters and of Puerto Rico as the film's setting worked in similarly paradoxical ways. While the film recognizes the island as a US possession, and thus as part of the American federation, it also promotes its reification by characterizing it as a lawless site of rampant crime and systemic ineptitude. In the film, the island is plagued by criminal gangs, corrupt officials and superstitious inhabitants. Thus, although the domestic setting offers the opportunity to showcase white American characters, it also provides a properly isolated and geographically detached dangerous 'exotic' location for a detective story to develop. Accordingly, the film manages to place both Asian immigrants and Puerto Ricans within the confines of the United States while simultaneously marking them as fringe elements, outsiders or simply foreign. Thus, I contend, *Mr. Moto in Danger Island* evidences the anxieties of an expanding empire in relation to who gets to be included in the American imagined community. Although the United States needed to make a claim to its growing geographic overseas territory and cultural influence, it also had to negotiate the presence of non-white residents (and would be citizens). Therefore, this film subtly displays discourses related to ongoing immigration battles or, as Joe Feagin describes them, the 'struggles over the composition and character of the nation' (1997: 15).

Further adding to the controversy over who got to be categorized as American, as the combination of *Mr. Moto in Danger Island*'s title character, a Japanese man, and its setting, Puerto Rico, signals, the spectrum of prejudices and anxieties present in the United States expanded and became more critical as the nation found itself on the brink of the Second World War. This unease is evident in the film's characterizations of its protagonist, Mr. Moto, as highly intelligent and resourceful but also as lacking the physical attributes or even personality that would make him attractive to women. Very problematically, Peter Lorre wears make-up for the role that darkens his complexion and makes his teeth protrude to give stereotypical 'authenticity' to the character (Thomas 2012: 69, 121). In addition, Lorre, like Warner Oland had done when earlier playing Charlie Chan, alters his accent to sound stereotypically 'East Asian' (2012: 67). Thus, Lorre's performance portrays Mr Moto in very unglamorous and highly prejudiced ways, and thus as 'alien' or improperly American. That is, his 'superb' brain cannot make up for his 'substandard' body. Similarly, his physical residence in the United States does not make him an American.

Further, the film's use of multiple 'ethnic' characters (including Irish, German, Japanese and Puerto Ricans) that have distinguishable flaws works to instruct the viewer on how to be a proper American citizen, rather than to portray a changing multiethnic society. That is, the film's diversity in characters and setting serve as an excuse to move forward traditional conceptions of Americanness, for as Stuart Hall argues, 'identity is always, in that sense, a structured representation that achieves its positive only through the narrow eye of the negative. It has to go through the eye of the needle of the other before it can construct itself' (1997: 174). Mr Moto and the other 'ethnic' characters, thus, serve as examples of what American citizens are not, in that way constructing an identity out of exclusions. Chiefly, Mr Moto's intellectual prowess but sexual undesirability define him as a non-threatening actor and as un-American. He seems to exist only as a worker, deciphering his case at all moments, since the movie does not afford him the opportunity to engage in any social act. For instance, even as Mr Moto attends a dance party full of women, he remains on the sidelines working on his case rather than connecting with anyone at a personal level. Throughout the whole film we see that Mr Moto can inhabit elite social spaces but only as an observer and not a participant (while his white assistant Twister McGurk flirts and then awkwardly dances with women). Thus, the idea of the self-effacing, hard-working immigrant, as expressed through the Model Minority Myth, as Lisa Lowe has very cogently expressed, 'requires acceding to a political fiction of equal rights that is generated through the denial of history, a denial that reproduces the omission of history as the ontology of the nation' (1996: 27). Through its representation of its characters, and what they can and cannot do, as well as its isolated island setting, *Mr. Moto in Danger Island* promotes an equally exclusionary and assimilationist vision of proper citizenship – a vision that both erases the historical contexts of migration and characterizes 'foreignness' as social inadequacy.

Performing proper Americanness

Remarkably, *Mr. Moto in Danger Island*'s concern with proper American masculinity also covers the portrayal of white men. In the dangerous, foreign-domestic setting even white subjects run the risk of compromising their values and thus transforming into reprehensible citizens. To offer its cautionary tale, apart from its non-white characters, from its beginning, the film also relies on a series of white characters that offer lessons on proper male behaviour. After the film's introductory shot of a geographically inaccurate map of Puerto Rico, which establishes the name and location of the 'dangerous' setting, the viewer is presented a perceptive Mr Moto; his comedic sidekick, Twister McGurk (Warren Hymer); and the sentimental belle of the film, Joan Castle (Amanda Duff). These three characters converge on a wrestling match amidst the ship that will take them to Puerto Rico where McGurk, a white man, rather unsuccessfully fights a 'West Indian' fighter. Since his original introduction, the film marks McGurk as well-meaning but completely inept. Unsurprisingly, McGurk, although white, is cartoonishly coded as ethnic (Irish in this case). McGurk has a clear desire to help thwart crime, constantly following leads, getting into fights and bringing forward theories. However, his hunches always prove to be misguided and his fighting technique seems to put him in peril more than save the day. Thus, even though McGurk possesses proper values that will guarantee his eventual entrance into American society, the film also represents him as currently coarse: an American in training rather than a full citizen.

Surprisingly, it is Mr Moto who is charged with training McGurk in the paradoxical foreign-domestic location in the proper ways to be both a man and an American. The men, thus, to become true citizens, need to exit the United States and enter also the American-in-training island of Puerto Rico. In the 'quarantine' location, Mr Moto's instruction covers both physical and mental attributes of proper masculinity. For example, in the initial wrestling-match scene, the 'West Indian' is clearly winning the competition until Mr Moto interrupts the action by commenting loudly to his distraught neighbour, Miss Castle, that the wrestlers have no real skills and thus cannot harm each other. The derogatory comments distract the 'West Indian' and McGurk manages to take the upper hand as Mr Moto sends him a conspiratorial wink.

The scene just described illustrates the main conventions of the film: the West Indies creates a problem, McGurk unsuccessfully fights the problem, Miss Castle laments the consequences and, finally, Mr Moto ingeniously solves the problem and teaches McGurk a lesson.

Nonetheless, despite Mr Moto's intelligence, patience and inventive use of his body, his portrayal of masculinity is not exactly exemplary. For instance, upon the trio's arrival at the San Juan port, Mr Moto quickly faints and McGurk has to carry him to an ambulance. Even though the fainting episode proves to be one of Mr Moto's clever plans to catch the criminals, the incident also serves to feminize him and showcase his fragile physique. The scene similarly offers an excuse for McGurk, who carries Mr Moto to the ambulance, to showcase his physical, masculine superiority. Consequently, the film makes use of Mr Moto's underwhelming physique to further its portrayal of him as a personification of intellectual knowledge (a brain without an appealing physical presence). Thus, Mr Moto can train the visibly white McGurk in proper Americanness but he himself can never become it.

The film presents the audience with another similarly problematic white character in the also ethnically coded Mr Sutter (Jean Hersholt). Mr Sutter, the film's ultimate villain, is an older gentleman with a vaguely stereotypical German accent and thus is also marked as a foreigner. As a contrast to McGurk, Mr Sutter is perfectly groomed and an exceedingly cordial man; however, his social performance is just a mask to hide his nefarious intentions. While Mr Sutter publicly performs the role of the concerned citizen, offering information, defending other characters and accounting for other people's flaws, he works behind the scenes to subvert the rule of law by breaking maritime and commercial regulations and by harming the island's agricultural sector (as the local plantation owner, Mr La Costa (Douglass Dumbrille), briefly points out). The film's presentation of Mr Sutter's evil doings hidden under a civilized, non-threatening mask could have perhaps worked as a political allegory about Germany's role in the First World War and the conflict currently brewing in Europe, from which Lorre himself was already a Jewish refugee. That is, although white Germany could arguably be conceived as an intellectual and cultural model, that high level of 'refinement' could also turn out to be aberrant if not properly assimilated into the American work ethic. Consequently, the portrayal of a villainous German reflects the growth in the United States of anti-German sentiments that persisted throughout a great part of the twentieth century. Hence, the film vacillates between lauding the intellectual and organizational capacity of the villain and ostracizing him for his lack of commitment to a shared national project. In an insidious way, that the film's criminal mastermind turns out to be an overly refined Western European instead of a Puerto Rican, while superficially seeming less prejudiced, could arguably yet support the idea that the white colonist has the mental superiority (even if used for evil). After all, such a successful crime could stem only from a twisted but civilized white mind.

Ultimately, the film settles on a traditional 'WASP-y' character, LT George Bentley (Robert Lowery), as the personification of proper American masculinity. Although not as effective in solving crimes as Mr Moto, LT Bentley manages to follow the rule of law even when it means questioning his own father-in-law and commanding officer's, Colonel Castle (Charles D. Brown), motives and whereabouts. That is, LT Bentley is able to be caring towards Miss Castle, his fiancée, listening to all her insights and theories, and to hold the suspected criminals accountable for their behaviour, following leads even when they implicate those who are personally close to him. Additionally, the film presents him not just as morally attractive but also as physically desirable since he manages to capture the heart of the most eligible bachelorette in the island, Miss Castle. Furthermore, LT Bentley is the only local official the film does not implicate in the crime (he never behaves suspiciously or excuses other people's behaviour). It is not surprising, then, that he is also the only character coupled and thus awarded the possibility of future procreation (or of making a new generation of citizens). Indeed, the colony as a murky racial space threatened the clear demarcation of racial markers of privilege. Ann Laura Stoler contends in relation to European colonists that 'the presence and protection of European women were repeatedly invoked to clarify racial lines. Their presence coincided with perceived threats to European prestige' (1997: 352). In a similar way, in *Mr. Moto in Danger Island* the coupling of American colonists with American (i.e. white) partners ensured the preservation of colonial privileges on the island.

Taming the exotic, mysterious location

Similarly to its presentation of ethnic characters as negatives from which to construct proper American masculinity, the film's choice of setting, Puerto Rico, can be seen as an entrance point to a discussion of the potential socioeconomic threat of incorporating the US territorial possessions into the federation. As a contrast to the unattractive Mr Moto, the film characterizes Puerto Rico as containing great physical beauty (with lush flora and opulent indoor spaces), but this beauty serves to hide its reality of rampant crime and ineffective management. Additionally, the film suggests that the failings of Puerto Rico are due to the inadequacy of its native population, which is incapable of understanding the rational, scientific progress of the West and instead clings to folk tales. Towards the beginning of the film, while Mr Moto is studying facts about the island's geography, and cultural history, particularly pirates, at a local library, the eventual villain Mr Sutter summarizes the island's problems in the following way: 'It is not only ghosts you have to contend with but the superstitions of a dangerously ignorant people.' Hence, the film manages to portray Puerto Rico as a paradoxical perilous paradise in need of profound cultural, economic and political transformation. Like McGurk, Puerto Rico also needs to be tamed and trained before it can be truly American. More specifically, while Puerto Rico offers economic possibilities, both to legitimate (Mr La Costa's plantations) and illegitimate (Sutter's diamond cartel) businesses, it needs to reorganize its institutions under the supervision of very involved American officials (such as LT Bentley). Just as the Courts had decided in the Insular Cases, the film ultimately suggests that Puerto Rico's beauty and resources can be a natural asset to the US expansionist project but only if the island's residents (particularly, native men) submit to American management and give in to complete sociocultural assimilation.

Nonetheless, the film presents that Puerto Rico's needed cultural assimilation will be an arduous process. As a contested site of the American colonial project, Puerto Rico serves as what Mary Louise Pratt terms a 'contact zone', that is, 'social spaces where disparate cultures meet, clash, and grapple with each other, often in highly asymmetrical relations of domination and subordination' (2008: 7). The unbalanced relations of power between Puerto Ricans and Americans that the film establishes rely on the use of the colonial space as a challenging location for the establishment of hierarchies of knowledge. Although Mr Moto and his white American counterparts certainly have the moral high ground, the natives have the upper hand when it comes to understanding the physical locality and the ruling corrupt system. For instance, the criminals can use the island's geography to hide their illicit activities. They can control both developed and underdeveloped territory: they kidnap Mr Moto and hide him in an urban space, but also conceal their operations and abduct Colonel Castle in the uncharted swamps. Thus, while Mr Moto and his American sidekicks work towards the establishment of an American rule of law, the natives operate to undermine that project through their concealment of knowledge (both geographic and political). Ultimately, however, American law and order wins, albeit through the mediation of an outsider to both cultures, Mr Moto. Therefore, the Japanese detective serves as an impartial judge establishing and defending the hierarchies of power of the contact zone.

Notwithstanding the challenges of the impenetrable location, throughout most of the film Mr Moto productively searches for answers to solve the murder of a detective that the local authorities believe was targeted by diamond smugglers after he discovered that the criminals were using Puerto Rico as an entrance into the United States. Through most of the film, the viewer also witnesses the smugglers make use of their knowledge of the island's metropolitan and isolated, natural spaces to hide their contraband. At the more sinister political level, the film also posits Mr Moto and his sidekicks (McGurk and Miss Castle) as uncovering legal corruption, while the local authorities constantly undermine their efforts through their obfuscation and outright concealment of facts (who knows what at what time). Remarkably, the film's suspects come from all sectors of the island's elite: maritime businessman Mr Sutter (Jean Hersholt), police commissioners Gordon (Richard Lane) and Madero (Leon Ames), plantation owner Mr La Costa (Douglass Dumbrille), and Miss Castle's father, Col. Thomas Castle (Charles D. Brown). Although the film takes place in Puerto Rico, only two of the characters are Puerto Rican (Madero and La Costa). With the exception of Madero, all the government officials implicated in the murder are American. Given that until 1952 the US president appointed the high-ranking government officers in Puerto Rico, including the governor, the film's characterization of these officeholders as

American is historically accurate. However, to justify the need and presence of Mr Moto in the dangerous island, the film also characterizes these US-born men as inept at their jobs because they cannot seem to understand the rules that govern the foreign space. Despite the inclusion of many white suspects, the film's narrative and its use of trite stereotypes invite the audience to believe that the Puerto Rican Madero is the murderer (though in the end we learn that it was all along the friendly and supportive Mr Sutter).

It is easy for the audience to buy into Madero's criminality because the film consciously plays with an already-cemented vision of Latinos as mysterious and violent (Jervinen 2012: 79; López 1991: 405). Through its blatant use of stereotypes, the movie vacillates between accepting the presence of immigrants and non-white nationals in American society and denying them the right to full citizenship. As I have already noted, the movie presents Mr Moto as the embodiment of the Model Minority Myth but also depicts Puerto Rico and particularly natives (the diamond smugglers, Commissioner Maderos and Mr La Costa) as criminally suspect and sexually aggressive. That is, although innocent, Madero's personality and physical appearance corroborate all prejudicial discourses about people from the tropics. He is well groomed and a seductive talker but also ethically suspect and physically aggressive. Throughout the course of the film, Madero tries to intercept notes, opens other people's offices, burns letters, shows broad knowledge of pirates and knives, and is constantly framed through close-ups of his conspiratorial, dirty looks. Whereas Mr Moto is open about his knowledge and restricted in his physical presence, Madero is excessively physical and intellectually mysterious. Although Madero is innocent, the fact that even the extra clever Mr Moto feels uneasy about him suggests a certain immorality of character. He might not be guilty of this crime, but Mr Moto still sees his potential to bend the rule of law. Thus, although both characters eventually prove to be ethically sound, the film also puts into question their performance of masculinity, and accordingly their right to citizenship.

Aside from being the home of distrustful locals, the film presents the island setting as containing the innate ability to transform normally trustworthy, professional men into criminal suspects. Even men who are traditionally tasked with preserving and moving forward the national project, like Colonel Castle, appear to degrade by virtue of the location they inhabit. The Puerto

Rican system, with its disorganization, ineffectiveness and possibility for corruption, taints the image of everyone involved in it. Thus, even though all the American officials (Colonel Castle, Commissioner Gordon and Governor Bentley) are ultimately absolved from any wrongdoing, the audience suspects them because of their already questionable decision to live in an amoral and dangerous location. The audience never sees any of the American characters perform any illegal acts. They only see mundane things, like possessing diamonds, as potentially criminal because the mysteriousness of the location and circumstances prompts them to question the disposition of the characters. Thus, it is the setting and not the men's personal characteristics that marks them as improper citizens.

Producing and exhibiting the colony

Despite the film's reliance on its setting to carry the plot forward, it shows very little care in representing Puerto Rico with any accuracy. First, the scenery of the film does not resemble Puerto Rico, suggesting rather a strange mix of New England and stereotypical Mexican architecture. In addition, much of the film's plot unfolds in the non-existent swamp of Salinas, characterized by quicksand, monkeys and boisterous parrots.[2] Although some Puerto Rican natural features can be dangerous, with treacherous currents and oppressive heat, the dangers presented in the film are not characteristics of this particular island. Similarly, the film's interior spaces embody a form of colonial architecture, albeit without interior gardens, a staple in the Spanish architecture of Old San Juan. As if realizing the inadequacy of the setting, the Set Decorator, Thomas Little, included a potted palm tree or other tropical greenery in the majority of the spaces to constantly remind viewers that the mysterious, dangerous actions are actually taking place in the lush Caribbean. Overall, the film's 'danger island', more than representing geographic fears about Puerto Rico, stands in for generalized worries about unknown tropical locations (whether they be in Asia, Africa or Latin America).

Although the misrepresentation of the setting can be attributed to the film's 'B' status (and its limited budget), the misrepresentation of Puerto Rico in Hollywood films was not particular to the Mr Moto series. On the contrary, most American productions of the 1920s and 1930s, like the top-grossing film of 1926 *Aloma of the South Seas*, relied on generic stereotypes about the tropics (such as grass skirts, wild animals and dangerous flora) in their representation of Puerto Rico (García-Crespo 2019: 106–13). And indeed, to this day, Hollywood films continue to substitute one tropical location for another (thus Puerto Rico has stood in for multiple locations from Iraq, in *The Men Who Stare at Goats*, to Brazil, in *Fast Five*). Accordingly, the film's representation of Puerto Rico says more about US discourses regarding the tropics than about the tropics themselves. In sum, as Alison Griffiths has argued in relation to early ethnographic films, *Mr. Moto in Danger Island* works as an 'elaborate spectacle of nationalism', a carnivalesque and easily consumable version of empire that both glorifies and justifies colonialism (2002: 326).

Although the film's discursive line worked to cement a vision of proper Americanness that excluded or indicted colonial and immigrant populations, as a business, Twentieth Century Fox was also concerned with promoting its product in the world cinema market, which included Puerto Rico. Unsurprisingly, US reviewers addressed the film's successes and failures according to its generic conventions rather than on its use of a colonial setting. For instance, *The New York Times* categorized the film as a failure because it found its villain far-fetched (1939 BC). Contrastingly, the *Chicago Tribune* praised the film precisely because of its surprising ending ('Mr. Moto in Danger Island'). Overall, reviewers in the United States considered the film passable, particularly in relation to the conventions already established by other titles in the Mr Moto series. Although *Mr. Moto in Danger Island* did play in theatres in Puerto Rico, I have found no reviews of it. Considering, as I have previously shown elsewhere, that the Puerto Rican press was known for covering extensively any film with a trace of Puerto Ricanness, it is quite surprising that this film did not receive that treatment (García-Crespo 2019). Perhaps, I wonder, the version that arrived in Puerto Rico did not signal its location as Puerto Rico?

Indeed, when the film was shown on the island, the title was translated to *Mr. Moto de Incógnito* (Mr. Moto Disguised) instead of *Mr. Moto in Danger Island* ('A dónde ir', 'Cartelera'). The Spanish title is not really supported by the film's plot but rather seems to have come about to avoid insulting Caribbean people, whose interest in this instalment of the series may have been heightened by the tropical setting. In fact, business might well have been negatively affected had the title explicitly categorized Puerto Rico or any neighbouring location as particularly dangerous.[3] In any case, despite its potential to generate controversy in the island, based on the, at best, scanty newspaper coverage the film received, it appears that, in this instance, the local reviewers and probably also viewers did not attend much to the particularities of the setting, any more than did the filmmakers and US reviewers. In general, from the lack of coverage, I can infer that the Puerto Rican public seemed disinterested in the film's lessons about citizenship and colonization, further implying that rather than the colony, the film aimed to address the concerns of the US public.

———

While *Mr. Moto in Danger Island* included a diverse list of characters (if not necessarily a diverse cast) and ventured to include Puerto Rico into its discussion of American values, it nonetheless silenced those underrepresented populations by ignoring their specificities. That is, the film represented the American empire but only to support prejudiced discourses that were already circulating inside the United States. Similarly to what Dennis Merrill contends in relation to US tourist narratives, *Mr. Moto in Danger Island* heightened the United States' value at the cost of its island colonies, because 'the national imagination prefers to define the American way of life as involving virtue, democracy, and wealth. [But] the history of cultural contact zones, however, links the pious rhetoric of empire to personal acts of insensitivity, global finance and trade to individual consumption, and the limits of U.S. power to host agency' (2009: 19). By marking the island as dangerous, corrupt and disorganized, the film justifies the US presence in its colonies. Similarly, by dehumanizing Mr Moto, transforming him into a kind of detective machine, the film marks him as foreign and thus improperly American.

Notes

1   Other titles in the Mr Moto series include: *Think Fast, Mr. Moto* (1937), *Thank You, Mr. Moto* (1937), *Mr. Moto's Gamble* (1938), *Mr. Moto Takes a Chance* (1938), *Mysterious Mr. Moto* (1938), *Mr. Moto's Last Warning* (1939) and *Mr. Moto Takes a Vacation* (1939).

2   Puerto Rico has neither quicksand nor native monkeys, and by the nineteenth century the Puerto Rican parrot's habitat was restricted to rain forests areas because of the deforestation caused by the proliferation of sugar plantations, of which the Central in Salinas was one of the largest.

3   Supporting this analysis, the Portuguese title of the film became *Mr. Moto na Ilha do Terror*, a literal translation of the English title, and in French, *Monsieur Moto en péril*, which made use of the 'danger' aspect explicit in the US title. See Matos (2003: 175) and Icart and Mischler (1983: 198).

References

'A dónde ir' (1939), *La democracia* (San Juan), 1 September: 6.

Aloma of the South Seas (1926), [Film] Dir. Maurice Tourneur, USA: Paramount Pictures.

Amor Tropical (1921), [Film] Dir. Ralph Ince, Puerto Rico: Porto Rico Photoplays.

B.C. (1939), 'The Screen', *The New York Times*, 20 March: 18.

'Cartelera' (1939), *La correspondencia* (San Juan), 8 September: 6.

Erman, S. (2019), *Almost Citizens: Puerto Rico, the U.S. Constitution, and Empire*, Cambridge: Cambridge University Press.

Fast Five (2011), [Film] Dir. Justin Lin, USA: Universal Pictures.

Feagin, J. R. (1997), 'Old Poison in New Bottles: The Deep Roots of Modern Nativism', in J. F. Perea (ed.), *Immigrants Out! The New Nativism and the Anti-Immigrant Impulse in the United States*, 13–43, New York: NYU Press.

Fojas, C. (2014), *Islands of Empire: Pop Culture and U.S. Power*, Austin: University of Texas Press.

García-Crespo, N. (2019), *Early Puerto Rican Cinema and Nation Building: National Sentiments, Transnational Realities, 1897–1940*, Lewisburg: Bucknell University Press.

Griffiths, A. (2002), *Wondrous Difference: Cinema, Anthropology, and Turn-of-the-Century Visual Culture*, New York: Columbia University Press.

Hall, S. (1997), 'The Local and the Global: Globalization and Ethnicity', in A. McClintock, A. Mufti and E. Shohat (eds), *Dangerous Liaisons: Gender, Nation, and Postcolonial Perspectives*, 173–87, Minneapolis: University of Minnesota Press.

Heart and Soul (1917), [Film] Dir. J. Gordon Edwards, USA: Fox Films.

How the Porto Rican Girls Entertain Uncle Sam's Soldiers (1899), [Film] Dir. F. S. Armitage, USA: American Mutoscope and Biograph Company.

Icart, R. and G. Mischler (1983), *Pour vous, Ciné-miroir, Cinémonde, 1929-1940: Index, Vol. II: Films américains de long métrange*, Paris. Cinémathèque.

Jarvinen, L. (2012), *The Rise of Spanish-Language Filmmaking: Out from Hollywood's Shadow, 1929–1939*, New Brunswick: Rutgers University Press.

The Liar (1918), [Film] Dir. Edmund Lawrence, USA: Fox Film.

Lowe, L. (1996), *Immigrant Acts*, Durham: Duke University Press.

López, A. (1991), 'Are All Latins from Manhattan? Hollywood Ethnography and Cultural Colonialism', in L. D. Friedman (ed.), *Unspeakable Images: Ethnicity and the American Cinema*, 404–24, Urbana: University of Illinois Press.

Matos, A. C. G. (2003), *A outra face de Hollywood: Filme B*, Rio de Janeiro: Rocco.

Meléndez, E. (2013), 'Citizenship and the Alien Exclusion in the Insular Cases: Puerto Ricans in the Periphery of American Empire', *Centro Journal* 25.1: 106–45.

The Men Who Stare at Goats (2009), [Film] Dir. Grant Heslov, USA: Smoke House Pictures.

Merrill, D. (2009), *Negotiating Paradise: U.S. Tourism and Empire in Twentieth-Century Latin America*, Chapel Hill: University of North Carolina Press.

'Mr. Moto in Danger Island' (1939), *Chicago Daily Tribune*, 31 May: 15.

Mr. Moto in Danger Island (1939), [Film] Dir. Herbert I. Leeds, USA: Twentieth Century Fox.

Nguyen, M. T. and T. L. Nguyen Tu (2007) 'Introduction', in M. T. Nguyen and T. L. Nguyen Tu (eds.), *Alien Encounters: Popular Culture in Asian America*, 1–32, Durham: Duke University Press.

Pratt, M. L. (2008), *Imperial Eyes: Travel Writing and Transculturation*, 2nd ed. New York: Routledge.

Romance Tropical (1934), [Film] Dir. Juan Viguié, Puerto Rico: Latin Artists Pictures Corp.

Stoler, A. L. (1997), 'Making Empire Respectable: The Politics of Race and Sexual Morality in Twentieth Century Colonial Cultures', in A. McClintock, A. Mufti and E. Shohat (eds), *Dangerous Liaisons: Gender, Nation, and Postcolonial Perspectives*, 344–73, Minneapolis: University of Minnesota Press.

Tents of Allah (1923), [Film] Dir. Charles A. Logue, USA: Edward A. MacManus.

Thomas, S. (2012), *Peter Lorre, Face Maker: Stardom and Performance between Hollywood and Europe*, New York: Berghahn Books.

Washing the Streets of Porto Rico (1898), [Film] USA: Selig Plyscope Company.

The Woman Who Fooled Herself (1922), [Film] Dir. Charles Logue, USA: Edward A. MacManus.

10

An archipelago of crossed gazes: Intersections of documentary media practices in Cuba and Puerto Rico

Juan Carlos Rodríguez

Rethinking the film archipelago in the Hispanic Caribbean is an invitation to elaborate frameworks that will allow us to understand the history of moving images in this part of the world as a series of currents, waves and flows between islands. Different gazes emerge in this archipelagic traffic, manifesting a desire to transform the sea and its islands into audiovisual projections that respond to diverse geopolitical and sociocultural imaginaries. In this chapter, I explore Cuban-Puerto Rican relations through documentary media practices by filmmakers from both islands after the Cuban revolution of 1959.[1] When considered through the lens of the documentary, Cuban-Puerto Rican relations constitute a complex audiovisual archipelago that has changed significantly over the past sixty years.

The question of the archipelago as a historical and aesthetic configuration is, among other things, a question of method (Martínez-San Miguel 2018; Stratford et al. 2011). In this essay, I would like to offer a methodological orientation to navigate the turbulent waters of this archipelago of crossed gazes. Caribbean writers (Bosch 1970; Glissant 1997; Palés Matos 1937; Walcott 1992) have contributed to multiplying the meanings of the Caribbean archipelago, while Caribbean scholars (Benítez Rojo 1989; Díaz Quiñones 2000; Martínez-San Miguel 2003; Torres-Saillant 2006; Quintero Herencia 2016) have elaborated frameworks to contextualize the Caribbean archipelago as a material, geopolitical and symbolic configuration. The discussion on the cultural intersections of Cuba and Puerto Rico has been dominated by a focus on literary and musical production in both islands. Exploring the intersections of documentary media practices in Cuba and Puerto Rico provides a new platform from which to think Cuban-Puerto Rican relations as an archipelagic sequence of moving images. It also invites us to rethink documentary as an archipelagic media practice that at times overlaps with, complicates or distances itself from the project of building a national cinema based on representing the reality of an island or on contrasting the realities of two islands. At other times, this archipelagic media practice allows for the emergence of diasporic and migrant gazes that follow the routes of this sea of images flowing through the screens of both islands.

Based on recent discussions in island studies and Caribbean studies, it is possible to explore the documentary production of Cuba and Puerto Rico as an island-to-island relationship. This approach allows for the study of the various rhetorical, pedagogic and epistemic strategies generated by documentary filmmakers and scholars in the Hispanic Caribbean, suggesting an archipelago of crossed gazes. As I argue, this archipelago began with Cuban representations of Puerto Rican realities, and has continued with Puerto Rican representations of Cuban realities. This archipelago of images represents the persistence and disappearance of gazes that at times have collaborated, confronted each other or spectrally overlapped. Although these gazes have not always coincided, they still constitute each other through operations of inclusion and exclusion.

Archipelagic relations in Cuban and Puerto Rican documentary

According to Elaine Stratford, 'island relations are built on connection, assemblage, mobility, and multiplicity' (2013: 3). The island-to-island approach serves to 'illuminate island spaces as inter-related, mutually constituted and co-constructed' (Stratford et al 2011: 113). This methodological approach allows us to investigate the connections and interrelations that highlight the specific areas of mutual constitution and co-construction within the multiple imaginaries created by Cuban and Puerto Rican documentary media practices. I would like to argue that in the case of Cuba and Puerto Rico, their island-to-island relations have been in part mediated by the different roles both islands have played in the global designs of the US imperialist imaginary and geopolitical mappings of the Cold War. As we will see when analysing Cuban documentaries produced during the Cold War, or Puerto Rican documentaries revisiting the history of the Cold War in recent years, the mutual constitution of island-to-island relations through moving images assumes the shape of a triangulated imaginary geography, underscoring the influence of the United States as a continental and metropolitan power in the political history of both islands (Roberts and Stephens 2017).

To investigate the intersections of Cuban and Puerto Rican documentary as a relationship between islands, I propose focusing on images of Puerto Rico created by Cuban filmmakers and on images of Cuba created by Puerto Rican filmmakers. During the Cold War, Cuba became the model of a socialist revolution in the Third World, while 'Puerto Rico was transformed into a Cold War "symbolic showcase" of U.S. developmentalist policies toward the periphery of the world-economy as opposed to the Soviet model' (Grosfoguel 2003: 2). The fact that both islands played opposing roles as symbolic showcases of US and Soviet superpowers during the Cold War has influenced not only the documentary production of each island but, more specifically, the production of documentary images that filmmakers from both islands have created of the other island. The images of Puerto Rico projected in Cuban documentaries were made almost exclusively during the Cold War and mainly reproduced the ideological polarities that structured the political and economic conflicts of the 1960s and 1970s: capitalism versus socialism; 'democracy' versus Communist Party politics. In contrast, the images of Cuba projected in Puerto Rican documentary belong to post-Cold War productions, some of which revisit the tensions of the Cold War by exploring the role of Cuba in the Puerto Rican pro-independence movement. Other productions made by Puerto Rican filmmakers in Cuba, however, explore the difficult realities of the Special Period and its aftermath from an ethical rather than political standpoint, engaging at times in a re-examination of the Cuban documentary tradition.

Puerto Rico in Cuban documentary:
Migrant flows in Cold War geopolitics

The history of the mutual constitution of Cuban and Puerto Rican documentary can be conceptualized in part as a flow of people and images.

With the creation of the ICAIC (Cuban Film Institute) in 1959, Cuba began to develop a national film movement that contributed important elements to the radicalization of documentary aesthetics around the globe. At first glance, images of Puerto Rico in Cuban documentary resemble a very small archipelago of film productions that appear as dispersed islands in the Cuban film archive: *Cerro pelado* (Santiago Álvarez, 1966), *Puerto Rico* (Jesús Díaz Rodríguez and Fernando Pérez, 1975) and *55 hermanos* (Jesús Díaz, 1978). Based on these films produced by the ICAIC, in only one of them, *Puerto Rico*, the US Commonwealth territory appears to play a prominent role. In contrast, the Puerto Rico explored in *Cerro pelado* and invoked in *55 hermanos* could be conceived as very small island fragments that somehow have been inserted into the archipelago of images and testimonies included in these films.

Cerro pelado shows the diplomatic battles of the Cuban delegation against the US Coastal Service days before the celebration of the 10th Central American and Caribbean Games in San Juan, Puerto Rico in 1966. Cerro Pelado, the ship that transported the Cuban delegation from Cuba to Puerto Rico, was not authorized by the US authorities to reach the Port of San Juan, so athletes had to complete their training in the ship before being transported in small boats to San Juan. Through a poetic treatment of the image that involves the creation of rhythmic patterns based on the Cuban athletes' body movements, the trip of the Cuban delegation on board the Cerro Pelado becomes in Santiago Álvarez's documentary the allegory of an athletic utopian society crossing the Caribbean Sea in order to defeat the political obstacles created by American imperialism.

Once the Cuban athletes and film crew reach the coast of Puerto Rico, the film underscores the contradictions capitalism produces in the US territory, emphasizing the contrast between the Americanization of San Juan by mass consumption and underdevelopment in the city's urban periphery, and offering a critique of American colonialism in Puerto Rico. The Puerto Rico Álvarez projects is an island full of bars, stores and military personnel, a contradictory landscape whose levels of poverty, made visible through images of urban slums, reveal cracks in the symbolic showcase of US developmentalism in the Caribbean. *Cerro pelado* registers how the Cuban community in exile in Puerto Rico receives the Cuban delegation with hostility. Puerto Rico is presented as an enemy territory in which Cuban athletes are exposed to various degrees of political manipulation. In spite of the tense political atmosphere, Cuban athletes accumulate a great number of victories and return to Cuba as heroes, having defeated not only their sport competitors but also their ideological enemies. The film helped promote the revolutionary rhetoric that framed Cuban sport victories as symbols of the triumph of Cuban socialism over American capitalism and imperialism. With *Cerro pelado*, images of Puerto Rico's American way of life enter Cuban screens to represent the dangers of US colonialism and capitalism in the Caribbean, as well as the threats posed by the Cuban exile. Puerto Rico is projected as a colonized, touristic, militarized and capitalist island that is the nemesis of Cuba. Álvarez uses the image of Puerto Rico not only to suggest the type of island Cuba refuses to become, but also to distinguish Cuba from other islands in the Caribbean while emphasizing the exceptional place of the Cuban Revolution within Cold War geopolitics.

A different image of Puerto Rico comes out of *55 hermanos*, a documentary about the Antonio Maceo Brigade's visit to Cuba, a brigade formed by young members of the Cuban exile which promoted a dialogue between Cubans in the island and in exile. The Brigade included various members of the Cuban exile community from Puerto Rico who discuss Puerto Rico's social problems, reaffirming the image of the island as a dangerous and deceptive US colonial and capitalist enclave. They also represent the ties between the Cuban revolution and the Puerto Rican pro-independence movement. Even if Puerto Rico, in the Cuban documentary imagination, continues to be represented as an illusory and deceitful symbolic showcase, in *55 hermanos* it is no longer the visible evidence of the colonized and capitalist island that serves to deliver this point, as in the case of *Cerro pelado*, but instead the very testimony of the young Cuban-Puerto Ricans members of the Brigade. Although the Puerto Rican reality can be deceptive, Cuban-Puerto Rican members of the Brigade associate the island with political hopes and utopian aspirations, expressing a commitment to the struggle for Puerto Rican independence. The broken mirror of US colonialism and capitalism projects a distorted image of Puerto Rico, while, in turn, the image of Cuba serves as a mirror from which to imagine the future utopia of a decolonized Puerto Rico. While *Cerro Pelado* offers a repulsive and abject image of Puerto Rico as enemy territory, *55 hermanos* reveals a contradictory island in which it is still possible to build solidarity networks between the Cuban revolution and the Puerto Rican pro-independence movement.

Prior to the Carter era, that facilitated the trips of the Brigade, restrictions imposed by United States and Cuba made it difficult to travel between Cuba and Puerto Rico. As Cuban film director Fernando Pérez suggests, the making of *Puerto Rico*, the only Cuban documentary focusing entirely on the US Commonwealth, overcame the limitations imposed by the tense political relationship between islands by relying on reconstructions of historical events and footage sent to Cuba by the Puerto Rican film collective Tirabuzón Rojo (Ramos 2013).

Puerto Rico explores 'the deep contradictions' of Puerto Rico's 'colonial modernization' as well as 'key counternarratives of the anticolonial struggle' (Ramos 2013). For Ramos, 'the fictionalization of Puerto Rico's clandestine struggles', including reconstructions of 'the Ponce massacre, the arrests of Hiram Rosado and Elías Beauchamp, and the Río Piedras massacre ... seem to have served as a workshop for the future elaboration of some shots and fundamental scenes of *Clandestinos*, the first feature film of Fernando Pérez' (Ramos 2013). *Puerto Rico* also includes a sequence in which we hear Nuyorican poet Pedro Pietri reading his poem 'Puerto Rican Obituary'. The inclusion of the Puerto Rican diaspora in *Puerto Rico* relates to co-director Jesús Díaz's later interest in promoting dialogues between Cubans in the island and the diaspora in *55 hermanos*, perhaps the first Cuban documentary that presented a positive image of the Cuban diaspora in Cuban screen culture.

During the 1980s, the image of Puerto Rico almost vanished from Cuban documentary. Conflicts in Central America and other parts of the Caribbean, including Grenada and Haiti, inspired Cuban filmmakers to turn their eyes in different directions in search for new topics. The image of Puerto Rico reappears almost randomly in a Cuban documentary of the 1990s, *La americana* (Luis Deulofeu, 1991), a film not produced by the ICAIC but instead by the Cuban Revolutionary Armed Forces Film and Television Studios (Estudios Cinematrográficos y de Televisión de las Fuerzas Armadas Revolucionarias). *La americana* focuses on the story of Sara, a woman from Puerto Rico who migrated to Cuba after living in the United States.

In *La americana*, Puerto Rico is less an enemy territory or a social reality under scrutiny than a vague reference in Sara's testimony: 'People sometimes tell me: Sara, will you ever return to Puerto Rico? I have three daughters in Puerto Rico, who are adults, married and with family. Nobody in Puerto Rico knows where I am' (my translation). When Sara confesses that nobody in Puerto Rico knows where she is, Puerto Rico becomes the place from which she has disappeared, while Cuba is presented as her new refuge, inverting the typical image of the Cuban exile seeking refuge in Puerto Rico. Sara's disappearance could be interpreted as an allegorical image not only of the secret migratory flows in the Caribbean archipelagos, but also of the disappearance and spectral returns of Puerto Rico in the Cuban film archipelago.

Sara's commitment to Cuba becomes evident when she discusses her contributions to Cuban schools and to the preservation of the lighthouse of Bahía Honda in Pinar del Río, where she serves as a guardian along with her husband. She mentions that, after moving to Cuba, she forgot about Puerto Rico and the United States, and explains that she does not feel comfortable when people call her 'americana': 'Sometimes I think that this people will never learn. Because I always tell them, I am not American, I am Puerto Rican, and it is true that, unfortunately, Puerto Rico belongs to the Americans.' Despite this affirmation of identity, the film ends in an enigmatic note that calls into question the fixity of national identities in the Caribbean. When the filmmaker asks Sara if it is appropriate to call her 'la americana', she answers: 'Never in my life I will be called 'la americana'. I am the Cuban, Rosario, the Cuban.' While the last words of the testimony celebrate Cuban national identity, it is also true that the uncertainty surrounding Sara's/Rosario's national identity highlights the ways in which migrant flows in the Caribbean destabilize notions of territory, belonging and community. It is never clear whether we are witnessing the story of an old woman with a complex identity or watching a mockumentary in which a film director invents a character to challenge the expectations of an audience willing to believe an old woman's testimony. *La americana* challenges the protocols of transparency associated with documentary, transforming nonfiction into an exploration of opacity (Glissant 1997).

The image of Puerto Rico in Cuban documentary at first appears, in *Cerro Pelado*, as that of an antagonistic island, an enemy territory and colonial nemesis that manifests the evils of US capitalism. In *55 hermanos* and *Puerto Rico*, however, the image of Puerto Rico assumes a dialectical character: the US Commonwealth continues to be represented as a colonial social reality, while

216 *The Film Archipelago*

the people of Puerto Rico are regarded as anticolonial political allies of Cuba. Puerto Rico is therefore constituted in the Cuban documentary imagination both as a social reality that has to be rejected and as an antiimperialist political promise. During this period, Puerto Rico also serves as a creative lab for Cuban filmmakers seeking to elaborate new expressive and thematic paths. Later, in *La americana*, Puerto Rico and Cuba appear as islands within a network of migrant flows and unstable identities that reveal an archipelagic imagination. It is not surprising that, as the political certainties and dialectical contradictions of the Cold War began to vanish, the image of Puerto Rico represented in *La americana* became more personal, elusive and ambiguous. Overall, in this period, the ambivalent image of Puerto Rico in Cuban documentary changes over time: it begins as the image of an antagonistic island in a tense archipelago dominated by Cold War politics, then transforms into a dialectical image that affirms the political anxieties and hopes of leftist politics in both islands, and later becomes an archipelagic image within a mutually constituted network of migrant flows and unstable identities that manifests the social and political uncertainties of the end of the Cold War.

Cuba in Puerto Rican documentary: A post-Cold War archipelago of political and ethical perspectives

As we have seen, the image of Puerto Rico in Cuban documentary belongs almost exclusively to the context of the Cold War and operates as a rhetorical construction of the Cuban revolution in the theatre of Cold War geopolitics. In contrast, the image of Cuba in Puerto Rican documentary belongs to the post-Cold War context. It is fair to say, however, that the Cuban and Puerto Rican documentary film traditions have a long history of interactions, political affinities and institutional links, as we have noted regarding the collaboration between Tirabuzón Rojo and ICAIC in the making of Pérez and Díaz's *Puerto Rico*.[2] For example, the Puerto Rican Diego de la Texera, director of *El Salvador vencerá* (1981), a documentary produced in collaboration with the Salvadoran political party Frente Farabundo Martí para la Liberación Nacional, received the Gran Coral prize at the 2nd Havana Film Festival (Festival Internacional del Nuevo Cine Latinoamericano de

La Habana). In 1983, the same festival gave an award to the Puerto Rican documentary *La operación* (1982) by Ana María García, a Cuban-Puerto Rican filmmaker who participated in the Maceo Brigade featured in Jesús Díaz's *55 hermanos*. In 1986, de la Texera became one of the co-founders of the Escuela Internacional de Cine y Televisión (EICTV) at San Antonio de los Baños, Cuba. As these examples suggest, the links between Puerto Rican and Cuban documentary in the 1980s have more to do with the expansion of exhibition and educational networks than with the creation of images of each island by Puerto Rican and Cuban filmmakers (Orozco Díaz 2012; Sánchez Pagán 2010).

Many young Puerto Rican filmmakers, including Maite Rivera Carbonell, Freddie Marrero, Kique Cubero, Tito Román and Margarita Aponte, studied at EICTV and have approached Cuban realities from interesting angles, documenting Cuba after the Special Period. Contemporary Puerto Rican documentary cannot be understood without considering the EICTV network and its contributions around the world. If we look at the images of Cuba created by Puerto Rican filmmakers from EICTV as a manifestation of an island-to-island relationship, we could identify at least two main representations: political documentaries recorded in Puerto Rico that include references to the Cuban Revolution, and social and cultural documentaries made in Cuba that explore the dynamics of the Special Period.

The image of Cuba in Puerto Rican political documentaries is an intermittent reference that provides context about the political history of Puerto Rico and the alliances and anxieties made possible by the Cold War. In other words, in these documentaries recorded in Puerto Rico and focusing on Puerto Rican political history, the influence of the Cuban Revolution is represented as a key element of Puerto Rican history. In contrast, the second representation of Cuba in Puerto Rican documentary mainly corresponds to social or cultural documentaries recorded in Cuba by Puerto Rican filmmakers who completed these productions while studying or teaching at EICTV. This second representation of Cuba focuses almost exclusively on the realities of the Special Period and is closer to an archipelagic co-production or collaboration that involves the crossed gazes of Puerto Rican filmmakers and Cuban social subjects. While the first image of Cuba in Puerto Rican documentary is political, and revisits the history of the Cold War in the post-Cold War

218   *The Film Archipelago*

period, the second image of Cuba in Puerto Rican documentary examines the dynamics of the Special Period from an ethical standpoint.

As we have already observed, in the Puerto Rican political documentaries made by EICTV graduates, the exploration of the intertwined histories of Cuba and Puerto Rico offers the opportunity to re-examine the impact and conflictive legacies of Cold War geopolitics in Puerto Rico. In these documentaries, the relationship with Cuba appears as a key element of Puerto Rico's political history. Juan Carlos García, the first Puerto Rican filmmaker to graduate from EICTV, made *Recordando a Carlos Muñiz Varela* (2007), a documentary on Carlos Muñiz Varela, a member of the Cuban exile community in Puerto Rico who was assassinated after travelling to Cuba with the Antonio Maceo Brigade in 1978. Other members of the Cuban exile community from Puerto Rico who opposed the dialogues between the Cuban regime and the younger generation of Cubans in exile during President Carter's administration allegedly killed him. *Recordando a Carlos Muñiz Varela* includes interviews with friends, family members and cultural personalities who speak about Muñiz Varela's life and contributions to the opening of dialogues between Cubans families in the island and in exile. The film explores the assassination plot, the reason why the criminal case remains unsolved, and the devastating consequences for Carlos's family and the Cuban exile in Puerto Rico. Although García's documentary discusses Muñiz Varela's case in the context of Caribbean Cold War politics, it also includes a call for justice and a commemoration of Carlos' life on behalf of his family, opening an ethical dimension that seems to challenge the Cold War rhetoric of Cuba and Puerto Rico as ideological and political enemies. This ethical dimension, present in Cubero's, Ramos's and García's works, has become a key element of Puerto Rican documentary practices that manifest an archipelagic perspective through the exploration of Cuban stories.

The denunciation of US colonial rule and the struggle for independence are political dramas of the Cold War and its aftermath that have served as master narratives in the development of contemporary Puerto Rican documentary. Recent documentaries by EICTV graduates, such as Maite Rivera Carbonell's *Las carpetas* (2011) and Freddie Marrero Alfonso's *Filiberto* (2017), articulate the history of Puerto Rico's anticolonial struggles as political persecution plots that take the shape of surveillance narratives. Through personal anecdotes, both documentaries reveal links of solidarity between the Cuban revolution, including Fidel Castro, and Puerto Rican freedom fighters. *Las carpetas* focuses on the discovery in 1987 of thousands of secret files used by the Puerto Rican police to persecute social activists and pro-independence militants, and explores the story of four activists who were subject to police surveillance. One of the characters, Providencia 'Pupa' Encarnación, shares her memories of a trip to Cuba in which she met Fidel Castro. The trip is part of an alternative political and public culture that defies the image of Cuba as taboo in the panoptic context of Cold War paranoia created by *las carpetas* (surveillance files).

Las carpetas develops its surveillance narrative through recreations of daily life that simulate surveillance acts, and nonfictional performances in which the victims challenge the files. *Filiberto*, in contrast, is a character-driven documentary that uses archival images recorded by FBI agents, and on location testimonies and interviews, to explore the assassination by the FBI in 2005 of Filiberto Ojeda Rios, the leader of the Ejército Popular Boricua Los Macheteros. The first part explores Filiberto's life in New York during the 1950s, his role as musician in different popular orchestras, including Quique Lucas's *La sonora ponceña*, and his decision to move to Cuba in the 1960s to work for the Cuban revolution. In 1968 Filiberto returns to Puerto Rico as a clandestine freedom fighter, and the film focuses on his role in Los Macheteros's military operations, and the internal conflicts that lead to the division of Los Macheteros into factions. The second part of the film focuses on the FBI persecution of Filiberto and his legal battles up to 1990, when he escaped from federal custody and lived clandestinely until his death in 2005. As Filiberto's biographical account suggests, the political history of Puerto Rico will be incomplete without considering, first, the key role played by the Cuban revolution in the political imagination of the Puerto Rican pro-independence movement, and, second, the key role of federal agencies in the persecution of Puerto Rican freedom fighters. In *Filiberto*, Cuba and Puerto Rico form an archipelagic image of Cold War geopolitics.

These surveillance narratives transform the islands of Puerto Rico, including Vieques, into ambivalent zones of political persecution and resistance, revealing the technologies of US colonialism in the Puerto Rican archipelago. These narratives suggest a sinister image of Puerto Rico's modernity under the tutelage of the United States, but also a critique of surveillance practices that

220   *The Film Archipelago*

simultaneously evokes ways of reversing, eluding or transgressing them. In *Las carpetas* and *Filiberto*, the mutual constitution of images of Cuba and Puerto Rico as an archipelago of crossed gazes at times goes through the visual field of a third eye and traverses the aural space of a continental ear, that define the panoptic sensorium of US surveillance technologies and practices in the Caribbean. The political force of *Las carpetas* and *Filiberto* is in part achieved through the reconstruction of a visual and aural map of the Caribbean archipelago's geopolitical conflicts. By exploring the archive of US political surveillance in Puerto Rico, both documentaries perform an 'archiveology' of the Cold War in the Hispanic Caribbean, a practice of collective memory that involves 'the reuse, recycling, appropriation and borrowing of archival materials' (Russell 2018: 1). In these documentaries, the archipelago of crossed gazes is an 'archival effect' (Barron 2014) that responds to a triangular structure created by the flows of documents and archival materials that belong to the culture of fear of the US continental power. The sense of paranoia, created by this flow of information, manifests the US archipelagic modes of control and surveillance in the Hispanic Caribbean.

Let us now look at the social and cultural documentaries recorded in Cuba by Puerto Rican students and educators affiliated with the EICTV. In 2009, Kique Cubero completed the One2One exercise as part of the second-year specialization programme in documentary production at EICTV. For the One2One, students travel to the Sierra Maestra and spend six weeks developing a documentary that must emerge from the encounter of the film director with their character (One2One). Cubero's One2One short documentary, *El almuerzo* (2009), explores the life of a couple living in a small hut in Sierra Maestra and follows their gendered routines. The woman shares with the man her frustration because he does not help her at home. He promises to help, then the camera follows him taking care of the land surrounding the hut. At the end we see the man leaving the hut once again as the woman sings a romantic tune, echoing the voice of someone who laments being abandoned by her lover. Cubero's documentary is not only a meditation on gender roles in the Cuban countryside but also a reflection on domestic labour in contemporary Cuba. This incursion into the realities of Sierra Maestra reveals another element of the archipelagic intersections of Cuban and Puerto Rican documentary: the role of Cuba as a learning landscape and as a pedagogically inflected human geography for Puerto Rican filmmaker.

Cubero's graduation project, the short documentary *Un peso más* (2010), explores the rise and fall of weightlifter and Olympic gold medallist Pablo Lara, and makes reference to Cuban Cold War rhetoric. It includes a sequence in which a Cuban athlete who defected the Cuban sport delegation before the Moscow Olympics in Mexico is treated by Fidel Castro and others as a traitor. But the documentary's rhetorical frame opens itself to new possibilities. Cubero's exploration of Lara's story, the sale of his Olympic medal, his time in prison and his integration to society as weightlifting trainer offer a glimpse into the challenges faced by some Cuban sport glories after the Special Period. In the process of casting a gaze towards a marginalized Afro Cuban athlete, Cubero invites audiences in Cuba and Puerto Rico to turn their gazes towards themselves, opening the possibility of transforming the archipelago of crossed gazes into an ethical act that interrogates the self as well as the other.

Puerto Rican intellectual Julio Ramos, who has taught at EICTV, has also contributed to the flows of images and knowledges that circulate in this archipelago of crossed gazes constituted at the intersection of documentary media practices in Cuba and Puerto Rico. With Cuban Filmmaker Raydel Araoz, Ramos co-directed *Retornar a La Habana con Guillén Landrián* (2013), an extraordinary cultural documentary about a Cuban filmmaker who was ostracized by the ICAIC in 1971, after battling with mental health problems. Araoz and Ramos's documentary can be seen as a creative complement to Ramos's critical work on Nicolasito Guillén Landrián (Ramos and Robbins 2013 and 2018). Before leaving the country in 1989, Nicolasito spent extended periods in Cuban prisons and psychiatric institutions. He lived in Miami with his partner, Gretel Alfonso Fuentes, from 1989 until 2003, when he died of pancreatic cancer at the age of 65. Araoz and Ramos's documentary is based on a long interview with Nicolasito's partner and footage of Nicolasito in his deathbed, days before passing away. Gretel revisits Nicolasito's life in Cuba when he was repeatedly persecuted and jailed by the Cuban state and describes their exilic life in Miami. She also narrates her return to Cuba with the filmmaker's corpse and the mourning process she experienced after the loss of her partner.

According to Ramos, the documentary was in part inspired by the fact that Gretel and Ramos decided to honour Nicolasito by commissioning an obituary plaque in stone to identify his tomb. He had been buried in Gretel's family tomb in Havana. The film combines images and sounds of the stone master chiselling the obituary plaque with images of Nicolasito's films, footage of his deathbed and newspaper clippings of his trajectory, all of which is held together by Gretel's testimony. The film ends with the placing of Nicolasito's obituary plaque in his tomb and footage of Nicolasito speaking from his deathbed. The film implicitly inscribes itself in the realm of Antigona's ethical act, as it narrates the story of a woman who, with the help of two filmmakers, tries to secure a respectful burial for her loved one. Against the forces of oblivion that conspire to keep Nicolasito's legacy buried in the mass graves of the Cuban film archives, *Retornar a La Habana con Guillén Landrián* is a commemorative documentary that symbolically performs a funeral ritual to honour the life and work of one of the most influential Cuban documentarians of all time (Goldberg 2014; Sánchez 2010).

Contemporary Puerto Rican documentaries redefine the intersections of documentary media practices between Cuba and Puerto Rico. The Cuban gaze cast over Puerto Rico in the 1960s and 1970s was framed by the geopolitical tension of the Cold War. The exploration of the Cold War has continued in recent Puerto Rican documentaries that focus on the intertwined political histories of Cuba and Puerto Rico. In contrast, recent Puerto Rican social and cultural documentaries made in Cuba, like the ones by Cubero, and Araoz and Ramos, resemble an archipelago of crossed gazes that re-examines, from an ethical standpoint, the paradoxes of the Cuban Revolution after the Special Period.

An elusive island in the archipelago of crossed gazes

As I have tried to suggest in this chapter, the history of the mutual constitution of Cuban and Puerto Rican documentary can be conceptualized as an inter-insular relationship made of flows of images, people, political rhetoric, learning experiences, new knowledges, ethical acts, archival spectres and runaway legacies. Some documentary intersections between Cuba and Puerto Rico respond to the political inflections of the Cold War context in Cuba (*Cerro Pelado, Puerto Rico,* and *55 hermanos*) and its aftermath in Puerto Rico (*Las carpetas* and *Filiberto*). Other intersections, most of them by Puerto Rican filmmakers, go beyond this polarized geopolitical configuration, aligning documentary with the possibility of generating an alternative archipelago of crossed gazes constituted by the imperative of ethical perspective (*Recordando a Carlos Muñiz Varela, El almuerzo, Un peso más,* and *Retornar a la Habana con Guillén Landrián*). In this context, the Cuban examination of contemporary Puerto Rico is still pending. This absent gaze affects the very constitution of this archipelago of crossed gazes.

In the first years of the revolution, Cuban filmmakers created documentaries in which Puerto Rico and its image played different roles (enemy territory, production partner, anticolonial symbol, home of socialist allies in exile, etc.). After the Special Period, these political frames vanished and have not yet been replaced. The disappearance of these frameworks has not yet inspired alternative Cuban approaches to look at Puerto Rican realities from a political or ethical standpoint. In contrast, contemporary Puerto Rican filmmakers have been elaborating an alternative framework to look at Cuba and Puerto Rico that depends on an ethical or political overlap of images and gazes from both islands. But even within the Puerto Rican documentary production, there are important distinctions. When images of Cuba and Puerto Rico appear in Puerto Rican political documentary, it is because Cuba continues to be an integral part of Puerto Rico's political history. When Cuban and Puerto Rican filmmakers collaborate in social documentaries, however, all the focus is on Cuba, and Puerto Rico does not seem to be part of the image of Cuba. While Cuban filmmakers have not elaborated images of Puerto Rico, Puerto Rican filmmakers continue to embark on the experience of travelling to Cuba, like pilgrims with a movie camera, in search of moving images of the other island that may speak to the self, to the point of displacing the subject like an elusive island floating on the waves.

These differences are important for our understanding of the archipelago of crossed gazes as a heterotopic space in which gazes at times coincide or miss each other, while mediating and remediating the always complex currents of documentary media practices in Cuba and Puerto Rico. On the one hand, these differences respond to political and economic factors. Puerto Rican filmmakers may have the material resources and institutional support to film in Cuba, while the possibility of filming in Puerto Rico is not within the reach of many Cuban filmmakers, due to visa restrictions, lack of material resources and limited institutional networks. On the other hand, these differences have to do with the dynamics of the Cuban exile. Except for the work of Ana María García, Puerto Rico has never played a prominent role in the documentaries of the Cuban exile. Although several young Cuban filmmakers have recently moved to Puerto Rico or visit the island frequently, to the best of my knowledge there are no post-Cold War documentaries on Puerto Rican issues made by Cuban filmmakers living in Puerto Rico. It remains to be seen whether or not the Cuban exile will develop a new documentary tradition based on the exploration of Puerto Rican realities.

Ultimately, an archipelago of crossed gazes invokes the idea that a gaze can never be equated to an island. It also highlights that our visual experience in the Hispanic Caribbean continues to be articulated by flows of desire and abjection. A desire for an elusive island that looks like an impossible gaze drives this archipelago of crossed gazes, but the subterranean currents of abjection at times turn the elusive gaze into an impossible island. After years of travel restrictions, the image of Cuba has become an object of desire for Puerto Rican documentary, a process driven by the fantasies of having access to an elusive island and elaborating what was before an impossible gaze. In contrast, the image of Puerto Rico elaborated in Cuban documentary during the Cold War was an ambivalent image, an island at once desired and rejected. As the horizons of Cuban documentary have expanded globally in recent years, Puerto Rico has disappeared from the map of the Cuban film imagination. In this sense, Puerto Rico has become an impossible island for an elusive gaze.

Although at first sight it might look like another discourse of transparency based on visible evidence, the film archipelago created by Cuban and Puerto Rican documentary media practices is an experience of divergent routes, encounters, gaps and multiple layers of opacity (Glissant 1997). The film archipelago is therefore not a collection of images of plenitude but rather an *efecto archipiélago* (archipelago effect) (Quintero-Herencia 2016), an intermittent flow of images constituted by a crack that frustrates the possibility of an insular closure of the Caribbean.

Notes

1 For a discussion on the historical similarities and differences between Cuba and Puerto Rico, see Scarano (2007).
2 For a history of Puerto Rican documentary, see Almodóvar Ronda (1994) and García (2014).

References

55 hermanos (1978), [Film] Dir. Jesús Díaz, Cuba: ICAIC.

Almodóvar Ronda, R. (1994), 'Archivo de la memoria: El documental, la animación y el cine experimental en Puerto Rico', in *Idilio tropical: la aventura del cine puertorriqueño*, 80–95, San Juan: Banco Popular.

La americana (1991), [Film] Dir. Luis Deulofeu, Cuba: Estudios de la FAR.

Barron, J. (2014), *The Archival Effect: Found Footage and the Archival Experience of History*, New York: Routledge.

Benítez Rojo, A. (1989), *La isla que se repite: El Caribe y la perspectiva postmoderna*, Hanover: Ediciones del Norte.

Bosch, J. (1970), *De Cristobal Colón a Fidel Castro: el Caribe, frontera imperial*, Madrid: Alfaguara.

Las carpetas (2011), [Film] Dir. Maite Rivera Carbonell, Puerto Rico: El Viaje Films and Producciones Lente Roto.

Cerro pelado (1966), [Film] Dir. Santiago Álvarez, Cuba: ICAIC.

Clandestinos (1987), [Film] Dir. Fernando Pérez, Cuba: ICAIC.

Chanan, M. (2003), *Cuban Cinema*, Minneapolis: University of Minnesota Press.

Díaz Quiñonez, A. (2000), *El arte de bregar*, San Juan: Ediciones Callejón.

El almuerzo (2009), [Film] Dir. Kique Cubero, Cuba: EICTV Producción.

El Salvador vencerá (1981), [Film] Dir. Diego de la Texera, El Salvador: Instituto Cinematográfico de El Salvador Revolucionario FMLN.

Filiberto (2017), [Film] Dir. Freddie Marrero Alfonso, Puerto Rico/Venezuela: Asoc. Coop. Perro Andaluz/Norte del Sur/Panafilms/Proyecto Chiringa/Villa del Cine.

García, J. (2014), *Historia del cine puertorriqueño*, San Juan: Palibrio.

Glissant, E. (1997), *Poetics of Relation*, Ann Arbor: University of Michigan Press.

Goldberg, R. (2014), 'Under the Surface of the Image: Cultural Narrative, Symbolic Landscapes, and National Identity in the Films of Jorge de León and Armando Capó', in V. Navarro and J. C. Rodríguez (eds), *New Documentaries in Latin America*, 59–74, New York: Palgrave.

Grosfoguel, R. (2003), *Colonial Subjects: Puerto Ricans in a Global Perspective*, Berkeley: University of California Press.

Martínez San Miguel, Y. (2003), *Caribe Two Ways: Cultura de la migración en el Caribe insular hispánico*, San Juan: Ediciones Callejón.

Martínez San Miguel, Y. (2018), 'El archipiélago pluriversal', *80 grados*. 6 April. Available online: https://www.80grados.net/el-archipielago-pluriversal/ (accessed 22 April 2021).

La operación (1982), [Film] Dir. Ana María García, USA: Latin American Film Project.

Orozco Díaz, A. L. (2012), '¿Quién es Diego de la Texera?' *Revista ENcontrARTE*, 15 October. Available online: https://arteyculturafmln.wordpress.com/2013/10/15/quien-es-diego-de-la-texera/ (accessed 22 April 2021).

Palés Matos, L. (1937), *Tun-tun de Pasa y Grifería*, San Juan: Biblioteca de autores puertorriqueños.

Puerto Rico (1975), [Film] Dir. Jesús Díaz and Fernando Pérez, Cuba: ICAIC.

Quintero Herencia, J. C. (2016), *La hoja de mar (:) Efecto archipiélago I*, Leiden: Almenara Press.

Ramos, J. (2013), 'Fernando Pérez o las alternativas del cine cubano', *80 grados*. 26 July. Available online: https://www.80grados.net/fernando-perez-o-las-alternativas-del-cine-cubano/ (accessed 22 April 2021).

Ramos, J. and D. Robbins (eds) (2013), 'Dossier: Especial Nicolás Guillén Landrián', *La Fuga* 15 (Primavera). Available online: https://lafuga.cl/dossier/especial-nicolas-guillen-landrian/15/ (accessed 22 April 2021).

Ramos, J. and D. Robbins (eds) (2018), *Guillén Landrián o el desconcierto fílmico*, Leiden: Almenara Press.

Recordando a Carlos Muñiz Varela (2007), [Film] Dir. Juan Carlos García, Puerto Rico: WIPR Canal 6/Prohibido Olvidar.

Retornar a La Habana con Guillén Landrián (2013), [Film] Dir. Raydel Araoz and Julio Ramos, Cuba: Producciones de otros.

Roberts, B. R. and M. A. Stephens (eds) (2017), *Archipelagic American Studies*, Durham: Duke University Press.

Rodríguez, J. C. (2018), 'Conversation with Kique Cubero', Facebook message, 26 November.

Russell, C. (2018), *Archiveology: Walter Benjamin and Archival Film Practices*, Durham: Duke University Press.

Sánchez, J. L. (2010), *Romper la tensión del arco: Movimiento cubano de cine documental*, La Habana: ICAIC.

Sánchez Pagán, M. (2010), 'Charla con Diego de la Texera', *Revista Surco Sur* 1.2: 65–9.

Scarano, F. A. (2007), '¿La isla que se repite? Contrapuntos cubano-puertorriqueños entre la Guerra Fría y el reencuentro', in F. A. Scarano and M. Zamora (eds), *Cuba: Contrapuntos de Cultura, Historia y Sociedad. Counterpoints on Culture, History, and Society*, 385–402, San Juan: Ediciones Callejón.

Stratford, E. (2013), 'The Idea of the Archipelago', *Island Studies Journal* 8.1 (May): 3–8.

Stratford, E., G. Baldacchino, E. McMahon, C. Farbotko and A. Harwood (2011), 'Envisioning the Archipelago', *Island Studies Journal* 6.2: 113–30.

Torres Saillant, S. (2006), *An Intellectual History of the Caribbean*, New York: Palgrave.

Un peso más (2010), [Film] Dir. Kique Cubero, Cuba: EICTV Producción.

Walcott, D. (1992), 'The Antilles: Fragments of Epic Memory'. Available online: https://www.nobelprize.org/prizes/literature/1992/walcott/lecture/ (accessed 22 April 2021).

11

'Irreducible memories' of Caribbeanness: Mariette Monpierre's *Le Bonheur d'Elza* (2011)

Sheila Petty

In his phenomenal body of work, Edouard Glissant argues for a 'Caribbean imagination' that visualizes culture and art production as an unfolding process, subject to both internal and external cultural contacts where the 'synthesis/ genesis' of identity and aesthetics are continually evolving (1989: 139). Working from the philosophy that the world is globalized, métissé and creolized (adding a layer of unpredictability), Glissant would often repeat, 'act in your location, think with the world' (2009: 87). Foregrounding a decentring of hegemonic and Eurocentric points of view and promoting interdisciplinarity, Glissant would also caution that while 'seeing and thinking large', it is important to take into consideration how the colonial past has informed present conditions of being (Imorou 2011: 34).

At approximately the same time that Glissant was expanding his theoretical framework through philosophy, prose and poetry, film theorist Hamid Naficy offered up a new method for engaging with postcolonial, exilic and diasporic forms of screen media. Naficy calls these texts 'accented cinema' and describes how their narrative, aesthetic and production contexts arise from feelings of displacement and an inherent sense of memory of 'the traditions of exilic and diasporic cultural productions that preceded them'. The filmmakers acquire two sets of voices from their heritage and lived experiences (Naficy 2001: 22). Such an approach is driven by aesthetic and narrative ingenuity, including 'self-reflexivity and autobiographical inscription, historicity, epistolarity' and 'multilinguality' and 'resistance to closure' (Naficy 1999: 131). More recently, Beti Ellerson has used the theoretical frame of 'accented cinema' to investigate the 'cinematic imaginary' of African women filmmakers born or raised in 'the host country of their immigrant parents' (2017: 273). Ellerson is particularly concerned with how these women filmmakers stage innovative journeys of identity and belonging and the ways in which they contribute to the canon of African and African diasporic cinema.

This essay will draw inspiration from Edouard Glissant's work on relational poetics and tout-mondism and Hamid Naficy's conception of accented cinema to probe the specifically Caribbean formulation of cinema aesthetics in Mariette Monpierre's first feature film, *Le Bonheur d'Elza* (France/Guadeloupe, 2011). In the film, Elza, a young Parisian woman, returns to her birthplace of Guadeloupe to search for the father of whom she holds distant memories. As an element of orality, memory or the personal recollection has a long history in Caribbean artistic practice. As Antonio Benítez-Rojo argues, the 'irreducible memory' of race is a recurrent 'theme' in the 'ethnographic, economic, political, and sociological terms' encompassing the shifting boundaries of Caribbean identity (2001, 202). By considering the film within its historical, cultural and production context and analysing its narrative through the relational auspices of plot, character, spectacle (cinematography and editing) and ideology, the essay will demonstrate how history and identity function as networks of meaning within Caribbean filmic memory-narrative.

Flows of transnational histories and accented production modes

Forged in the crossfire of slavery and the global economic impulses that drove it, Caribbean cultures have long been actively aware of globalization and its effects. As Glissant suggests, 'the dialectic between inside and outside is reflected in the relationship of land and sea' where a 'multiple series of relationships' brought to the island by European, African, Indian and other migrations create 'a Caribbean imagination' that 'liberates us from being smothered' under the weight of discordant histories and oppressions (1989: 139). For Glissant, this multiplicity of cultures spurs Caribbean writers and artists to repudiate Western universalisms as 'edict[s] that summarized the world as something obvious and transparent, claiming for it one presupposed sense and one destiny' (1997: 20). From this perspective, models of theory that insist on universal application and Western historical underpinnings are clearly in conflict with the hybrid cultures and histories of the Caribbean. As Glissant further suggests, such 'generalization[s]' are fundamentally flawed because they represent 'one side of the reports, one set of ideas' which are then 'export[ed] as a model' specifically geared to masking voices of resistance (1997: 20–1). In order to 'help to correct whatever simplifying, ethnocentric exclusions may have arisen' from such models, Glissant argues for a view of historical interaction that 'reproduces the track of circular nomadism' which 'abolishes the very notion of center and periphery' by redefining its boundaries in response to local imperatives (1997: 21, 29). Referring to this as a 'poetics of Relation', this concept sees meaning, history and identity functioning as a 'network inscribed within the sufficient totality of the world' in a set of flexible 'dialectics between the oral and the written, the thought of multilingualism, the balance between the present moment and duration' and 'the nonprojectile imaginary construct' (27, 29, 35). Meaning, then, is contextual and relational and to unpack a Caribbean specificity within a global frame, Glissant sees the necessity to 'return to the point of entanglement' (Puri 2004: 77).

Guadeloupe is often described as one of France's 'vieilles colonies' (old colonies) along with Martinique, Guyane and Réunion. Originally populated by Indigenous Arawaks and then handed over to Carib natives and the Spanish before France claimed control in 1635 and exterminated what was left of indigenous populations, Guadeloupe's history has been fraught at the very least. For two centuries slaves imported from Africa during the transatlantic slave trade produced goods (mostly from sugar plantations) for export to metropolitan France. In particular, the enormous Darboussier Sugar Factory in Pointe-à-Pitre transformed the island into a place of great wealth for the French colonialists. When France officially declared slavery abolished in its own colonies in 1848, freed slaves received nothing as reparation while former slave owners were generously compensated for simply agreeing to the abolishment of slavery. Furthermore, affranchised slaves were not even allowed to remain in their huts and cultivate their own gardens to ensure their livelihoods unless they continued to work on the plantations where they lived. Slavery was replaced with a new form of indentureship which forced entire families (including children) to work on the plantations for a third of the produce they reaped.[1] And to ensure that families stayed put, Napoleon III allowed immigration of Indian, Chinese, Japanese and African workers, further reducing remuneration received by former slaves for their labour (Gautier 2003: 580–1). Maddy Crowell points out that 'much of the local economy is still controlled by *békés*, descendents of white French slave owners who received reparations from the French government after 1848 after losing their livelihoods' (2018).

In 1946, Guadeloupe was created an Overseas Department of France (DOM) with a locally elected government that reports to the president of France in Paris. Unlike other Caribbean nations that sought independence, it remains, like Martinique, intimately connected to France. This is not to say that Guadeloupe and Martinique have been immune to the flows of political thought and activity occurring in other parts of the Caribbean. For example, the assassination of Walter Rodney in Guyana in 1980 and the Duvalier dictatorship and reign of terror in Haiti for nearly thirty years until the mid-1980s are but a couple of examples of historical moments that would help forge new forms of political consciousness. This rise of political awareness would collide with a sweeping downturn in the economic stability of the Caribbean as structural adjustment programmes controlled monetary currencies; increased emigration to Canada, the United States, Europe and the United Kingdom of nurses and teachers, in particular, resulted in a significant 'brain drain' of professional expertise; and depreciating infrastructure would all contribute 'to impose severe limitations on many Caribbean nations and individuals' (Cham 1992: 3). Shalini Puri has argued that:

> the French DOM's have led to social formations that are comparably contradictory: they are not even nominally independent politically or economically; they hold strategic and symbolic value for the metropolitan states; and they are characterized by little local agricultural or industrial production, dense urban populations, a high standard of living relative to many independent Caribbean islands, and high unemployment offset by large metropolitan transfers. In both islands, the debate is often framed as a problem of balancing economic survival against cultural assimilation by the metropoles.
>
> (2004: 230, n17)

This is the political and economic context within which cinema production was forged in the Caribbean and, as Mbye Cham argues, these 'currents' would provide filmmakers with 'subject matter, and, in some cases, aspects of these currents manifest themselves in matters of form, style, and orientation' (1992: 5). A major goal within cultural production was a sense of identity reflecting the diversity of the Caribbean: 'diversalité' versus 'universalité' (4). A singular, collective Caribbean identity is not being sought. Rather, the specific histories of individuals lead to diverse experiences of meaning.

Within Naficy's frame of 'accented cinema', meaning arises from 'interstitial' spaces within 'social formations and cinematic practices' (Naficy 2001: 4). Naficy contends that screen media produced in this context are 'simultaneously local and global.[...] and signify upon the conditions both of exile and diaspora and of cinema' (4). The narrative modes and aesthetic strategies of these accented texts often reflect a blending of all the artistic influences embraced and experienced by their makers. In the case of Caribbean cinema, attempts to define it, or even understand its evolving complexities, have led scholars to describe it as a 'push-me, pull-you' configuration, a 'tension between national borders and diasporic connections' and a constant reconfiguring of its 'geocultural scope' to account for transatlantic movement between the Caribbean archipelago and North and South America and Europe (Bryce 2019: 123). Martinican Filmmaker Jérome Kanapa has even declared, according to Meredith Robinson, that 'the difficulty in talking about Antillean cinema is that one never knows when it began, and with whom' (Robinson 2010: 45).

In his pioneering contribution to Caribbean film studies, Mbye Cham attempts to define 'indigenous film practice', which he describes as Caribbean production by Caribbeans living in the Caribbean (1992: 5, 8). He concludes that until Euzhan Palcy's 1983 Martinican blockbuster film *Rue case-nègres/ Sugar Cane Alley*, based on Aimé Césaire's novel of the same title, knowledge of indigenous or local cinema tended to be limited to Perry Henzell's *The Harder They Come* (1972), which popularized Jimmy Cliff's reggae music in Jamaica. Interestingly, the film's narrative structure follows actual reggae rhythms and is an excellent example of intangible cultural expression providing a platform for expression of the tangible (cinema) and the political. Cham goes on to describe how work during the same decade by Guadeloupian 'pioneers' such as Gabriel Glissant and Christian Lara was not well known at all (5). Meredith

234   *The Film Archipelago*

Robinson cites Guadeloupian film scholar and journalist, Osange Silou, who, in turn, attributes the first 'Antillean film, *Lorsque l'herbe* to Christian Lara, in 1968' (2010: 47).

Lara's early production seems to fit into Cham's rubric of 'indigenous' production and, as Robinson asserts, he is the most prolific of the 'French-Caribbean' directors with an extensive repertoire of more than twenty-four relatively big-budget feature films. Robinson further describes how Lara's work, despite its lavish production values and valorization of Guadeloupian history in order to catalyse political consciousness, has been largely ignored by scholars or described negatively by reviewers as 'imitative and unoriginal with a tendency to reinforce the exotica of Euro-American productions about the Caribbean and to unconsciously subvert its avowed militant pro-Antillean pretentions' (Cham 1992: 23; Robinson 2015: 68). Thus, according to Robinson, Lara 'straddles a precarious position in French-Caribbean filmmaking' because he eschews Eurocentric perceptions of non-Western production values while creating political statements (2015: 68). In fact, one could argue (as Robinson does for Lara) that both Lara and Euzhan Palcy create political films because they espouse 'new interpretations of historical events' (68). With his films such as *Sucre amer/Bitter Sugar* (1998) and *1802, L'Epopée Guadeloupéenne/1802, The Guadeloupean Epic* (2004) that stage events around the Guadeloupian rebellion against the French in 1803, Lara is reaching out to Guadeloupians to reconsider their collective memory around French involvement in their history, politics, economics and culture. Robinson further opines that this disconnect between lavish production values and political intent confounds Westerners. Perhaps Western filmgoers cannot reconcile lavish aesthetics and non-classical Hollywood-style narrative structure. With episodic form and structure, the narrative is more akin to oral storytelling forms.

Cham acknowledges the difficulties inherent in categorizing Caribbean film production since most filmmakers born in the Caribbean live and work in larger centres. Christian Lara, for example, discloses that he was born in Guadeloupe, spent his childhood and youth in Africa, and moved to Paris to work as a journalist and filmmaker (Cham 1992: 280). He thus joins the ranks of other filmmakers of Caribbean descent living and working in the African and Caribbean diasporas, as well as filmmakers of African descent working in independent production contexts on themes of Black solidarity and resistance to colonialism, slavery and oppression. Cham points to the 1979 film *West*

Indies: Les Nègres Marrons de la Liberté/West Indies: the Fugitive Slaves of Liberty, by Mauritanian filmmaker Med Hondo, as an example of 'tout-mondisme' because Hondo, as an African, creates transnational flows of Black culture and history by deconstructing and reconstructing Caribbean history drawing on the play *Les négriers/The Slavers* by Martinican Daniel Boukman to expose, via the musical comedy genre, the appalling legacy of the slave trade (8). What Cham is grappling with in the 1990s in terms of 'this question of belonging' and 'requisite conditions' (10) for films to be classified as Caribbean is similar to the questions film scholar Hamid Naficy began to probe in the late 1990s and early 2000s concerning films that arise from expatriation and displacement of the filmmaker who works in alternative production contexts, with migration movement and exile as common themes (2001: 4–20).

Mariette Monpierre falls squarely within Naficy's description of accented filmmakers, but also, to a certain extent, within Lara's framework of what qualifies as a Caribbean film and a Caribbean filmmaker. He maintains that a production's director must be from the Caribbean; the story must be Caribbean; the lead actor must be Caribbean; the production unit should be Caribbean and Creole should be spoken (at least some of the time). However, he does concede that, although this is the ideal situation, it might be rare for all five conditions to exist in any single case (Cham 1992: 10). Born in Guadeloupe and raised in Paris, Monpierre completed a master's degree in media & languages at the Sorbonne University and Smith College in Massachusetts and moved to Manhattan where she began her filmmaking career as a producer of award-winning short films and commercials for companies such as Pepsi Cola, Visa, Campbell's, Pizza Hut, Gillette and FedEx. In 2002, her short film *Rendez-vous* about a woman seemingly waiting for someone or something as she observes clients entering a restaurant was nominated for the Djibril Diop Mambety Award in partnership with the Directors Fortnight in Cannes. The film experienced a successful run in several major international film festivals such as Toronto International Film Festival, Official selection of the Marrakech Film Festival, The African Diaspora film Festival in New York, Montreal World Film Festival, Panafrican Film Festival of Ouagadougou, the International Women's Film Festival in Seoul, among others.

In 2017, Monpierre directed a fifty-two-minute documentary titled, *Entre deux rives: de Saint-Domingue à Pointe-à-Pitre: Between Two Shores* for the *Archipels* documentary TV series. The documentary uncovers the complicated process of immigration within and between Caribbean islands as two women, Johanna and Cristina, fight to bring back their children left in the Dominican Republic to Guadeloupe where they emigrated to in search of better lives. The story of these two women reflects a strand of Monpierre's personal history. Although the context and time periods are different, Monpierre's own mother had left Guadeloupe for France in search of better opportunities for her children, who she left with their grandmother until it was financially possible for her to send for them.

Little by little, through each of her film projects, Monpierre braids together her complicated family history into that of Guadeloupe, the Caribbean and the Black Atlantic. In 2018, she developed the first episode of a television comedy series, *Caribbean Girl NYC* (25 mins/episode), which follows the lives and exploits of four twenty something Caribbean women living in New York City.[2] Interestingly, the main character, Isabelle, effects a reverse journey to that of Elza, whereby she leaves Guadeloupe and the Caribbean in pursuit of the American dream, Caribbean style.

'Caribbeing' memory narrative and aesthetics

With *Le Bonheur d'Elza*, the central task facing Monpierre is the need to go beyond 'the long and painful quest' of creating identity schema in 'opposition to the denaturing process introduced' by the Caribbean's colliding histories of colonialism (Glissant 1997: 17). Yet, paradoxically, this cannot be achieved without addressing 'the processes of identification or annihilation triggered by these invaders' whose actions fundamentally shaped the political, historical and economic contexts of Caribbean nations (17). To bridge this seeming contradiction, Monpierre chooses to view Caribbean experience as a 'rhizome' comprised of global flows of history highlighting 'the knowledge that identity is no longer completely within the root but also in Relation' between creolized viewpoints of that experience (18). Such a strategy undermines linear Eurocentric depictions of Caribbean histories by positing identities that arise from these histories as multifaceted and multidimensional.

This strategy also works in concert with the interstitial accented production context of *Le Bonheur d'Elza* in which several conditions are 'rhizomatically

'Irreducible Memories' of Caribbeanness   237

interlinked' (Naficy 2001: 43). For example, Naficy argues that an interstitial context involves operating 'both within and astride the cracks of the system, benefiting from its contradictions, anomalies, and heterogeneity. It also means being located at the intersection of the local and the global, mediating between the two contrary categories', and, as a result, identities as filmmakers and roles within the productions become 'interstitial, partial, and multiple' (46–47). With *Le Bonheur d'Elza*, Monpierre acts as director, co-screenwriter and actor in the film, fulfilling Naficy's 'multiple functions' criterion. The choice of Mama Keïta as co-screenwriter and executive producer provides an added layer of interstitiality and transnationality. Born in Dakar, Senegal, to a Vietnamese mother and a Guinean father, Keïta studied law at the University of Paris I before becoming a film director and producer of many feature films, including the 2009 award-winning film *L'Absence/The Absence*. His work often deals with issues of mixed race relations, human rights and transnationality within the globalizing African diaspora. Valorization of Black culture and African heritage is central to his films' narratives and it appears, in the opening scenes of *Le Bonheur d'Elza*, that this will again be the case.[3]

Le Bonheur d'Elza opens very unconventionally (in terms of classical Hollywood narrative style precepts) with extreme close-up shots of a mass of hair twists as the opening credits roll. An off-screen male voice asks, 'So, Elza ... the usual?' Elza Béranger, the main character, lifts her head and faces the camera in direct address, agreeing with the request. The opening scene depicts Elza in a Parisian Black hair salon having her hair straightened and pulled back into a tight bun. An extreme close-up of the stylist's hand foregrounds a gold slave bracelet featuring an African continent ornament as she styles Elza's hair, while reggae strains of 'Caribbean people .... one nation' are heard on the music track. References to the Black Atlantic slave trade and the links to Africa, symbolized by the thin gold chains crossing the hand and attaching the ornament to the bracelet, are visual reminders of the slave trade routes and flows of history. While this opening scene serves to introduce Elza as the main protagonist, it also centres Africa as the world within the local. In her work on African American women and the effects of white standards of beauty on their body and hair images, Tracey Owens Patton maintains that 'haircare and styling' are a performance and that hair is 'performed' as a way 'to become centered in a world of beauty that tends to not value' Black expressions of hair norms (2006: 36). This opening 'performance' is followed by a scene of Elza, her sister and mother (played by Monpierre) in their apartment as they celebrate Elza's successful university graduation. She has just passed the Agrégation – the highest French teaching degree obtained by an elite handful whose exact number is determined by the Ministry of Education depending on how many are needed. This qualification is typically only open to holders of master's degrees or higher. But rather than immediately embark on a teaching career, Elza decides to 'return' to Guadeloupe.

Elza's journey is a journey of identity that provides the narrative quest of the film, acting as a structuring metaphor. Following the opening hair salon scene, Elza returns to the family apartment for the celebration and as her mother congratulates Elza on her success, she presents her with a gift of money. Her sister asks what Elza will do with it and when Elza replies that she will travel to their homeland, a fierce argument ensues. These shots are intercut with close-ups of Elza in a tour bus in Guadeloupe as she recalls the heated opposition of her mother: 'What are you looking for? No one is waiting for you there!' The intercutting of these shots sets up a 'push me-pull you' dynamic that orders the narrative for the duration of the film, much like the tension embodied by the 'national borders and diasporic connections' of Caribbean cultures (Bryce 2019: 123).

Naficy cautions that accented filmmakers' journeys are more than just 'physical and territorial', but are also 'psychological and philosophical' (Naficy 2001: 6). He maintains that a significant aspect of the journey is the quest for identity, sloughing off the old one and forging a new one – identity as an ongoing process of becoming – a performance whereby 'each accented film may be thought of as a performance of its author's identity' (6). Indeed, Monpierre has disclosed the autobiographical nature of her film when she states the following:

> This movie for me is like therapy and a form of catharsis. It cost me a lot of money you know. It was very expensive therapy. But it was all worth it. Because I had to confront the issues I had with my father; that he abandoned me, and when I came to see him years later, he rejected me. So I had to take a look at that and come to terms with it.
>
> (Mims 2017)

In this interview, Monpierre not only reveals her objectives in making the film, but she also exposes a further characteristic of the interstitial production mode whereby accented filmmakers often must invest significantly in their own productions (or fundraise as producers) to move them forward to completion. By performing multiple functions in the production process, filmmakers become, in Naficy's schematic, the true authors of their productions (Naficy 2001: 47, 49).

Within Naficy's frame of interstitiality, accented filmmakers are often 'ironically' critical of both home and host cultures as they navigate new identities (53). In *Le Bonheur d'Elza*, the protagonist will find that her return to her roots involves an unravelling of many painful aspects of personal and national histories. The return to the source trope was seen as a decolonization strategy in early African film criticism, where it was deemed that political and cultural emancipation of new nation states was only possible through the valorization of indigenous cultural tradition (Diawara: 1992: 140). Elza's 'return to the source' does not occur in an uncomplicated, linear line of action. In fact, the story strands are braided as in oral tradition. When she arrives at the Désiré estate, she is mistaken (based on her dark skin colour and kinky hair, no longer tied back in a bun) by Madame Désiré for the new babysitter the family had advertised for. Elza is promptly hired to care for Caroline, the Désirés' granddaughter. Elza takes on the name 'Marie-Line' and forms a close bond with Caroline as she navigates the family's complicated relationships. The Désirés have two daughters: Christine, who is married to Bernard, a white French man; and Marie, Caroline's unwed mother. Christine and Bernard live with the family while Marie is recovering from the trauma of forced separation from Jean-Luc, Caroline's Black labourer father, in a long-term care home. Both Bernard and Désiré are womanizers, and Marie-Line must ward off Bernard's sexual advances while Désiré spends as much time as possible with Sophie, the glamorous young Black wife of Léopold, his white banker, rather than with his own white wife.

Elza's quest exposes the nature of race relations on the island with each character representing different threads of Caribbean culture history. Race is a marker of culture in Caribbean nations where race, initially proscribed by colonialism and slavery and later by the importation of waves of indentured labourers, has meant an ongoing struggle against systemic dehumanization.

The body, on which these histories of 'creolization' are inscribed through discourse, therefore remains evocative of 'the unceasing process of transformation' at the centre of Caribbean identities (Glissant 1989: 142). Even concepts of 'social class', according to Benítez-Rojo, entrenched in many other societies, are 'displaced by "race," or in any event by "skin color"' (2001: 200). This 'double conflict of the skin' in Caribbean culture is embodied most clearly in the film through the character of Désiré (201). He has married a white French woman and has two mixed-race legitimate children. Bernard tells Elza that Désiré pretends to be a good Catholic, but has bastard children all over the island, before asking Elza if she is one of them (implying the children are dark-skinned). When Elza meets Jean-Luc at a bar to tell him she gave Caroline the birthday gifts he brought to the house (that were thrown in the rubbish bin by Madame Désiré and subsequently rescued by Elza), he confides in her that he had wanted to marry Marie but Désiré considers him too black and just a common labourer. A strike at Désiré's factory, where Jean-Luc was working, went 'haywire' and Jean-Luc hurt a policeman in self-defence. He was imprisoned and Marie suffered a nervous breakdown. Jean-Luc is now fighting for the legal custody of Caroline, but fears that due to his status as a labourer on a fishing boat and more significantly, his skin colour, he will not win because the historical divisions of plantation cultures still obtain. Shalini Puri has written that 'the antagonism between a racialized "us" and "them"' lies in 'the series of oppositions' used to justify the importation of Indian labour by stereotyping Afro- and Indi-Caribbeans as 'the thriftless African/the thrifty Indian; the lazy African/the hard-working Indian; [and] the childlike African unable to control his sexual appetites/the calculating and ascetic Indian' (2004: 172–3). In doing so, white planters were successful in polarizing the two cultures and thus prevented a challenge to their authority.

Elza's quest exposes a further story strand of continued exploitation of factory workers employed by Désiré. The scenes of picketing workers appear at three intervals, and in the third sequence, the workers threaten to kidnap Caroline for ransom, although there is mitigated support for this idea as many workers (all dark-skinned and most with dreadlocks) are still loyal to Jean-Luc. It is worthwhile posing the question whether the labour unrest thread is a nod to history. For example, in 2009, Guadeloupean labour unions and others known as the Liyannaj Kont Pwofitasyon went on strike for higher wages that would provide them with a decent level of living. A forty-five-day national struggle against colonial exploitation ensued led by trade union leader, Domota. The Sarkozy government sent soldiers to Guadeloupe to suppress the protest and all that was eventually conceded was a plan for higher wages, although the legacies of slavery and colonialism and the racial hierarchies fostering discrimination were exposed leading to important questions around social and political agency (Crowell 2018).

The camera in *Elza* is used as a motif for agency. Elza uses her camera to document her trip from the moment she arrives in Guadeloupe, as if she were compelled to record the results of her quest, from scenes of lush landscape to shots of her father's indiscretions. Her mother's searing question at the beginning of the film, 'What are you looking for?', comes to mind. Is her camera a weapon, or a means to record and thus prove her identity? She gives Jean-Luc photos of Désiré with Sophie Léopold ('with this he can never touch you'); yet, the photos Elza throws at Désiré near the end of the film are old photos of Elza and her sister. What is she, indeed, looking for? At many points throughout the film, she tries to get close to him – while he pretends to be sleeping in a lawn chair, she places his glasses on the table beside him. And while Elza is 'looking at' Désiré, he is also surreptitiously looking at her. The first time Elza, as 'Marie-Line', takes Caroline to the beach, he gazes at her from the window as they leave the estate, although he had ignored her while she was in the house. When Elza takes the bus to Capesterre to visit the house she lived in with her sister and mother as a small child, Désiré follows her. When she returns to the Désiré estate, she is confronted by both Madame Désiré and Christine who have learned of her true identity and order her to leave. She storms into Désiré's study and cries, 'I really needed to tell you how much my sister and I missed you.' At this point, Désiré is gazing out the window with his back to Elza, refusing to look at her and retorting, 'With your kinky hair, you couldn't possibly be my daughter.' Elza throws her old family photos on his desk snapping back, 'Like it or not, we are your family too. Please look at me!' A reverse medium two-shot frames Désiré's face pensively gazing out the window on frame right, refusing to look at her, while Elza stands behind him in the background. Incredibly, the aesthetics of the natural lighting emphasize his 'whiteness' versus Elza's 'blackness'. This visual aesthetic presentation recalls Trinidadian filmmaker Yao Ramesar's cinematographic philosophy. In an aesthetic that he terms 'Caribbeing', Ramesar advocates the use of natural elements in the filmic storytelling process. He explains that 'the choice of camera and other materials is specifically made within the context of filming (often on exterior locations) with the expectation that elements in situ, including though not solely naturally occurring elements such as sun/moon light, water, and earth/landscape, will be incorporated into the process of the storytelling within and beyond the frame' (2019: 167–8).

The physical landscape of Guadeloupe plays a powerful role in Monpierre's aesthetic project. Glissant contends that 'the inescapable *shaping force* in our production of literature is what I would call the language of landscape' (1989: 145). Ramesar takes this a step further in his own film work by 'using the Caribbean landscape as both character and cinematographic tool' (2019: 172). Similarly, in her filmic depiction of Guadeloupe, Monpierre places a strong emphasis on landscape as a bearer of history and a portal to memory. Water, waves and bright sunlight on clear blue oceanscape and beaches provide blissful moments when Elza experiences a sense of freedom. For example, when she arrives in Guadeloupe, she jumps off the tour bus and rushes into the ocean, her hair still tightly bound in her Parisian (diaspora) bun. She emerges from the waters liberated in the homeland's (Guadeloupe) 'boundlessness and timelessness' (Naficy 2001: 5). But images of waves, cliffs and rocks also stir up images of the past, and several times throughout the course of the film Elza dreams of this very seascape where the saturated images of the water and rocks contrast with the crisp whiteness of the shirt Désiré wears as he twirls an infant Elza lovingly in his arms. Following the scene in which Bernard queries Elza's paternity, flashes of the seascape memories are intercut with shots of Elza's mother demanding to know why she is determined to resurrect the past. The shots that follow depict Elza screaming in anguish, curled up on the beach. This sequence is highly reminiscent of the climax of Med Hondo's *Soleil Ô* which frames the protagonist's profound psychological disjunction within the transnational context of the Black Atlantic as he symbolically 'vomits' all that he has ingested since his arrival in France (Cottenet-Hage 1996: 182). In the end, the protagonist positively reclaims his own subjectivity and moves on to redefine Black experience within evolving contexts and global flows of experiences.

In the end, the final scenes of reconciliation between Elza and her father leave some room for interpretation as it is not entirely clear if Elza's relationship with

'Irreducible Memories' of Caribbeanness

243

her father has been satisfactorily resolved. Elza is at the airport, about to board her plane back to Paris when she decides to return to Désiré, who has suffered a heart attack. She is asleep in a chair beside his bed when he awakens, puts out his hand, and calls her 'Elza', as he caresses her face. She awakens and their hands lock. The final shots are in slow motion as father and daughter dance in the garden – Elza in a black dress and Désiré in a white shirt and white pants. The continued emphasis on Elza's 'blackness' versus Désiré's 'whiteness' gives pause for thought. Is this about coming to terms with one's own identity within the global flows of passion and conflict of families in transition? Monpierre views her own quest as something larger than her personal relationship with her father, who is now dead – she was able, ultimately to discover and connect with her father's larger, extended family – something she now cherishes. The 'boundlessness and timelessness' (Naficy 2001: 5) of the film's family connections are made all the more evident through Monpierre's dedication to her son at the opening of the film and to her deceased mother, Man Dédée, at the end of the film. The journey has come full circle.

Notes

1   It is no wonder that Caribbean filmmakers have taken up the infamous legacy of the sugar trade and slavery in their productions. See, for example, Christian Lara's 1998 *Bitter Sugar (Sucre Amer)*. This new form of slavery is also staged brilliantly in Euzhan Palcy's 1983 film, *Sugar Cane Alley*, as well as, of course, in the novel by Aimé Césaire, on which the film is based.

2   An interesting comparison can be made to Fatima Sissani's *Les Gracieuses* (France, 2014) which follows the lives of six young thirty-something women who are all of different ethnic backgrounds and who were all born in the same apartment building in the suburbs of Champigny Sur Marne, France. The feature-length documentary explores race, class and gender relations and identities in contemporary France as French youth debate and reassess established forms of French republicanism.

3   This is also the case in *Sugar Cane Alley*. During the opening of the film, Euzhan Palcy initially stakes out an ideological position with strong overtones of Negritude: through a series of sepia postcards and photographs, Palcy depicts life in 1930s Martinique, focusing on images of black Martinicans in street scenes,

family portraits and at work. In addition to setting the time period, the images signal Palcy's intention to valorize black Martinican experience by foregrounding their culture as central to the film's narrative. The most explicit statement aligning the sequence with Negritude is Palcy's dedication of the film, which occurs over an image of a black man driving an ox cart. The words 'Dedicated to the world's Black Shack Alleys' place the film in a Panafrican context by linking the Caribbean experience to black Africa and the diaspora.

References

1802, L'Epopée Guadeloupéenne (2004), [Film] Dir. Christian Lara, France/ Guadeloupe: Bicéphale Productions.

L'Absence (2009), [Film] Dir. Mama Keïta, France/Guinea: Kinterfin.

Benítez-Rojo, A. (2001), *The Repeating Island: the Caribbean and the Postmodern Perspective*, Durham: Duke University Press.

Le Bonheur d'Elza (2011), [Film] Dir. Mariette Monpierre, France/Guadeloupe: Tu Vas Voir Productions/Aztec Musique/ OverEasy Productions/ France Télévisions (co-production)/ Canal Plus Overseas (co-production)/Région Guadeloupe (support)/Morgane Production.

Bryce, J. (2019), 'Close-Up: Caribbean Cinema as Cross-Border Dialogue: Introduction', *Black Camera: An International Film Journal* 11.1: 123–9.

Caribbean Girl NYC (2018), [TV pilot series] Dir. Mariette Monpierre, USA: Flow/ Caribbean Tales International/Overeasy Productions.

Cham, M. (ed.) (1992), *Ex-Iles: Essays on Caribbean Cinema*, Trenton: Africa World Press.

Cottenet-Hage, M. (1996), 'Decolonizing Images: *Soleil Ô* and the Cinema of Med Hondo', in D. Sherzer (ed.), *Cinema, Colonialism, Postcolonialism: Perspectives from the French and Francophone Worlds*, 173–87, Austin: University of Texas Press.

Crowell, M. (2018), 'The Island Where France's Colonial Legacy Lives On', *The Atlantic*, 21 April. Available online: https://www.theatlantic.com/international/ archive/2018/04/france-macron-guadeloupe-slavery-colonialism/557996/ (accessed 4 December 2019).

Diawara, M. (1992), *African Cinema: Politics and Culture*, Bloomington: Indiana University Press.

Ellerson, B. (2017), 'African Women in Cinema Dossier: Traveling Gazes: Glocal Imaginaries in the Transcontinental, Transnational, Exilic, Migration, and

Diasporic Cinematic Experiences of African Women', *Black Camera: An International Film Journal* 8.2: 272–89.

Entre deux rives: de Saint-Domingue à Pointe-à-Pitre (2017), [Film] Dir. Mariette Monpierre, France/Guadeloupe/Dominican Republic: Art & Vision Productions/ Les Films Jack Febus.

Gautier, A. (2003), 'Femmes et colonialisme', in M. Ferro (ed.), *Le livre noir du colonialisme. XVIe – XXIe siècle: de l'extermination à la repentance*, 569–607, Paris: Éditions Robert Laffont.

Glissant, E. (1989), *Caribbean Discourse: Selected Essays*, Charlottesville: University Press of Virginia.

Glissant, E. (1997), *Poetics of Relation*, trans. B. Wing, Ann Arbor: The University of Michigan Press.

Glissant, E. (2009), *Philosophie de la Relation*, Paris: Gallimard.

Gott, M. and T. Schilt (eds) (2018), *Cinéma-monde: Decentred Perspectives on Global Filmmaking in French*, Edinburgh: Edinburgh University Press.

The Harder They Come (1972), [Film] Dir. Perry Henzell, Jamaica: International Films/Zenon Pictures.

Les Gracieuses (2014), [Film] Dir. Fatima Sissani, France: 24images/Girelle Production.

Imorou, A. (2011), 'Du Tout-monde comme objet d'étude: postcolonialisme, histoire globale et poétique de la relation', *Africultures* 87: 34–42.

Lorsque l'herbe (1968), [Film] Dir. Christian Lara, Guadeloupe.

Mims, S. (2017), 'Interview: Getting Personal with Mariette Monpierre, Director of "Elza" (At PAFF LA Feb 10 & 13)', *Shadow and Act* (20 April). Available online: https://shadowandact.com/interview-getting-personal-with-mariette-monpierre-director-of-elza-at-paff-la-feb-10-13 (accessed 31 December 2019).

Naficy, H. (1999), 'Between Rocks and Hard Places: The Interstitial Mode of Production in Exilic Cinema', in H Naficy (ed.), *Home, Exile, Homeland: Film, Media, and the Politics of Place*, 125–47, New York: Routledge.

Naficy, H. (2001), *An Accented Cinema: Exilic and Diasporic Filmmaking*, Princeton: Princeton University Press.

Patton, T. O. (2006), 'Hey Girl, Am I More than My Hair?: African American Women and Their Struggles with Beauty. Body Image, and Hair', *National Women's Studies Association Journal* 18.2 (Summer): 24–51.

Puri, S. (2004), *The Caribbean Postcolonial: Social Equality, Post-Nationalism, and Cultural Hybridity*, New York: Palgrave MacMillan.

Ramesar, Y. (2019), 'Close-Up: Caribbean Cinema as Cross-Border Dialogue: Caribbeing Continuum: Progression of a Cinema Eyealect in the Motion Picture

Feature *Haiti Bride*', *Black Camera: An International Film Journal* 11.1 (Fall): 167–79.

Rendez-vous (2002), [Film] Dir. Mariette Monpierre, USA.

Robinson, M. N. (2010), '*Ciné woulé, ciné en progrès*: An Investigation of the Francophone Caribbean Film Circuit, 1968–2010', *Small Axe* 33: 45–68.

Robinson, M. (2015), 'Christian Lara: Reconciling Vision and Execution in Sucre Amer and 1802, l'Epopée Guadeloupéenne', *Imaginations* 6.2: 68–83. Available online: DOI: 10.17742/IMAGE.CCN.6-2.7 (accessed 8 November 2019).

Rue case-nègres (1983), [Film] Dir. Euzhan Palcy, France: Sumafa Productions/Orca Productions/NEF – Nouvelles Éditions de Films (Paris).

Soleil Ô (1969), [Film] Dir. Med Hondo, Mauritania/France: Grey Films/Shango Films.

Sucre amer (1998), [Film] Dir. Christian Lara, Canada/France/Guadeloupe: Films Stock International Inc./Guadeloupe Films Compagnie (GFC)/R.F.O./Tesson.

West Indies: Les Nègres Marrons de la Liberté (1979), [Film] Dir. Med Hondo, France/Mauritania: Les Films Soleil Ô/Yanek/Ipc/R.T.A./Onmc.

12

Documenting lifestyle migration:
Anayansi Prado's *Paraíso for Sale* (2011)

Carolyn Fornoff

Surrounded by water and detached from the mainland, islands have long been conceived as spatially and conceptually set apart from the rest of society. This distance has made the island the perfect staging ground for envisioning utopia, where, following Thomas More, 'the best state of a commonwealth' can be founded.[1] In the twenty-first century, one neoliberal manifestation of the quest for a paradisiacal blank slate is lifestyle migration. Primarily undertaken by retirees from the Global North, lifestyle migration – otherwise known as residential tourism – is the practice of 'consumption-led migration' southward, driven by the search for an inexpensive and warm leisure destination to live out one's later years (McWatters 2009: 3). Since the turn of the twenty-first century, lifestyle migration has been rewriting the demographics of Latin American coasts, displacing and dispossessing (often Indigenous or Afro-descendant) local populations who have occupied the land for years, yet whose claim to it is not legally protected. In countries like Panama, residential tourism has been pursued as a development strategy. In order to court foreign investment, the Panamanian state has promoted the idea that its pristine coasts are an empty paradise awaiting future inhabitants – erasing locals from the frame.

Anayansi Prado's 2014 documentary, *Paraíso for Sale*, dramatizes the racialized and spatialized conflicts set in motion by the influx of semi-permanent, older white residents to the Panamanian archipelago Bocas del Toro. Prado, a Panamanian filmmaker based in Los Angeles, sheds light on the vexed transformation of the island chain as North American retirees and developers rushed to buy land in the 2000s. Her documentary presents residential tourism as a form of neoliberal imperialism that activates conflicts

248 *The Film Archipelago*

around land rights, not just between locals and foreigners, but also between Panama's Ngäbe-Buglé and Afro-Panamanian populations. In this chapter, I explore how *Paraíso for Sale* unpacks the inequities arising from the discourse of development and destabilizes the normative tourist gaze that typically frames the island space. I propose that Prado's decision not to dwell on the aesthetic beauty of the islands or on the Caribbean Sea's clear waters (eschewing for instance, the bird's-eye view) upends archetypal touristic visualizations of archipelagos and instead provides a terrene-oriented sense of place.

Who deserves a view?

About halfway through *Paraíso for Sale*, one of the documentary's protagonists, Ngäbe activist Feliciano Santos, joins an Indigenous group that is blocking the road in protest of the demolition of their homes. Emotions run justifiably high: the land underlying their sixty homes has been claimed by an Afro-Panamanian man. The man holds a land title that dates back to the 1950s, but he has never lived there. Now that its value has skyrocketed, he plans to sell the parcel to developers. To get the best price, he needs to evict the Indigenous community that inhabits it. Although they have lived there for longer than the fifteen years required by the state to stake legal claim to the parcel, the government has turned a blind eye to the enforcement of laws protecting Indigenous land rights, and instead favours the archipelago's development and the nation's welcoming reputation to outside investors.

The roadblock is the Ngäbe's only remaining recourse, a way to make their voices and frustration visible to the public. As a visual artefact, *Paraíso for Sale* expands and extends this visibility through time and space by registering these efforts and repackaging them for a transnational audience, a group that Prado purposefully targets for driving Bocas del Toro's increased desirability as a retirement destination, and who may be persuaded to see the harm underlying lifestyle migration. This cinematic focus on righteous local anger counters normative colonial imagery of the tropical Caribbean, which, as Krista Thompson has shown, relies on images of 'disciplined "natives"' to market the locale as a tourist attraction in which locals are merely another element of local colour, rather than agents whose desires might threaten travellers' safety or enjoyment of their tropical escape (2006: 7). In effect, Prado's film shifts the imagery linked to Bocas in the foreign viewer's imagination from serene tropical views to a close-up of the inland roadblock, recentring the justifiably wrathful Ngäbe subject.

The roadblock encapsulates the film's theme of racial inequity: specifically, the inequity that crops up around the question of access to land with proximity to the sea. Carrying a banner that reads, 'No displacement, humiliation, or injustice on our own land', the Ngäbe protestors decry their dispossession.[2] Two interviews are sequentially shown. The first woman angrily explains in Spanish, 'I want to live by the ocean, not just whites want to live there, not just Blacks.' A second woman adds, 'white people want to live there and not see us at all.'[3] These animated statements get at the crux of *Paraíso*'s driving question: who is allowed to desire a view? The first woman's insistence upon her inclusion within the framework of desire for ocean proximity reveals its exclusionary logic. Her demand for incorporation within the affective economy of desire for place negates the notion that Bocas' recent 'discovery' by residential tourists means that it was not a previously valued or valuable landscape, while also affirming her agential claim, as an Indigenous woman, to desire a view. The second interviewee elaborates that the tourist attraction to paradisiacal space is a fantasy contingent upon expunging Indigenous subjects from the frame. As the women make clear, both the desire for landscape and the desired landscape have been conceived of in ways that require the stripping of agency and the dispossession of Indigenous subjects.

In order to understand these two vectors – the desire for landscape and the desirable landscape – it is helpful to parse them apart. First, I discuss the phenomenon of lifestyle migration and how Prado tackles it in *Paraíso* through a tripartite structure. Second, I touch on the tourist gaze that has framed Bocas as an aspirational, unpopulated landscape in order to demonstrate how Prado troubles this imaginary by pointedly redirecting the frame away from untouched sandy beaches and back towards the land and the subjects that have long lived there.

Migrating south

The term migration, or the movement of people across or within borders, immediately conjures up preestablished ideas about directional flows from south to north, motivated by economic factors. Copious cinematic work – fiction and nonfiction – is dedicated to this subject. This includes films directed by Prado, who has completed three documentaries profiling undocumented migrants in the United States.

Prado's debut film, *Maid in America*, follows the lives of three Latina domestic workers in Los Angeles. Broadcast in the PBS series Independent Lens in 2004, the hour-long documentary is aimed at a general public and advocates for undocumented workers' rights by revealing the hardships the protagonists endure to provide for their families. Because *Maid in America*'s pedagogical goal is to promote the compassionate and ethical treatment of these labourers, their depiction is resoundingly positive. The women are defined by their sentimentalized roles as caretakers, and their exemplary behaviour is deployed to justify their deserved entrance into the US citizenry. Irune del Rio Gabiola rightly notes that this representation of the women as 'ideal maternal bodies' or easily assimilable 'maternal heroines' is problematic (2013: 119). In spite of this, as a whole Prado's film successfully illuminates the gendered and racialized exploitation of domestic labourers at the turn of the twenty-first century.

In subsequent films, Prado has delved into other aspects of US immigration, cementing her reputation as a 'transnational feminist filmmaker' (Palmer 2011). Her documentary short *Children in No Man's Land* (2008) focuses on unaccompanied minors, and her feature *The Unafraid* (2018), co-directed with Heather Courtney, investigates access to higher education for DACA (Deferred Action for Childhood Arrivals) students in Georgia.

Expanding upon her commitment to the intersection of social justice and migration, Prado's 2014 documentary, *Paraíso for Sale*, echoes a shift that is also occurring within the field of migration studies: the recognition that migration not only courses from south to north, but also inversely from north to south. Whereas northbound migration is often characterized as forced – the migrant is compelled to leave their home because of insecurities linked to violence, environmental conditions or unemployment – southbound migration is decidedly voluntary. Like most migrants, these southbound travellers are inspired to relocate in search of a better life. What differentiates them is that they are already relatively affluent individuals from the Global North who are not driven by employment opportunities, but by the search for a more affordable lifestyle that enables their self-actualization.

Lifestyle migration is generally motivated by two factors: the desire for a better location with specific aesthetic and climatic properties, and improved consumption practices or greater purchase power in the local currency. Additionally, lifestyle migrants are often interested in places that promise a more 'authentic' way of life, one that diverges from the fast-paced experience of neoliberal modernity in the location of origin. This can manifest through the romanticized aspiration for pastoral life, such as that expressed by British migrants who move to rural southern France, or for spaces that supposedly 'escape' modernity, like Mazatlán, Mexico or southern Spain.

Lifestyle migration to Latin America is motivated by not only a desire for authenticity, natural beauty and warm weather, but also greater affordability. Lifestyle migrants are usually retired or self-employed; they generally do not need to generate income while in the destination country, but instead dedicate themselves to leisure activities or the task of self-realization. While lifestyle migrants are privileged subjects who are affluent in the global sense, they largely self-identify as middle class and had professions considered as such in their countries of origin (Benson 2013: 503). Matthew Hayes has demonstrated that North American lifestyle migrants to Ecuador are increasingly motivated by economic factors, such as the 2008 financial crisis and a subsequent loss in savings (Hayes 2015). Research by Omar Lizarraga, Alejandro Mantecón and Raquel Huete has shown that North Americans who choose to relocate to Mexico often report incomes lower than their British counterparts who move to France or Spain (Lizarraga, Mantecón and Huete 2015). These destinations' lower cost of living makes them attractive options for middle-class US retirees.

Other terms used to describe the practice of lifestyle migration include residential tourism, second-home tourism, retirement tourism or migration tourism. Residential tourism is the most common of these monikers and is used to describe the resulting practices of lifestyle migrants in the host country. Michaela Benson and Karen O'Reilly argue however that we should purposefully use the term 'migrant' – rather than terms like expatriate or residential tourist – when describing these privileged migrant subjects in order to expand our association of migration beyond a delimited set of people and motives. Underscoring the ease with which these subjects migrate south troubles the 'white normativity' that typically excludes white subjects from the category of the migrant and lays bare 'the inequalities and asymmetries that exist and are (re)produced within contemporary migration regimes and governance' (Benson and O'Reilly 2018: 10). Indeed, patterns of north to south lifestyle migration alter existing political, economic and social structures, just as migration northward does.

In Panama, the number of permanent and semi-permanent foreign residents exploded at the turn of the twenty-first century. This influx was the product of the expanding cohort of North American baby-boomers nearing retirement age, combined with Panama's economic and governmental stability relative to the rest of Latin America, and its implementation of a series of tax breaks in the late 1990s designed to attract foreign residents. One of these strategies, the *pensionado* [retirement] visa programme, grants permanent residency to any foreigner residing in Panama who receives a monthly pension of at least US$1,000. It also applies to those with monthly pensions of at least $750, as long as they own Panamanian real estate valued over US$100,000.[4] This visa brings with it a host of benefits in addition to legal residence: tax and duty exemptions, and discounts on transportation, hotels, restaurants, utilities, and health care. Panama's retirement visa was modelled after Costa Rica's, which was established in the late 1970s, and successfully induced a tsunami of lifestyle migrants. However, as Mason McWatters notes, at the same time that Panama began implementing incentives to attract foreign retirees, Costa Rica was scaling its policies back in response to rising tensions between local and foreign residents (2009: 70). Even though Panama was aware of these policies' foreseeable downsides, they were cast aside as insignificant collateral damage in the pursuit of economic growth.

The inflow of relatively privileged migrants to a host country unsurprisingly creates friction with native residents. While the influx of foreigners boosts GDP through consumer power and property investment, at the same time, their arrival exacerbates preexisting social inequities, effectively propelling what Thomas Sigler and David Waschmusch term 'transnational gentrification', which creates an economic chasm between foreign residents and locals (2015).

This influx dramatically changed Bocas del Toro, a province on northwestern Panama's Caribbean coast composed of an archipelago and adjacent mainland. While Bocas is now one of the most touristed areas in Panama, this was not always the case. Historically the region received its greatest migrant influx in the late nineteenth century, when the United Fruit Company (UFC) established operations there. After UFC's withdrawal inland in 1910, the archipelago was left to its own devices. UFC's departure, combined with the ripple effect of the Great Depression and the outbreak of Panama Disease (a fungus affecting bananas), meant that the islands proceeded largely undisturbed by outsiders for much of the twentieth century (Guerrón Montero 2015: 198). The region was also ignored by the state. As Carla Guerrón Moreno describes, at the national level Bocas 'was portrayed as a dangerous, unappealing and unwelcoming place due to its geographic isolation and primarily Afro-Antillean and indigenous populations' (2015: 199).

The Ngäbe-Buglé (previously known as the Guaymí) are two separate linguistic/ethnic groups that together compose Panama's largest Indigenous population. In 1997, as required by Panama's 1972 constitution, land from Bocas del Toro and neighbouring provinces Chiriquí and Veraguas were carved out to create the Ngäbe-Buglé Comarca, an autonomous administrative region with substantial Amerindian peoples, essentially the equivalent of a province. Yet the most developed and touristy parts of Bocas del Toro were not included within the bounds of the Comarca, in spite of the fact that the Ngäbe-Buglé make up more than 70 per cent of the archipelago's population and were the first peoples to inhabit it (Contraloría 2010). This is yet another example of the ongoing, systematic marginalization of originary peoples in Panama. The Ngäbe-Buglé continue to struggle with the entrenched legacies of colonial racism, including the occupation of their lands by settlers, subpar access to health care and education, and limited economic opportunities.

The archipelago's Afro-Antillean presence is composed both of the descendants of the enslaved forcibly brought from the Antilles to Panama in the early 1800s, and the descendants of Antillean migrants who arrived to work for UFC at the century's close. After slavery was abolished in 1852, Afro-Antilleans established villages along the coast and lived off subsistence agriculture, small banana plantations and turtle fishing. Between the Afro-Antilleans and the Ngäbe-Buglé peoples, the former had the economic upper hand throughout the twentieth century, thanks to their ability to speak English and their racialized reputation as more reliable labour. As a result, today Afro-Antillean residents are more likely to occupy positions of governmental power and possess land titles than their Ngäbe-Buglé counterparts.

254 *The Film Archipelago*

In the 1990s, the tourism industry was established in the islands and rapidly took off. The archipelago has been marketed as the 'Galápagos of the Twenty-First Century', an ecotourist destination with high biodiversity, unique flora, coral reefs and pristine beaches. Bocas has been advertised in ways that highlight its ecological and ethnic diversity, as a destination that is 'off the beaten path', and 'the ultimate tropical and sunny location' (Guerrón Montero 2015: 200), in spite of the fact that it is often rainy.

Paraíso for Sale: *A Trefoil*

Paraíso for Sale explores how policies encouraging elite migrants to settle in Bocas del Toro have unsettled life on the islands, and resurfaced centuries-old disputes and inequities that are both race- and class-based. Mirroring Prado's debut documentary *Maid in America*, *Paraíso* is structured around three subjects who individually represent broader sectors of the population: Feliciano, a Ngäbe activist, Darío, an Afro-Panamanian tour guide and mayoral candidate, and Karan, a white Californian woman who has retired in Bocas with her husband Willy. All three are involved in land disputes with developers. Although they come from different racial and socioeconomic backgrounds, the trio's interwoven struggles combine to piece together a comprehensive portrait of the havoc inflicted by Panama's weak land laws, which benefit corporate developers and leave individuals with little recourse. However, in spite of the similar struggles that unite the three subjects, their disparate responses reveal the racialized fault lines that underlie Panama today.

The first of the documentary's three structural pillars is the aforementioned Feliciano Santos, a Ngäbe land rights activist.[5] As previously mentioned, Panamanian law gives rights of possession to any person who occupies or cultivates a piece of land for more than fifteen years. In theory, this law should protect the Ngäbe, who have long lived on Panama's Caribbean coast, but rarely possess titled land. In practice, this law is not observed. Panamanian courts regularly side with developers or lifestyle migrants who have purchased titles from (usually Afro-Panamanian) individuals who have not lived there for years, or who have manufactured fraudulent titles. This problem is exacerbated by the fact that Panama last conducted an official land census in 1970, meaning there is no state-documented evidence to prove long-term land occupation. As a result, Ngäbe homes are easily legally dismissed as trespassing and torn down by titleholders. These forcible displacements are presented in *Paraíso* as the neoliberal continuation of processes of Indigenous dispossession ongoing since the colonial period.

Feliciano and his neighbours are caught up in one such conflict. A North American developer, James Crabtree, purchased the beachfront property where Feliciano and his neighbours have lived for over twenty years. While there is no documentation to legally prove their occupation of the land, in one scene Feliciano points to mature coconut trees and describes how his family planted them there years ago. He explains that when they first arrived to the plot, it was a wasteland and local trash dump. Together they cleared the ground, planted trees and cleaned up trash. These practices of care and cultivation, although visibly evident on screen for the viewer, do not count as evidence in Feliciano's legal dispute with the developer.

Feliciano's description of the history of the environment where his family lives, and the way that it has changed due to human intervention – be it negative (its use as a trash dump) or positive (its cultivation) – illustrates that there is no such thing as 'nature' outside of human intervention. Therefore, while the developer or lifestyle migrant might be drawn to Bocas for its seemingly 'untouched' natural beauty, the archipelago's picture-perfect coastline is an illusion that glosses over decades or even centuries of care performed by subjects that are invisible to the tourist gaze. Feliciano's testimony of his family's cultivation of this spot troubles the presentation of Panama's coastlines as readymade, empty paradisiacal spaces that await the insertion of human bodies for their enjoyment. To the contrary, Feliciano situates what we can see as the result of practices of care that give shape to the pristine coastlines that are then coveted by 'imperial eyes' (Pratt 2008). The coconut trees shading the seashore that Feliciano and his family planted are naturalized as innate to the landscape and commodified into a currency that buoys Panama's amenable reputation to foreign developers.

Feliciano differs from the other two primary subjects in his affective demeanour. Unlike Darío's generally jovial bearing and Karan and Willy's relaxed optimism, Feliciano can be described as a killjoy. At one local hearing, Feliciano brings up the land struggles faced by the Ngäbe. From the opposite side of the room, his legal opponent speaks up, visibly irritated: 'He's on my property. He's been there for two years. I bought it legally five years ago. He's bothered me for five years. He's complained to every government agency … and I've beat him every time. He thinks I'm stealing his land, which he never owned.' The developer's comment suggests that Feliciano's presence is ubiquitous, an unreasonable nuisance to his rightful claim to the land. Feliciano fits the figure of the killjoy described by Sara Ahmed: a person who brings up an existing societal problem. In the act of voicing the problem, the killjoy becomes perceived as the problem's source. As Ahmed puts it, 'It is as if these problems are not there until you point them out; it is as if pointing them out is what makes them there' (2017: 39). Feliciano's insistent presence and unrelenting recourse to different institutional spaces to argue his case, even in the face of indifference and failure, transforms him into a disturbance. It makes his body visible as one that is supposedly in the way, blocking Panama's development and future economic prosperity.

In *Paraíso*, Prado presents disruption through killjoy visibility as one of few tools Indigenous subjects have at their disposal when seeking to counter their erasure by the state and developers. After Feliciano joins up with the roadblock, one woman explains that she was born in this village thirty years ago, so for the courts to affirm that she has no proof that she has lived there for over the required fifteen years is equivalent to the denial of her very self. With no institutional recourse, protest or contentious action is the only avenue through which Indigenous subjects can insert themselves into processes of governance and make their unhappiness visible. Feliciano explains, 'As Indigenous people, we are being incited to violence. However, we are very respectful of the law. But I insist: the only future that awaits us, if we see no progress on this issue, is one that invites us to do something that we don't want to do.' Reframed this way, acts of violent disruption like roadblocks are not a 'problem' that is located in the Ngäbe body, but the result of policies that force or, in Feliciano's words, 'invite' violence as the only possible response to dispossession.

Of the three subjects, Feliciano's concluding arc is the most dire. After his case is dismissed in the developer's favour, his house, along with those of his neighbours, is demolished, and their possessions set ablaze. Shots of a sneaker amid a pile of rubble and a newly emptied sandy stretch where their homes used to be underscore how Bocas' picture-perfect untouched wilderness is manufactured through dispossession. This portrait of loss – of the irreversibility of policies that privilege lifestyle migration over Indigenous rights – markedly contrasts with Feliciano's final scene, in which he travels to the United States to testify at a United Nations meeting on Indigenous Issues and at a congressional hearing. At the hearing, he calls for international pressure on the Panamanian government to comply with laws protecting Indigenous claims to the land that they have occupied since pre-Columbian times. This is one of the only scenes that takes place outside of Panama. This spatial displacement illustrates the extent to which Feliciano, as a representative of Ngäbe land rights writ large, has exhausted potential national forums in which to argue his case. He is literally left without place in his country, a 'developmental refugee' or 'uninhabitant' that bears the consequences of the pursuit of modernity (Nixon 2011: 150). By concluding Feliciano's story on this note, Prado ambivalently posits the United Nations and the US Congress as an effective reparative forum for Ngäbe visibility and agency, even if it does not result in the desired change. This concluding sequence also signals the extent to which her argument against lifestyle migration is directed towards a North American audience that holds these institutions in high regard.

The second subject profiled in *Paraíso* is Darío Vanhorne. Darío is an upbeat Afro-Panamanian man who is a tour boat guide and has been an activist since the onset of residential tourism in Bocas. He cofounded Boteros Bocatoreños, an organization established with the explicit goal of creating space for local guides at the marina. Darío is also involved in a land dispute with a resort that has claimed ownership of a small island that has long been in his family. However, unlike Feliciano, Darío's narrative arc does not revolve around this legal battle, but instead focuses on his campaign to become mayor, where he believes he can affect the most change. Viewers follow him as he wins the primary, registers rural voters and campaigns for office. Scenes demonstrating Darío's dedication to his campaign encourage viewers to see him as meriting leadership: he finances his run for office through a second job, seeks out Indigenous support and ferries voters himself to the polls.

Unlike Feliciano's scepticism of Panamanian institutions, Darío remains optimistic that in order to transform the system, one must first gain admittance. Their divergent modes of activism in turn reflect the relative permeability of institutional power for Indigenous and Black subjects in Panama, which has historically favoured the latter. While Darío needs the Indigenous vote to gain power – as they comprise 50 per cent of the electorate – this voting bloc remains rightly distrustful of political promises, which, as Feliciano explains, have yet to pan out in its favour.

Darío's arc concludes with the election. The viewer is primed to expect his success – we have watched him drum up support among diverse voters and persevere in the face of economic obstacles – but he loses by a narrow margin. Darío's reaction to this loss is of bitter disenchantment. He explains, 'I will never even vote again, because to vote you have to believe in the system. And if you find out that the system ... is a total fraud, why would I even give somebody my vote?' Unlike the rich contextualization of Feliciano's disenchantment, *Paraíso* leaves Darío's sudden change of heart unexplored. The subtext is that fraud has occurred, but neither the interviewed subject nor the documentary fleshes out what precisely went wrong. What is salient is Darío's affective slippage from optimism to deep cynicism – from a future-oriented space of affirmation to one of suspension and withdrawal from political life.

The third profiled subject of *Paraíso* is Karan Schreiber, a lifestyle migrant from California who has retired in Bocas with her husband Willy. They explain that they were drawn to Panama's Caribbean coast for its scenery, warm climate and affordable health care. Karan clarifies that they were aware of land dispute issues in Bocas and were advised to only buy titled land. They did so, and built their dream house, designed by Karan, just a few steps from the ocean. Karan describes it as a 'colonial Caribbean house' that looked 'like it belonged' and 'like it had probably been here for 100 years if you didn't know any better'. Her wording unwittingly places her home within a long history of US intervention in Panama, as well as colonial and postcolonial settler occupation of the archipelago. Her emphasis on authenticity and replication of existing culture is not so much an accurate statement, as later footage of bocatoreño homes show them to be smaller and more rustic, but rather reflects the couple's self-fashioned identity as ideal lifestyle migrants. Karan and Willy stress their appreciation of the archipelago's cultural diversity and their attempts to integrate within established cultural norms. They actively volunteer with a charity, BESO (Bocas Educational Service Organization), that gathers funds from residential tourists to benefit local students (through scholarships) and schools (providing them with cement floors and first aid kits).

Their account of themselves as responsible elite migrants – who recognize that there was an existing society before they arrived, and who take responsibility for improving that society – is not disputed by the documentary. BESO's charitable work is represented in a positive light as a necessary supplement to lapses in governance. Prado includes scenes of other lifestyle migrants advocating for native interests against exploitative development projects, like a planned yacht marina that would displace local fishermen. Such scenes suggest that lifestyle migrants are not inherently good or bad but can choose to actively operate as allies instead of turning a blind eye to politicized local concerns. Prado's stance effectively attributes complexity to the phenomenon of lifestyle migration, but also puts more stress on the personal integrity of individual migrants, rather than the systemic structural issues that perpetuate residential tourism's drawbacks.

Karan and Willy define themselves in opposition to big developers, who Willy explains are 'money-hungry people – that's not us'. They too are swept up in a land dispute. Although they bought titled land, when their neighbour sells her plot to a developer, the developer claims that the title also covers Karan and Willy's plot. After spending much of their savings in the pursuit of legal protection, Karan and Willy ultimately prevail. Yet in spite of this victory, at the end of *Paraíso*, they leave Bocas for another region in Panama. They explain this decision as a reaction to what is happening to the island; growth has transformed it into something different from the 'calm, peaceful, easy-going' way it used to be. Willy furthers, 'Call me selfish, but I don't like to share this beauty with big developers.' This dynamic gets at the heart of one of the paradoxes of consumption-driven lifestyle migration. Lifestyle migrants are drawn to a space because of its real or imagined properties that differentiate it from the country of origin. Yet their migration there changes the very properties desired in the first place – causing the place to rise in price, become more crowded and lose its 'authentic' difference. Karan and Willy are, of course, sad to abandon the house they built for retirement. Yet their ability to pick up and move also reflects their economic mobility and loose affective kinship with the community. Unlike Feliciano and Darío, they give up the fight altogether, revealing their relatively detached relationship with the archipelago.

Redirecting the tourist gaze

Following the highly competitive and labour-intensive financing scheme pursued by most independent documentarians in the United States, Prado funded *Paraíso for Sale* through a series of grants. These were obtained from public and private sources, echoing general trends in which government agencies fund preproduction, and private sources provide completion funds (Rosenthal 2005: 175). Distribution rights were folded into grants from Latino Public Broadcasting, which pre-sold the film's television rights to PBS for five years, guaranteeing it circulation (Case Study). After its successful debut at the Los Angeles Film Festival, *Paraíso* went on to screen at several other festivals, and then to distribution with New Day Films, an educational DVD distributor. Prado also took the film on a screening tour in Panama, funded by an online crowdsourcing campaign through IndieGoGo, so that the communities shown on screen could see the final product.

These funding and distribution sources indicate that *Paraíso* was conceived as an educational documentary and framed for consumption by a general public located in the United States.[6] Because of this, it can be situated within the expository subgenre. In his definition of the expository mode, Bill Nichols explains that it is structured by a 'more rhetorical or argumentative frame than an aesthetic or poetic one' (2001: 105). Prado's didactic argument clearly targets PBS viewers. While parts of the film denounce the Panamanian government's inaction with respect to Indigenous rights, its larger argumentative framework addresses North American viewers who might be interested in retiring in the Global South and glosses over complex local issues, such as the alleged fraud experienced by Darío in the mayoral election. It aims to educate North American viewers to look past Panama's commoditized beauty, and instead see the people displaced by lifestyle migration. The trailer tagline illustrates this messaging and its assumed audience: 'What price would you pay for your own piece of paradise? And who would you take it from?'[7] This direct challenge to viewers to reflect on their participation in structures of power that perpetuate inequity echoes the guiding principles of Third Cinema, the political and aesthetic project that took off in the 1960s and 1970s that utilized film to challenge existing beliefs and increase social consciousness about ongoing processes of historical oppression.

Part of the challenge for Prado then is to not reproduce views of the Panamanian coast that furthers its commodification, while still informing viewers – who are likely unfamiliar with the region – about why North American retirees are drawn to it. Prado resolves this by including only a few select shots that echo the sweeping panoramic views of the lush coast and its crystal blue waters, shots typical of imagery used to advertise the archipelago. These shots are largely confined to the documentary's introductory sequence and serve to contextualize the region's desirability.

The task of not propagating imagery that aestheticizes the Panamanian coast is particularly difficult because since the birth of cinema, cinema and tourism have been mutually reinforcing. Both fulfil the desire for mobility: the aspiration to see and consume new places. According to Jeffrey Ruoff, cinema can be theorized as 'a machine for travel' or 'a machine for knowing the world' (2006: 1). It provides the viewer with a way to experience movement on screen, and to become mobile themselves, virtually whisked off to remote lands. In all likelihood, PBS viewers of *Paraíso* are initially piqued to view the film not just to learn about lifestyle migration, but by the desire to witness the appeal of this in-demand destination.

Cinema and tourism have often conjoined to imagine, market or brand a space in a way that ignites the interest of outsiders. In his analysis of early travelogues, Tom Gunning writes that seeing images of far-off places spurred the desire to visit them and made the possibility of getting there seem more tangible (2006: 28). Gunning furthers that the eagerness to consume images of remote places went hand-in-hand with imperial aspirations to know and possess the world. Specific visualization techniques perpetuated the sense that the viewer could visually master a foreign landscape. The panorama, for instance, overwhelmed the viewer with its sweeping sense of scale, and the travelling shot carried her into the space, seemingly reenacting 'the actual penetration of space that traveling involves' (2006: 36). As cinema evolved, techniques that encourage the audience's scopic fascination with a totalizing view of a landscape have only become more ingrained. We can think for instance of the characteristic bird's-eye establishing shot of Manhattan skyscrapers at the beginning of a Hollywood rom-com, or an aerial view of the pristine blue expanse surrounding palm-studded islands in films set in the Caribbean. Such techniques mirror and perpetuate the 'tourist gaze' as defined by John Urry, a gaze that commodifies the setting for its distinctness from the viewer's everyday life (Urry and Larsen 2011).

According to Urry's pioneering definition, the tourist gaze is marked by leisure (separate from work) and movement to locations outside the normal (2011: 22). The places captured by the tourist gaze have been already anticipated as sites of pleasure, rejuvenation, adventure and difference. This prior work of imagination is mediated by other non-tourist representations of place: virtual travel through film, television and books (2011: 4). Landscape is central to this act of imagination: a commodity marketed 'as a destination or as an experience' (Leotta 2012: 2). Traditionally, landscapes are represented from the viewpoint of an external observer, one who is not enmeshed within the depicted material universe. The abstracted vantage that the concept of landscape implies, Jens Andermann notes, gives the sense that the viewer and the viewed space are disconnected, rather than entangled (2018: 8).

The tourist gaze is critiqued by the aforementioned Ngäbe roadblock protestor, who condemns lifestyle migrants for desiring the landscape she stands in, but only as long as she is not included within the frame. The presence of Indigenous and Black subjects disrupts the tourist gaze of the archipelago – envisioned as a blank slate, a deserted paradise. If the tourist gaze builds upon prior imaginative work that constructs an idea of a place before experiencing it first hand, *Paraíso* redirects this imagining from one that focuses on the coast's aesthetic properties to shots brimming with people. This is clear in the documentary's final scene. Initially, the camera lingers on waves lapping against the sandy beach: a classic view of Bocas' paradisiacal and empty landscape. Yet as it pans left, a dock comes into view. Three Afro-Panamanian teenage boys cavort on the dock and jump into the sea. The concluding shot refuses to allow the viewer to linger too long with the landscape as a depopulated space, instead insisting through the pan – the slightest horizontal movement – that the space is already inhabited.

Thus, while *Paraíso* must address the aesthetic paradigm that has presented Bocas del Toro as an alluring paradise for lifestyle migrants, it actively eschews participating in and perpetuating the tourist gaze. The cinematographer, Victor Mares, rarely uses bird's-eye view or totalizing shots of the ocean or jungle, which would further commodify the landscape as an object of aesthetic fascination. This rejection of aerial visualization techniques is undoubtedly linked to budget constraints, but also has the effect of pushing back against the viewer's consumption of the documentary as a form of virtual tourism. Conforming to the expository mode, *Paraíso*'s lack of aesthetic interest in Bocas del Toro directs the viewer to focus on the film's argument: on its subjects, rather than the landscape's beauty.

Paraíso for Sale broadens Anayansi Prado's commitment to treating migration through the language of documentary cinema. It inverts normative understandings of migration as flowing unidirectionally from south to north, and instead centres southbound lifestyle migration as another form of settler colonialism that has reshaped the archipelago Bocas del Toro. Promoted by the developmentalist model of national growth, lifestyle migration is motored by the quest for a 'blank slate' that demands the active unimagination of island inhabitants. Cinema has historically been implicated in promoting this blinkered tourist view through montage that assembles aerial shots of pristine beaches and lush forests and cuts locals out of the frame, crafting an image of tropical paradise amenable to the desires of investors, developers and potential lifestyle migrants. Countering this paradigm, *Paraíso for Sale* redirects the tourist gaze from commodifiable features of the landscape and back towards the roadblock representative of the socioeconomic asymmetries produced by the influx of privileged migrants. Through a tripartite structure, Prado foregrounds how Indigenous, Afro-Panamanians and lifestyle migrants are swept up in land disputes with developers backed by the state, demonstrating the foreclosure of Bocas del Toro to life forms that come in the way of capital.

Notes

1   The original title of More's *Utopia*, translated from Latin, is 'On the Best State of a Commonwealth and on the New Island of Utopia' (More 2016).

2   All translations are mine or are pulled from the film's subtitles.

3   These women's idiosyncratic Spanish reflects their bilingualism. The Ngäbe people speak Ngäbere; the Buglé speak Buglére. The Panamanian educational system has not prioritized literacy among originary groups. Public education has mostly been in Spanish, an approach that perpetuates the asymmetrical,

colonial valorization of Spanish above other cultural modes. Recent efforts by the Ngäbe to resist this colonizing linguistic paradigm have sought to revitalize the study of Ngäbe orthography. See Sánchez Arias, Miranda (Tido Bangama), and Brody 2019.

4   These numbers have gone up since the plan was first implemented in the 1990s, when the required pension was at least US$500 monthly (McWatters 2009: 70).

5   Feliciano Santos is the founder of MODETEAB (Movimiento por la Defensa del Territorio del Ecosistema del Archipelago de Bocas del Toro), an organization that advocates for Indigenous and land rights.

6   While Prado's primary audience is composed of PBS viewers, the film is also accessible for Spanish-speaking viewers. All dialogue in English is subtitled in Spanish, and vice versa.

7   One downside of this framing is that it somewhat reductively places the majority of the blame for Panama's land conflicts on US developers, rather than on a more complicated network of culpability stemming from the model of tourist development pursued by the Panamanian state. For more on development in Bocas del Toro, see Thampy (2013).

References

Ahmed, S. (2017), *Living a Feminist Life*, Durham: Duke University Press.

Andermann, J. (2018) 'Introduction', in J. Andermann, L. Blackmore and D. Carrillo Morell (eds), *Natura: Environmental Aesthetics after Landscape*, 7–16, Zurich: Diaphanes.

Benson, M. (2013) 'Living the "Real" Dream in *la France profonde*?: Lifestyle Migration, Social Distinction, and the Authenticities of Everyday Life', *Anthropological Quarterly* 82.2: 501–25.

Benson, M. and K. O'Reilly (2018), *Lifestyle Migration and Colonial Traces in Malaysia and Panama*, London: Palgrave Macmillan.

'Case study: *Paraíso for Sale*', Film Independent (IFP), http://www.anayansiprado. com/case-study-paraiso-for-sale.html (accessed 26 June 2019).

Children in No Man's Land (2008), [Film] Dir. Anayansi Prado, USA: Chicken and Egg Films.

Contraloría General de Panama (2010), Censo 2010, Instituto Nacional de Estadística y Censo (INEC).

Del Rio Gabiola, I. (2013), 'Globalizing the Care Chain: Representations of Latinas in *Maid in America*', *Chasqui* 42.1: 119–30.

Guerrón Montero, C. (2015), 'Building "The Way": Creating a Successful Tourism Brand for Panama and Its Consequences', in A. Panosso Netto, L. Gonzaga and G. Trigo (eds), *Tourism in Latin America: Cases of Success*, 191–205, New York: Springer.

Gunning, T. (2006), '"The Whole World within Reach": Travel Images without Borders', in J. Ruoff (ed.), *Virtual Voyages: Cinema and Travel*, 25–41, Durham: Duke University Press.

Hayes, M. (2015), 'Moving South: The Economic Motives and Structural Context of North America's Emigrants in Cuenca, Ecuador', *Mobilities* 10.2: 267–84.

Leotta, A. (2012), *Touring the Screen: Tourism and New Zealand Film Geographies*, Bristol: Intellect.

Lizarraga, O., A. Mantecón and R. Huete (2015), 'Transnationality and Social Integration within Lifestyle Migration. A Comparative Study of Two Cases in Mexico and Spain', *Journal of Latin American Geography* 14.1: 139–59.

Maid in America (2004), [Film] Dir. Anayansi Prado, USA: Impacto Films.

McWatters, M. R. (2009), *Residential Tourism: (De)Constructing Paradise*, Bristol: Channel View Publications.

More, T. (2016), *Utopia*, G. M. Logan (ed.), trans. R. M. Adams, 3rd ed., Cambridge: Cambridge University Press.

Nichols, B. (2001), *Introduction to Documentary*, Bloomington: Indiana University Press.

Nixon, R. (2011), *Slow Violence and the Environmentalism of the Poor*, Cambridge: Harvard University Press.

Palmer, L. (2011), 'Neither Here nor There: The Reproductive Sphere in Transnational Feminist Cinema', *Feminist Review* 99: 113–30.

Paraíso for Sale (2014), [Film] Dir. Anayansi Prado, USA: Impacto Films.

Pratt, M. L. (2008), *Imperial Eyes: Travel Writing and Transculturation*, 2nd ed., New York: Routledge.

Rosenthal, A. (2005), 'Staying Alive', in A. Rosenthal and J. Comer (eds), *New Challenges for Documentary*, 2nd ed., 167–79, Manchester: Manchester University Press.

Ruoff, J. (2006), 'The Filmic Fourth Dimension: Cinema as Audiovisual Vehicle', in J. Ruoff (ed.), *Virtual Voyages: Cinema and Travel*, 1–23, Durham: Duke University Press.

Sánchez Arias, G. A., M. Miranda (Tido Bangama) and M. J. Brody (2019), 'Ngäbere: An Orthography of Language Revitalization in Western Panama', in A. Sherris and J. Kreeft Peyton (eds), *Teaching Writing to Children in Indigenous Languages: Instructional Practices from Global Contexts*, 218–34, New York: Routledge.

Sigler, T. and D. Wachsmuth (2015), 'Transnational Gentrification: Globalisation and Neighborhood Change in Panama's Casco Antiguo', *Urban Studies* 53.4: 705–22.

Thampy, G. (2013), *Indigenous Contestations of Shifting Property Regimes: Land Conflicts and the Ngobe in Bocas del Toro, Panama*, Columbus: Ohio State University Press.

Thompson, K. (2006), *An Eye for the Tropics: Tourism, Photography, and Framing the Caribbean Picturesque*, Durham: Duke University Press.

The Unafraid (2018), [Film] Dir. Anayansi Prado and Heather Courtney, USA: Presente Films.

Urry, J. and J. Larsen (2011), *The Tourist Gaze 3.0*, 3rd ed., Los Angeles: Sage.

13

Raoul Peck's archipelagic cinema: Island contestations of the international order in *Assistance mortelle* (2013)

Jana Evans Braziel

'What persists' in modernity, Adrian Parr writes in *The Wrath of Capital*, 'is the condition of violence embedded in neoliberal capitalism as it robs each and every one of us (other species and ecosystems included) of a future' (2012: 2), Like Parr, who foregrounds the infinite and universal ravages, or the 'wrath,' of capital, Peck too isolates the ravenous and violating forces of capitalism as having been uniquely destructive in his home country of Haiti. Peck, in 'Les liaisons dangereuses' (his Préface to Ricardo Seitenfus's *L'échec de l'aide international à Haïti*), also bemoans the avaricious and rapacious exploitation of Haiti in which the country was 'rendered' poor – radically, if not inexorably, transformed (through centuries of greed, wars, imperialist threatens and diplomatic blackmail) from the 'pearl of the Antilles' into the 'poorest country in the western hemisphere'. Peck similarly laments that the post-quake condition in Haiti has even further immiserated his island homeland: 'These words should be titled "ticket to a world with no return," or, closer to the truth, "macabre chronicle of a country that no longer exists"' (2010: 43). Except: Haiti does exist. Peck himself, of course, reiterates this point again and again in 'Les Liaisons dangereuses' and in 'Dead-end in Port-au-Prince'. Below I further explore this tension – that between hope and despair, between ravaged and immiserated present versus heroic, revolutionary past – as a cinematic lens through which to analyse Peck's filmic deconstructions of capitalism and the possible futures (one bleak and unequal, another hope-suffused and egalitarian). I do so by examining his two documentary takes (or reverse angle shots) on capital: first in *Le Profit et rien d'autre!* (2001) and second in *Assistance mortelle* (2012).

Raoul Peck's *Le Profit et rien d'autre!* (2001) is a searing and directorially deliberate takedown of the 'new world order' that emerged after 1991 with all that entailed historically: the presumed 'death' of communism (concomitant with the geopolitical and economic collapse of the USSR) and the prematurely celebrated 'triumph' of capitalism that reigned – or ran amuck! (depending on who you asked) – in the neoliberal restructuring of global capitalism. Peck's derisive if lugubrious documentary reveals the palpable (and even, at times, ruinous) consequences of unfettered, unregulated, market-driven capitalism in a world of uneven geographies, profound economic disparities, and unstable and unequal 'states' of power, precariousness and political influence – in some cases, that is, Haiti: grinding poverty. With Haiti as its geopolitical and archipelagic point of departure and small-place or small-island perspective, Peck dismantles the ideological myths of capitalism – as equal prosperity, as opportunity, as possibility, as economic growth for all. As I have explored elsewhere, the film radically deconstructs the post-1991 'new world order'. The film is as stunningly beautiful as it is painfully arresting: 'Visually breathtaking and rhetorically moving', the documentary is a 'cinematic montage' of Haiti 'adrift in a globe that is capitalistically-striated, a film both cerebral and aesthetic, intellectually arduous and yet starkly beautiful' (Braziel 2003: 144). Peck's documentary redirects 'our eyes toward poor Haitian peasants who starve while the world's wealthy daily discard food' and exposes the deleterious impacts of international financial institutions (IFIs) on Haiti and other small states that are subject to neoliberal strictures and structural adjustments (2003: 144).

Peck's *Assistance mortelle* (2012) is also a documentary tour de force and, with *Le Profit et rien d'autre!*, launches a scorching and extended filmic intervention in global capitalist economic systems. *Assistance mortelle* is a cinematic *métissage* of multiple and mixed filmic forms – documentary, digital footage, hybrid montage, epistolary tragedy, part *cinema vérité*, part subjective film essay – which was filmed in the two years immediately following the 2010 earthquake in the director's home country and detailing the catastrophe in striking images, haunting soundtrack, cutting words and startling juxtapositions (of *au courant* digital footage, eyewitness testimonials, journalistic 'breaking stories', press statements by world political leaders, round table discussions among IHRC members, NGO public community meetings, commentary by involved Haitian political leaders and USAID workers, and mournful, even funereal, directorial reflections and narration). Peck's grave and lugubrious film hits hard on and against the international aid system, as well as its ultimate and intermediary failures.[1]

In line with Moyo's economic ideas and building on the earlier filmic arguments made in *Le Profit et rien d'autre!* (2001), Peck titled his documentary about the failures of international aid in Haiti post-earthquake *Assistance mortelle* (2012). The Caribbean, long the all-inclusive resort for the rich and famous, then all-too-frequent site of offshore banking for corporate wealth, has now entered a perilous period of absolute necrocapital destruction before (and perhaps for) profit.

Drawing dynamic, critical and incisive energy from Peck's cinematic deconstructions of capital as filmed in *Le Profit et rien d'autre!* (2001) and *Assistance mortelle* (2012), I organize my core analyses around three interrelated geopolitical themes or filmic *scenes*: (1) body counts, (2) disposable people and (3) dead aid. First, I forward key media moments, or what I define as *obscenes*, followed by a theoretical setting of the *scene* in which these three salient themes – body counts, disposable people and dead aid – are visibly manifest. The isolated *obscenes* are also examples of what Marcel O'Gorman defines as *necromedia*: not only the collision of technologies and death, but also the death blow, or the coup de grâce, *necromedia* is manifest in what Baudrillard isolates as 'symbolic exchange and death', the gift which can never be paid back. By theoretical extension, the *obscene* is a necromedia framing of death, disposability and amassed bodies that is exploitative and reductive, debased and dehumanizing, although intended, simultaneously and counter-productively, to evoke sympathy (if only superficially) for human suffering.

Finally, I detail Peck's filmic reversals, or his cinematic *reverse angle shots* on these *scenes* or *obscenes*, these moments of media and geopolitical obscenity. I deploy *reverse angle shot* metaphorically and ideologically, not purely cinematically. In cinematography, a 'reverse angle shot' is a second shot taken at a 180° angle from the one immediately preceding it: cinematographers and directors use the reverse angle shot to highlight the contrasting angles and a character's filmed response to the first shot. In Peck's *reverse angle shots*, I am gesturing more expansively towards the director's ideological and epistemic, as well as intellectual, political and cinematic reframings of historical events, particularly those related to global capitalism and international geopolitics and the consequential, damaging impacts wrought by these macro-machinations on vulnerable, small places – small island or exploited (i.e. underdeveloped) states and territories. To signal all the ways these necromedia *obscenes* have now almost entirely eclipsed other ways of seeing, I end with reflections on necrocapitalism and Peck's (imagined) *reverse angle shots* (to come), or archipelagic revisioning, of alternative futures beyond this 'dead-end'.

Sistèm Lan [= The System]: *Body counts: Biopolitics of disaster*

Obscene 1. *16 January: four days after the earthquake: Secretary of State Hillary Rodham Clinton arrives in Port-au-Prince. With a team of staff members, including Cheryl Mills and other volunteers, the Secretary of State helps unload (at least for a photo-op moment) a truck filled with donated relief food.*

Scene 1. Following natural disaster, politicians and policymakers, community workers and activists, scholars and governmental officials begin tallying the losses, counting donations, accounting for damages – at times, a seemingly endless inventory – and calculating the impacts of the disaster. Yet body counts, unlike insurance estimates of reconstruction costs (and actual claims) are often contested and open to contentious debate: in Haiti, following the 12 January 2010 earthquake, initial reports of the estimated death toll were only a fraction of the final count. According to Timothy Schwartz, conducting a study for USAID, a report that was later scuttled, the death toll was estimated at 60,000. Disputed by national and international officials, this initial estimate was later revised to the now almost universally accepted estimate of 240,000–316,000 deaths. Questions persist, thus, and return: What is the calculus of disaster? What is its accounting? How are the losses tallied? And how to calculate the biopolitics of disaster, the body counts, the death counts and the necropolitical sums of loss?

Reverse angle 1. In stunning, visual imagery, first-account observation and compelling eye-witness testimony, Peck's *Assistance mortelle* gives viewers a close-up vision of death following the earthquake. In addition to the narrator's voice that inflects sorrow and sarcasm into this subjective documentary essay, the film is also punctuated by letters written by an unnamed *she* and *he*, addressed to *Chèr ami/Chère amie*, Dear Friend. In the French edition of the film (*Assistance mortelle*), the epistolary voice-overs are read by Peck himself (the *he*) and by Céline Sallette (the *she*) and, in the English language edition, by the director's brother Hébert Peck and by Natalie Paul. According to the film credits included at the end of both editions – *Assistance mortelle* and *Fatal Assistance* – the letters are based partially on Peck's diary of the disaster and its aftermath, partially on correspondence between himself and Mary Bowman, a senior aid worker based in the country during the period of post-quake reconstruction. The film, strikingly, is also multi-linguistic, featuring interviews, commentary, speeches and newscasts in Kreyòl, French and English, as well as fragments in other languages, and it also features a spectacular soundtrack with original compositions by Alexei Agiui. Suffice it to say, sound in Peck's cinema plays as beautifully as image and idea. The film is also polyphonic, at times cacophonic, as Peck foregrounds multiple voices and perspectives through engaged dialogue with several key interlocutors – foremost among them are Joséus Nader, Jean-Max Bellerive, Ricardo Seitenfus and Priscilla Phelps, all of whom were directly involved in the reconstruction process. It is the polyphony of diverse and divergent voices in Peck's film that multi-tonally, if not symphonically, contests the monolithic account and accounting of the capitalist system.

Assistance mortelle also features videotaped footage taken from 'a surveillance camera inside the collapsing National Palace' (Vitello, 48) in both its opening and closing sequences – underscoring the devastation wrought by the quake and its aftermath (a point to which I will return). Whereas the aid accounting system tallies up its donations, accomplishments, buildings repaired, houses constructed, pounds of rice donated, bottles of water delivered, Peck's reverse angle shot casts this account (and accounting) into different light. In the opening scenes of *Assistance mortelle*, Peck foregrounds a native voice, a Haitian voice and someone who witnessed and survived the devastating earthquake on 12 January 2010 and has dedicated all his time, energy, effort and expertise to the rescue, recovery and rebuilding process: in Peck's reverse angle shot, we hear and see the events and its aftermath through the words and eyes of Joséus Nader, the director of Public Works for

272   *The Film Archipelago*

the Haitian Government, an engineer and a civil servant. As the film opens, we hear Nader recounting the earthquake, stating:

> I wasn't in shape that morning. Something was troubling me. I didn't know what exactly, but something was up. I couldn't stay at work. Something drove me to get in the car and quickly get where I was going. At the corner of Janvier Street and Réunion, I heard and felt something hit the car: BOOM!

The shattering and cataclysmic violence of this moment, recounted by Nader, is underscored through the incorporated live footage of the earthquake. Only after this opening scene with Nader does Peck incorporate the video footage: we see a dust cloud suffusing a courtyard; shelves tumbling; walls falling; a woman running then falling to the ground as the plume of dust envelops her and the courtyard. Immediately after the video footage of the *bagay*, the 'thing', as some Haitians refer to the earthquake in Kreyòl, the camera returns to Nader who is driving along Route 1 north of the capitol towards Titanyen, the site of mass burials post-quake.

Nader continues his account: 'We didn't move the bodies in one go. It took fifteen days to move them all. Some had just died; others were from the morgue, but since no one came for them, they were dumped back into the streets.' Nader (and Peck through him) offers another account and accounting: that of the victims who died during and after the earthquake. Nader also reminds viewers that the rescue teams were overwhelmed by the sheer numbers of bodies, their removal from the amassed debris, their transportation to Titanyen, their mass burial and the incapacity – of the drivers, at the morgue, in the streets – to properly care for the dead. (It is worth noting also that the Desounen rituals for burial in Vodou are quite elaborate and extremely important, and these rituals were not likely performed among the Vodouissant dead, nor were rituals for Catholic, Protestant or Muslim burials.) Nader continues his harrowing account: 'The drivers wouldn't get out. Imagine how the bodies fell out of the dump truck .... There wasn't time to cover them before more arrived.' He laments in recalling, 'The first two days were horrible.'

To further counter the calculus and capitalist accounting, Peck also uses what Vitiello aptly calls 'Godard-like intertitles in red, grey, and white that carry shocking information about the quake' to offer a radically different accounting from that tallied by the international community and its 'Republic of NGOs' – the number of dead, injured, homeless: '230,000 *dead*'; '300,000 *wounded*'; '1,500,000 *homeless*'.

By critical, cinematic juxtaposition, Peck also reminds viewers of the international community's economic system of accounting, its tallying of donated dollars and assessed damages: '5 billion *in 18 months*'; '11 billion *in 5 years*'. These at-odds and oppositional modes of accounting for disaster and post-disaster reconstruction point us towards another organizational logic of neoliberal, global capitalism – that of disposable people, or *moun ki jetab*, 'throw-away people'; those so-called or presumed 'surplus populations' within capitalist calculations; those deemed to be in excess of or outside of the productive or profitable systems of economics and exchanges. To fully understand the obdurate and obfuscatory accounting of neoliberal, global capitalism – or what Henry A. Giroux accurately calls the 'violence of organized forgetting' – delineated in *Obscene/Scene 1: Body Counts*, we need to return to the machinations and ruinations wrought by neoliberal disposability.[2]

Moun ki jetab [Throw-Away People]: *The necropolitics of disposable people*

Obscene 2. *March 2010: two months post-quake: Former Presidents Bill Clinton and George W. Bush arrive in the capitol as representatives of the Clinton-Bush Haiti Relief Fund. Greeting Haitians, walking amid the rubble, shaking hands, the two former presidents arrive on the* scene *to deliver aid; notoriously, and candidly captured in televisual footage, former President Bush wipes his hand on former President Clinton's shirt after shaking hands with an individual in the crowd.*

Scene 2. In Haiti, as Sybille Fischer explains, one glimpses 'fantasies of bare life', what Peck excoriates as 'humanitarian pornography' in *Assistance mortelle*, or what I define and differentially reference as *obscenes* that are profligately captured, obscenely circulated and then endlessly recirculated within *necromedia*. Haiti offers, tragically, a compelling case study in the nefarious machinations of necrocapitalism and its devouring of so-called disposable people.[3] The devastating 2010 earthquake in the country killed between 240,000 and 316,000 people, most of whom were buried in mass

274 *The Film Archipelago*

graves or simply dumped at Titanyen, a historical dump site where the Duvaliers also notoriously left bodies exposed in the combustible, oppressive Caribbean sun to rot. As Alex Dupuy indicts the contemporary, collapsed state of Haiti: in his estimation, the World Bank and other IFIs have both 'abet[ed] dictatorship and undermin[ed] democracy'.[4] Or as Robert Fatton similarly laments: Haiti remains 'trapped' in the 'outer periphery'.[5] In addition to the staggering death toll, there are the injured survivors: the earthquake left many more maimed, mutilated and severely injured (crushed limbs and amputations were common), not to mention traumatized, and ultimately, it resulted in approximately 1.5 million internally displaced persons (IDPs) living in make-shift tent camps for almost two years.

Within the contemporary and variably local contexts of twenty-first-century global necrocapitalist economies, the extensions of late consumer capitalism, there is a fine and ever-more-tenuous, ever-more-transient line between commodity and waste. In a world of disposable commodities bought-sold-discarded by consumer-shoppers, it is increasingly difficult to discern product and waste-product. Disposable economies – of food, clothing, housewares and gadgets – also increasingly inform the bodies of the consumer-shopper who buys, uses, then trashes those commodities; and disposable economies come to define the consuming body as a stable entity among so many discarded objects. But what becomes of those bodies that fall outside of the productive mechanisms and profitable systems of consumer capital? Those who are unemployed, homeless, hungry, illiterate, without cultural or financial capital (to evoke the terms of Pierre Bourdieu): they are increasingly regarded, I argue, as throw-aways, discards, one more bit of refuse in a world of abundant refuse; they are deemed *throw-away people*; when considered at all, they are deemed all the same and nevertheless to be living *disposable lives*; they are, within global networks of production, labour and financial flows, seen as expendable and disposable. Capitalist destruction is predicated upon waste, expendability and the inhumane rendering of some human beings into 'throw-away people' treated (by the necropolitical powers that be and who reign with imperial sovereignty) as if they were living *disposable lives*.

Reverse angle 2. Like the body counts that define *Assistance mortelle* and its filmic documenting of disaster, disposable bodies are also a recurrent cinematic motif in the film. In this section, I focus on Peck's scenes from

Assistance mortelle that are set at and comment upon Camp Corail-Cesselesse. Peck's documentary reveals the failures of the tent camps, particularly the one at Camp Corail. From the privileging of house and school construction over debris removal, which negatively impeded human movement (through streets and alleys) and also negatively impacted well-being, to the subhuman living conditions in IDP tent camps, particularly in Corail, the policies and decisions set and made by the IHRC for Haitians and the Haitian Government reinforced the regrettable idea that Haitian lives did not matter – or, at least, did not fully matter. As Prime Minister Jean-Max Bellerive attests midway through the film, reflecting on the failures at Camp Corail, 'no one want[ed] to live in tents'. Gérald-Emile Bun, an engineer with the Nabutec Corporation, similarly states of the constructed shelters:

> Without electricity. No green areas and with minimal furnishings. The essential is to build a solid shelter – generally a block with minimal openings to the outside. But inside, there's nothing – no drinking water, no sanitation nor kitchen. There are no interior furnishings as in a decent, comfortable house.

Jean-Ronald Merisma, a section leader in the Onaville camp (located at Corail-Cesselesse), impugns, 'we're struggling to avoid slums but the way they're building is even worse … they wouldn't let their animals live in them', he laments, about the small constructed sheds built at the camp. The dumping of dead Haitian bodies and the mass burial of them at Titanyen are mirrored, in fact, in the *en masse* relocation – without forethought, without long-term planning, without considering the social and familial ramifications – of thousands of homeless Haitians in October 2010 to Corail, a site 11 miles north of Port-au-Prince, the capitol city where commerce occurs, buying and selling happens and what limited resources that are available to Haitians are doled out. This mass relocation happened, of course, just as the cholera outbreak erupted in the country: brought in by Nepalese UN soldiers who dumped raw sewage into the river near Mirebalais, almost 10,000 Haitians eventually died from the outbreak, the first cholera outbreak in Haiti in over a hundred years. Peck's camera lens (and his documentary *Assistance mortelle*) actually zoom in on these failures, rather than zooming out: his lens and his documentary ultimately reveal that international aid amounts to 'fatal assistance', to 'dead aid'. Giorgio Agamben's ideas are certainly provocative ones for thinking through

the post-earthquake tent camps in Haiti following the 2010 natural disaster –
as Valerie Kaussen (2011) has persuasively demonstrated in the essay 'States of
Exception – Haiti's IDP Camps'. Agamben's text also provides conceptual tools
for understanding the ways in which entire countries, perhaps even continents,
exist as if camps for internally displaced persons, or IDPs. To fully understand
these horrific accounts and body counts in documented disasters, however, we
need to articulate and then conceptualize necropolitics and necropower as the
foundations of global necro-capitalism, or *Necro-Capital, Inc.*, which I do in
the third section below.

Machin Èd [= Aid Machine]: *Dead aid: From necropolitics to Necro-Capital, Inc*

*Obscene 3. 31 March 2010: 'Haiti, OPEN for business'. HRC. Michel Martelly.
UN-sponsored International Donors Conference 'Towards a New Future for
Haiti'. $9.9B pledged from 59 donor states; documented for perpetuity, for
better, for worse by C-SPAN. A forum sponsored by the Centre de Facilitation
des Investissements (CFI), 'The one-stop for investors' – say no more. Seriously,
please – say no more.*

Scene 3. 'Haiti, Open for Business'? We must ask: what is being bought?
What is being sold? Or, more precisely, what is being traded? By whom, and for
whom? In Haiti, amidst grinding poverty, it seems (obscenely) that everything
is still for sale or simply up for grabs to the highest bidder (rarely Haitian):
reconstruction contracts; housing plans; portable toilets; steel rebar; concrete
cinder blocks; trash removal; dump trucks; purified water; imported rice; but
also, and more expensively, international agribusiness deals; transnational
free trade zones; mining rights for gold, silver and copper; expansive tracts of
prime real estate for tony hotels and extravagant resorts; and the list goes on.
One can only sardonically ask: Will Port-au-Princian poverty be the final and
perpetual commodity for sale in the international aid and global financial debt
markets? Or as Fidelis Bagolun decried in *Adjusted Lives*, 'the garbage heaps of
the increasingly rich' have become 'the food table of the multiplied population
of the abjectly poor'. Striking and salient parallels to Renzo Martens' *Enjoy
Poverty! Episode III*, particularly its sardonic, cinematic positioning of the global

'war on poverty', the purported labour of ostensible non-profits and the mobile machinations of INGOs as, contrarily, a massively profitable transnational industry are, of course, completely and entirely apropos. We are inexorably, or so it seems, in the bog-down and quicksand terrains of *Necro-Capital, Inc.* – the dazzling rich, the disposable poor. While some have defined technology as the 'master of war' and the distributor of death,[6] I argue that it is the nefarious mechanisms (production, circulation, investiture, divestiture, privatization, consumption and disposal) of for-profit destruction, disaster and disposability that define the 'death phase' of neoliberal, late expenditure capitalism – or what I am designating as *necrocapitalism*. It deals in death. It deals out death. Its death blows strike at point a and blowback to point b and so on; *und so weiter* (Johnson 2004). It miasmically spreads. And like other neoliberal malaprops and geoeconomic misnomers – strikingly, 'cat bonds' (instead of catastrophe bonds)[7] and *Citizens United* (with its legal transformation of corporations into juridically protected persons in the United States): these are the machinations of death-for-profit incorporated: *Necro-Capital, Inc.* These are the biopolitics of disaster, the necropolitics of savage capitalism – *necrocapitalism*.

Reverse angle 3. Body counts. Disposable bodies. Peck's documenting disaster reveals the larger machinations of disaster capitalism and how the post-disaster period of reconstruction can also yield disastrous, unforeseen consequences. Peck's film – particularly its focus on the *machine d'aide* (the 'aid machine' or in Kreyòl, 'machine lèd') – reveals the myriad ways that humanitarian aid (even non-profit) nevertheless still profits from poverty, suffering and even, at times, death. As Peck writes in his essay 'Beyond Help', the machinations of the 'aid machine' are deleterious to the very idea of assistance or help; it has become (or perhaps has always been) 'assistance mortelle' or 'dead aid':

> To this we need to add a series of epiphenomena which have become for me [Peck] completely intolerable today: the waste of resources, the meddling, the arrogance, and the blindness ... the cyclic repetition of errors, of mea culpas, and then the same errors, which are repeated with just as much zeal.
>
> (2015a)

As Peck continues towards the logical culmination, he writes: 'In the meantime, people are dying. Lives are shattered, children will never grow up, dreams will never be realized.' Peck excoriates the ways that the 'machine

278   *The Film Archipelago*

d'aide', particularly the ways that NGOs are inextricably bound to capitalism and capitalist economic structures, function as long-arm tentacles of affluent, dominant, foreign states (those which fund NGOs, as well as control and set policy) and effectively replace state institutions – through an NGO-ization of the state – of weak, fragile, vulnerable, failed or apparent states, states such as Haiti or even aspirational ('non-sovereign'; Bonilla 2015) states like Puerto Rico. All of these interrelated dimensions of the 'aid machine' – capitalist structures, foreign control, NGO-ized states – were, in fact, strikingly manifest in the post-earthquake reconstruction of Haiti and also in Peck's documentary film *Assistance mortelle*.

Beginning with early debates about debris removal – who would pay, facilitate and complete – versus those wishing to allocate funds instead for home and school construction, and continuing through the temporary establishing of IDP camps (mostly tent or tarp camps), and culminating in the disastrous relocation of a very large camp (initially set up on a Pétionville golf course) to Corail, a barren and arid site 11 miles north of Port-au-Prince, it is not difficult to discern and to decry the 'aid machine' as driven by something other than human (or Haitian) interest. Even into late 2012, the vast majority of donated emergency, relief and reconstruction funds remained undistributed and unspent. After the earthquake, international donors and aid organizations pledged $16.3 billion for relief and reconstruction: of that total, $2.4 billion in relief funds, was disbursed in the months following the disaster; and by December 2012, only $7.5 billion of the total pledged had been disbursed, approximately $1.2 billion allocated to relief and temporary tent camps and only $215 million of the dispersed funds allocated or expended for permanent safe housing (Sontag 2012). Housing that was built post-earthquake was not only exorbitantly priced (around US$1,000+ per month as opposed to a typical Haitian house that a family may rent for US$500 annually), but also almost exclusively reserved for and rented out to North American and European non-governmental workers. The Clinton Fund also strategically diverted funds, when finally released, towards building a multinational corporation 'free trade' zone, the Korean-based Sae-A, in northwest Haiti, far removed from the disaster zone and situated near a mangrove ecological preserve, later scuttled altogether. To boot: the vast majority of dispersed funds were released to NGOs, not to the Haitian government.

Filmed interviews for *Assistance mortelle* with Prime Minister Max Bellerive and Joël Boutroue, former UN Resident and Humanitarian Coordinator and adviser to the prime minister, affirm that the international community (or core group: a special representative of the United Nations secretary-general; a special representative of the Organization of American States; and the ambassadors of Brazil, Canada, France, Germany, Spain, the European Union and the United States of America) systematically, strategically and deliberately funnelled the overwhelming majority of international donations through international non-governmental organizations (IGOs), headquartered and effectively controlled by foreign states and foreign investors, rather than allocating donated funds and the control of those funds to the Haitian government. As Prime Minister Bellerive decries in *Assistance mortelle*, 'they', referring to the international community, 'prefer to give to UNICEF or Doctors without Borders or to WHO, not to the Department of Public Health'. Endlessly trapped, or so it seems, in historical cycles and past accusations of corruption, Haiti stands indicted of the future crime (or offence) before it can even possibly be committed. As Boutroue exclaims, and as Peck captures on films, 'it seems that Haiti always stands accused. Prove to us that you're not corrupt'. And as structural adjustment and international assistance increase, sovereignty diminishes. International aid further immiserates Haiti, 'renders' the country poor, broke, broken, with only illusions of sovereignty, staggering debt, grinding poverty and the seeming impossibilities of non-sovereign futures. I end by returning to Peck's archipelagic, cinematic deconstructions of global and international 'aid' capitalism and its nefarious ends.

Disaster capitalism has indeed entered a lethal phase: that of necrocapitalism. To conceptualize how we have historically moved from necropolitics to the echoing death chamber of necrocapitalism, I formulate urgent questions that exigently demand answers: have we now entered the stage of capitalism that may be aptly defined as necrocapitalism and that hyper-produces unneeded commodities, absurd consumer and fashion fetishisms, infinitely disposable products and also, unforgivably, disposable people, disposable lives? Have economic frames become indistinguishable from political ones, and the economy indistinct from the necropolitics of perpetual war (Vidal 2002)? What happens, moreover, when biopolitical governmentality becomes necropolitical rule by ongoing, constant warfare not only against terrorist organizations, rogue states (Derrida 2004), citizens and publics, but against life itself and especially in 'inconvenient continents' and disposable 'shithole' countries where lives are rarely documented by censuses and deaths too infrequently tallied? What happens, in short, when biopower nefariously becomes exercised as necropower? Is neoliberal, late expenditure capitalism, then, predicated upon necrocapital, the profit from death and destruction? Is not disaster capitalism, then, by default, by definition, and by extension actually necrocapitalism?

Other questions also demand to be asked: What does it mean, for example, to 'capitalize' death? What does it mean when profits are intensively and inextricably entangled not only with destruction and disposability, but also with death? Why are there speculative markets that wager losses and gains in death and destruction? And are there futures in death profits? War and its surplus capital offer only one model. But what of deaths wrought through natural disasters, and the capital gained from post-disaster reconstruction? What of mortal, manmade disasters caused by a strategic decades-long dismantlings of the state, the public and welfare across the globe? What of the rapid descent to the bottom of increasingly low-wage and ever-outsourced labour pools internationally that has left abandoned warehouses, defunct mills and empty factories standing – or dilapidated and collapsing – like the very skeletal remains of industrial capitalism on almost every continent on earth? And what happens to those laid-off labourers? Where are toxic chemicals dumped and why? In a now infamous (yet still no less shocking) memorandum, Lawrence Summers actively and coldly advocated for toxic dumping in poor countries, rationalizing that the lives of people living there were both shorter in duration and less valuable in monetary calculations. What, finally, of the brink-of-disaster and dreadful near-point of no-return for the earth's ecology? Parr (2012) has aptly diagnosed this as *The Wrath of Capital*, and Klein correctly, if also scarily, notes that *This Changes Everything*. Corporate 'solutions' to ecological degradation, of course, equal 'hijacking sustainability', as Parr (2009) notes. And what of cost/benefit analyses that determine CEO decisions to divest in some regions, countries or even large swaths of entire continents rendering those areas and the people living in them as *expendable* and *disposable*?

We can easily imagine, of course, Peck's final *reverse angle shot* and its searing critiques of small island fragility and the larger forces of hemispheric imperialism that impose fiscal austerity through international financial institutions on the already-indebted and grindingly poor and to the interest-rate advantage of those sitting affluently, comfortably at centre of the international core. Peck's critiques of neoliberal, global capitalism – or more simply: *le système*, or *sistèm lan* – offer vital and incisive lessons for Haiti, for inter-island politics, for trans-archipelagic relations and for potential sovereign or non-sovereign futures in the Caribbean archipelago.

Notes

1   Mark Schuller has been one of the leading critical voices decrying the infractions, inefficiencies and failures of international aid: his books repudiating the NGO industry and 'aid' business include his post-quake ethnographies *Killing with Kindness* (2012) and *Humanitarian Aftershocks in Haiti* (2016) and his co-edited book *Tectonic Shifts* (2012). Schuller's scholarly books, like Katz's (2013), parallel Peck's film in significant and striking ways: all three deride the 'humanitarian business', or what Peck derisively calls 'humanitarian pornography'; all three detail the devastating unnatural disasters – financial, organizational, governmental, nongovernmental, social and human – left in the wake of the actual natural disaster, the earthquake.

2   The 'politics of disposability' was first conceptualized as the plight of precarious labour in the postmodern, late capitalism, informatized economies by Hardt and Negri (2000), though the term arguably derives from Bales (1999), manifest in the 'ungrievable' losses of the global terror war as documented by Butler (2004), more fully elaborated in Bauman (2004), and further developed in Giroux (2006), as well as centrally important in the collaborative and extended 'Disposable Life' project of Brad Evans, notably in *Disposable Futures* (2015), co-authored with Giroux, and particularly chapters two and three, 'The Politics of Disposability' and 'The Destruction of Humanity'. Also Klein's references to 'the disposable poor' (2008: 18).

3   These intellectual threads and key ideas – disposability, disposable economies, disposable people and *necrocapitalism* – also genealogically emerged from concepts such as *biopower*, *biopolitics*, *bare life* and *necropolitics* by Foucault, Agamben, Mbembe among others.

4   See Dupuy's *Haiti: From Revolutionary Slaves to Powerless Citizens*, especially chapters 5 and 6.

5   Fatton, *Haiti: Trapped in the Outer Periphery*.

6   Henry (2014) argues that technology will overtake and eventually dominate capitalism, and when this technological triumph transpires, we will pass from the 'capitalist world to the world of technology' in which the 'power for destruction and death' will 'dramatically increase'.

7   Online financial articles on catastrophe bonds, or cat bonds, which have boomed since their introduction onto financial markets in 1997, are exemplary of *necromedia* and *necrocapitalism*, the buying-and-selling, trading-and-investing, profiting-and-speculating in death: death-capital. Administrative accounting that does not and cannot account for death are wilful forgetting, a will-to-ignorance à la Charles Mills' *The Racial Contract*, an inadmissibility of death counts, body counts, precisely because there can be no accounting of disposable bodies consumed by disposable economies. I more fully address cat bonds as exemplary disaster capitalism in a book manuscript-in-progress tentatively entitled *Global Studies: Lessons from Haiti and Puerto Rico*.

References

Agamben, G. ([1995] 1998), *Homo Sacer: Sovereign Power and Bare Life*, trans. D. Heller-Roazen, Stanford: Stanford University Press.

Assistance mortelle (2013), [Film] Dir. Raoul Peck, France: ARTE.

Baggesgaard, M. A. (2015), 'The Migrating Earth: Cinematic Images of Haiti after the 2010 Earthquake', in S. P. Mosland, A. R. Petersen and M. Schramm (eds), *The Culture of Migration: Politics, Aesthetics and Histories*, 309–26, London: I.B. Tauris.

Bales, K. (1999), *Disposable People: New Slavery in the Global Economy*, Berkeley: University of California Press.

Barnes, H. E. (1947), *Perpetual War for Perpetual Peace*, Caldwell: Caxton Printers.

Baudrillard, J. (2017), *Symbolic Exchange and Death*, London: Sage.

Bauman, Z. (2003), *Wasted Lives*, London: Polity Press.

Bonilla, Y. (2015), *Non-Sovereign Futures? French Caribbean Politics in the Wake of Disenchantment*, Chicago: University of Chicago Press.

Braziel, J. E. (2003), '"*Profit and Nothing But!*" (*Le Profit et rien d'autre!*): Raoul Peck's Impolite Thoughts on the (Haitian Diasporic) Class Struggle', *Journal of Haitian Studies* 19.2 (Fall): 141–76.

Braziel, J. E. (2008), 'From Fort Dimanche to Brooklyn: Transnational Regimes of Violence, Duvalierism, and Failed Heteromasculinity in Raoul Peck's *Haitian Corner*', in *Artists, Performers, and Black Masculinity in the Haitian Diaspora*, 59–81, Bloomington: Indiana University Press.

Butler, J. (2004), *Precarious Life*, New York: Verso.

Cortés, J. (2018a), 'Necromedia, Haunting, And Public Mourning in The Puerto Rican Debt State: The Case of 'Los Muertos', *Journal of Latin American Cultural* 27.3: 357–69.

Cortés, J. (2018b), 'Puerto Rico: Hurricane Maria and the Promise of Disposability', *Capitalism Nature Socialism* 29.3: 1–8.

Derrida, J. (2004), 'The Last of the Rogue States: The "Democracy to Come," Opening in Two Turns', *South Atlantic Quarterly* 103.2/3 (spring/summer): 323–41, trans. P.-A. Brault and M. Naas.

Dupuy, A. (2013), *Haiti: From Revolutionary Slaves to Powerless Citizens: Essays on the Politics and Economics of Underdevelopment, 1804–2013*, London: Routledge.

Evans, B. and H. A. Giroux (2015), *Disposable Futures: The Seduction of Violence in the Age of Spectacle*, San Francisco: City Lights Books.

Fatton, R. Jr. (2014), *Haiti: Trapped in the Outer Periphery*, Boulder CO: Lynne Rienner.

Foucault, M. (1978), *The History of Sexuality*, trans. R. Hurley, New York: Pantheon Books.

Foucault, M. (2008), *The Birth of Biopolitics: Lectures at the Collège de France, 1978–79*, trans. G. Burchell, ed. M. Senellar, New York: Palgrave Macmillan.

Giroux, H. A. (2006), *Stormy Weather: Katrina and the Politics of Disposability*, Boulder: Paradigm.

Hardt, M. and A. Negri (2001), *Empire*, Cambridge: Harvard University Press.

Henry, M. (2014), *From Communism to Capitalism: Theory of a Catastrophe*, London: Bloomsbury.

Johnson, C. (2004), *Blowback: The Costs and Consequences of American Empire*, New York: Holt Books.

Katz, J. (2013), *The Big Truck that Went By: How the World Came to Save Haiti and Left behind a Disaster*, New York: Palgrave Macmillan.

Kaussen, V. (2011), 'States of Exception—Haiti's IDP Camps', *Monthly Review* (1 February). Available online: https://monthlyreview.org/2011/02/01/states-of-exception-haitis-idp-camps/ (accessed 22 April 2021).

Klein, N. (2007), *The Shock Doctrine: The Rise of Disaster Capitalism*, New York: Metropolitan Books.

Klein, N. (2018), *The Battle for Paradise: Puerto Rico Takes on the Disaster Capitalists*, Chicago: Haymarket Books.

'Le Combat Par Le Cinéma de l'Haïtien Raoul Peck: Une Rétrospective au Forum Des Images' (2010), *Le Monde*, 3 February. Available online: https://www.lemonde.fr/cinema/article/2010/02/02/le-combat-par-le-cinema-de-l-haitien-raoul-peck_1300108_3476.html (accessed 22 April 2021).

Livesey, J. (2015), 'Fatal Assistance', *Visual Anthropology Review* 31.1 (May): 115–17.

Mbembe, A. (2003), 'Necropolitics', trans. L. Meintjes, *Public Culture* 15.1: 11–40.

McAuley, C. and C. Michel (2003), 'Filmer sans compromis: Interview avec le cinéaste, Raoul Peck', *Journal of Haitian Studies* 9.2 (fall): 128–40.

N'Zengou-Tayo, M.-J. (2004), 'The Tree That Does Not Hide the Forest: Raoul Peck's Aesthetical and Political Approach to Cinema', *Caribbean Quarterly* 50.4 (December): 63–71.

O'Gorman, M. (2015), *Necromedia*, Minneapolis: University of Minnesota Press.

Parr, A. (2009), *Hijacking Sustainability*, Cambridge: MIT Press.

Parr, A. (2012), *The Wrath of Capital: Neoliberalism and Climate Change Politics*, New York: Columbia University Press.

Parr, A. (2017), *Birth of a New Earth*, New York: Columbia University Press.

Peck, R. (1998), *Monsieur le Ministre … jusqu'au bout de la patience*, Port-au-Prince: Velvet.

Peck, R. (2010), 'Dead-end in Port-au-Prince', in M. Munro (ed.), *Haiti Rising: Haitian History, Culture and the Earthquake of 2010*, 43–8, Liverpool: Liverpool University Press.

Peck, R. (2015a), 'Beyond Help?' in T. Pressley-Sanon and S. Saint-Just (eds), *Raoul Peck: Power, politics, and the cinematic imagination*, 273–80, Lanham: Lexington Books.

Peck, R. (2015b), 'Préface à l'edition Haïtienne: *Les liaisons dangereuses*', in R. Seitenfus, *L'échec de l'aide international à Haïti: Dilemmes et égarements*, trans. P. Reuillard. Éditions de l'Université d'État d'Haïti. 8–14

'Peck, Raoul' (2002) *Current Biography International Yearbook*, 1 January 2002.

Pressley-Sanon, T. and S. Saint-Just (eds) (2015), *Raoul Peck: Power, Politics, and the Cinematic Imagination*, Lanham: Lexington Books.

Riep, D. M. M. (2011), 'Visual Revision: Intersecting Art and Film in the Work of Jean-Marie Teno and Raoul Peck', *Journal of African Cinemas* 3.1 (January): 81–92.

Schuller, M. (2012), *Killing with Kindness: Haiti, International Aid, and NGOs*, New Brunswick: Rutgers University Press.

Schuller, M. and P. Morales (eds) (2012), *Tectonic Shifts: Haiti since the Earthquake*, Sterling: Kumarian Press.

Seitenfus, R. (2015), *L'échec de l'aide international à Haïti: Dilemmes et égarements*, trans. P. Reuillard. Éditions de l'Université d'État d'Haïti.

Sontag, D. (2012), 'Rebuilding in Haiti Lags After Billions in Post-Quake Aid', *New York Times*, 23 December.

Taylor, C. (1996), 'Autopsy of Terror: A Conversation with Raoul Peck', *Transition* 69 (1 April): 236–46.

Vidal, G. (2002), *Perpetual War for Perpetual Peace*, New York: Nation Books.

Part Four

Reimagining islandscapes

Part Four

Reimagining landscapes

14

Notes on an island film: A journey to Martín García

Edgardo Dieleke

I travel for the second time to Martín García Island, in the Río de la Plata, about 30 miles and a three-hour sail aboard a catamaran from Buenos Aires.[1] The island is tiny, less than one square mile, and a privileged location for a film project, a place somewhere between a ruin and the future. However, I travel without a clear idea of what I would like to do. The island was a prison for Argentina's most popular presidents, Hipólito Yrigoyen and Juan Domingo Perón; it has a strange and decadent theatre with Masonic ornaments, which was abandoned many years ago; most of the crosses in the cemetery are slightly bent, probably also a Freemason remnant. There are very few houses and in the central square stands the old prison, in ruins, overrun by vegetation.

It is autumn, a good time to film: not too cold, the sunlight is not too intense and there are few visitors. Very few people live on the island, between 100 and 120, a figure that doubles on the days when tourist groups visit the place. There is another, not to be overlooked benefit to filming here: it is possible to travel the whole island on foot, from the pier to the other end, in no more than half an hour. And there are very good reasons to walk around the island. Martín García is for me the capital of a country that was not, a modernity that did not happen, a sort of uchronia. For all these reasons, I travel to explore the island during four intense days together with Daniel Casabé, with whom we directed *La forma exacta de las islas* (The exact shape of the islands), shot in the Malvinas Islands. Will we find a movie here?

Martín García is a ghost island, an Argentine ghost, a forgotten place in the history of South America and a site where many anonymous people have left their trace and many political prisoners in the nineteenth and twentieth centuries suffered, not to mention those who were imprisoned there during colonial times. Some of these names are famous, but many more have been forgotten. Domingo Faustino Sarmiento chose this place as the location for his utopian city Argirópolis, which would be the capital of the future United States of South America. A few years after writing the small book bearing the name of his imaginary city, once he became the president of Argentina, Sarmiento founded here a lazaretto for people infected with yellow fever and to hold immigrants who arrived on quarantined ships before they could enter the port of Buenos Aires. At the same time as it functioned as a lazaretto, the island was also a prison for the Ranquel chieftains and their clans after their defeat in the military campaign infamously known as the 'Conquest of the Desert'. A few years later, in 1895, the Nicaraguan poet Rubén Darío visited the island and wrote a three-part chronicle for the newspaper *La Nación*; during his stay, he composed the poem 'Marcha Triunfal' (Triumphal March). In 1930, after the first military coup in Argentina, a group of members of the Radical Party were imprisoned in Martín García, including ex-presidents Yrigoyen and Marcelo de Alvear, with their ministers and some followers, as well as Ricardo Rojas, the author of the eight-volume *Historia de la literatura argentina* (History of Argentine Literature).[2]

For such a small place, the island contains a lot of history: ruins that seem inadequate, barely visible commemorative plaques, some busts in poor

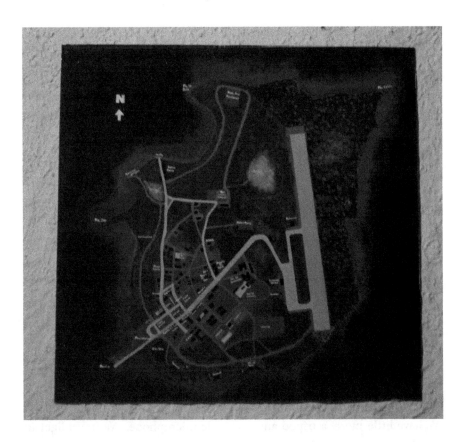

condition, not enough inhabitants to convey the history of the island. What to do in Martín García? What films are there to be uncovered? We went there without any clear plans, to look for images and maybe some order, a story, a possible film. It must be a film about a quest. I record here, in this text, alternately, the diary of that journey and some ideas thought out later, after our visit. Maybe these notes are better, more adequate, than a possible film. The process of writing expands, while the image at times fixes and discards what was of no use.

Day 1 // Thursday, 31 May 2018

We leave the port of Tigre, on a rainy day, aboard the Hercules catamaran of the Cacciola tourist company, the only one that makes the Buenos Aires to

Martín García route four times a week. There is a group of teachers who go for the day to work in the school, about four or five local inhabitants, a couple of tourists, the guide who takes them on a short tour and hardly anybody else – about ten or fifteen in total. On weekdays almost no one travels; on weekends, Saturdays and Sundays, about 100–150 people, nostalgic for the country that was not, go for the day to visit the places where illustrious politicians once dwelled, perhaps to feel a slight relief, or to think that at some point there were great leaders of the nation, great speakers. *Ubi sunt* is the condition of this island!

The catamaran, with its mythical name Hercules, seems hardly tossed by the waves of the Río de la Plata, even though they are high and it is quite windy. The sky is grey and it blends with the dark brown colour of the river. We leave the Tigre Delta, sail up the Sarmiento River onto the Paraná, and then to the Rio de la Plata. The boat is run by the 'Cacciola' agency – an indication that the immigrants who arrived to the islands were not the Scots and Danes that Sarmiento wanted. The long journey provides us with a good opportunity to familiarize ourselves with the new camera I bought recently. We hardly carry anything with us: a Sony A7, a photo camera that can also film, with an old Canon 50 lens which gives a less digital finish to the image. We have little more, a tripod and a reliable microphone. We travel light to be able to move around without attracting attention. We prefer to be taken for photographers, as if this were less dangerous or invasive than shooting moving images.

The catamaran is the first thing that surprises me, its interior decoration a perfect location to start a cinematic journey: angled windows, blue and modern plastic tables, like a 1960s nightclub or spacecraft. In *Argirópolis* (1850), Sarmiento, with his excessive fascination with rivers, imagined hundreds of ships, boats and schooners navigating on the Rio de la Plata. All along the way there are hardly any vessels aside from the wooden boats used for public transport in the region, which are more than sixty years old. We make some shots of the interior, fixed shots and some views of the river. It is a good start to arrive to the nineteenth century in this almost empty boat from the future. The pier is long, more than 200 yards perhaps. On my previous trip to the island – on a Saturday – there were many tourists and getting off the catamaran took some time. This time around, we leave the ship quickly, looking for shelter from the rain and the strong wind. At the pier stands a young coast guard and also a van where a series of boxes, water bottles and other basic necessities are loaded. We linger on and film the disembarking, a good shot for an observational documentary, or even a fictional one, edited with images of the island.

Towards the end of the pier there is a small natural elevation and a few buildings; further down, in the main square stand some cannons. To the left and right, the waves of the Rio de la Plata hit the pier hard, just as they hit the shores, with trees and plants that have been coming down for hundreds of years from the Argentine coast. Martín García is the only island that is not strictly part of the delta; it is a rocky island and its soil is one of the most ancient in Argentina. Slowly but steadily, islets and water hyacinths from the Paraná and the Uruguay Rivers approach the island and pile up on its shores. From the pier you can see the Uruguayan coast on the right, and although barely, you can also see the paper mill plant, one of

Figure 14.3 'Muelle de atraque de la Isla Martín García, 1936'. Archivo General de la Nación, fondo Acervo Gráfico Audiovisual y Sonoro. Código: AR-AGN-AGAS01-Ddf-rg-2248-138852.

292 *The Film Archipelago*

Uruguay's most thriving foreign investments. Despite being closer to the Uruguayan coast, the island is Argentinian, as determined by a 1973 treaty in which the two countries also agreed that it should be a nature reserve. This is why they have set a limit to the number of inhabitants and visitors to the island.

Some of the first prisoners of Martín García, the Ranqueles, defeated in the so-called 'Conquest of the Desert' by the Argentine State, must have walked along this same pier, or perhaps not exactly the same, but in the same area. Hundreds of indigenous people, great captains and leaders such as Pincén or Epumer Rosas, along with their families, were the first political prisoners on this island, and they were here for years, doing forced labour in the quarry, in the hospital and then in the lazaretto founded during the Sarmiento administration. Many died of smallpox, from the cold; most were given away as slaves and rural pawns to families of the military and the Buenos Aires aristocracy. Apparently, president and general Julio Argentino Roca, in charge of the 'Desert Campaign' of 1879, sent one of the most famous chieftains of the time, Pincén, to his estate. Did he have him there to show him as a trophy? To humiliate him? Did his decision entail a slight show of camaraderie between rivals, taking him to his estate to enjoy greater comforts than in a prison like Martín García, surrounded by water, without horses, without pampas? What would Pincén recognize as familiar on the island? The song of some birds, perhaps? What was it like for him to see Roca again, if the encounter ever happened?

In Martín García there is very little to be seen of that past. The island's primary school is called Pincén. The cemetery where the Ranquel and other leaders were buried has disappeared; some locals say a flood washed it away. Pincén can be found in the tiny historical museum of the island: he appears in a photograph taken in Buenos Aires in the studio of Antonio Pozzo. In that image he poses as an 'Indian', with a prop spear and a prop rock in the ground, the photo later to circulate as a postcard for the Centennial Celebrations of the Argentine Independence in 1910. The first photographs of indigenous people establish the documentary gaze: they create the other, deliberately. How to show any of this in a film shot here?

294   *The Film Archipelago*

In their research on this period of Martín García, historians Mariano Nagy and Alexis Papazian retrieved letters from the military in charge of the indigenous people. I copy here one of the letters:

'Buenos Aires, April 7, 1879

To the Commander of Martín García Island:

Please make the due provisions to hand over to the bearer of this letter ten indigenous families consisting of the indio, his woman and their children, arranging that unwed females take a husband from men on the island 40 years old or older. Eight of the families are for Don Gregorio Torres and two for Don Carlos Casares.

May God guide you'

Historians also list the names of the prisoners: I copy some here as well. I think of using some of those names, quoting them in the film, bringing their names to the screen, although these are probably not their real names, or maybe some are. In the words of the island authorities, this is a partial list of 'prisoners and indigenous people living outside the lazaretto' (sic):

Pancho Rosas / (NN) / Máximo / Luciano Migoya / Luciano López / Ceferino Artigo / Arriola Alvarez / Santos Pérez / Pacheco Nicolás / Alejo Acosta / José González / Pulquichea / Saturnino López / Jacinto Molina / Juan Centeno / Ignacio Centeno / Arriola / Marcelino Calfunel / Manuel Guenpuí

Who were Pancho Rosas, Migoya, Pulquichea, Calfunel? Taken away from the pampas, from a life of nomadism and tolderías (encampments), they ended up imprisoned in Martín García. In his essay 'The Desert Island', Gilles Deleuze suggests that humanity's imagination is tied to islands, that to some extent human philosophy has to do with the way we imagine islands, what we project onto them, what is not on them but is assumed about them. There is a fragment of the essay that can be useful for a script, to get some ideas:

To that question so dear to the old explorers – 'which creatures live on deserted islands?' – one could only answer: human beings live there already, but uncommon humans, they are absolutely separate, absolute creators, in short, an Idea of humanity, a prototype, a man who would almost be a god, a woman who would be a goddess, a great Amnesiac, a pure Artist,

A Journey to Martín García at the top

a consciousness of Earth and Ocean, an enormous hurricane, a beautiful witch, a statue from the Easter Islands.

(Deleuze 2004: 10)

I find this passage very productive to imagine fictions located on this island: a group of artists hiding here organizing a meeting of utopianists in the wonderful abandoned theatre or a storm raging over the island that alters the climate of the Rio de la Plata forever. We could also use something closer to the Latin American recent years and the prison condition that the island used to have. Lula imprisoned in Brazil, Evo Morales exiled from his own country after another coup d'etat. Why not imagine a uchronia, a divergent reality on this island, a contemporary prison for a popular leader who must be sent into exile to a not too far away place? Martín García can be a repeating island.

I think that this should be a fiction film because maybe there is too much history, but at the same time there are hidden stories. Perhaps a film about this island, on this island, should be more universal, less national. I also think that the Ranqueles imprisoned here would not share Deleuze's ideas about islands. What would be their deserted islands? Why would they imagine an island?

Day 1 // Thursday, 31 May 2018

Along the pier you can read, in reverse chronological order, short texts about the 'famous' prisoners held on the island: first the last one, Arturo Frondizi, president of the Radical Party, deposed by the military in 1962. Juan Domingo Perón detained on the island for a few days before the historic 17 October 1945, the day Peronism was born. Yrigoyen, the first democratic president, imprisoned after the first military coup in 1930; Alvear, a member of the Radical Party, also imprisoned in those same years. There is hardly anything about other political prisoners such as the indigenous people; not only the warriors were imprisoned here, but their children as well. Nothing on the common prisoners either. The signs are strange. The island is famous for being a prison of popular politicians, the most popular in modern Argentine history. Political imprisonment as something to be proud of for the tourist. A voice-over at the beginning of the film could promote it: 'Come and know the place where Argentina's most powerful politicians were detained. All in one place! Come and learn in less than a day the best kept secret of Argentine politics.'

We leave our bags at the inn, the only one on the island. It used to be a building for navy officers. Twelve rooms. My friend Daniel and myself are the only guests. Other guests are expected to arrive on Saturday, the only day the inn is full. We are greeted by A., the manager. She is a lady in her fifties, with intense black hair and a very lively face; she probably has indigenous ancestors. Could she be a character in the film? We will try to film her later. She will be here until we leave. We go for a walk, under a drizzle rain and a strong southerly wind. It is not that cold and the light is perfect.

On the first day we have time to walk about a good portion of the 'inhabited' section of the island, a few blocks around the main square. The square is almost the same as any other square in Argentina: the flag, a statue of a military hero, a grid design. Except it is a square with no people on it and an excessive military presence: cannons pointing at the river, the ruins of the old prison and the old house for the navy commander of the island. This building is today a park ranger station and a post office with a beautiful semi-abandoned garden and an overgrown swimming pool. Despite it being late autumn, everything is green in Martín García: many evergreen trees, palm trees, green grass and the orange trees with fruits on the ground. Even more: the intense red of the poinsettias – known as 'federal stars' – the flowers worn by followers of the nineteenth-century caudillo Rosas and of the montoneros in the twentieth. Humidity is a constant on the island, and the vegetation seems to be taking over.

As we walk along the main streets, we stop and make many fixed shots of nature, the wind bending the elastic structure of the palm trees, the clouds moving quickly, the waves forcefully hitting the pier. The very few people we come across look at us at a distance; they seem to know already who we are. We cross paths with several officers from the Naval Prefecture – the border patrol. Filming on a small island, as we already know from our experience on the Malvinas, has the advantage that the stories come to you: the inhabitants and potential characters are curious, they do not quite get why you come to such a small island. In general, if you are a good conversationalist, they will want to talk with you. My co-director, Daniel, is very nice and friendly. As for me, like him, I seem harmless.

Today we hardly talk with the locals, we walk around, get acquainted with the island and visit the ruins of the strangely called 'Chinese quarter' or old village. We then walk all the way to the area of the abandoned crematorium, its oven and a high chimney a standard feature of the oldest photos of the island. As we reach the northeast end of the island, facing the Uruguayan coast, we shoot some images of the airstrip. It is a perfect location; on the weekend we will come again to check out the small planes flying in from Buenos Aires.

Day 2 // Friday, 1 June 2018

The night on Martín García is astonishing: the silence is almost absolute, only the wind, a TV or radio from a house and little else. In the distance, depending on the wind, you can hear the engine of the power station that supplies electricity to the island. The few houses and some buildings have their yellow lights on and cast shadows of the vegetation, which move with the wind and seem to be about to walk into the houses. The plant world is replicated on several of the buildings of the island: fleur-de-lis, circular flowers and other Freemason ornaments. Where are the Freemasons nowadays? Will the few inhabitants who live on the island have some kind of secret lodge?

Sarmiento distributed copies of his Argirópolis *before defeating Rosas, but according to scholar Adriana Amante, he strangely did so anonymously. This book is one more example of Sarmiento's 'geographical' thinking. This new 'City on the Rio de la Plata', capital of the imagined United States of South America, was conceived to overcome not only the political problems of South America, the caudillismo of Rosas in Argentina and of Francia in Paraguay, but also the ills of the 'pampa': its size and the indolence it produced. He projected that there would be citizens in this future capital, who, as in Genoa or Valparaiso, would be*

overwhelmed by a lack of space and thus would be forced to socialize, consume and establish links, instead of indulging in barbarous gaucho customs.

However, the plan, which Sarmiento sent to General Urquiza and for which he sought sponsorship in France, is scrapped and it ends up as a minor text in his oeuvre. There is a timeworn bust of Sarmiento in the streets of Martín García, without plaque, his gaze always stern. It is actually the less preserved statue of all. The people who live in this place have their movements restricted; they have to request permission to leave, as they are employees of the Government of the Province of Buenos Aires. They do not long to live in a big city, quite the opposite. Here the red of the poinsettia flowers seems more intense than the presence of Sarmiento, or of his influence.

Day 3 // Saturday, 2 June 2018

Today we rush to film the landing and take-off of planes. We were able to film almost head-on the take-off of a plane, a few yards away. The pilots and passengers who come are mostly men; they eat in the *Solís* dining room, the only restaurant on the island; they have some wine, dessert perhaps, and then they fly back. What they do is much less interesting than the image it evokes: a group of mysterious airplanes landing on a semi-deserted island. What do they come here for? What are they up to? Is there always something being planned on an island?

Very close to the *Solís* dining room – actually here the notion of what is close or far away changes – is Dr Prudencio Plaza's old house. He was the doctor in charge of the hospital and the lazaretto in 1895. The poet Rubén Darío stayed in this house for a few weeks. We take some shots of the house – it is pretty run down – and focus on the verdigris bronze bust of Rubén Darío. What are we going to make this bust say in the film? Maybe just the sound of the wind, of the waves of the Río de la Plata. Maybe some fragments of his poem 'Marcha Triunfal' but not using this shot. The entire island is a museum, a kind of museum for the future; the busts, those of Brown, Artigas, Perón, Darío Sarmiento, San Martín, will survive, next to the plaques and strange crosses in the cemetery. The visitors of the future will have the impression that very important persons lived here once. The bust of Darío is the most accomplished.

In the inn, after dinner, we resume the conversation with A. She looks shy; she finally makes up her mind to let us film her, and off-camera we keep on chatting with her. She leads a peaceful life with her daughter; she is a single mother. She does not fear for her daughter or for herself; there is no insecurity, and the island is cheap. They do not have to pay for gas electricity or transportation to move around; everything is covered by the state. They lead a simple life, following the rhythm of nature: they go to bed early and get up early. Before dawn, light is cut off until later in the morning; no one needs it. The only concern is health emergencies and – I imagine – alcoholism, a common phenomenon on the nearby islands of the Tigre Delta as well as in the Malvinas.

A. would never leave the island; she would like to live here forever. Maybe she is concerned that children, like her own daughter, are too naive, and once they leave the island, they will have to face a very different world. A. tells me that there are no conflicts on the island, that this is a very good community. She also gives me a bit of very valuable information: about twenty years ago, the island had a special semi-open prison programme and some convicts were able to live here with their partners and families. That programme lasted a few years, but some ex-convicts remained on the island. She says they adjusted very well and that the locals do not let tourists know who the former inmates are. She does not reveal anything to us either. It is now impossible for us to walk around the island without wondering who could have been inmates and what crimes they may have committed. The documentary filmmaker is always a bit of a detective.

Films about islands 1: Films about islands, on islands; there are many. I watch again the short film Nueva Argirópolis *by Lucrecia Martel, released in 2010 and available on YouTube. It is amazing, like everything Martel does. It is a counter-narrative to Sarmiento's utopian vision for Argentina. Yet, it is not filmed on this island, but on the shores of Formosa. Strange boats come downriver, with women and children speaking in an indigenous language that Navy officials don't understand. The people on the boat smile, and the authorities seem to suspect a conspiracy. On a screen, an indigenous leader spreads a message on YouTube that is not intelligible to Spanish speakers as there is no translation until suddenly one clear sound can be heard, Nueva Argirópolis. A new society taken by the original settlers? In Martín García there are remains of artefacts that belonged to the Guarani people, who occasionally navigated to the island in their canoes.*

I go back to Deleuze's quote, to the reference to the beautiful sorceress on an island. I had thought of that before looking at this essay, which I had already read and even quoted in the film we made with Daniel Casabé and Julieta Vitullo, La forma exacta de las islas (*The exact shape of the islands*). *Deleuze says there are derived islands, a bit like ideas. That is an idea I play with for now, while we review the material that we filmed on Martín García: the island, a semi-deserted island, far from the big cities, difficult to reach, almost without tourism, begins to receive an increasing number of visitors.*

At first, the inhabitants themselves are surprised, but everyone suspects the reason why more and more visitors, almost like pilgrims, come to the island. Most come by day, go to a lost house in the bushes, in a high place that never floods. There lives a woman, neither very young nor very old; all kinds of rumours begin to spread about her. Rumours that travel fast. The lady always greets visitors with red flowers, poinsettias, that surround the house for protection; the lady in whose there is a series of clearly Masonic symbols, circular figures that are never completely symmetrical, the cemetery of crooked crosses, where many Freemasons are buried; the lady whose house, they say, is built on the old indigenous burial site.

One day, before so many of the growing numbers of followers of this new cult started to visit the island in chartered boats to see her, the lady had started to officiate a service, on Saturdays, in the old Teatro General Urquiza, the beautiful

302   *The Film Archipelago*

decadent theatre with Masonic symbols, today in disuse. A theatre dominated by circular figures, presided over by the indigenous face of Antonio Verdi, the patron of this new religion. Who can this lady be? Maybe just a voice? Or maybe, she does not talk, she does not say anything?

Day 3 // Saturday, 2 June 2018

We carry out a series of interviews. We are not interested in showing 'talking heads'; we look rather at historical busts, and in that line, we make filmed portraits, with almost one minute in-camera shots of the inhabitants of the island. We talk to them before and after making the portrait, we take notes, record them to see if anything about their lives and their experiences would help us think of a documentary we could shoot here. The location, the whole island and even their faces seem more suited for a fiction film. It feels as if a documentary would not do them justice – it would reduce them to their reality, which is less expressive than what they could actually do on this island.

We talk with the two park rangers of the island, two women, one of them perhaps thirty-something, who has just been assigned to the island, and her boss. The ranger in charge of the island, a woman in her forties, is a mother and is raising her children on the island. She spent her childhood here; her father was a prison guard, during the last stages of the special programme for prisoners. Since that childhood on the island, she has been looking for ways to return. Back then, in the 1990s, the island had a limited population. The park ranger smiles to the camera – a bit too much. She is very happy on the island. Maybe too happy to be a character in the film. The other one is more interesting; she doesn't want us to film her.

Because of this conversation with the park rangers, we are late to meet the historic tour guide and her husband, our second fixed appointment. They are perhaps the people who know most about the place and they enjoy talking to us, telling us about life on the island. He, a man in his sixties, has a great face, great gestures; he is thin and he was probably very attractive as a young man, a proper heartthrob. She overflows with joy; she is perhaps a little less interesting as a character, but is very good on camera. They are very friendly, and open the Urquiza Theatre for us, a decadent stage built in 1915, now abandoned, which

A Journey to Martín García

was sometimes used in the past for school events. I'm still toying with the idea I had a while ago: to organize a conference of utopianists on this stage, a group of artists and intellectuals planning future projects for this island. The more impossible to put into practice, the better.

Movies on Islands 2: As I write this, as we ponder with my partner Daniel what to do with the recorded material, especially with the fixed-camera shots, the portraits and little else, I watch a film shot on another island: El viento sabe que vuelvo a casa (The wind knows that I'm coming back home) *by Chilean director José Luis Torres Leiva, featuring filmmaker Ignacio Agüero. He plays a film director who arrives on an island in the Chiloé archipelago and says he is there to make a film. A film about a love story, a kind of Romeo and Juliet, of forbidden love between an indigenous young woman and a white man, and this quest opens the way to explore the island, using a fictional device presented as true. I think of the possibility of not filming anything else, of making a formal restriction and only using the shots, mostly without movement, without interviews, and create out of them a story. Only through voices? I think of mixed narratives, the portraits sharing their thoughts more than their testimonies, the busts unloading on us the weight of their historical burden. A dialogue between busts, some of flesh and blood, some made of metal. I keep on thinking, I keep on writing down ideas.*

Writer Sergio Chejfec and scholar Graciela Montaldo are admirers of Martín García. She has written an excellent article on it; he published a small author's book El mes de las moscas (The month of the flies), *with a story written about a visit to the island. Chejfec gives me a clue, a tip I want to explore further. Apparently, in 1973, when the island became a nature reserve, the historical inhabitants of the island were forcibly displaced. Chejfec tells me that there is a group that meets and vindicates its historical and cultural right to populate Martín García. I'm going to look for them and their descendants. Maybe they are organizing something, maybe they are preparing to take the island, maybe I should just listen to their claims, I could populate with voices the images that we shot there, almost without people, in ruins. At the same time, I think this would have to be something fictional, a group of people who have organized to return to their island; the reason they were expelled is never entirely clear, like legal verdicts, like the justice that was applied to so many prisoners who were sent to Martín García.*

Day 4 // Sunday, 3 June 2018

On the last day, we film mostly close-ups of people's faces. We film the oldest inhabitant of the island. We film the mother of the employee at the power station, who we had filmed yesterday. We film a couple of men we suspect are two ex-cons, although this intuition is largely prejudice. Everyone's faces are great, generally more interesting than their life stories.

We move around the island avoiding the groups of tourists, who are steered, mindfully, from the dining room where they are given a barbecue, to the main square, the old prison, the sites of interest. We stay clear of their presence and we hardly shoot anything with the group on it. The last two places we film are the cemetery and the old bakery founded by Italians. Both are large locations, a cemetery in the middle of the woods, with its crooked white crosses, the vegetation close by about to creep in and cover the tombstones. The old bakery has an oven that is over seventy years old. The baker tells me she used to bake bread for more than 3,000 sailors, when there was a navy detachment here. In the past, everything was better and bigger in Martín García.

I go back to the notes, I check the photos. We have to make a film in the future tense, without the burden of the past; history should not be the motor force of fiction. We should imagine here an alternate time, perhaps a conspiracy; perhaps the history of another island but with the faces of the

current inhabitants. Not a counter-narrative or a revision of Sarmiento's utopia; perhaps a minor island, with smaller, more personal stories, and at the same time, a ruin of what never was.

Translated from the Spanish by Erna von der Walde

Notes

1   I have written a previous text after my first visit to Martín García, a sort of travelogue and research text, published in 2019 (see references).

2   Many of these references come from a wonderful text on the island Martín García written by Graciela Montaldo (2019). I wish to thank her for some of the conversations we had and for some of the insights she gave me for this project.

References

Amante, A. (2007), 'Prólogo. El letrado y el poder', in D. F. Sarmiento (ed.), *Argirópolis*, 9–32, Buenos Aires: Editorial Losada.

Chejfec, S. (2016), *El mes de las moscas*. La Plata: Oficina Perambulante.

Darío, R. (2013), 'Cartas del Lazareto', in G. Montaldo (ed.), *Viajes de un cosmopolita extremo*, 55–74, Buenos Aires: Fondo de Cultura Económica.

Deleuze, G. (2004), 'Desert Islands', in D. Lapoujade (ed.), *Desert Islands and Other Texts, 1953–1974*, 9–14, trans. M. Taormina, Los Angeles: Semiotext(e).

Dieleke, E. (2019), 'La capital de una nación que nunca existió: viaje a la isla Martín García, Argentina', in I. Depetris Chauvin and M. Urzúa Opazo (eds), *Más allá de la naturaleza. Prácticas y configuraciones espaciales en la cultura latinoamericana contemporánea*, 353–67, Santiago: Ediciones Universidad Alberto Hurtado.

Masotta, C. (2011), 'El atlas invisible. Historias de archivo en torno a la muestra «Almas Robadas - Postales de Indios» (Buenos Aires, 2010)', *Corpus* 1.1. Available online: https://doi.org/10.4000/corpusarchivos.963 (accessed 3 May 2021).

Montaldo, G. (2019), 'Complot y castigo: la condición transnacional de la isla Martín García', *Revista de estudios hispánicos* 53.2: 449–71.

Nagy, M. and A. Papazian (2011), 'El campo de concentración de Martín García. Entre el control estatal dentro de la isla y las prácticas de distribución de indígenas

(1871–1886)', *Corpus. Archivos Virtuales de la Alteridad Americana* 1 (2). Available online: http://journals.openedition.org/corpusarchivos/1176 (accessed 2 March 2018).

Nueva Argirópolis (2010), [Film] Dir. Lucrecia Martel. Argentina: Ministerio de Cultura.

Sarmiento, D. F. (1850), *Argirópolis*. Available online: http://www.cervantesvirtual. com/obra/argiropolis-o-la-capital-de-los-estados-confederados-del-rio-de-la-plat (accessed 2 March 2018).

El viento sabe que vuelvo a casa (2016), [Film] Dir. José Luis Torres Leiva, Chile: Globo Rojo Films.

15

Letters from the islands:
A visual essay

Antonio Traverso

Introduction

This visual essay is presented as a series of textual and photographic fragments that illustrate an unfinished 'epistolary film' (Naficy 2001; Rascaroli 2017), *Letters from the Islands*. The visual essay, with its implicit film, seeks to contribute to the work of excavation in the present of a hidden colonial past delineated by a racialized imaginary that systematically transformed the islands of the Pacific into carceral territories, such as penal and leper colonies as well as correctional and isolation prisons, and which perpetuates carceral colonial ideology with regard to the lives of Indigenous people and people of colour today. The visual essay's imagined film addresses an approach to film style that Griselda Pollock and Max Silverman (2011) name as 'concentrationary'. This film style, according to Pollock and Silverman, is characterized by the use of 'radical techniques of montage and [disorienting] camera movements,' as it seeks to incite 'disturbing juxtapositions and prolonged visual attentiveness' in order to 'expose invisible knowledge' (2011: 1–2) buried underneath normative histories and naturalized documentary representation, while 'shock[ing] us out of comforting dichotomies that keep the past "over there"' (2011: 2). Films concerned with histories of oppression that subscribe to this style encourage a critical viewing position of interrogation of the legacies of the past in the present. Such films ostensibly contribute to the cultural articulation of 'a memory that purposively erodes divisions between past and present, using specific histories to become a constant probe with which to interrogate the present for any current affinities with absolute horror and aspirations towards total domination' (Pollock and Silverman 2014: 1). The political core of the concentrationary film aesthetics is therefore its agitational drive: to render visible in the present the normalized legacies of 'l'univers concentrationnaire', a phrase coined by David Rousset in 1946 (cited in Pollock and Silverman 2014: xv, 1) that describes not only a site and regime of incarceration but more broadly a normalized dictatorial model of society. The concentrationary universe is thus not an overt but naturalized totalitarian system of social engineering produced and reified as an effect of the historical synergies of colonialism, modernization and capitalist expansion. This understanding of modern society as essentially 'carceral' recalls Michel Foucault's analysis of modernity, which in *Discipline and Punish* (1979) he famously illustrates through the figure of the 'carceral archipelago', a concept inspired in Alexander Solzhenitsyn's *The Gulag Archipelago* (1974), where the Russian writer bears witness to the minutia of the Stalinist prison. While Foucault describes the conceptual design and operation of the modern penal system, which is ordered according to an archipelago-like structure, that is, as a series of carefully planned compartments or islands, this is not just a theory of the modern prison but an encompassing allegory of modern society. According to Foucault, 'this great carceral network reaches all the disciplinary mechanisms that function throughout society [...] the carceral archipelago transported [the penitentiary technique] from the penal institution to the entire social body' (1979: 298). Foucault defines the 'islands' that make up the 'carceral archipelago' as a 'carceral continuum' (1979: 303) deeply traversing modern society.

Many disenfranchised filmmakers from the Global South have precisely sought to explore and render visible the historical synergies of the modern concentrationary universe and the post-colonial carceral system with films that focus on islands or distant, isolated locations that have been used as gaols. Recent concentrationary island films include *La cárcel del fin del mundo*/The Prison at the End of the World (Lucía Vassallo, Argentina 2013) and *Tierra sola*/Solitary Land (Tiziana Panizza, Chile 2017), which reflect on the carceral past and present of, respectively, Ushuaia, southern Argentina and Rapa Nui/ Easter Island, by juxtaposing archival and actuality film. Another example of a concentrationary island film is *Chauka, Please Tell Us the Time* (Behrouz Boochani & Arash Kamali Sarvestani, PNG/Australia/Netherlands, 2017), shot clandestinely on a smartphone over several months by Kurdish-Iranian refugee writer and journalist Behrouz Boochani (2018), incarcerated at the Australian offshore detention centre of Manus Island, northern Papua New Guinea, between 2013 and 2017. *Chauka, Please Tell Us the Time* describes through audio and visual impressions only, without narration, refugees' experience of long-term incarceration in the detention centre's everyday. These films, like this visual essay, suggest that the concentrationary aesthetics proposed by Pollock and Silverman includes but does not limit itself to rapid, shocking and forcefully disorienting cinematic techniques. On the contrary, concentrationary cinema does also make frequent use of minimalist stylistic approaches characterized by silence, incompleteness and evocation, which can be equally disconcerting and defamiliarizing, while shocking us out of internalized aesthetic comfort zones. Similarly, this visual essay imagines a multi-layered epistolary cinematic fiction, which, not unlike many of the films discussed by Laura Marks in *The Skin of the Film* (2000), seeks to excavate a landscape of voids and silences. The visual essay juxtaposes intervened still images recovered from the author's own personal photographic archive and original segments of fictional writing. While largely non-autobiographical, the narrative and poetic contents of the essay are derivative of actual historical context and evocative of personal experience. As it depicts a single moment of a larger epistolary exchange, the temporality of this imagined conversation is multiple: while the text that constitutes the narrative basis of the piece is patently presented as written in 2020, the address also contains references to earlier, some distant and some no so distant, correspondence, as well as to shared memories of events in Chile, and of travel to Australia in the 1980s. These are experiences of political action and exilic wandering, all infused by the carceral aesthetics of a timeless concentrationary universe.

Letters from the islands

It was good to speak with you online the other night after such a long time. You know, besides the spread of death, fear, hopelessness, Covid also forced us, at least for a while, to pause, to take a distance from the vertiginous stream of the present, to reconnect with some of the traces and the people of our many pasts. You only mentioned your sister once but I haven't been able to stop

thinking about her, about everything that went on, since we spoke. Perhaps you won't remember but the first time I wrote you about her, after receiving the email where you gave me the news of her passing, I told you about a long letter she'd sent me many years earlier relating her journey to Australia, when she was released and allowed to leave the country in the mid-eighties. Planes flying across the Pacific between Chile and Australia at the time had to stop on as many islands as it was possible: Rapa-Nui, Tahiti, Aotearoa. I'd been on that endless trip myself a few months before she did. I don't think I gave you much detail then. She told me about the short stopover on Eastern Island. She wrote that it was her third time on a plane but the first time she'd landed in daylight. She said that as they descended rapidly towards the ocean, she was startled as the cliffs suddenly came into view in the window, and that she felt (she said she only thought about this later) that the plane was about to crash. She said that for a split second the hair on her skin rose anticipating the indifferent, incommensurable heaviness of sharp and bulky volcanic rock indistinctly swallowing all matter in her and around her: flesh and metal, blood and plastic, bone and glass. Everything erased absolutely in an absolute instant of silvery haze. She didn't say it exactly like this but it's how I remember it.

She told me that she came out of the plane into a wide, iridescent day and went down the narrow ladder, step by step, shaken by a blast of humid hot air, the kind of light and heat she'd never experienced before, and then walked on the bitumen to the Mataveri airport, a mere hangar, which in a moment was replete with in-transit passengers. She said that they had to reboard in one hour. Among the arts-and-crafts stalls, some of the islanders were offering a swift trip to the shore to see *moais* for five US dollars a head. She went along on an impulse, she wrote, as she was only carrying a hundred dollars into exile. She sat in one of two vans packed with over excited Chilean families, the women holding on to children, the men clasping photographic cameras. When they got there, a young woman asked her to take a photo of her and her husband standing in front of the statues. She wrote that children were climbing the stone foundations, then embracing and kissing the *moais* while their parents took pictures. She noticed a man and his son. The child repeatedly crawled under a wire fence in order to climb a small ornamental statue out of the man's reach. She said that the boy's father would call out to him angrily saying that if he didn't come back, the plane would leave and he would be left alone on the island. She wrote: the wind is blowing hard, I feel awkward and ashamed,

impatient to get back to my seat on the plane. She said she imagined the boy stranded and scared. She imagined herself surrounded by insurmountable masses of water. Imprisoned again, this time for ever. She said that when the plane was taking off she thought that the *moais* had seemed false to her but I've never understood what she meant by that.

    She said that in her first year in Australia she started to write and draw, and that, on weekends, she'd take day trips to nearby locations she'd read about. She visited a historical museum known as the Round House in Fremantle, a port city of the Western state, where she lived then. She described it as a small limestone panopticon that had been a security prison in the past. She wrote that she spent a long time inside the dark, minute isolation cells made for prisoners deemed problematic. She said she'd read elsewhere that many of the captives had been young Aboriginal men forcefully removed from their remote communities, accused of crimes they didn't understand. She wrote that a man had signalled to her to take his photograph inside the museum and that later, as she looked at the ocean outside, he had approached her again pointing towards a ship parked at the nearby port, speaking with a strong accent in a broken English that she could not fathom. She said she would have gone with him anywhere that day if he had asked, or if she had been able to understand. She said that the distant smells and noises the wind brought to her from the port made her think of rusty metal in the central coast of Chile. Corroded sections of ships and trains, decaying on rocky edges in San Antonio, Cartagena, Valparaiso, Ritoque, Quintero. Dark railways cutting across the hot, oil-smeared sand. Smelly train stations filled with lethargic people waiting in silence besides cardboard boxes carefully tied up with rope. Ghostly, motionless railway wagons that seemed to have always been there, never gone anywhere since coming into existence. Wrecked wooden fishing boats, slowly rotting away, eroded by the sun and the sandy wind. A salty taste in the back of her tongue, gasping, panting, swallowing fearful dry saliva. Shadows that become images even in the darkest, most unctuous of blindfolds. Distant seagull cries and the sound of ocean waves crushing nearby, marking the passage of time. Mechanical and electric things starting, stopping and starting again.

She wrote that as she walked through empty streets undergoing construction works, she saw the following scene: a young Aboriginal boy was musically strolling right in the middle of the road while confidently defying the camera lens of a man with the tallest backpack she'd ever seen. She asked me if I remembered a project we had been working on for one of our university

courses before I had to leave Chile, the year the riots started. She said it was something about the return of the gaze in ethnographic cinema that we never got to finish. I couldn't recall any of it.

She wrote that afternoon I caught a ferry from Fremantle to Rottnest Island. During the half-hour crossing, she read on a brochure that the name Rottnest means 'rat nest' in Dutch, which was coined by Dutch navigators who encountered the island on their reconnaissance trips in the seventeenth century, misidentifying the *quokkas*, small local marsupials. In her letter, she traced a series of ellipses around 'misidentifying'.

She wrote that on the island, she joined a tour she had signed up for before and learned from a *Noongar* elder that Rottnest Island's real name is *Wadjemup*, which means something like 'home of the spirits across the water'. The man told the group of tourists that in spite of being a deeply spiritual place for his people, the island had been used as an isolation penal camp for Aboriginal prisoners dragged there from remote regions between the early nineteenth and early twentieth centuries. They walked to a bushy area where there was a modest plaque informing visitors that on that ground lay the unidentified remains of many Aboriginal men and boys, most of whom had died of cold, hunger and European diseases, like influenza. The man told them

that there were many more unmarked collective graves around the island and that some prisoners had managed to escape on stolen or makeshift boats. She said that even though many fugitives had drowned, some had actually made it to the mainland.

She read that when the gaol was closed in the first half of the twentieth century, much of the prison infrastructure continued to be used as holiday accommodation for middle-class white Australians and foreign tourists until recently. She wrote: I stand here on my own holding on to my sketch book. I imagine all those holiday makers, like the ones I see in front of me now, sleeping with their golden children in whitened rooms that only a fraction of time before had been dirty dark cells restraining black bodies in pain.

The day after we spoke, I wrote to her Chilean friend, who still lives in Perth. At first I said I was writing to ask how she was doing in the midst of the pandemic. It had been a while since we last communicated. Eventually I did say I had spoken with you and that I'd been thinking about your sister. I wondered how she was coping with the loss. Soon it will be three years since she decided to take her own life, if that is actually what happened. She most enigmatically wrote back: I'm an old woman now and sometimes I think I've seen it all. But, of course, life always proves me wrong. She attached some pictures of a public art action she'd attended in Fremantle in support of the BLM movement. One night back in June, a group of activists projected the names of many of the Aboriginal people who have died in custody in Western Australia since the early 1990s onto a large rainbow-shaped public sculpture built to celebrate the city's heritage as a significant port of the Indian Ocean. She wrote: she would have been there by my side that night had she still been

around. Looking at the pictures with the projected names, many of them of women, I found myself foolishly searching for her name.[1]

Notes

1 The author would like to thank Dr Pilar Kasat and Professor Suvendrini Perera for their assistance in the production of this piece.

References

Boochani, B. (2018), *No Friend but the Mountains: Writing from Manus Prison*, trans. Omid Tofighian, Sydney: Picador.

La cárcel del fin del mundo (2013), [Film] Dir. Lucía Vassallo, Argentina: Habitación 1520 Producciones.

Chauka, Please Tell Us the Time (2017), [Film] Dirs. Behrouz Boochani and Arash Kamali Sarvestani, Netherlands.

Foucault, M. (1979), *Discipline and Punish: The Birth of the Prison*, New York: Vintage Books.

Marks, L. (2000), *The Skin of the Film: Intercultural Cinema, Embodiment, and the Senses*, Durham: Duke University Press.

Naficy, H. (2001), *An Accented Cinema: Exilic and Diasporic Filmmaking*, Princeton: Princeton University Press.

Pollock, G. and M. Silverman (eds) (2014), *Concentrationary Memories: Totalitarian Terror and Cultural Resistance*, London: I.B. Tauris.

Pollock, G. and M. Silverman (eds) (2011), *Concentrationary Cinema: Aesthetics as Political Resistance in Alain Resnais's Night and Fog*, New York: Berghahn Books.

Rascaroli, L. (2017), *How the Essay Film Thinks*, Oxford: Oxford University Press.

Solzhenitsyn, A. (1974), *The Gulag Archipelago*, New York: Collins & Harrill Pr.

Tierra sola (2017), [Film] Dir. Tiziana Panizza, Chile: Domestic Films.

Index

Boldface locators indicate figures; locators followed by "n." indicate endnotes

Aboriginal people 23, 312–14, 316
accented cinema 229–30, 233, 238
Acción 56
aesthetics 5, 14, 33, 37, 44–5, 55, 75, 89,
    91, 124, 127, 209, 212, 229, 233–4,
    248, 251, 260–3, 268
  Caribbean cinema 230
  'Caribbeing' memory narrative and
    236–43
  of choral euphoria 13
  concentrationary film 308–9
  of cultural representation 98
  of hunger into garbage 137–8
  Latin American cinema 24
  of sublime 38, 46, 51 n.11
affect 18, 43, 81, 89, 91–4, 99, 102, 136,
    138, 144, 148, 181, 183, 205, 223,
    257
  archive 106
  climate change 144
  global capitalism 133
  Global South 140, 142, 146
  island imaginaries 18
  radioactive contamination (Goiânia)
    132
  United States 191–2
affective mappings 91, 94
  mobile landscapes and 90–2
  poetic ethnography and 105–7
The African Diaspora film Festival (New
    York) 235
Afro-Antilleans 253
Afro-Panamanians 248, 254, 257, 262–3
Agamben, G. 275–6, 281 n.3
Agiui, A. 271
Agüero, I. 303
Aguilar, G. M. 32, 43, 45
Aguilar Camín, H. 119
Ahmed, S. 256

Alaimo, S. 139–40, 144
  'trans-corporeality' 133–4, 136–7, 139
Alcatraz island 167 n.8
Alicia (*Magic Magic,* 2013) 58–68
Allende, S. 67–8, 69 n.2, 73
Allende's deputies 83, **85**
Almodóvar Ronda, R. 225 n.2
Aloma of the South Seas (Tourneur, 1926)
    194, 204
Alonso Marchante, J. L. 81, 87 n.8
Álvarez, S. 212–13
Alvear, M. de 288, 295
Amado, A. M. 32
Amante, A. 297
Amaro Castro, L. 167 n.4, 167 n.7
American citizenship 22, 192–3, 196
American imagination 4
Ames, L. 201
Andermann, J. 39, 61, 184 n.1, 262
Ángel Negro (Olguín, 2000) 58
Anthropocene 132–4, 137, 142, 146, 149 n.2
  capitalism and 133, 137
  racial dimension of 149 n.3
Antigona 222
Antillean cinema 233–4
Antonio Maceo Brigade 213–14, 217–18
Antonioni, M. 20
Aón, L. 167 n.2
Aonikenk people 80
Aotearoa 310
Aponte, M. 217
Appadurai, A. 6, 24
  imaginary landscapes 6
Aranzuela (*La hija del penal,* 1949) 121–2
Araoz, R. 221–2
Aravamudan, S. 11
Araya (Benacerraf, 1959) 149 n.2
archipelagic thinking 2
  stage of 10

Index

archival images (exposed insularity) 141–7
archive 3, 22, 31, 59, 67, 90–1, 98–101,
    103, 105–6, 110, 129, 142, 184 n.1,
    212, 222, 309
    Argentine 38–9, 41, 43, 49, 50 n.1
    of Chilean histories 78
    ethnographic 94, 96
    US political surveillance (Puerto Rico)
        220
archive effect 106, 220
Argentina 15, 19, 40, 154, 158, 160, 166,
    171, 185 n.4, 287–8, 291, 296–7,
    308
    cultural production 157
    as deserted landscape 31–2
    as homogeneous national body 164
    Independence bicentennial (2010) 154
    indigenous communities 154, 160,
        167 n.1
    military junta (1982) 35–6
    political imprisonment 295
    post-dictatorship 56
    Salinas Grandes 39
    Sarmiento's utopian vision 300
Argentine cinema 12, 31, 37, 49 n.1, 51
    n.8, 73, 175–6. *See also specific*
    Argentine films
    Argentine literature 39, 46, 50 n.1, 51
        n.9, 51 n.11, 153
    dictatorship 32
    ex-combatant filming 36, 46–8, 49 n.1
    of Malvinas/Falkland Islands 19, 31, 49
        n.1, 51 n.9
Argentine Civil Wars 155
Argentine Confederation 156
Argentine Hijos por la Identidad y la
    Justicia contra el Olvido y el
    Silencio (H.I.J.O.S.) 56
Argentine National Anthem (1813) 165
Argentine Naval Prefecture 163
Argentine settlement 35
Argirópolis (1850) 21, 154–6, 160, 162,
    164–5, 167 n.7, 290
Argirópolis Island 154–5, 158, 161–2, 166,
    288, 297
Arias, L. 49 n.1, 153
Ariel-Caliban opposition 11–12
Artigas 299
Asian-Americans 194

Assistance mortelle (Peck, 2013) 22, 268–9
    reverse angle shots 270–1, 274–5,
    278–9
    scenes 273
Atacama Desert 73, 76–80, **78**
Attenborough, D. 145
Australia 23, 97, 308–10, 312, 316
Avelar, I., *The Untimely Present:*
    Postdictatorial Latin American
    Fiction and the Task of Mourning
    (1999) 67
Aventuras de Robinson Crusoe (Buñuel,
    1954) 11
Azores 134

Baer, W. 132
Bagolun, F., *Adjusted Lives* 276
Bahía Honda (Pinar del Río) 215
Baker, J.
    intentional disruption 5–6
    La sirène des tropiques (1927) 5
    Zouzou (1934) 5
Baldacchino, G. 108 n.1
Bales, K. 281 n.2
Balseros (Bosch, 2002) 14
balseros crisis (1994) 14–15
Balzac vs. People of Puerto Rico 193
Bandeira, M. B. L. 132–3, 135, 147
bare life 273–4, 281 n.3
Baron, J. 106, 220
Barraza, V. 57
Bartles, J. 15, 19
Base de Submarinos de la Armada
    Argentina 44
Base Naval 44
Bassi, E. 43
Battaglino, J. 35
Battle of Coronel 15
Battle of the Falkland Islands 15
The Battles of Coronel and Falkland Islands
    (Summers, 1927) 15
Baudrillard, J. 269
Bauer, T. 49 n.1
Bauman, Z. 281 n.2
Beagle, H. M. S. 34
Beauchamp, E. 214
Belem Novo 143
Belgium 97
Bell, L. 140. *See also* waste theory

320   *Index*

Bellerive 279
Bellerive, J.-M. 271, 275, 279
Benacerraf, M. 149 n.2
Benítez-Rojo, A. 209, 230, 240
   irreducible memory 230
Benjamin, W. 91, 95
   'The Task of the Translator' (1923) 160
Benner, W. 9, 20
Bennett, J. 97. *See also* vibrant matter,
   concept of
Bennings, J. 183
Benson, M. 251–2
Berg, C. R. 128
Bermejo river 157
Bernades, H. 51 n.7
Bernard (*Le Bonheur d'Elza,* 2011) 239–40
bilingualism 263 n.2
biopolitics 116, 120, 126–7, 129, 270–3,
   277, 279, 281 n.3
biopower 280, 281 n.3
Bitter Sugar/Sucre Amer (Lara, 1998) 234,
   243 n.1
Black Atlantic 236–7, 242
black Martinicans 243–4 n.3
Black Shack Alleys 244 n.3
Black solidarity and resistance 234
BLM movement 315
'Blue Marble' photograph 145
Boca de lixo (Coutinho, 1993) 138, 149 n.2
Bocas del Toro 21, 247–8, 252–4, 262–4,
   264 n.7
Bocas Educational Service Organization
   (BESO) 258–9
Bojórquez, D. 115
Bond, J. 5
Bongie, C. 172
Bonilla, Y. 278
Boochani, B. 308–9
Borensztein, S. 49 n.1
Bosch, C. 14
Bosch, J. 209
Boteros Bocatoreños 257
Boukman, D. 235
Bourdieu, P. 274
Boutroue, J. 279
Bowman, M. 271
Braniff, S. 35
Braziel, J. E. 17, 22, 268
Brazil 8, 69 n.3, 131, 148, 204, 279, 295

debt crisis 132
democratization 132
economic miracle 138
landfills 138
social inequality 132, 138
tropicalismo counter-culture 137
Brazilian cinema 137, 145
Bresson, R. 175, 180
Brink (*Magic Magic,* 2013) 58, 63, 65–6
Brody, M. J. 264 n.3
Brown, C. D. 199, 201, 299
Browning, E. 58
Brugués, A. 15
Bruno, G. 96, 108 n.5, 173, 176, 181, 185
   n.6
   Atlas of Emotion (2002) 96
Bryant, L. R. 135
Bryce, J. 233, 238
Buenos Aires 48–9, 154–6, 171, 287–9,
   292, 294, 297, 298
Bun, G.-E. 275
Buñuel, L. 11, 117, 119
Burke, E. 37
Bush, G. W. 273
Busquets, N. 128
Butler, J. 281 n.2

Cabellos Damián, E. 149 n.2
Cacciola 289–90
Cadena perpetua (Ripstein, 1978) 116,
   128–9
caesium (*Ilha das Flores*) 136, 139, 147–8
Calama 74, 79, 85
Calderón, M. G. 76, 81
Calveiro, P. 50 n.3
Camila (Bemberg, 1984) 32
Campbell, R. 102–3
Camp Corail-Cesselesse 275
Canada 96, 232, 279
Canary Islands 134
Canclini, A. 50 n.2
Canto del cisne (Fontán, 1994) 184 n.2
capitalism 18, 131–4, 137–40, 146, 149 n.2,
   267, 270, 273–4, 280–1, 282 n.6
   colonialism and 212–13
   disaster 277, 279, 282 n.7
   in environmental issues 133, 138–40,
   146, 183
   ideological myths of 268

triumph of 268
vs. socialism 211
capitalist destruction 274
Capitalocene 137
Carbonell, M. R. 217, 218
carceral archipelago 308
Caresani, L. 37
Caribbean cinema 233–5
Caribbean Girl NYC (Monpierre, 2018)
    236
Caribbean imagination 229–30
Caribbean island 8, 14–15, 21, 43, 134,
    191, 193, 203–4, 224, 232, 236, 239,
    244 n.3, 261, 269
  Cold War politics 218
  colonialism and capitalism in 213, 236,
    258
  diversalité *vs.* universalité 233
  film archipelago 21–2, 209, 215, 220,
    233, 281
  identity 230, 233, 240
  as structural adjustment programmes
    232
  US developmentalism in 212
'Caribbeing' memory 236–43
Carrasco, G. 89
cartography 61, 107
  embodied 91
  of imperialism 134
  modern 94
  and travelogue 95–7
  as 'way of writing' 107
Casabé, D. 23, 31, 45–6, 48–9, 287, 301.
    See also La forma exacta de las islas/
    The Exact Shape of the Islands
    (2013)
Castillo, C. 56
Castro, F. 219, 221
Cera, M. 58
Cerro pelado (Álvarez, 1966) 212–13, 215,
    223
Cerutti Guldberg, H. 167 n.7
Césaire, A. 233, 243 n.1
  Cahier d'un retour au pays natal (1939)
    10
  Une tempête (1969) 10
CGI 9
Chacabuco concentration camp (Atacama
    Desert) 79

Chaco 154
Cham, M. 232, 235
  indigenous film practice 233–4
Champigny Sur Marne 243 n.2
Chan, C. 191, 194, 196
Chanan, M. 13, 86 nn.1–2, 90
Chapa (Alejandro Cobo) 121–2
Chauka, Please Tell Us the Time (Boochani
    and Sarvestani, 2017) 308–9
Chejfec, S., *El mes de las moscas* (The
    month of the flies) 303
Chicago Tribune 204
Children in No Man's Land (Prado, 2008)
    250
Chile 15, 19–20, 69 n.3, 73, 84, 86 n.1, 86
    n.4, 86 n.7, 93, 96, 103, 108 n.3,
    308–10, 313
  archipelagos (*El botón de nácar*) 20, 76,
    77, 80–1
  Concertación 55–7, 66
  cultural and natural residue 74–6,
    78–81
  geographic insularity 75–7
  islands of 76–7
  legacy of Pinochet and neoliberalism
    69 n.2
  Patagonia 55–6, 60–1
  Pinochet dictatorship in 55, 78–9, 82
  public protest in 56
  recurrence of oppression 75
*Chile, la memoria obstinada/Chile, the
    Obstinate Memory* (Guzmán, 1996)
    86 n.1, 86 n.3
Chilean cinema 57, 69 nn.3–4, 100. *See
    also* contemporary Chilean cinema
  dearth of critical reception 55
  neoliberal culture 58
Chiloé Island 76, 303
China 191–2, 232
Chinese Exclusion Act (1882) 193–4
'Chinese quarter' 296
Chiriquí 253
Chonos Archipelago 76
Choropampa, el precio del oro (Cabellos
    Damián, 2002) 149 n.2
Cinema Novo 137
cinematic imaginary 11, 229
Cineteca Nacional 100
Citizens United 277

Clandestinos (Pérez, 1987) 214
Claudio 110 n.9
Cliff, J. 233
climate change 22, 133, 137, 144–6, 148
Clinton, B. 273
Clinton, H. R. 270
Clinton Fund 278
Cobo, A. 121
Cobo, R. 117
cognitive geography 90
Cohen, M. 44
Cold War 5, 13–14, 22, 210–11, 216,
    218–24
Cold War geopolitics 216, 218–19
    impact and conflictive legacies 218
    migrant flows 211–16
Collor de Melo, F. 132
Combatientes (2013) 51 n.8
community isolation 78–83
Compañía Explotadora de la Isla de Pascua
    (Easter Island Exploiting Company)
    93
concentrationary cinema 23, 307–9
Conde, A. G. 124
Confederación General del Trabajo (CGT)
    50 n.3
Confederate States of the Río de la Plata
    155–6, 166
Conley, T. 108 n.5
'Conquest of the Desert' 288, 292
'Con razón' (*Pedropiedra*, 2011) 65
consumption-led migration 247
contemporary Chilean cinema 68, 82, 85
    reckoning with state terror 55–7
contemporary neoliberalism 18
Conti, H. 153
continental/derived islands 153, 161–3, 301
'continentally oriented' modernity 134
Contraloría General de Panama (2010) 253
Cooke, S. 139
Cooper, M. C. 8
Corbin, M. 52 n.12
Corrientes 154
Costa Rica 8, 252
costumbrismo 32–3
costumbrista gaze 41
Couret, N. 74
Courtney, H. 250
Coutinho, E. 138, 149 n.2

Crabtree, J. 255
Creole 235
Crichlow, M. 25 n.1
Crichton, M., *Jurassic Park* 8
Criscenti, J. T. 167 n.7
Crosby, A. W. 134
Crowell, M. 232, 241
Crutzen, P. 132
Cruzado Plan 132
Cuba 8, 10–17, 21–2, 86 n.1, 193, 211,
    223–4, 225 n.1
    Haitian community in 13–14
    insularity 13
    as learning landscape 221
    in Puerto Rican documentary 216–22
    Special Period 217–18, 221–3
Cuba documentary
    archipelagic relations in 210–11
    media practices 210, 222–4
    Puerto Rico in 211–16, 224
Cuban Adjustment Act (1995) 14
Cuban Institute of Cinematographic Art
    and Industry (ICAIC) 13–14, 212,
    214, 216, 221
Cuban-Puerto Rican relations 209–10
Cuban Revolution 10, 12, 209, 213–14,
    216–17, 219, 222
Cuban Revolutionary Armed Forces Film
    and Television Studios 214
Cubero, K. 217–18, 220–2
cultural and aesthetic primitivism 5
Cumbite (Gutiérrez Alea, 1964) 13–14
'Cycle of the Paraná Delta' 177
'Cycle of the River' 177, 184 n.2

D'Alessandro, N. 4, 9, 21
Danes 290
Darboussier Sugar Factory 231
Darío, R. 254–5, 257–60, 288, 299. *See also*
    Boteros Bocatoreños
Darwin, C. 34
Davidovich, K. 52 n.12
Davis, N. Z. 8
Dawson Island
    Allende's deputies 83, **85**
    indigenous peoples 83, **84**
    Pinochet incarceration, survivors 84–6,
    85
death-capital 282 n.7

Debs, S. 141
defamiliarizing techniques 57, 309
Defoe, D., *Robinson Crusoe* (1719) 10–11, 157
de la Texera, Diego 216–17
Deleuze, G. 55, 295, 301
  Cinema 2: The Time-Image (1985) 65
  'continental/derived islands' 153, 161–2, 301
  'The Desert Island' 107 n.1, 294
  Desert Islands and Other Texts 153
  A Thousand Plateaus 107
D'Elia, A. 149 n.2
DeLoughrey, E. 133–6
del Rio Gabiola, I. 250
Demaría, L. 41
Demos, T. J. 24, 132
Denmark 79
Depetris Chauvin, I. 10, 20, 47, 51 n.10, 89, 94, 185 n.2
Derrida, J. 280
  The Beast and the Sovereign 153, 157
'Desert Campaign' (1879) 292
desert/deserted islands 11, 15, 19, 33, 39–40, 107–8 n.1, 294, 298, 301
  Argentina as 31–2
  claiming 34–6
  Malvinas/Falklands as 33–5, 45, 49
de-subjectivizing sublimity 38
Deulofeu, L. 214
Diawara, M. 239
Díaz, J. 14, 212, 214, 216–17
Díaz, P. 116
Díaz Espinoza, E. 56
Díaz Quiñones, A. 209
dictatorship 31–3, 36, 40, 42–3, 45–6, 49, 73, 274
  Brazil 138
  Duvalier (Haiti) 232
  Pinochet (Chile) 55–7, 66–8, 69 n.2, 74–5, 78–80, 82–4, 86 n.3
Didi-Huberman, G. 55, 175
  Being a Skull: Site, Contact, Thought, Sculpture (2016) 62
  The Eye of History: When Images Take Positions (2018) 63–4
Dieleke, E. 9, 23, 31, 45–6, 48–9. *See also La forma exacta de las islas*/The Exact Shape of the Islands (2013)

Diestro-Dópido, M. 57, 69 nn.3–4
digital technologies 9, 57
di Lauro, J. 100
disaster capitalism 277, 279, 282 n.7
disposability 269, 273, 277, 280, 281 nn.2–3
disposable economies 274, 281 n.3, 282 n.7
'Disposable Life' project of (Evans) 281 n.2
disposable people 269, 273–6, 279, 281 n.3
dispossession 162, 247, 249, 255–7
distribution rights 260
documentary/documentary films 3, 5, 9, 18–22, 33, 37, 45–6, 48, 57, 73–6, 80, 82, 90, 107, 142, 145, 218, 221, 260–3, 268, 275, 291, 302, 307. *See also specific documentary films*
  core and formative indexicality 142
  environmental 145
documents 105, 109 n.7, 118, 220
  expressive nature 100–4
  types 105
Dogme 95 movement 16
Donde cae el sol (Fontán, 2002) 184 n.2
Duff, A. 197
Dumbrille, D. 198, 201
Dunn, C. 137
Dupuy, A. 274
  Haiti: From Revolutionary Slaves to Powerless Citizens 281 n.4
Duvalier dictatorship 232

'East Asian' 196
Easter Island 10, 20, 76, 89, 93, 95, 106, 108 n.3, 109 n.7, 295, 308, 310
Echeverría, E., *La cautiva* (1837) 39
ecocinema 146
ecocriticism 131–3
Edmond, R. 25 n.1, 172
efecto archipiélago (archipelago effect) 224
Efron, F. 96
Egypt 191
Ehrmantraut, P., *Masculinidades en guerra* (2013) 50 n.1
1802, L'Epopée Guadeloupéenne/1802, The Guadeloupean Epic (Lara, 2004) 234
El almuerzo (Cubero, 2009) 220, 223
El árbol (Fontán, 2006) 184 n.2

324 *Index*

El botón de nácar/The Pearl Button
(Guzmán, 2015) 20, 73–7, **77,** 80–3,
85, 86 nn.3–4, 86 n.7, 149 n.2
'El Comodín' (*La hija del penal,* 1949) 122
El día nuevo (Fontán, 2016) 184 n.2
Elegía de abril (Fontán, 2010) 184 n.2
El estanque (Fontán, 2016) 184 n.2
El golpe de estado/The Coup d'Etat (1976)
86 n.1
Ellerson, B. 229–30
El limonero real (Fontán, 2016) 21, 173,
176–7, 179–82, **180, 182,** 184,
184 n.2
El paisaje invisible (Fontán, 2003) 184 n.2
El poder popular/Popular Power (1979)
86 n.1
*El rostro/*The Face (Fontán, 2014) 21, 173,
176–9, **177,** 184, 184 n.2, 185 n.7
El Salvador vencerá (de la Texera, 1981) 216
elusive island 222–5
El viento sabe que vuelvo a casa (Leiva,
2016) 303
El visitante (Olivera, 1999) 49 n.1
Elza Béranger (*Le Bonheur d'Elza,* 2011)
230, 236–43
embodied cartography 91
empty land- and seascapes (films) 31, 33,
262
La campana (2010) 42–5
La deuda interna (1987) 39–42
La forma exacta de las islas (2013) 49
site of memory 47
*Entre deux rives: de Saint-Domingue à
Pointe-à-Pitre: Between Two Shores*
(Monpierre, 2017) 235
environmental thinkers 135
epistolary film 229, 268, 271, 307, 309
Epps, B. 75
Epumer Rosas 292
Erman, S. 192
Ernesto (*La hija del penal,* 1949) 121–2,
126
erosion 24, 153, 155, 161
erotics of art 181
Escobar, A., *redes* 17
Escollera Norte 44
Escollera Sur 44
Escuela Internacional de Cine y Televisión
(EICTV) 217–18, 220–1

Esposito, R., progressively desocialized
spaces 120
Esses, C. 172
Estamira (Prados, 2004) 138
ethics 14, 136, 199
ethnic representation 7, 18, 20, 191–2,
196–7, 200, 243 n.2, 253
ethnographic cinema 23, 97–8, 105, 107,
108 n.4, 109 n.7, 204, 314
ethnographic spectacle 108 n.4
ethnography 90, 98, 101, 107, 109 n.7
classical 94
culture and 109 n.7
experimental 90, 95, 98–9, 106–7
indigenous 5, 101
poetic 105–7
reinvention of 105
sensory 97
Ette, O. 172
Europe 75, 165–6, 198, 232–3
Evans, B., *Disposable Futures* (2015) 281
n.2
Evtushenko, E. 14
Exclusion Acts 192–4
expenditure capitalism 277, 280
experimental ethnography 90, 95, 98–9,
106–7
exposed insularity 21, 133–4, 137
of Ilha das Flores 140
through archival images 141–7

Fabian, J., *Time and the Other: How
Anthropology Makes Its Object*
(1983) 102
Fábula 57, 69 n.4
Falkland Islands. *See* Malvinas/Falkland
islands
Fanon, F. 10
Farnhout, J. 97
Fast Five (Lin, 2011) 204
Fatton, R. Jr., *Haiti: Trapped in the Outer
Periphery* 274, 282 n.5
'federal stars' 296
Feierstein, D. 61
Feliciano Santos (*Paraíso for Sale,* 2011)
248, 254–5, 257–9
human intervention 255
killjoy 255–6
Felipe (*Islas Marías,* 1951) 116, 125–6

Fernández, E. 21, 116, 123–9. *See also Islas Marías* (Fernández, 1951)
Fernández, J. 123
Fernández Retamar, R., *Calibán* (1971) 10
Fernández Reyes, Á. 118
Figueroa, G. 123–5
Filiberto (Alfonso, 2017) 218–20, 223
film archipelago 3, 6, 8, 23, 25, 73, 76, 92, 102, 224, 259
  carceral 308
  Chile 77, 80–1
  of crossed gazes 209, 220, 222–5
  in Hispanic Caribbean 209–10
  as ideological and social template 134
  islands 131
  Latin American 1, 9, 17, 25
  post-Cold War 216–22
films about islands. *See* island films
financial crisis (2008) 251
First World 17
Fischer, S. 273
FitzRoy, R. 31, 34
55 hermanos (Díaz, 1978) 212–15, 217, 223
Flaherty, R. J. 5
Flatley, J. 91, 94–5
floating signifiers (islands) 92
Fogwill, R. E., *Los Pichiciegos* (1982) 50 n.1
Fojas, C. 193
Fontán, G. 17, 21, 173–5, 177–81, 184 n.2, 185 n.5, 185 n.7. *See also specific Fontán's films*
  advancement of time 182
  'Cycle of the River' 184 n.2
  islands (in films) 183–4
  phantasmagoric 178
  poetic-cinematic 174–6, 183
forced disappearance 55, 66–7
Formosa 167 n.1, 300
Fornoff, C. 10, 17, 22
Foucault, M. 118, 120, 281 n.3
  Discipline and Punish (1979) 308
  modernity 308
fracture 16, 142, 153–5, 161–5
France 50 n.2, 86 n.4, 230–2, 236, 243 n.2, 251, 279, 298
Francis, T. S. 5
Freemason ornaments/remnant 287, 297

Fremantle Island 312, 314, 316
French island films 5, 93
Frente Farabundo Martí para la Liberación Nacional 216
Friedrich, C. D., *The Monk by the Sea* (1809) 44
Frondizi, A. 295
Fuckland (Marqués, 2000) 16
Fuegians 76, 80, 87 n.8
  oppression and 81, 83, 86
  water-based lifestyles 76
Fundación Pinochet 69 n.2
Furtado, G. P. 142
Furtado, J. 21, 131–5, 137–8, 140–8, 148 n.1. *See also Ilha das Flores* (Furtado, 1989)

Galápagos of the Twenty-First Century 254
Gamerro, C., *Las islas* (1998) 50 n.1
garbage (in film) 134, 138, 140, 144
  as exposure 139
  island of 137–41, 147
García, A. M. 217, 224
García, J. 225 n.1
García, J. C. 218
García, M. 109 n.8, 110 n.9
García Borrero, J. A. 13
García-Crespo, N. 9, 22, 193, 204
García Yero, O. 14
Garrido Díaz, M. 100
Gauguin, P. 5
Gautier, A. 232
gazes 209–10
  costumbrista 41
  diasporic and migrant 210
  film archipelago of crossed 209, 220, 222–5
  haptic 176
  optic 185 n.6
  tourist 260–3
  web of textures 98–100
  zenithal 97
Generation of '37 (*Generación del 37*) 39, 51 n.6
geographic imaginaries 2, 60, 90, 92–3, 148, 209–11
Germany 86 n.4, 279
  First World War 198

Getino, O. 16, 73–4, 149 n.2
Ghosh, A. 24
Gillis, J. R. 108 n.1
  Islands of the Mind 34
Gilroy, P. 51 n.4
Ginsburg, F. 101, 109 n.7
Giroux, H. A. 281 n.2
  Disposable Futures (2015) 281 n.2
  violence of organized forgetting 273
Gleyzer, R. 16
Glissant, É. 133–8, 209, 215, 224, 229–30,
    236, 242
  'archipelagic thinking' 2, 10
  Caribbean imagination 229
  generalization 231
  'poetics of Relation' 133
  'right to opacity' 2
  Treatise on the Whole-World 1
Glissant, G. 233
Global North 138, 140, 142, 247, 250
Global South 3, 10, 18, 23, 140, 260, 308
  capitalism in Anthropocene 133, 142,
    149 n.2
  environmental justice 146
*Global Studies: Lessons from Haiti and
    Puerto Rico* 282 n.7
global terror war 281 n.2
Godoy, C., *La construcción. Metales
    radioactivos en las islas del Atlántico
    Sur* (2014) 50 n.1
Goiânia 132, 136, 139
Goldberg, R. 222
Goldman, N. 167 n.3
Gomes, C. 144
Gomes, E. 34
Gómez, L. 167 n.2
Gómez, S. 13–14
Gómez Cruz, E. 128
González, J. V., *Mis montañas* (1893) 41
Good Neighbor policy 191–2
Gordon, R. 46
Granada 214
Gran Chaco (Van Esso, 2015) 149 n.2
Graziadei, D. 172
Gretel Alfonso Fuentes (*Retornar a La
    Habana con Guillén Landrián*,
    2013) 221–2
Griffiths, A. 204

Guadeloupe 9, 21–2, 230–2, 234–6, 238,
    241–2
Guaíba estuary 21, 131, 133–5, 138, 141,
    143–4, 148, 148 n.1
Guam 192–3
Guaraní language 154, 159–60, 164–5,
    300
Guattari, F., *A Thousand Plateaus* 107
Guayaneco Archipelago 76
Guber, R. 35, 50 n.3
Guerra, J. de 34
Guerrón Moreno, C. 253–4
Guillén Landrián, N. 221–2
Gunning, T. 261
Guterl, M. P. 5
Gutiérrez Alea, T. 74
  Cumbite (1964) 13–14
  Memorias del subdesarrollo (1968) 12,
    14, 73–4
Guzmán, P. 9, 20, 56, 73–82, 84, 86 n.1,
    86 n.3, 86 n.7, 149 n.2. *See also El
    botón de nácar/The Pearl Button*
    (2015); *La cordillera de los sueños*
    (2019); *Nostalgia de la luz/Nostalgia
    for the Light* (2010)

'Hacia un tercer cine'/Towards a Third
    Cinema (Solanas and Getino) 74
Haiti 13, 21–2, 214, 232, 267–70, 273–6,
    278–9, 281
  cinematic montage 268
  impacts on IFIs 268
  necrocapitalism 273
Haitian film 13–14, 268–9, 273–5
Hall, S. 196
Halperín Donghi, T. 51 n.6
Han, B. C., *Saving Beauty* 38
handycam films 45–7
Hanga Roa Museum 109 n.7
haptic 176–7, 185 n.6
haptic gaze 176
haptic vision/visuality 109 n.6, 173–4, 176,
    181
  optical and 99–100
Haraway, D. 133
The Harder They Come (Henzell, 1972)
    233
Hardt, M. 108 n.2, 281 n.2

Harper, G. 6
Haush 80
Hawai'i 193
Hay, P., 'A Phenomenology of Islands' 36
Hayes, M. 251
Heart and Soul (Edwards, 1917) 194
Hemingway, E. 12
Henry, M. 282 n.6
Henzell, P. 233
Hernández Adrián, F.-J. 25 n.1
Herrera, M. 13
Hersholt, J. 198, 201
Hijos-Chile 56
Hipócrita (Morayta, 1949) 118
Hispanic Caribbean 209–10, 220, 224
Historia de la literatura argentina/History of Argentine Literature 288
historiography 90, 95
Hollweg, B. 86 n.7
Hollywood 9, 13, 22, 24, 192, 234, 237, 261
  as ethnographer 7–8
  misrepresentation of Puerto Rico 203–4
Holmes, A. 9, 20
Holocene 131
homogeneous national map 154–5, 161, 164
Hondo, M. 235, 242
How the Porto Rican Girls Entertain Uncle Sam's Soldiers (Armitage, 1899) 193
Huete, R. 251
humanitarian business 277, 281 n.1
Hymer, W. 197

Icart, R. 206 n.3
identity 6, 11–12, 17, 60–7, 92–3, 108 n.2, 109 n.7, 125, 142, 161, 196, 216, 237–9, 241, 243, 243 n.2, 258
  Caribbean 215, 229–30, 233, 236, 240
  as transactional 63
Ilha da Casa da Pólvora 131
Ilha da Pintada 131
Ilha das Flores 131–6, 141, 143, 148, 148 n.1
Ilha das Flores (Furtado, 1989) 21, 131–2, 137–8, 148
  'Blue Marble' photograph 145
  caesium (toxicity) 136, 139, 147–8

consumerism and waste disposal 133, 140–1
  epistemic stance 143
  Holocaust 144, 147
  indexical power 143
  names and definitions, choice 146–7
  performing exposure 144
  photographic images 142
  syllogism 142–4, 146
Ilha das Garças 131
Ilha do Pavão 131
Iluminados por el fuego (Bauer, 2005) 49 n.1, 51 n.8
imaginary islands/islandscapes 4–7, 8, 36–7, 60, 93, 134, 138, 140, 147–8, 155–6, 161, 307
IMDb sites 86 n.5
immigrants/immigration 192, 194–6, 202, 204, 230, 232, 236, 250, 288, 290
Immigration Act (1924) 194
Imorou, A. 229
Import Substitution Industrialization (ISI) 119
indetermination 185 n.4
'Indian hunters' 81
IndieGoGo 260
Indigenous Arawaks 231
indigenous communities 21, 23, 32, 38–40, 42, 61, 80–2, 108 n.4, 159, 248, 292, 294–5, 307
  American 167 n.8
  Argentina 161–4, 167 n.1
  Dawson Island **84**
  dispossession 255–7
  Fuegian 83, 87 n.8
  and land rights 248, 257, 260, 264 n.5
  oppression 82
  Panama 253
  Paraná Delta 154
  Patagonia 74
  victims and Allende's deputies 83–4
  Yámana 83
indigenous film practice 233
indigenous media 109 n.7
Infante, P. 116–17, 123, 127
The Inhabitants (Peleshian, 1970) 174
Instituto Geográfico Militar de Chile 86 n.6

328 *Index*

Insular Cases 192–3, 200
insularity 2–4, 10–18, 20–1, 23, 25, 107,
    135, 153, 156, 158, 162, 165
    and ecology 133
    exposed 133–4, 140–7
    geographic (Chile) 76–7
    hermetic isolation 134
    of Lago Ranco 64
    of memories 75
    Nueva Argirópolis 156, 160–2
    Western imaginary of 147
insular states 92–5
insurgency and resistance, spaces 175
Intercontinental Dictionary Archive 87 n.9
international aid economies 269, 275–6,
    279, 281 n.1
International Atomic Energy Agency 132
international film festivals 33, 235
international financial institutions (IFIs)
    268, 274, 281
international nongovernmental
    organizations 277, 279
International Women's Film Festival
    (Seoul) 235
Iruya River 157
Isla de Pascua (Yankovic and di Lauro,
    1961) 100
Isla Grande de Tierra del Fuego 76
island(s) 1–2, 5, 7, 9, 20–2, 25 n.1, 33, 36,
    153, 176, 219, 247, 253–4, 294–5,
    308, 310. *See also specific islands*
    and archipelagos 4
    British chose to colonize 50 n.2
    of Chile 76–7
    desert/deserted (*see* desert/deserted
        islands)
    as detachment and fracture 154, 161–5
    epistemological power 108 n.2
    as floating signifiers 92
    of garbage 137–41
    landscape 55, 59–61, 63, 67–8, 138, 179
    letters from 309–17
    literary and cultural studies 172
    lives, filming 17–19
    loom as 176
    and memories in suspense 45–9
    memory 75, 83–6
    nostalgia for 23–5
    staging 10–17

visual unrepresentability of 156–61
island effect 92, 108 n.2
island films 1–2, 6, 31, 37, 45, 118, 295,
    300, 303. *See also specific films*
    concentrationary 308
    ethnographic thinking 7–10
    French 5, 93
    Latin American 1–4, 19–23
    on Martín García (*see* Martín García
        Island)
    subgenres 4–5
Island Observed (Lemieux, 1965) 96
island studies 36, 133, 137, 210
island-to-island relations 210–11
Islas de Sansón 34
Islas imaginadas 50 n.1
Islas Marías archipelago 12, 21, 115–17,
    120–4, 126, 129
    fictionalizations 128
    films about 118
    as *tableau* 124
Islas Marías Federal Prison 116
Islas Marías (Fernández, 1951) 21, 116,
    119, 123, 125, 127–8
islets 76, 172, 291
Itaú Cultural 132

Jamaica 8, 233
Japan 194–5, 232
Jean-Luc (*Le Bonheur d'Elza*, 2011) 239–41
Jemmy Button (Yámana, *El botón de
    nácar*) 80–1, 83
Jervinen, L. 202
Jewett, D. 34
Jiménez, C. 56
Joan Castle (*Mr. Moto in Danger Island*,
    1939) 197–9, 201–3
José, A. 137
journey 10, 23, 43–4, 51 n.10, 89, 91, 103,
    107, 108 n.5, 124, 141, 148, 173,
    236, 243, 290
    of identity 230, 238
    to Islas Marías 118
    to Martín García (*see* Martín García
        Island)
Joyce, J. 157
Juan de los muertos (Brugués, 2011) 15
Juan Fernández Islands 76
Jurassic Park (Spielberg, 1993) 8

kai kai (Rapa Nui practice) 100–1
Kalatozov, M. 14
Kamin, B. 49 n.1, 153
Kanapa, J. 233
Kant, I. 37, 51 n.4
Kapstein, H. 162
Karan Schreiber (*Paraíso for Sale,* 2011) 254–5, 258–9
Karl, I. 167 n.1
Kasat, P. 317 n.1
Katz, J. 281 n.1
Kaussen, V., 'States of Exception – Haiti's IDP Camps' 276
Kawéskar 76, 80–1, 87 n.8
Keïta, M. 237
Kiarostami, A. 171, 183
Kinane, I. 165
King Kong (Cooper and Schoedsack, 1933) 8
Klein, N. 280, 281 n.2
   This Changes Everything 280
Kohan, M. 50 n.1
   Ciencias morales (2007) 49 n.1, 50 n.1
Koza, R. 175, 185 n.4, 185 n.8
Krassa, M. 96
Kreyòl 271–2, 277

La americana (Deulofeu, 1991) 214–16
La batalla de Chile/The Battle of Chile (Guzmán, 1970s) 73–4, 86 n.1, 86 n.3
L'Absence/The Absence (Keïta, 2009) 237
La campana 42
*La campana/*The Diving Bell (2010) 31, 33, 51 n.7
   empty seascapes in 42–5
*La cárcel del fin del mundo/*The Prison at the End of the World (Vassallo, 2013) 308
La casa (Fontán, 2012) 184 n.2, 185 n.2
La ciénaga (Martel, 2001) 158
La cordillera de los sueños (Guzmán, 2019) 149 n.2
La deuda (Fontán, 2019) 184 n.2
*La deuda interna/*Internal Debt (1987) 31–3, 43
   empty landscapes in 39–42, 45
*La forma exacta de las islas/*The Exact Shape of the Islands (2013) 31–3, 45, 287, 301

aesthetic innovations (NCA) 45–6
empty land- and seascapes 49
suspension 46
Lago Ranco 58, 64
La hija de la laguna (Cabellos Damián, 2015) 149 n.2
La hija del penal (Soler, 1949) 20–1, 116, 119–20, 123–7
La historia oficial (1985) 32
La hora de los hornos/The Hour of the Furnaces (Solanas and Getino, 1968) 73, 149 n.2
La insurrección de la burguesía/The Bourgeois Insurrection (1975) 86 n.1
La isla más isla del mundo (Efron and Krassa, 1970) 96
La madre (Fontán, 2009) 184 n.2
La mirada invisible (Lerman, 2010) 49 n.1
La Nación 288
La Nana (Silva, 2009) 58
land/oceanscape 1, 16, 34, 42–3, 91–2, 194, 230, 242, 248–9, 254, 257
land property conflicts 10, 264 n.7
landscapes 2, 5, 18, 42, 47, 95, 97, 102, 124–5, 176–7, 181, 184 n.1, 212, 221, 241–2, 255, 261–3, 309. *See also* empty land- and seascapes (films)
   act of imagination 262
   body becoming 64–8
   desirable 249
   imaginary 6
   living and sensorial 90
   mobile 90–2
   performative 55, 59–64
   as physical archive 184 n.1
   wind-swept 35
Lane, R. 201
language of cinema 185 n.4, 263
La noche de los lápices (1986) 32
La operación (García, 1982) 217
'La oreja de Bresson' 185 n.4
La orilla que se abisma (Fontán, 2008) 177, 184–5 n.2, 185 n.5
La pampa antes de 1879 40
Lara, C. 233–5, 243 n.1
Lara, P. 221
Larraín, J. de D. 57, 69 n.4. *See also* Fábula
Larraín, P. 56–7, 69 n.4. *See also* Fábula

Larsen, J. 262
Las carpetas (Carbonell, 2011) 218–20, 223
La sirène des tropiques (Étiévant and Nalpas, 1927) 5
La sonora ponceña (Lucas) 219
Latin America 148, 157, 203, 247, 252
  lifestyle migration to 251
  and prison condition 295
Latin American cinema 1–4, 9, 23–5, 69 n.3, 142
  as altering environments 18
  categories and practices 2
  'contact zones' 18
  documentary filmmakers 149 n.2
  filmmaking, literary tradition and politics 12
  islandscapes 6, 9
  'peripheral displacements' 7
  political scenario of 4
  provisional parameters 3
  "spectacular experiments" 7
  traits 3
  watching 19–23
Latino Public Broadcasting 260
L'Avventura (Antonioni, 1960) 20
Lawner, M. 79
Le Bonheur d'Elza (Monpierre, 2011) 22, 230, 236–7, 239
Leeds, H. I. 22, 194. *See also Mr. Moto in Danger Island* (Leeds, 1939)
Lefebvre, M. 39, 55
  Landscape and Film (2006) 59
A Lei da Água (D'Elia, 2015) 149 n.2
Leiva, J. L. T. 303
Lejanía (Díaz, 1985) 14
Lelio, S. 56
Lemieux, H. 96
Le Profit et rien d'autre! (Peck, 2001) 268–9
Lerman, D. 49 n.1
Les Gracieuses (Sissani, 2014) 243 n.2
Les négriers/The Slavers (Boukman) 235
Letter from Siberia (Marker, 1958) 98
Levinson, B. 68
lifestyle migration 22, 247, 259–61, 263
  factors 251
  migrating south 249–54
  as neoliberal imperialism 247–8
  over Indigenous rights 257
  practice of 251

L'Île de Paques (Storck and Farnhout, 1935) 97
Lillo, G. 40
liminal islands 20, 108 nn.1–2, 131
Lingenti, A. 185 n.7
linguistic transcription 87 n.9
Little, T. 203
'living and sensorial landscapes' 90
Liyannaj Kont Pwofitasyon 240
Lizarraga, O. 251
Lluvias (Fontán, 2015) 184 n.2
López, A. 202
López, A. M. 7, 86 n.2
  'peripheral displacements' 7
López Balló, J. F. 56
Lorenz, F. G. 34, 36
Lorre, P. 191, 195–6
Lorsque l'herbe (Lara, 1968) 234
Los Angeles Times 58
Los chicos de la guerra (Kamin, 1984) 49 n.1, 51 n.8, 153
Los olvidados (Buñuel, 1950) 117, 127
Lowe, L. 192, 196
Lowery, R. 199
Lucas, Q. 219
Lula 295
Luquín, E. 116, 123–4
Luz de otoño (Fontán, 1992) 184 n.2

MacDougall, D. 96
Madame Désiré (*Le Bonheur d'Elza,* 2011) 239–43
Magallanes, F. de 34
Magic Magic (Silva, 2013) 9–10, 20, 55–6, 58–61, 63–8, 69 n.3
Maid in America (Prado, 2004) 250, 254
Malecón of Havana 13, 15
Malm, A. 133
Malosetti Costa, L. 40
Malvinas/Falkland islands 10–17, 31–2, 36, 38, 153, 287, 296, 300
  as deserted islands 33–5, 45, 49
Malvinas/Falklands War (1982) 31, 35, 40, 42, 49–50 n.1, 51 n.9, 153
Mandolessi, S. 51 n.11
Man of Aran (Flaherty, 1934) 5
Mantecón, A. 251
'mantra,' idea 110 nn.9–10
Manus Island 309

maps/mapping, films and 108 n.5. *See also* affective mappings
of nocturnal space 109 n.8
paralytic map 90
Mapuche community 61, 66
'Marcha Triunfal' (Triumphal March) 288, 299
Marechal, o la batalla de los ángeles (Fontán, 2001) 184 n.2
Mares, V. 262
Marginal Cinema movement 137
María (*La hija del penal,* 1949) 116, 119–22, 125–6
Marín, P. 57
Marker, C. 98
Marks, L. 99–100, 109 n.6, 173, 176, 181, 185 n.6, 309
Marqués, J. L. 16
Marrero Alfonso, F. 217–18
Marshall Islands 139
Martel, L. 9, 21, 153–9, 162–4, 166, 167 n.2, 300
Martelly, M. 276
Martens, R., *Enjoy Poverty! Episode III* 276
Martin, D. 154–5, 165, 167 n.2
preeminence of orality 158–9
Martín, S. 299
Martínez-San Miguel, Y. 209
Martín García Island 9, 23, 154–6, 167 n.6, 287, 291, 305 n.2
artefacts 300
catamaran 290
'Conquest of the Desert' 288, 292
'Muelle de atraque de la Isla Martín García, 1936' **291**
mysterious airplanes landing 298
park rangers of 302
Pincén 292
political imprisonment 295
prisoners and indigenous people 294
semi-open prison programme 300
Solís dining room 298–9
Ubi sunt 290
Martinique 231–2, 243 n.3
Martin-Jones, D. 78
Martins, L. M. 17, 21, 185 nn.2–3, 185 n.9
masculinity 191, 197–200, 202
Masonic ornaments 287
Matos, A. C. G. 206 n.3

Mazatlán (Mexico) 251
Mbembe, A. 134, 281 n.3
McAuley, R. 97
McEwan, I., *Machines Like Me* (2019) 50 n.1
McMahon, E. 134, 137
McWatters, M. R. 247, 252, 264 n.4
mediascapes 24
Meléndez, A. 115
Meléndez, E. 193
Memoria del saqueo (Solanas, 2004) 149 n.2
Memorias del subdesarrollo/Memories of Underdevelopment (Gutiérrez Alea, 1968) 12, 14, 73–4
memory 3, 17, 20, 23–5, 56, 65–8, 69 n.1, 73, 78, 93, 178–9, 220, 234, 242, 307, 309
aural 103
and choice 68
cultural articulation 307
dictatorship and oppression 73, 75, 80
and identity (inhabitants) 92
irreducible 230
islands 75, 83–6, 109 n.7
in natural elements surfaces 79–81
politics 55
of senses 99–100, 174, 229
in suspense 45–9
territorial 106
memory-narrative 230, 236–43
memory studies 92–3, 103
Mendoza, D. H. de 116
The Men Who Stare at Goats (Heslov, 2009) 204
Merisma, J.-R. 275
Merrill, D. 205
Metzger, S. 25 n.1
Mexican American War 118
Mexican cinema 12, 21, 124, 126, 129
'Mexican miracle' 119
Mexican Revolution 115, 127
Mexico 21, 69 n.3, 116–17, 126–7, 221, 251
culture 115
modernization 128–9
social transformations 123
Meyer, L. 119
migrant(s) 18, 117, 166, 210, 251, 259

Antillean 253
flows in Cold War geopolitics 211–16
influx 252
lifestyle 251–2, 254–5, 258–9, 262–3
in United States 250
migration tourism 251
90 millas (Rodríguez Fernández, 2005) 14
Miller Klubock, T. 74, 86 n.3
Mills, Charles., *The Racial Contract* 282
n.7
Mills, Cheryl 270
Mims 238
Minas de Leão 138
Minh-ha, T. T. 102
Ministerio de Cultura 153
Miranda, M. (Tido Bangama) 264 n.3
Mischler, G. 206 n.3
mise-en-abîme (mirroring effect) 32, 46,
48
Missile Crisis (1963) 13
Mistral, G. 90–1, 107
Mitchell, D., *Black Swan Green* (2006) 50
n.1
Moana (Flaherty, 1926) 5
mobile landscapes and affective mappings
90–2
'mobile markers' 43
Mocha Island 76
Mocoví language 160, 164–5
Model Minority Myth 196, 202
'modern Polynesian' music and dances 103
modus operandi 143, 176
Molloy, C. 146
Monpierre, M. 22, 230, 235–9, 242–3
Monsieur Moto en péril 206 n.3
Monsiváis, C. 123
Montaldo, G. 303, 305 n.2
Montiel, G. 115
Montreal World Film Festival 235
Monumento a los Caídos en Malvinas 48
Moore, J. W. 131, 133, 137
Morales, E. 295
Morales, P., *Tectonic Shifts* (2012) 281 n.1
Morayta, M. 118
More, T., *Utopia* 155, 166, 247, 263 n.1
Morton, A. D. 119
motionless railway wagons 313
Movimiento por la Defensa del Territorio
del Ecosistema del Archipelago

de Bocas del Toro (MODETEAB)
264 n.5
Mr. Moto in Danger Island (Leeds, 1939)
22, 191–2
foreign, domestic subject 194–6
historicizing colony 192–4
performing proper americanness
197–9
producing and exhibiting colony 203–5
series 205 n.1
taming exotic, mysterious location
200–3
Mr. Moto na Ilha do Terror 206 n.3
multivalenced site of memory 48
Muñiz Varela, C. 218
Muñoz, A. 172
Munro, K. 97
Murnau, F. W. 5
music 103–4, 237
modern Polynesian 103
in Rapa Nui language 94

Nader, J. 271–2
Naficy, H. 229–30, 233, 235, 237–9, 242–3,
307. *See also* accented cinema
Nagi, M. 167 n.6, 294
Nancy, J. L. 171
Nanook of the North (Flaherty, 1922) 5
Napoleon III 232
Nasty Baby (Silva, 2015) 57
nation 4–6, 8, 12, 15, 24, 31–3, 39–43, 45,
49, 89, 119, 126–7, 132, 148, 154–6,
161–6, 195–6, 232, 236–7, 239, 290
national cinema 1, 3–4, 12, 24, 31, 137,
210
national crises 8, 118
national identity 6, 161, 215
natural disasters 132, 138, 148, 270–3,
276–8, 280, 281 n.1
natural elements, memory 75, 79–81, 242
natural residue 75–6, 78–83
Navarino 76
Navarro, V. 145
Nayarit 116
necrocapitalism 270, 273, 277, 279, 281
n.3, 282 n.7
necromedia 269–70, 273, 282 n.7
Negri, A. 281 n.2
Negritude 243–4 n.3

Negroni, M. 176
neoliberal economics 8, 18, 55–6, 58, 61, 68, 69 n.2, 268, 273, 277, 280–1
nesostalgia 23–5
New Latin American Cinema 74, 86 n.2
The New York Times 204
Ngäbe-Buglé Comarca 253
Ngäbe/Ngäbe-Buglé (Guaymi) 248–9, 253–7, 262, 263–4 n.3
NGO-ized states 278
Nguyen, M. T. 194
Nguyen Tu, T. L. 194
Nichols, B. 143, 260
    'commonsense assumptions' 141
Nivaclé language 167 n.1
Nixon, R. 148, 257
    Slow Violence and Environmentalism of the Poor 139, 146
Nora, P. 47–8
Norse 'water-land' 92
North America 75, 165, 233, 260–1, 278
    lifestyle migrants to Ecuador 251
Nosotros los pobres (Rodríguez, 1948) 117
Nostalgia de la luz/Nostalgia for the Light (Guzmán, 2010) 20, 73–6, 78–81, 85, 86 nn.3–4, 149 n.2
    Atacama Desert as island **78**
    awards 75
    cultural residue 78
Nouzeilles, G. 60–1
Nubia 8–9
Nuestras Islas Malvinas (Gleyzer, 1966) 16
Nueva Argirópolis 154, 157
Nueva Argirópolis (Martel, 2010) 9, 21, 153, 167 n.2, 300
    camalote 157, 159–63
    indigenous communities, struggle 154, 161
    islands as detachment and fracture 161–5
    25 miradas, 200 minutos project 153–4
    national foundation and progress 155
    new map and textual gaze 165–7
    non-translation mechanisms 160
    organizational and political divisions (territory) 163
    visual unrepresentability, islands 156–61
    'What is an island?', question 157, 160

Nueva historia argentina 167 n.3
Nuevo Cine Argentino (NCA) 32–3, 45–6
Núñez, L. 79

O'Brien, A. 5
observational filmmaking 96
'ocular focus' 185 n.6
Official selection of the Marrakech Film Festival 235
O'Gorman, M., necromedia 269–70
O Guaraní (Gomes) 144
Ojeda Rios, F. 219
Oland, W. 195
Olascoaga, M. J., *Choyque-Mahuida* (1880) 40
Old San Juan 203
Olguín, J. 58
Olivera, J. 49 n.1
One2One 220
online financial articles (catastrophe bonds) 282 n.7
oppression 20, 73, 75–6, 80–2, 84–5, 93, 134, 145, 230, 234, 253, 260, 274, 307
optical and haptic vision 99–100, 109 n.6, 176
'optic gaze' 185 n.6
orality 158, 160, 230
O'Reilly, K. 251–2
Orozco Díaz, A. L. 217
Ortiz, J. L. 153, 173, 185 n.2
Ottone, G. 57
Oubiña, D. 32, 181, 183
Overseas Department of France (DOM) 232
'ownerless islands' 157–9, 161–3, 166

Pacific Garbage Patch 138
Pacific Ocean jail 115
Palcy, E. 233–4, 243–4 n.3, 243 n.1
Palés Matos, L. 209
Pampas 38–40, 43–4
Panafrican Film Festival of Ouagadougou 235
Panama 21–2, 255–8, 260
    educational system 263 n.3
    Indigenous population 253
    land conflicts 264 n.7

permanent/semi-permanent foreign
    residents 252
residential tourism 247–8
rights of possession 254
Panama Disease 253
Panizza, T. 20, 89–90, 93, 98, 101–3,
    105–7, 109 n.9, 308
    Bitácora (Logbook) 89
    spatial practice 97
    super 8 camera, use 98, 100
Papazian, A. 167 n.6, 294
Papua New Guinea 309
Paraguay 154, 297
Paraíso for Sale (Prado, 2011) 17, 22, 247
    desirable landscape 249
    desire for landscape 249
    inequities 248–9
    killjoy visibility 256
    tourist gaze 260–3
    trefoil 254–9
    visual artefact 248
parallax effect 101, 109 n.7
paralytic map 90
Paraná Delta 154–7, 163, 166–7, 171–3,
    176–7, 183, 184 n.1, 185 n.2, 290–1
    'Cycle of the Paraná Delta' 177
    ecosystem 184
Paranaguá, P. A. 7
Parr, A., *The Wrath of Capital* 267, 280
pascuenses (Easter islanders) 108 n.3
Pasolini 185 n.4
Patagonia landscape 55–6, 60–1, 64, 66–8,
    74, 156
patautau 100, 103
Paterito, G. 76, 81
Patton, T. O. 237
Paul, N. 271
PBS series Independent Lens 250
Peck, H. 271
Peck, R. 17, 22, 267–9, 281 n.1. *See also*
    reverse angle shots (Peck); scenes/
    obscenes (Peck)
    'Beyond Help' 277
    humanitarian pornography 281 n.1
Peleshian, A. 174
penitentiary reform 116
pensionado (retirement) visa programme
    252
Pepe el Toro trilogy 119

perceptive will 176
Pereira, M. 31. *See also La deuda interna/
    Internal Debt (1987)*
Perera, S. 317 n.1
Pérez, F. 212, 214
Perez, G., *The Material Ghost* 175
Pérez Trujillo, A. 21
performative landscape in film 59–64
Perón, J. D. 287, 295, 299
Peronism 295
Petty, S. 9, 22
Phelps, P. 271
Philippines 192–3
photographs, reproduction 141–2
Piccato, P., 'criminal literacy' 118
Pietri, P. 214
Pilagá language 160, 164–5, 167
Pincén 292
Pineda Barnet, E. 14
Pink, S. 97
Pinochet, A. 56, 69 n.1, 69 n.2
    coup d'état 73
    Fundación Pinochet 69 n.2
Pinochet dictatorship 55, 57, 66–7, 74–5,
    78–80, 82–3, 86 n.3
    Dawson survivors of 84–6, **85**
Planet Earth series 145
Podalsky, L. 9
poetic-cinematic 174–6, 183, 185 n.4
poetic ethnography 105–7
poetic principle 178
'poetics of Relation,' concept 231
Pointe-à-Pitre 231
political prisoners 78, 85–6, 287, 292, 295
politics 12, 20, 24, 35–6, 51 n.11, 55, 86,
    136, 160, 184 n.1, 194, 234
    Caribbean Cold War 218
    of disposability 281 n.2
Polizzotti, M. 117
Pollock, G. 307–9
Polynesian Triangle 108 n.3
Ponce massacre 214
Pons, M. A. 125–6
Pontecorvo, G. 8
Porfirian regime 115
Port-au-Prince 270, 275–6, 278
Porto Alegre 131–2, 135, 138, 140–1, 143
post-cold war archipelago 216–22
post-dictatorship studies 56, 66

post-quake ethnographies 281 n.1
Pozzo, A. 292
Prado, A. 22, 247, 249–50, 259, 261, 263, 264 n.6. *See also specific Prado's film*
Prados, M. 138
Pratt, M. L. 18, 255
   'contact zone' 200–1
   Imperial Eyes: Travel Writing and Transculturation (2007) 60
Provincias Unidas del Río de la Plata 34
'Publicidad. El derecho de elegir' (campaign) 68
Puerto Rican documentary 224, 225 n.1
   archipelagic relations 210–11
   Cuba in 216–22
   media practices 210, 224
   Tirabuzón Rojo 214, 216
'Puerto Rican Obituary' (Pietri) 214
Puerto Rico 21–2, 191–5, 200, 206 n.2, 225 n.1, 278
   American colonialism in 212
   colonial modernization 214
   in Cuba documentary 211–16
   documentary practices 22
   as paradoxical perilous paradise 200
Puerto Rico (Díaz Rodríguez and Pérez, 1975) 212, 214–16, 223
Puerto San Julián 34
Pulido Esteva, D. 115, 117
Puri, S. 231–2, 240

Qawaskar language 87 n.9
Qom community 154, 167 n.1
Queimada/Burn! (Pontecorvo, 1969) 8
Quintero Herencia, J. C. 209, 224

The Radiological Accident in Goiânia 132, 136
rails monument (Villa Grimaldi Peace Park, Santiago) **83**
Ramesar, Y. 241–2
Ramos, J. 214, 218, 221–2
   fictionalization of Puerto Rico 214
   Retornar a La Habana con Guillén Landrián (2013) 221
Ranqueles 292, 295
Rapa Nui/Easter Island 20, 23, 94, 97, 100, 108 n.3, 109 n.9, 308, 310
   culture 98

history 93
kai kai 100–1
phonographic records (songs) 102
Rapu, A. 93
Rascaroli, L. 307
Rattenbach Commission 35
Ratto, P., *Trasfondo* (2012) 50 n.1
Rayner, J. 6
'reading of the space' 96
real islands 36–7
Rebolledo, J. 82
Recordando a Carlos Muñiz Varela (García, 2007) 218, 223
Redes (1936) 122
Rendez-vous (Monpierre, 2002) 235
residential tourism 247, 249, 251, 257–9. *See also* lifestyle migration
retirement tourism 251
Retornar a La Habana con Guillén Landrián (Araoz and Ramos, 2013) 221–3
reverse angle shots (Peck) 269–70
   biopolitics of disaster 270–3
   necropolitics of disposable people 273–6
   necropolitics to Necro-Capital, Inc. 276–81
Revueltas, J. 115–16
   'Los muros de agua' 116
Revueltas, R. 123
Rezende de Carvalho, E. 167 n.7
Richard, N. 74–5
Río de la Plata 43, 154–5, 157, 171, 287, 290–1, 295, 297, 299. *See also* Martín García Island
Rio Grande do Sul 131
Río Piedras massacre 214
ripple effect 253
Ripstein, A. 116, 128–9
Ritos de paso (Fontán, 1997) 184 n.2
Rivas, M. 56
Roberts, B. R. 25 n.1, 134
robinsonades 5, 11
Robinson, M. 233–4
Roca, J. A. 292
Rocha, G. 137
Rocha Dallos, S., 'cinematic profilaxis' 117
Rodney, W. 232
Rodó, J. E., *Ariel* (1900) 10

Rodríguez, F. A., *Un desierto para la nación* 38
Rodríguez, I. 117
Rodríguez, J. C. 22
Rodríguez Fernández, F. 14
Rojas, R. 288
Rojo, R. 121
Román, T. 217
Romantic sublime 33, 37–8, 41–5, 95
Roosevelt, F. D. 192
Ros, A. 56, 67, 69 n.2
Rosado, H. 214
Rottnest Island 314
Roumain, J., *Gouverneurs de la rosée* (1944) 13
Round House in Fremantle 312
Rousset, D. 308
Rue case-nègres/Sugar Cane Alley (Palcy, 1983) 233, 243 n.1, 243 n.3
Rugendas, J. M. 40
Ruiz, R. 56
rumba 125
Ruoff, J. 261
Russell, C. 95, 98, 101, 106, 220. *See also* experimental ethnography

Saavedra, V. 79
Saer, J. J. 153
    El limonero real 171, 173, 179
Sagaón, R. 124–6
Saint-Domingue 8
Salazar, G. 77
Salinas 203, 206 n.2
Salles, M. 7
Sallette, C. 271
Salta region 39, 154, 158
Sánchez, C. 56
Sánchez, J. L. 222
Sánchez Arias, G. A. 264 n.3
Sánchez Pagán, M. 217
Sánchez Prado, I. M. 11–12, 20
Sandino Moreno, C. 58
San Francisco 167 n.8
Santa Fe 154, 167 n.1, 179
Santiago Villa Grimaldi Peace Park 82, **83**
Santos, F. 248, 254, 264 n.5
Sarmiento, D. F. 21, 39–40, 156–8, 167 n.7, 288, 292, 297–8, 299, 305

Argirópolis o la capital de los Estados Confederados del Río de la Plata (1850) 21, 154–5, 160–2, 164–5, 167 n.7
civilization/barbarism 160, 164
Facundo 43
gaucho naval transformation 156, 164
geographical thinking 297
homogenizing effect 156, 162–3
institutional labyrinth 163
new map and textual gaze 165–7
Sarvestani, A. K. 308
Sassen, S. 25
Scarano, F. A. 225 n.1
scenes/obscenes (Peck) 269
    biopolitics of disaster 270–3
    necropolitics of disposable people 273–6
    necropolitics to Necro-Capital, Inc. 276–81
Schenoni, L. L. S. 35
Schoedsack, E. B. 8–9
Schuller, M. 281 n.1
    Humanitarian Aftershocks in Haiti (2016) 281 n.1
    Killing with Kindness (2012) 281 n.1
    Tectonic Shifts (2012) 281 n.1
Schwartz, T. 270
Scots 290
seascapes 32, 44, 48–9, 107, 242. *See also* empty land- and seascapes (films)
    sublime 36–9, 44–5, 48
second-home tourism 251
Second World War 195
'seismic human' community 89
Seitenfus, R. 271
    L'échec de l'aide international à Haïti 267
Selknam 80
Seminci Film Festival in Spain (2017) 69 n.3
sensory ethnography 97
Ser Tão Velho Cerrado (D'Elia, 2018) 149 n.2
Shell, M. 92
Sherlock Holmes 191
Sierra Maestra 220
Sigler, T. 252

Silou, O. 234
Silva, A. 58
Silva, S. 9–10, 20, 60–2, 68, 69 n.3
   defamiliarizing techniques 57
   performative filmic landscape 55
   Sundance Film Festival Grand Jury
      Prize and Directing Award 58
   and transnational filmmaking 57–9
Silva Rey, A. 179
Silverman, M. 307–9
Simpson, T. 18, 25 n.1
Sissani, F. 243 n.2
site of infamous torture centre 82
site of memory 47–8, 52 n.12
   multivalenced 48
   Plaza San Martín (Buenos Aires) 48
sites of fluctuation and transit 134–5
Skidmore, T. E. 132
The Skin of the Film (Marks, 2000) 309
small-island states 5, 131–2, 212, 268, 270,
   296
Smith, V. 25 n.1
social class 132, 141, 240
social justice 69 n.1, 132, 250
social reformation 20, 115–16, 118, 122–3,
   127
   affirmation 117
   crime 119
   faith in 128
   liminal space of 117
social reorganization 115
Solanas, F. 73–4, 149 n.2
Soleil Ô (Hondo) 242
Sol en un patio vacío (Fontán, 2014) 184 n.2
Soler, A. 121
Soler, F. 20, 116, 129. *See also La hija del*
   penal (Soler, 1949)
solitary land 93
Solzhenitsyn, A., *The Gulag Archipelago*
   (1974) 308
Sontag, D. 278
Sontag, S. 142, 185 n.9
   Against Interpretation (1966) 181
Sophie Léopold (*Le Bonheur d'Elza*, 2011)
   241
Sotomayor, D. 56
South America 9, 132, 156, 161, 233,
   287–8, 297

sovereignty 16, 20, 116, 118, 274, 279
Soy Cuba/I Am Cuba (Kalatozov, 1964)
   14
Spain 69 n.3, 86 n.4, 87 n.10, 251, 279
Spanish-American War 192–3
Spielberg, S. 8
Stahl, J., Jr 128
Stam, R., Tropical Multiculturalism 137
Staniscia, S. 108 n.2
'state machiner' 159
Steinberg, P. E. 43
Stephens, M. A. 25 n.1, 134
Stern, S. 56, 69 n.1
Stites Mor, J. 32
'stolid monadism of the island' 137
Storck, H. 97
Stormer, E. 132
Stratford, E. 209
sublime 19, 31, 41, 44, 46–7, 49, 51 n.4,
   51 n.5
   land- and seascapes 36–9, 44–5, 47–8
   rhetoric of 51–2 n.11
   Romantic 33, 37–8, 41–5, 95
Sucesos intervenidos (Fontán, 2014) 184
   n.2
Summers, W. 15
Sundance Film Festival (2013) 58
super 8 format 89, 94, 98–100, 107, 110
   n.9
Switzerland 86 n.4

Tabu: A Story of the South Seas (Murnau,
   1931) 5
Tahiti 103, 310
Tambogrande: mangos, muerte, minería
   (Cabellos Damián, 2007) 149 n.2
Teatro de guerra (Arias, 2018) 49 n.1, 153
technology 219–20, 269, 282 n.6
   digital 9, 57
   as distributor of death 277
   as 'master of war' 277
   of social reformation 123
Telenoche (news show) 16
The Tempest (Shakespeare, 1610) 10–11
Temple, J. 58
temps mort 59–64
territorial distributions 154
territorial memory 106

Texas 118
Thailand 191
Thales of Miletus 101
Thampy, G. 264 n.7
Thank You, Mr. Moto (1937) 205 n.1
Think Fast, Mr. Moto (1937) 205 n.1
Third Cinema 90, 260
Third World 8, 17, 211
Thomas, S. 191
Thompson, K. 248
'threshold,' notion 110 n.10
Tierra del Fuego 76, 80
Tierra en movimiento (Panizza, 2014) 89
Tierra sola/Solitary Land (Panizza, 2017)
20, 89, 92–5, 97, 109 n.7, 308
expressive nature of documents 100–4
frame from **104, 105**
gazes (web of textures) 98–100
historical facts 96
sensitive maps 105–7
Tigre Delta 300
Toba language 154, 160, 164–5
Tobing Rony, F. 108 n.4
Toronto International Film Festival 235
Torres, F. 31. *See also La campana*/The
Diving Bell (2010)
Torres-Saillant, S. 209
Totaro, D. 173, 174
Tote Tepano 109–10 n.9
tourism, cinema and 261, 263
tourism industry 254
tourist gaze 248–9, 255
redirecting 260–3
'tourist utopias' 18
transatlantic movement 233
trans-corporeality 133–4, 136–7, 139
transnational gentrification 252
travelogue 89, 105, 107, 261, 305 n.1
cartography and 95–7
travel space 107
Traverso, A. 23
Treaty of Paris (1898) 192
Trecartin, R. 183
Troy 167 n.8
Tsing, A. L. 133
Twentieth Century Fox 191, 204
Twister McGurk (*Mr. Moto in Danger
Island,* 1939) 196–8, 200

udigrúdi 137
The Unafraid (Prado and Courtney, 2018)
250
Un cuento chino (Borensztein, 2011) 49
n.1, 51 n.8
Une tempête (Césaire, 1969) 10
unitarios and *federales* 155, 167 n.3
United Fruit Company (UFC) 253
United Kingdom 15, 19, 35, 37, 49 n.1,
232
United States 50 n.2, 58, 191–7, 199, 201,
204–5, 211, 214–15, 219, 232, 250,
257, 260, 277, 279, 288, 297
colonialism and capitalism 213
imperialism and capitalism 212–13
Puerto Rico's modernity 219
'Wet Feet – Dry Feet' policy 14
Universidad Nacional Tres de Febrero 153
unnatural disasters, devastating 281 n.1
Un peso más (Cubero, 2010) 221, 223
Urry, J. 262
Uruguay 154–5, 291–2, 296
USAID 269–70
Ushuaia 308

Van Esso, L. 149 n.2
Vassallo, L. 308
Vázquez, K. E. 58
Veraguas 253
Verdad y Justicia 56
Verdi, A. 302
Vergès, F. 149 n.3
Vernet, L. 34–5
Verónico (*La deuda interna*) 40–2
vibrant matter, concept of 97
Vidal, G. 279
Vidaurrázaga, T. 101
Vieques 219
Villa Grimaldi Peace Park (Santiago) 82,
83
Villavicencio, S. 167 n.4, 167 n.7
visual anthropology 101
visual essay 23, 307, 309
Vitullo, J. 33, 45–9, 50 n.1, 51 n.9, 271–2,
301
von der Walde, E. 107, 305
Voyage to the Tip of the Earth (McAuley,
1968) 97

Wadjemup/Rottnest Island 314
Waissbluth, A. 56, 57, 69 n.3
Walcott, D. 209
Waschmusch, D. 252
Washing the Streets of Porto Rico (1898) 193
waste 21, 131, 133, 135, 137–41, 146–8, 274, 277
waste theory 140
Western civilization 77
Western occularcentrism 97
West Indies: Les Nègres Marrons de la Liberté/West Indies: the Fugitive Slaves of Liberty (Hondo, 1979) 234–5
'Wet Feet – Dry Feet' policy 14
Wichi language 160, 164–5, 167

Williams, S. 36
Willy (*Paraíso for Sale,* 2011) 255, 258–9
Wood, A. 56
Woolf, V. 157

Xavier, I. 137

Yámana 76, 80–1, 87 n.8
Yankovic, N. 100
Yrigoyen, H. 287–8
Yucatecan Casta Wars 118
Yusoff, K. 149 n.3

Zama (Martel, 2017) 158
zenithal gaze 97
Zouzou (Allégret, 1934) 5

Printed in the USA
CPSIA information can be obtained
at www.ICGtesting.com
LVHW050538300723
753749LV00004B/95